Intelligibility, Oral Communication, and the Teaching of Pronunciation

A proper understanding of intelligibility is at the heart of effective pronunciation teaching, and with it, successful teaching of speaking and listening. Far from being an optional, "add it on if we have time" language feature, pronunciation is essential because of its tremendous impact on speech intelligibility. Pronunciation dramatically affects the ability of language learners to make themselves understood and to understand the speech of others. But not all elements of pronunciation are equally important. Some affect intelligibility a great deal, while others do not. With a strong emphasis on classroom practice and how pronunciation teaching can be more effectively approached in different teaching contexts, this book provides an important resource for pronunciation researchers, with a distinctly practical focus. It shows how intelligibility research informs pronunciation teaching within communicative classrooms, enabling language teachers to incorporate intelligibility findings into their teaching. Professionals interested in oral communication, pronunciation, and speech perception will find this book fascinating.

John M. Levis is Angela B. Pavitt Professor of TESL and Applied Linguistics at Iowa State University. He is coeditor of *Social Dynamics in Second Language Accent* (2014), *Handbook of English Pronunciation* (2015), and *Critical Concepts in Linguistics: Pronunciation* (2017), and is the founding editor of the *Journal of Second Language Pronunciation*.

THE CAMBRIDGE APPLIED LINGUISTICS SERIES

The authority on cutting-edge Applied Linguistics research

Series Editors   2007–present: Carol A. Chapelle and Susan Hunston
                        1988–2007: Michael H. Long and Jack C. Richards

For a complete list of titles please visit: www.cambridge.org

Recent titles in this series:

Intelligibility, Oral Communication, and the Teaching of Pronunciation

John M. Levis
Iowa State University

CAMBRIDGE
UNIVERSITY PRESS

CAMBRIDGE
UNIVERSITY PRESS

University Printing House, Cambridge CB2 8BS, United Kingdom

One Liberty Plaza, 20th Floor, New York, NY 10006, USA

477 Williamstown Road, Port Melbourne, VIC 3207, Australia

314–321, 3rd Floor, Plot 3, Splendor Forum, Jasola District Centre,
New Delhi – 110025, India

79 Anson Road, #06–04/06, Singapore 079906

Cambridge University Press is part of the University of Cambridge.

It furthers the University's mission by disseminating knowledge in the pursuit of
education, learning, and research at the highest international levels of excellence.

Information on this title: www.cambridge.org/9781108416627
DOI: 10.1017/9781108241564

© Cambridge University Press 2018

First published 2018

Printed in the United Kingdom by TJ International Ltd. Padstow Cornwall

A catalogue record for this publication is available from the British Library.

Library of Congress Cataloging-in-Publication Data
Names: Levis, John (John M.), author.
Title: Intelligibility, oral communication, and the teaching of
   pronunciation / John M. Levis.
Description: Cambridge, United Kingdom ; New York, NY : Cambridge University
   Press, 2018. | Series: Cambridge applied linguistics series |
   Includes bibliographical references and index.
Identifiers: LCCN 2018010106 | ISBN 9781108416627 (hardback) |
   ISBN 9781108404013 (pbk.)
Subjects: LCSH: English language–Pronunciation. | Speech, Intelligibility of. |
   English language–Pronunciation–Study and teaching–Foreign speakers.
Classification: LCC PE1137 .L448 2018 | DDC 421/.52071–dc23
   LC record available at https://lccn.loc.gov/2018010106

ISBN 978-1-108-41662-7 Hardback
ISBN 978-1-108-40401-3 Paperback

Contents

Figures

Tables

Series Editors' Preface

Speakers of different languages regularly connect with each other through oral communication using a lingua franca, either face-to-face or remotely through the Internet. Using a spoken lingua franca for conducting business, gaining an education, or engaging in social interaction has become commonplace, elevating the role of oral language to a position of unprecedented importance in the fabric of life. Accordingly, the teaching of spoken communication skills requires serious reconsideration by a profession that was once satisfied with the idea that students would pick up these skills on their own if they were provided with enough opportunity to hear the language. John M. Levis engages with this reconsideration by placing intelligibility at the center of the matter and by carefully considering what should be taught to help students make their speech intelligible. What, on the surface, may seem to be a straightforward issue is appropriately problematized by Levis, who identifies the issues that impinge on achieving a simple solution. For example, how can norms of intelligibility legitimately be identified in a world in which many different native varieties of a language thrive? How should researchers and educators take into account the fact that much of the oral communication in the world today takes place between nonnative speakers? How can language teachers plan to teach what their students need to develop intelligible speech without overwhelming them with all of the detail of the sound system of the language? Levis argues that the complexity of such issues necessitates an intelligibility-based approach to oral communication. This book outlines this argument based on a thorough treatment of the detail of pronunciation for the contexts in which speakers need to be intelligible. *Intelligibility, Oral Communication, and the Teaching of Pronunciation* addresses crucial questions for teachers of English today and is a most welcome addition to the Cambridge Applied Linguistics Series.

Author's Preface

Since finishing my dissertation, no other project besides this book has given me an equivalent level of enjoyment and procrastination. I think it has also taken nearly as long. A book like this could not come about without the inspiration and help of many people. My interest in pronunciation teaching and research came first from Wayne Dickerson, who taught me in my first semester of graduate school, mentored me in teaching pronunciation, and later directed my dissertation. If one person can be said to change the trajectory of a professional life, it was Wayne who changed mine. A second influence was Braj Kachru, whose evangelistic fervor for World Englishes has influenced the way I view English-language teaching. When I was in his class, I was too inexperienced and naïve to understand the implications of what he said. But the seeds he planted finally took root, and it is impossible for me to see English, and its pronunciation, without seeing its ubiquitous contexts of use. Another influence has been Jennifer Jenkins, whose work on pronunciation in lingua franca contexts has continually challenged and inspired my thinking. I still regularly go back to her book, *The Phonology of English as an International Language* (2000), as I grapple with issues related to intelligibility. In this book, I often critique Jenkins and the reasoning underlying her influential Lingua Franca Core (LFC), but my critiques are those of a true fan. I simply cannot think of pronunciation apart from Jenkins and her work. Although Jenny has not done much in the past decade with pronunciation issues related to English as a lingua franca, her work on pronunciation remains required reading for anyone who is interested in intelligibility.

More recent influences on my thinking, who have been even more central to what I have written in this book, are Tracey Derwing and Murray Munro. Their work on intelligibility, comprehensibility, and accentedness rightly dominates research on L2 pronunciation, and provides a way for me to try to explain how pronunciation impacts the understanding of speech. Although I am not equivalent to them as a researcher, their support, friendship, and willingness to help have much to do with any success I have had. They encouraged and supported my development of the Pronunciation in Second Language Learning and Teaching conference, the *Journal of Second Language Pronunciation*, and a hundred smaller undertakings. Needless to say, my mistakes in this book should not be laid at their feet; they simply demonstrate that I remain an imperfect student.

In addition to these, there are too many people to name who have encouraged me to finish this book, and from whom I have learned so much, but the following must be mentioned: Judy Gilbert (who praised my first TESOL presentation in 1992 and took me out for coffee to talk afterwards), Ron Thomson, Jennifer Foote, Pavel Trofimovich, Dorothy Chun, Anne Wichmann, Sinem Sonsaat, Alif Silpachai, Kimberly LeVelle, Carol Chapelle, Alene Moyer, Marnie Reed, Shannon McCrocklin, Monica Richards, Ghinwa Alameen, Manman Qian, Edna Lima, Mary O'Brien, and Beth Zielinski.

I am also deeply grateful to my in-laws, Burt and Jackie Muller, who have been endlessly interested in my career and the things that I have to talk about. If I am half as interested in others as they have been, I will find that my life was well worth living. And finally, I would not be in the career I am without my wife, Greta. She encouraged me to leave my first career as a supermarket manager, then helped me see ESL (English as a second language) as a possible path, then joined me on that path. I now have a partner who is interested in many of the same things I am, and with whom I can talk shop. And because she is usually more perceptive than I am, this book shows the marks of her influence throughout.

Abbreviations

AOA	age of arrival
AWL	Academic Word List
BE	British English
CEFR	Common European Framework of Reference
CLT	communicative language teaching
CV	consonant/vowel
DSL	Dutch as a second language
EIL	English as an international language
EKB	Early Korean English bilingual
ELF	English as a lingua franca
ESL	English as a second language
ESOL	English for speakers of other languages
FL	functional load
FTA	foreign teaching assistant
GA	General American
HP	high proficiency
IP	intermediate proficiency
ITA	international teaching assistant
LFC	Lingua Franca Core
LKB	late Korean English bilingual
LOR	length of residence
NNS	nonnative speaker
NS	native speaker
NTA	native teaching assistant
RA	research assistant
RP	received pronunciation
SE	Singapore English
TA	teaching assistant
TESOL	teaching English to speakers of other languages
TL	target language
TOEFL	test of English as a foreign language
VOT	voice onset time
VP	verb phrase

Introduction

Purpose of the Book

This book argues that pronunciation is a central element in effective language teaching in all approaches, but especially in the teaching of speaking and listening skills. Although pronunciation is a servant skill, existing not on its own but in relation to other aspects of spoken language, it is far from being an optional, "add it on if we have time" language feature. Rather, pronunciation is essential because it has the greatest impact on speech intelligibility, dramatically affecting the ability of language learners both to make their speech understood and to understand the speech of others. In addition, pronunciation is an important element of comprehensibility, or the amount of work that listeners have to do to understand speech.

This book is intended for those who are interested in the teaching of pronunciation, and especially for those interested in the reasons that certain features of pronunciation should and should not be taught. Although I have tried to be practical, as this is how I tend to think, the book is not practical in the sense that it provides specific activities to use in the classroom. There are plenty of other books on the market to meet this need, and it was not my intention to duplicate them. I expect that the audience for this book will be professionals interested in the teaching of pronunciation and oral communication, and those interested in speech perception. The book will be appropriate to those teaching courses in applied phonology and related areas, because of its focus on intelligibility.

Intelligibility is important because spoken language is the heart of human interaction. According to a recent study, native speakers (NS) of English produce, on average, at least 16,000 words per day (Mehl, Vazire, Ramírez-Esparza, Slatcher, & Pennebaker, 2007). Assuming 16 waking hours, this is an average of 1,000 words per hour, or more than 16 words every waking minute, day after day after day. The ubiquity of spoken language is possible because of mutual intelligibility between speakers and listeners. Spoken communication is fast, flexible, and variable, yet it is also extremely efficient for most aspects of oral communication. The mutual intelligibility of speech clearly depends upon, among other things, shared norms in lexis, grammar, semantics, conversational structure, and phonological and phonetic form. Phonological and phonetic knowledge, this last factor, allows speakers and listeners to use their implicit knowledge of phonemic categories and allophonic variation, as well as the categorical and gradient aspects of suprasegmentals, to communicate varied levels of meaning, to interpret the information structure of discourse, to communicate nuanced pragmatic messages, to express attitudes, and to establish and express individual and group identity (Celce-Murcia, Brinton, Goodwin, & Griner, 2010). Such shared norms of pronunciation are essential to successful NS–NS communication, yet their power in facilitating communication is often hidden, noticed only when unexpected variations alert speakers and listeners to the existence of regional and social accents.

For nonnative speakers (NNS) of English, however, the lack of shared pronunciation norms with NSs means that spoken communication is sometimes unsuccessful when NS listeners cannot easily decode or interpret the pronunciation deviations of NNSs. As Hinofotis and Bailey said long ago, "there seems to be a threshold of intelligibility ... up to a given proficiency level, the faulty pronunciation of a non-native speaker can severely impair the communication process" (1981, p. 124). In study after study examining factors that make nonnative speech unintelligible, pronunciation is overwhelmingly the dominant factor, with other errors, such as those related to grammar or lexis, playing a relatively minor role in loss of intelligibility (e.g., Gallego, 1990; Jenkins, 2000; Munro & Derwing, 1995).

Prosody appears to be heavily implicated in loss of intelligibility in some studies (Derwing & Rossiter, 2003), but other studies indicate that errors in vowels and consonant sounds dominate the causes of unintelligibility (Munro & Derwing, 2006). Yet other studies have found that combinations of prosodic and segmental errors are most likely to impair intelligibility (Zielinski, 2008). What all these findings have in common is pronunciation's power to either facilitate or impair communication.

Mismatches between the phonological systems of NSs and NNSs impact the ability of NS listeners to understand nonnative speech, but they also mean that nonnative speakers of English often cannot understand native speakers, indicating another source of unintelligibility.

Difficulties in NNS listening comprehension are frequently phonological in nature, and can only be remedied when learners are able to recognize and interpret details of phonological form that are produced by their interlocutors (Alameen & Levis, 2015; Field, 2003; Gilbert, 1995). Not only is pronunciation central to the success of NS–NNS interactions, it also appears to be the central factor in the intelligibility of NNS–NNS spoken communication (Jenkins, 2000). The spread of English as an international language means that many, if not most, interactions in English around the world take place without the involvement of a native speaker. Rather than diminishing the importance of pronunciation in international communication, current evidence (Lewis & Deterding, 2018; Low, 2014; Sewell, 2017) suggests that pronunciation, especially the pronunciation of word-based errors involving vowel and consonant sounds, are a major cause of unintelligibility in NNS–NNS interactions.

While intelligibility has been a central paradigm of pronunciation teaching for several decades, it has largely not been used to inform the teaching of listening and speaking. Effective teaching of these skills is central to communicative language teaching (CLT), yet pronunciation has historically been neglected within CLT (Levis & Sonsaat, 2017), as if one could speak without pronouncing or understand others without successfully decoding phonological form. Drawing on research into, and pedagogical treatments of, pronunciation, listening, and speaking, and building on discussions of intelligibility by Smith and Nelson (1985), Munro and Derwing (1995), and Derwing and Munro (1997), this book presents a case for pronunciation as a critical but badly neglected part of the teaching of spoken language skills in a communicative approach. It provides a framework for an intelligibility-based approach to oral communication by providing: principles for understanding intelligibility; specific discussions of the role of segmentals, clusters and syllable structure, word stress, rhythm, prominence and intonation; and discussion on teaching in an intelligibility-based approach.

Contents of the Book

The first two chapters frame the general need for intelligibility as the central principle for including pronunciation in language teaching. Chapter 1, "Intelligibility, Comprehensibility, and Spoken Language," defines the key terms used throughout the book. Intelligibility and comprehensibility, the two key terms, are used in varied ways throughout the research literature, but this book follows the operational definitions of Munro and Derwing (1995), in which intelligibility refers to whether a listener understands a speaker, and comprehensibility is a judgment of how easy it is to understand. These concepts undergird the justification for using an intelligibility-based approach to teaching, in which pronunciation affects understanding of words and discourse, which is simply any kind of language beyond the level of the phrase or sentence.

Chapter 2 reviews priorities in pronunciation teaching. Implicit in any kind of teaching is the need for teachers and materials developers to emphasize certain features and deemphasize or ignore others. An intelligibility-based approach to teaching makes this practice explicit by describing how decisions about intelligibility are made, how such decisions vary according to the pronunciation features involved, and how decisions are context-dependent. For example, an intelligibility-based approach is likely to look quite different for beginning and advanced students, for a class of mixed L1 backgrounds and a class of the same L1 background, and for L2 speakers who are primarily likely to use English as a means of communication with other L2 speakers, as opposed to L2 speakers who will regularly communicate with L1 English speakers (i.e., native speakers).

The next section looks at intelligibility and word-based pronunciation features, focusing primarily on English. This is a limitation of the book, of course, as English is neither more nor less important than other languages. Instead, English pronunciation is both the area I know best, and the language that has been most researched. For example, Lee, Jang, and Plonsky (2015), in a meta-analysis of eighty-six pronunciation instruction studies, noted that eighty-three were on English. I look forward to future work that can remedy this limitation of my book.

Word-based pronunciation features primarily affect intelligibility in the most obvious way, in the difficulties that listeners have in identifying the word that was said. Chapter 3 is about segmentals and intelligibility. This chapter includes a discussion of research on vowels and consonants. While these categories have much that is distinct (e.g., vowels are largely continuous in nature whereas many consonants have distinct points and manners of articulation), both segmental categories also have much in common. Both vowel and consonant contrasts can be understood in relation to their functional load, that is, the amount of work the contrast does in the language. Both types have allophones that may be more or less important for understanding. Both can create loss of intelligibility at the word level, impairing lexical access for listeners. Errors early in a word are more likely to cause loss of understanding, and consonant and vowel errors in stressed syllables are more likely to create unintelligibility than errors in unstressed syllables (Zielinski, 2008).

The next chapter is related to segmentals, but also to suprasegmentals because of its connection to syllable structure (Cardoso & Liakin, 2009). It focuses on consonant clusters and grammatical morphemes with morphophonological variants (such as the [d], [t], and [əd] pronunciations for <ed> morphemes). Such morphemes, in addition to being interesting for issues related to L2 acquisition, are also connected to the pronunciation of final consonant clusters. English does not have the most complex syllable structure among the world's languages, but it is far more complex than many languages, allowing syllables to have at least three consonant sounds before and after the vowel (e.g., *sprints*), placing it at the more complex end for syllable structure. This complexity creates intelligibility problems for learners from different L1s. As a result, consonant clusters that are formed with and without grammatical morphemes are environments that are ripe for two types of adjustments in L2 speech: vowel epenthesis (such as when some Spanish speakers say sC words with an initial vowel; *school* → *eschool*; *speak* → *espeak*) or deletions of sounds (such as when Vietnamese speakers say *clasps* as *cas*). Any change to expected syllable structure is likely to affect intelligibility, making it important to account for the pronunciation of consonant clusters.

Chapter 5 discusses intelligibility related to word stress. Word stress is closely tied to questions about lexical access (how listeners identify words in the stream of speech). In pronunciation teaching, word stress has long held a central place, although this place has been questioned by Jenkins (2000) and others. I argue that word stress is central to intelligibility in both ESL and ELF (English as a lingua franca) contexts, although not all word stress deviations are important, including many that are included in teaching materials (such as noun–verb pairs – e.g., *INsult–inSULT* – and stress deviations that do not change vowel quality). Word stress also cannot be separated from segmentals in native Englishes, but even where other Englishes do not have such a tight connection between vowel quality and stress, word stress remains important to intelligibility.

The next section is about discourse-based features and intelligibility. Some pronunciation features rarely affect the identification of individual words, but instead affect intelligibility at the level of the message being communicated or at the level of the intentions of the utterance (i.e., its illocutionary force). Chapter 6 addresses rhythm and intelligibility. This is the chapter I had not wanted to write, hoping to hide its recommendations in the chapter on word stress. In this, I had been affected by my agreement with Jenkins' (2000) recommendations for her LFC, which argues that elements related to rhythm are as unimportant for production yet essential for perception. But there are reasons to question such a black-and-white judgment of rhythm. Like other phrase-level suprasegmentals, rhythm is unlikely to affect intelligibility at the word level, but this is only the most basic level of speech understanding. Research indicates that rhythm is essential to how listeners process speech and segment the stream of speech into identifiable words and messages. This, then, indicates that rhythm is likely to be critical for intelligibility, but that rhythm alone will not be a direct cause of unintelligible words. Rhythm shapes words in discourse, and the vowels and consonants that make them up (that is, it affects connected speech). Different rhythmic structures across languages almost guarantee that rhythm will affect how listeners and speakers understand each other. In other words, rhythm will be important for intelligibility, though perhaps not in the ways that we typically think of intelligibility.

The next chapter addresses the role of intonation in judgments of intelligibility. The chapter first describes what intonation is, then addresses the connection of prominence and intelligibility. Prominence is perhaps the most studied suprasegmental in regard to intelligibility, and there is abundant evidence of its importance in ESL, EFL (English as a foreign language), and ELF contexts. Prominence is the only suprasegmental feature included in the LFC. Its placement in phrases is tied to how information is structured in discourse, and to how categories are implicated in the use of contrasts. After prominence, the chapter addresses the connection of tune, or final intonation, to intelligibility, arguing that the beliefs that intonation is unimportant are due largely to our word- and sentence-based way of teaching pronunciation.

The last section of the book addresses teaching issues. The primary purpose of the book is to offer a strong justification for an intelligibility-based approach to teaching spoken language, and to argue for why this is important. The last three chapters describe what is meant by such an approach. The first of these chapters addresses principles for intelligibility-based teaching. Teaching for intelligibility can never ultimately be a recipe with all features measured out carefully, but is instead heavily dependent on the context in which learners learn and teachers teach. The principles in Chapter 8 are meant to provide a kind of policy statement of what to look for in a teaching/learning context. The set of six principles is unlikely to be complete, but they are based on both research and experience.

The next teaching chapter imagines what an intelligibility-based classroom might look like, and as such is an attempt to put flesh on the principles presented in Chapter 8. Pronunciation, while long neglected in language teaching, is making a comeback, but the way it has traditionally been taught – with a heavy emphasis on minimal pair exercises, on segmentals that mark nonnative accents, and on trying to develop native-like pronunciation – all continue to influence our pedagogy. All of these elements should be questioned in a classroom meant to promote intelligibility, and Chapter 9 explores what such an approach to teaching might look like.

The final chapter is perhaps the antithesis of the six principles in Chapter 8, in that it summarizes how features are both important for, and peripheral to, teaching for intelligibility. My recommendations are likely to be contentious (such lists are always a source of contention), especially in that many of the features listed in Chapter 10 are both important and unimportant. My reading of many of the studies discussed in this book, and my experience, convinces me that every general feature (such as consonants or word stress) includes both important and unimportant aspects. For example, /l/ is an important consonant in English, but initial /l/ (as in *lot*) is more important than final /l/ (as in *tall*). Part of this is a matter of initial consonants being more important than final consonants, since they define the universe for the words that are activated in the listener's mind. Part of it is related to the allophonic variation of the final /l/ being less critical for intelligibility. The final /l/, or dark [ɫ], is not a phoneme and does not carry contrastive meaning, and in final position may even lose its identity of sounding like /l/ at all. It may also be that my list will be compared to influential lists of "core" features, like the LFC (Jenkins, 2000). That would be an honor, quite frankly, since Jenkins' LFC has influenced me greatly in my thinking, in how I consider pronunciation issues, and in many of the arguments in this book.

What the Book Does Not Include

This book also does not address some important issues, such as an extensive discussion of the research on intelligibility, comprehensibility, and accentedness. Fortunately, this is far more expertly addressed by Derwing and Munro (2015), who offer an essential and clearly written book for anyone interested in pronunciation research and teaching. Second, this book does not address the importance of intelligibility for the assessment of spoken language. I originally planned to include this, but in the time since this book was planned, Isaacs and Trofimovich (2017) recruited assessment experts to write chapters on this very topic. Rather than do an inadequate job of the same topic, I recommend that readers interested in intelligibility and language assessment read their book, which can be either purchased or downloaded under Open Access licensing at http://discovery.ucl.ac.uk/1528781/1/Isaacs-TrofimovichOA.pdf. Finally, the book does a cursory job of treating the two concepts of comprehensibility and accentedness, the first because it includes many features beyond pronunciation (my focus), and the second because, while it is closely related to pronunciation, it is relatively unimportant for the teaching of L2 pronunciation because of its inability to distinguish more important from less important features.

Part I

A Framework for the Teaching of Spoken Language

1 *Intelligibility, Comprehensibility, and Spoken Language*

The language of adult foreign language learners, even those who reach advanced proficiency levels, is rarely native-like. The vocabulary range of such individuals may be impressive but still have significant gaps, both in the words they know and in their sensitivity to subtleties in meaning. Their grammatical knowledge may allow them to write and be published in their foreign language, yet their grammatical intuitions do not appear to be the same as those of native speakers (NSs) (Coppieters, 1987). Nowhere is their lack of native-likeness as apparent as in their pronunciation. Foreign-accented speech is the overwhelming norm among adult learners of foreign languages, and even foreign language learners who are far advanced in their grammatical knowledge and ability to use their new language are likely to have a noticeable accent, yet be largely intelligible. By intelligibility, we mean that "a speaker's message is actually understood by a listener" (Munro & Derwing, 1995, p. 76). The presence of a foreign accent is often attributed to critical period constraints on acquiring a second language phonological and phonetic system (Lenneberg, 1967; Scovel, 2000). The evidence for the critical period is far more uncertain than is commonly believed, with some older learners reaching native-like status with pronunciation, and some young learners never achieving a native accent (Coppetiers, 1987; Flege, Frieda, & Nozawa, 1997; Moyer, 2014). But in general, achieving native-like pronunciation is relatively uncommon for adult language learners and may be related to how closely related the L1 and L2 are (Bongaerts, Van Summeren, Planken, & Schils, 1997). Despite the unlikelihood of sounding native, many learners continue to desire such an achievement, and many teachers believe it is achievable.

This focus on reaching native levels of language achievement sometimes masks the fact that second-language speakers do not need to be native-like to be effective communicators. Their vocabulary does not have to match that of an NS to get their message across. Indeed,

11

any two educated NSs are unlikely to have exactly the same vocabulary knowledge. Many second-language speakers can write, read, speak, listen, and effectively communicate in a wide range of contexts, despite having less than perfect grammar. Such speakers can also be understood even though their pronunciation differs markedly from what NSs expect of other NSs. Listeners are remarkably flexible in deriving messages from widely varying phonetic and phonological input, and people can communicate, and communicate well, even when their speech does not match a particular model or does not fit the stereotypical expectations of a listener. In other words, nonnative speakers can be highly intelligible even when their speech is strongly accented.

The specific aspects of such understanding, and the relationship of intelligibility to pronunciation, is the primary topic of this book. I'm using a broad definition of intelligibility here, one that includes both actual understanding (at the lexical, semantic, and pragmatic levels) and the degree of effort involved in understanding (called comprehensibility). These two types of understanding overlap, yet are distinct (Munro & Derwing, 1995). A speaker can be fully intelligible, but listeners may have to work hard to understand. Because the vast majority of the research on intelligibility and comprehensibility has focused on English language acquisition, this volume is about intelligibility primarily related to English and English language teaching. These principles are likely to be relevant to other languages as well, but the questions about intelligibility and teaching have been asked most often about English because of the dominance of English as a lingua franca around the world. The book's overall emphasis is the role of pronunciation in intelligibility, even though other areas of language structure are also important to intelligibility and comprehensibility. The use of the wrong word in describing something can confuse a listener (for example, when a British English speaker talks about the *boot* of a car to an American English speaker, who calls the same thing a *trunk*). In such a case, misunderstanding, or even partial or delayed understanding, is directly related to word choice. However, some research has shown that loss of intelligibility is more closely tied to pronunciation deviations (e.g., Jenkins, 2000). In the *boot–trunk* example, both speakers can pronounce English accurately, albeit differently, but misunderstanding occurs because *boot* has different meanings in the two varieties of English. In contrast, if a speaker pronounces *boot* as *voot*, the word not only may be unfamiliar to the listener, but the listener also has to decode it to fit a possible English word. Even if the listener can decode the word and guess what the speaker means, the amount of time and energy the listener must use to process the speech changes the nature of the interaction. In other words, such deviations also begin to affect comprehensibility. The effect of a phonetic deviation may be multiplied by the 200–300+ syllables that can be spoken each minute by NSs (Cruttenden, 2014), and the opportunity for misunderstanding grows exponentially with greater numbers of unexpected deviations.

Given the possibilities for misunderstanding based on pronunciation differences, it is surprising that foreign-accented speech often loses little or none of its intelligibility. Many variations in pronunciation are not hard to interpret. In this, foreign-accented speech is similar to NS speech, which is also full of variability. Speakers of different dialects can have large numbers of systematic differences in their speech yet still understand one another. Such differences in pronunciation are more likely to cause a loss of intelligibility if they are beyond the range of expected variation, but the ability of NSs to understand each other despite significant variations in their pronunciation shows that people typically demonstrate a great deal of flexibility in communication. Unlike machines, people are flexible listeners.

But listeners' flexibility, while still operative, may be somewhat impaired when exposed to nonnative accents, in which pronunciation variations are more likely to be unexpected or outside the range of familiar NS dialects. In addition, the speech of nonnative speakers may contain other features of language structure that are unexpected, so pronunciation variations can combine with grammar and word choice differences to cause an overload that leads to a loss of intelligibility (Varonis & Gass, 1982). For example, speakers who pronounce the stressed vowel in *bed* and *letter* as [aɪ] (*bide, lighter*) rather than [ɛ] will be more difficult for listeners to understand than speakers who use perceptually close vowels such as [e] (*bade, later*) or [æ] (*bad, latter*). The sheer unexpectedness of the erroneous pronunciation [aɪ] coupled with the fact that it often sounds like another word causes a consistent loss of intelligibility.

Reasons for an Intelligibility-Based Approach to Teaching

In 1981, when pronunciation was not being widely taught during the early days of the Communicative Approach, Hinofotis and Bailey conducted research into the effectiveness of foreign teaching assistants (FTAs) in US universities. Foreign teaching assistants (now usually called ITAs, or international teaching assistants) often taught or assisted in introductory-level classes in academic fields such as chemistry or math. It was important for these FTAs to be understandable. In their research, Hinofotis and Bailey found that although some FTAs were sufficiently expert in the course content and that their overall language proficiency was advanced, they were still not easily understood. The researchers argued that their results meant that speakers must have a threshold level of pronunciation ability to communicate and that pronunciation had a special role in promoting intelligibility.

Hinofotis and Bailey (1981) questioned the dichotomy of native and nonnative speech, suggesting instead that we need a more nuanced continuum. Foreign language learners may not be able to achieve the pronunciation abilities of NSs, but progress in pronunciation is both possible and essential. Learners must have sufficient command of pronunciation or else their speech will not be sufficiently understood. It will not matter if they speak fluently (smoothly and without unnecessary hesitations), have sufficient vocabulary, use perfect grammar, or are pragmatically appropriate in their language use.

An intelligibility-based approach to oral communication is thus the pursuit of skilled rather than native speech. While pronunciation is important in speaking (after all, one cannot speak without pronouncing), it is not the only component of effective speech. Speakers must choose appropriate vocabulary and grammar, and must speak with sufficient fluency to communicate. All elements of speech are important in getting one's message across, and all must combine in such a way that they are within a listener's expected range of production. None of these elements of speech needs to be perfectly native-like, but they all need to be good enough. But what is good enough?

Since 1981, research and many teaching materials have sought to define what features are important in developing a threshold level of intelligibility, typically centered on the rough dichotomy of suprasegmentals (stress, rhythm, intonation) and segmentals (consonants, vowels). Many have advocated greater emphasis on suprasegmentals than segmentals (e.g., McNerney & Mendelsohn, 1992) to promote intelligibility because of the belief that suprasegmentals lead to faster improvement in comprehensible speech. Because time and energy for pronunciation instruction is always limited, this faster rate of improvement is important. Derwing and Rossiter (2003) found that comprehensibility ratings for learners who were taught with a more global approach (focusing more heavily on suprasegmentals) improved significantly more than did those for learners who were taught with a focus on consonants and vowels (a segmental approach).

Research has also found a differential importance for errors. Some errors cause greater impairments to intelligibility than others, a fact that is at the heart of the suprasegmental–segmental question. The principle of differential importance also applies within categories of errors. For example, Munro and Derwing (2006) examined the principle of differential importance by looking at the comprehensibility ratings of two kinds of consonant errors: /θ/–/f/ (as in *think–fink*) and /l/–/n/ (as in *light–night*). They found not only that the /l/–/n/ errors had a greater effect than /θ/–/f/ on listeners being able to understand a sentence, but also that one /l/–/n/ error had a greater effect than a combination of two or three /θ/–/f/ errors. This is attributed to the different functional load of the two types of errors. The first has few minimal pairs, and so has a low functional load, while the second has many minimal pairs, and a high functional load with greater opportunities for confusion.

This principle of differential importance applies in many contexts outside language teaching. It is known as the Pareto principle, or the 80–20 rule. The principle may suggest, for example, that 20 percent of workers create 80 percent of the wealth, or even that 20 percent of the students take up 80 percent of a teacher's time and energy. Applied to pronunciation teaching, then, we can guess that the largest improvement in a learner's intelligibility may come from improvement in a minority of the learner's errors.

If we can determine which errors constitute that important minority of errors, we can target our teaching toward the few vital errors, and deemphasize or ignore the other, less important errors, either because they will not make a difference or because many of them will be remedied in the normal course of development (as with some vowel errors or consonant errors; see Munro & Derwing, 2008 and Munro, Derwing, & Thomson, 2015, respectively). Almost all pronunciation materials focus overwhelmingly on vowel and consonant sounds, including sound contrasts that are unlikely to be a problem for any learner or listener. For example, one can find exercises teaching the difference between the interdental fricatives /θ/ and /ð/, as in *ether–either*, despite the lack of evidence that it is worthwhile to teach this contrast. Most learners of English have plenty of trouble with both sounds, but the two sounds are potentially confusable with only a few infrequent words, and if learners have trouble with either sound, they are likely to confuse it with other sounds such as /s, t, f/ and /z, d, v/, not with the other interdental fricative.

What Is Intelligibility?

Intelligibility is widely agreed to be the most important goal for spoken language development in a second language – both for listening and speaking – no matter the context of communication. In ESL (English as a second language) contexts, in which learners are surrounded by the target language outside the classroom, and in

English as a lingua franca (ELF) contexts, where nonnative speakers communicate primarily with other nonnative speakers, researchers have called for a focus on intelligibility.

But what is intelligibility? This is not an easy question to answer, it seems, because the word has often been used with two distinct but related meanings. Munro and Derwing suggested that "intelligibility may be broadly defined as the extent to which a speaker's message is actually understood by a listener" (1999, p. 289). This broad description of intelligibility presumes that listeners understand speech in a variety of ways: that they can identify the words that are spoken, that they understand the message, and that they understand the intent behind the message (Smith & Nelson, 1985). Broadly or narrowly conceived, intelligibility does not include speech that is irritating or socially unacceptable. For example, the use of taboo words in some contexts may be socially unacceptable but not unintelligible. The overuse of filler words such as *like* or *umm* may be irritating, but it does not necessarily create problems with understanding. However, intelligibility may be compromised by other features of the communicative environment, such as noise (Munro, 1998) or a speaking rate that is challenging (Munro & Derwing, 1998).

Munro and Derwing (1995), whose model of spoken language understanding is based on the work of James Flege, include three distinct but partially overlapping types of judgments that listeners make about L2 speech. These are intelligibility, comprehensibility, and accentedness (Figure 1.1).

Intelligibility means both the extent to which a speaker is understandable, and whether the particular words used by a speaker are successfully decoded (the lexical level of intelligibility). In the narrow sense, intelligibility may be measured through transcription or dictation tasks, in which listeners are asked to write down exactly what they heard. If listeners cannot successfully decode particular words, the words are defined as unintelligible. In a broader sense, listeners may be asked to answer comprehension questions or provide

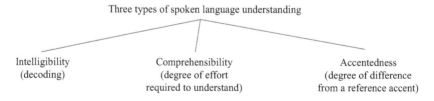

Figure 1.1 Three types of spoken language understanding (Munro & Derwing, 1995)

summaries of what they understood (e.g., Hahn, 2004), thus demonstrating intelligibility at the semantic level.

The second type of understanding is comprehensibility, defined as the amount of work that listeners need to do in understanding a speaker. This is often measured via a Likert scale, on which 1 = *extremely easy to understand* and 9 = *impossible to understand* (Munro & Derwing, 1999, p. 291), or through continuous sliding scales on a computer (e.g., Crowther, Trofimovich, Saito, & Isaacs, 2015). Thus comprehensibility taps into listeners' overall sense of how easy speech is to understand and highlights difficulties in speech processing, feelings about how difficult it is to listen to a speaker, and "factors . . . that [do] not necessarily determine whether an utterance [is] fully understood" (Munro & Derwing, 1999, p. 303). Listeners are very reliable with these kinds of holistic ratings. Tapping into NSs' intuitions also has a long history in linguistic research.

What is the relationship between intelligibility and comprehensibility? Munro and Derwing (1999) found that there was a correlation between ratings of intelligibility and ratings of comprehensibility, but that the two dimensions did not measure the same things. It was not uncommon for listeners to transcribe speech perfectly (that is, to find it completely intelligible) and yet perceive it to be difficult/effortful to understand.

Finally, accentedness is important to consider because accent is commonly appealed to, both popularly and in research, for its presumed connection to whether speech is understandable and its potential usefulness in assessing spoken language (e.g., Ockey, Papageorgiou, & French, 2016). Clearly, accent can interfere with intelligibility, but research has shown that speakers can be perfectly intelligible (in that all of the words they speak are understood) while being simultaneously judged as having a very strong accent. Accentedness is also scalar, and is defined as the degree of difference between speech and a local or reference accent (Munro & Derwing, 1995). Because it is scalar, an assumption demonstrated by Derwing and Munro (2009), it is possible to talk about listeners hearing speech as more or less accented in comparison to the reference accent or in comparison to another accent. However, describing accents as thick, heavy, or light without some kind of measured judgment task is unhelpful. Accentedness judgments of this sort seem particularly prone to bias based on stereotypes and other social judgments, perhaps leading to perceptions of accented speakers being less truthful (Lev-Ari & Keysar, 2010), less understandable (Rubin, 1992), or having poorer teaching skills (Major, Fitzmaurice, Bunta, & Balasubramanian, 2002).

In summary, listeners' ability to decode words successfully does not guarantee that speech will be easy to understand. This kind of intelligibility is not only a matter of how many words are not understood, but also *which* words. Misunderstood function words may have less impact than misunderstood content words (Zielinski, 2006). It is likely, however, that speech will be less comprehensible if words are frequently unintelligible. What we do not know is how many words can be missed by a listener before overall understanding is severely impaired. Nation (2002) suggested that nonnative listeners need to understand at least 95 percent (nineteen of every twenty words) or perhaps 98 percent (forty-nine of fifty words) of the content words in running speech in order to have excellent comprehension and be able to guess the meanings of unknown words. The threshold for NSs, with better guessing skills and faster processing of their first language, is likely to be lower, but we do not know how much lower.

A potential confusion of intelligibility and comprehensibility comes from Smith and Nelson (1985), who divided their concept of "international intelligibility" into three different types of understanding, which they named intelligibility, comprehensibility, and interpretability (Figure 1.2). International intelligibility is listed as an overarching term based on Smith and Nelson's attempt to describe understanding across different varieties of world Englishes. It is important to note that, despite the terms used, all three types of understanding in Smith and Nelson's work are types of intelligibility – that is, they are all types of actual understanding. None of them is the same as comprehensibility as discussed by Munro and Derwing (1995).

Smith and Nelson (1985) define *intelligibility* as a listener's ability to decode the words that are spoken. In other words, this is lexical intelligibility. From the speaker's point of view, this is the ability to say words in such a way that listeners can successfully decode them. For example, I once was listening to a talk given by the Australian applied linguist, Wilga Rivers. I had no difficulty understanding anything she said even though her accent was largely unfamiliar to me at

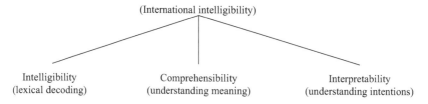

Figure 1.2 Three types of understanding thought to constitute international intelligibility (Smith & Nelson, 1985)

the time. Then she used a word that I didn't understand at all – [kə'ɹɑlɹi]. I spent almost a minute trying to decode the word, during which time I did not hear any of the rest of her talk. First, I searched my mind for any word that seemed to fit. Finding none, I spelled out the sounds I heard <c_rol_ry> and then visually was able to see a word that fit: *corollary*. Then, and only then, did I realize that I had heard that British-influenced varieties of English used this stress pattern for this word that is pronounced in North American English as [ˈkʰɔɹəˌleɹi]. The speaker's unexpected stress pattern and consequent vowel and consonant pronunciations of this word caused a loss of intelligibility in that I was not able to successfully decode the word in real time.

In Smith and Nelson's work, *comprehensibility* involves the ability of a listener to understand a spoken message. Again, this use of comprehensibility is not the same as that of Munro and Derwing (1995). Comprehensibility in this model refers to "the meaning of a word or an utterance" (Smith & Nelson, 1985, p. 334). A text is comprehensible if the listener can make sense of or paraphrase it. Smith and Nelson's (1985) third type of understanding, *interpretability*, refers to understanding the "meaning behind the word or utterance" (p. 334). The interpretability of a spoken text is high if the listener is able to understand the speaker's intentions in uttering the message in a particular context. Interpretability refers to another type of intelligibility, pragmatic intelligibility, but this type of intelligibility can be extremely variable. It is also difficult to determine whether a listener has misunderstood the meaning behind the word or utterance. Listeners may think that they understand, and a speaker may think that a listener has understood the meaning that the speaker intended, only to find out later that the listener's understanding was quite different from the speaker's intended meaning. Interpretability has not played a significant role in research involving pronunciation. In one study that suggests a role for this type of intelligibility, Low (2006) described how given information is marked as (non)prominent by British English (BE) and Singapore English (SE) speakers. It is typical for BE speakers to make given information less prominent when it is repeated (e.g., the second use of "car" in the example below). SE speakers, rather than making car less prominent, appear to make it prominent again. Low suggested that this difference caused a loss of interpretability, in that inner-circle speakers misunderstood the communicative intent of SE speakers:

the Singapore English speaker's reaccenting of old information causes a British interlocutor in at least a few instances to misunderstand the SE speaker's communicative intent ... Anecdotally, a compromise in interpretability makes sense. In cases where I merely reaccented repeated words, for example, *I looked around for the car but there was no car;* I have often been asked by foreigners whether I was angry when my communicative intent has been far from conveying the feeling of anger.   (Low, 2006, pp. 756–7)

This book is primarily about intelligibility, but it is also about comprehensibility. When the word *intelligibility* is used, it is used to mean understanding of a spoken message, either in regard to lexical identification, meaning, or intention. When I speak of comprehensibility, I mean the degree of difficulty a listener has in understanding. Loss of intelligibility can happen between two NSs, and in fact any mismatch between a listener's expectation and the speaker's production can cause it (Zielinski, 2008). However, mismatches do not always impair understanding. They may, however, make a difference in how easily a listener understands a speaker, and consequently how likely a listener is willing to communicate with different individuals. If it takes extra effort to understand someone, interlocutors may avoid contact.

Intelligibility and Teaching Pronunciation

In teaching pronunciation in relation to discussions of intelligibility, we often make assumptions about who the listener and the speaker are in an interaction. Typically, we assume that the listener is an NS while the speaker is a nonnative speaker (NNS). Thus, we assume that the NNS bears the burden for being understood, while the NS, who has a command of the language and is able to determine whether an NNS is intelligible, bears less of a burden. Because any interaction involves both speakers and listeners playing both roles, this need not be the only, or even the most helpful, way to understand intelligibility. As I have written elsewhere (Levis, 2005a), intelligibility can be understood through a matrix of possible relationships between listeners and speakers.

Figure 1.3 delineates possible relationships between listeners and speakers, and each of the relationships has implications for intelligibility, and in turn for pronunciation instruction.

In Quadrant A, both the speaker and listener are NSs. Implicitly, communication in this quadrant should be easy and successful since both the listener and speaker share not only the same linguistic code but many of the same rules for using it as well as intuitions about its unspoken rules. Unfortunately, we do not know how far we can expect such success to reach. Native speakers come in many flavors, with wide varieties of dialects and ways of speaking. It is not hard to recall interactions between NSs that include a loss of intelligibility. Once, while playing golf in Scotland, I played with two other golfers,

LISTENER			
		Native speaker	Nonnative speaker
SPEAKER	Native speaker	(A) NS–NS	(B) NS–NNS
	Nonnative speaker	(C) NNS–NS	(D) NNS–NNS

Figure 1.3 Speaker–listener intelligibility matrix (Levis, 2005a)

one native to Scotland and the other native to the north of England but who had lived in Scotland for decades. More than once, their speech became increasingly unintelligible to me, especially as topics became more emotionally charged. I didn't understand many words, the meaning, or the intent of the messages being communicated.

Quadrant B, with native speakers and nonnative listeners, is often found in language classrooms and when NNSs interact with NSs in second-language contexts. This is the flip side of typical intelligibility research which focuses on nonnative speakers and native listeners. In this quadrant, NNS listeners are tasked with understanding normal NS speech, with all its variations, in real time. A lack of intelligibility in this case means that NNSs cannot understand. In other words, the NS may be unintelligible to the NNS. From the viewpoint of a pronunciation teacher, the goal must be to help learners decode and process speech as quickly and easily as possible. In real-world communicative interactions, NSs must carry a large part of the burden for intelligibility, not only in phonology but also in adjustments, speech rate, etc., if some interactions are to be successful.

Quadrant C reflects the bulk of the research on intelligibility, in which NNSs are the speakers and NSs the listeners. The artificial division between Quadrant B and Quadrant C is unfortunate, because in reality any interaction between NSs and NNSs means that NSs and NNSs will play both roles. The important thing to notice, though, is that it is possible for both NSs and NNSs to be unintelligible when communicating, and conversational adjustments are common by NSs (for an early review, see Long, 1983). In Quadrants B and C, the NS often places the responsibility for success on the NNS, but the NNS cannot be fully responsible for successful communication. Success in any communicative interaction involves the ability to speak and listen and to adjust if communication is not happening. If NSs cannot adjust, they are also partly responsible for a lack of intelligibility.

Finally, Quadrant D involves speakers and listeners who are both NNSs. This is typical of the ELF setting. This quadrant describes the widespread use of English as a medium of communication for speakers who have different non-English first languages. In a smaller way, it also reflects the need for learners in a second-language classroom setting to communicate with other learners of different L1s. I have often had students ask if they could practice with me in class and not with other learners, because they believed the other learners' grammar and pronunciation were bad. This request presumes a kind of osmosis in that other learners' errors will somehow rub off and ruin their progress, while my native speech will rub off and lead to the kind of improvement they desire. Such osmosis is unlikely to work – either for good input or for bad. Findings about correction show that learners don't seem to correct fellow students' errors, and thus presumably they don't notice them (Long & Porter, 1985).

All four quadrants reflect different intelligibility issues. Intelligibility is always a two-way street, and both NS and NNS interlocutors carry the responsibility for successful communication. It is only by recognizing the contexts in which we talk about intelligibility issues that we can achieve greater success in our teaching.

Pronunciation and Oral Communication

Although this book is primarily about the role of pronunciation in intelligibility, it is impossible to discuss pronunciation outside the larger context of oral communication. Pronunciation, with all its intricacies and interesting features, does not exist on its own. It is a servant skill. We pronounce as a byproduct of speaking, and we pronounce within the context of the communicative acts or the speaking task we are involved in. We pronounce if we are fluent, and we pronounce if we are not fluent. We pronounce with our particular lexical and grammatical skills. Likewise, we process the pronunciation features of others' speech, presented to us within the fluency, speed, grammar, and lexis of their speech. Sometimes the speech will be more careful, and sometimes it will be more casual. Pronunciation (or its primary correlate, accent) seems to play such an outsized role in intelligibility because it is a first stop for listeners, and many of its features are those that listeners are very good at noticing. We notice small deviations of vowel and consonant sounds even when listening to other NSs, and we often make social judgments about others because of these differences. For example, the insertion of /ɹ/ into the word *wash* so that it is pronounced *warsh* is immediately noticed by most US speakers and is almost always criticized as sounding uneducated. Likewise, the deletion of [h] in words like *house* and *hospital* in British English has historically been highly stigmatized, indicating social class distinctions (Mugglestone, 1996), despite the fact that other [h] deletions in function words (e.g., *Did he give him the book?*) are usually unnoticeable in normal conversational speech.

Word-Based and Discourse-Based Features

What are the features of pronunciation and how do they fit into Munro and Derwing's (1995) intelligibility/comprehensibility research? First, let's look at the kinds of features that are usually associated with pronunciation teaching. I will divide these into word-based and discourse-based features, although it is notoriously difficult to divide English pronunciation into discrete categories. The stress and rhythm of English affect the ways that vowels and consonants are pronounced, and the clarity of a word's pronunciation is influenced by its location in the discourse. Likewise, vowels are spoken with different pitch levels, thus influencing pitch range and intonation. Many of these variations are ignored by NSs because they are allophonic, or characteristics of different registers, or irrelevant noise, but we should not consider that such variations are heard in the same way by learners, for whom the variations are likely to affect how they process speech.

To native listeners, intelligibility and comprehensibility mean the extent to which they can understand the speech of others, or the extent to which they need to work in understanding. Both types of understanding for native listeners are by and large unconscious and noticeable only when understanding is challenging. Native listeners also tend not to recognize their own role in promoting understanding while communicating with nonnative speakers. However, when native listeners do take on the role of an active participant in the interaction, even difficult speech can become more understandable. In one study, social work students were given training on listening to Vietnamese-accented speech. The training led to increased confidence in their ability to understand immigrant clients compared to a group with cross-cultural training and a control group (Derwing, Rossiter, & Hannis, 2000; Derwing, Rossiter, & Munro, 2002).

To nonnative listeners, especially those at lower proficiency levels, negotiating the intelligibility of speech is a conscious process, sometimes painfully so, during casual speech or in a communicative situation in which messages are partly masked by noise. Intelligibility is important for nonnative speakers in their own speech and in listening to the speech around them. The speech of NSs can sound excessively fast, a rapid fire of foreign and strangely distributed sounds that they can barely process.

Word-Based Features

Word-based features include segmentals and word stress. These features are most likely to affect intelligibility at the lexical level. In some languages (e.g., Mandarin, Vietnamese, Kikuyu), this category would also include lexical tone. First, some justification of my classification is in order. Typically, pronunciation features are described as being either segmental or suprasegmental. This classification scheme is central to teaching materials, but it creates an unnatural division in discussing intelligibility. Consonant and vowel errors primarily cause listeners to have trouble decoding individual words. This is the logic behind the use of minimal pairs in teaching pronunciation. For example, the numerous research studies that have examined the difficulty that Japanese learners of English have with /l/ and /ɹ/ all reflect the many minimal pairs that these two phonemes have in English. Brown (1988), extending Catford (1987), described one effect of the number of minimal pairs that two phonemes have as functional load. Functional load is measured by the numbers of minimal pairs that exist for a contrast (e.g., [p]/[b]) initially and finally, and the likelihood that the contrast is enforced in all varieties of English. Minimal pairs of segments with a high functional load are thought to be more likely to cause loss of intelligibility.

In addition to minimal pairs, another segmental feature that can cause difficulties in understanding words involves allophonic variations. For example, voiceless stops and affricates ([p], [t], [k]) in inner-circle English varieties are aspirated at the beginning of stressed syllables. If the sounds are not aspirated, there is a strong chance of unintelligibility because inner-circle listeners are likely to hear them as their voiced counterparts ([b], [d], [g]).

Vowel reduction is also a strong candidate for intelligibility problems, especially from the second-language learner's point of view. Because English NS speech is full of vowel reduction (Woods, 2005), L2 learners of English may find NS speech unintelligible when they cannot easily connect the speech signal to the written representation of the words.

Likewise, word-stress errors also cause trouble with intelligibility at the lexical level. Stressing a word incorrectly can not only mask the identity of the word (Zielinski, 2008), it can also change how the vowels and consonants are pronounced. Although word stress is typically considered a suprasegmental feature, I will treat it similarly to segmentals in its effect upon intelligibility. In other words, the kinds of interpretive problems related to word stress are likely to be related primarily to intelligibility at the lexical level.

Discourse-Based Features

Most suprasegmental errors are unlikely to cause listeners to misidentify words, but may cause loss of intelligibility in understanding the message or the speaker's intent. They may also cause decreased comprehensibility by increasing the effort listeners put forth in understanding speech. Most suprasegmental features, unlike segmental features, carry their meaning beyond the sentence level. As such, these features are part of the overall structure of spoken English, allowing it to be spoken with its characteristic rhythm and melody, and creating meaning that is pragmatic, attitudinal, and connected to the communication of information structure.

Unlike word-based features, discourse-based features in English are rarely right or wrong. If a Korean speaker who does not consistently distinguish the sounds [p] and [f] says the name *Pat* as *fat*, there is a clear sense of right or wrong. However, if the same Korean speaker asks the question, "Is Pat available to talk?" with falling rather than rising intonation, the difference in meaning is far more subtle. We know from research that both intonations are perfectly acceptable and may be equally common for yes-or-no questions (Thompson, 1995), so any interpretive issues are likely to be pragmatic in nature rather than related to basic speech decoding.

Intonation is thus the first suprasegmental feature that is unlikely to cause difficulties with word intelligibility. Although we do not hear differences in intonation as right or wrong as with mispronounced words or segmentals, this does not mean that intonation is unimportant since it is more likely to affect intelligibility in terms of the message or the intent. In one well-known example, Gumperz (1982) described a misunderstanding that occurred due to misperceptions of intonational meaning. British Airway employees (primarily native speakers of English) who ate at a company cafeteria thought that the servers (largely women of Indian and Pakistani descent) were rude and sullen. This perception was so strong that it caused a barely simmering revolt on both sides: The airline staff felt they were being treated badly by those they perceived as being beneath them in status, and the cafeteria workers felt those they were serving were rude and angry. Gumperz discovered that the problem had its roots in the use of intonation. When serving, the Pakistani and Indian women would offer things to the employees with a falling intonation (e.g., Gravy↘), while the employees, having English-language expectations, expected rising intonation (e.g., Gravy↗). In the Indian and Pakistani women's L1s, the use of falling intonation was polite and appropriate, while for the native English-speaking employees it was heard as rude. In other words, the English-speaking employees did not hear the intonation as linguistically wrong, like a phoneme error; rather, they considered it to be a social failing.

In another study, Hahn (2004) found that misplacement of sentence focus caused listeners difficulties in recalling information from a lecture. The study examined three conditions in which a Korean English bilingual presented the same information: correct focus placement, incorrect focus placement, and no focus placement at all. All three conditions included a text that was, technically, perfectly intelligible. However, when unexpected words were given special emphasis, or when no emphasis at all was used, listeners did not recall the information with the same degree of success. In addition, the speaker was heard as more or less likable, depending on the emphasis pattern.

Another suprasegmental feature is phrasing, or juncture, in which speakers' pauses have more than one effect on how well listeners interpret speech. In Example (1.1), juncture plays an obvious role in differentiating between the meanings of the two sentences. There is no necessary difference in intelligibility, because both sentences use the same words. The entire difference in meaning is one of intelligibility, although phrasing differences are rarely so clear as in this example.

(1.1)

"Joe said his wife was away" versus "Joe, said his wife, was away".

A third suprasegmental feature is rhythm. Although closely related to word stress in its ability to affect the pronunciation of vowels and consonants, phrase rhythm in English affects the overall structure of the discourse. Function words, such as single-syllable prepositions (e.g., *in, at, on, with, by*), determiners (e.g., *the, a, some, an, his*), and auxiliary verbs (e.g., *have, can, could, would, is, did*) are almost always unstressed in discourse, and thus can be difficult to process for learners of English. On the other hand, the same learners' tendency to pronounce function words as full forms rather than reduced (e.g., *can* as [kʰæn] rather than [kən]) sometimes causes difficulties for native North American English listeners, who associate the full vowel pronunciation with the negative, *can't*. Additionally, spoken language with too many stresses can overload the circuits of native listeners, causing them to pay attention to too much informational content, thus making it hard for them to select key words from the stream of speech. Interestingly, Jenkins (2000) argued that pronouncing all segments with full forms is unlikely to lead to loss of understanding in ELF communication, in which NNSs speak primarily to other NNSs. This remains an open question for research in ELF.

Rhythm also has the potential to affect intelligibility, especially for nonnative listeners. Rhythm in English leads to pronunciation adjustments both within and across word boundaries, especially in informal casual speech. The word *polite* is likely to lose its initial unstressed syllable, being pronounced *p'lite*, which in discourse can be misunderstood as *plight*. Native listeners are likely to pay attention to an additional cue, the length difference for the stressed vowel, but there is no guarantee that nonnative speakers will pay attention to or produce this cue consistently. Palatalization across word boundaries along with reductions can mask the identity of words completely, so that sentences like *Did you eat yet?* may sound like *Didja eat yet?* or even *Jeechet?*

Other Features

The flow of speech (fluency) appears to affect comprehensibility more than intelligibility. Fluency is a bundle of different features, and it is notoriously difficult to define precisely (Riggenbach, 2000). It includes, at the very least, speech rate, phrasing, grammatical grouping, and final lengthening, all mixed up in a soup pot with just the right amount of timing. Even NS speech may be judged as not fluent, since native speakers may have excessive and badly placed filled pauses (e.g., um) or pathological conditions such as stuttering. For listeners who are native speakers of English, disfluent speech interrupts their processing of the message. Likewise, overly fast speech, without appropriate pauses and emphasis, can also make a speaker's message hard to understand. For listeners who are nonnative speakers of English, excessively fluent speech may be hard to process simply because of its speed. Slower speech, and speech that is less fluent, may be easier to process. From the point of view of speaking, fluency in nonnative speech is likely to develop along with proficiency and practice. A focus on language chunks may be helpful in developing fluency, but fluency is primarily a result of greater speech automaticity, in which all the elements of language do not have to be thought about equally during communication (Gatbonton & Segalowitz, 1988, 2005).

Speech rate is closely related to fluency. Although some L2 speakers talk at an excessively fast speech rate (Munro & Derwing, 2001), many more speak with rates that are too slow for native listeners. While it may appear to some North American English listeners that some second-language speakers speak too quickly (such as Indian speakers of English), the perception of a fast speech rate may also come from an unfamiliar rhythmic pattern in which more syllables are strongly stressed than expected.

Another global feature of pronunciation, voice quality (Esling & Wong, 1983), may play a role in judgments of comprehensibility, either by facilitating understanding (if the voice quality is familiar and comfortable for a listener) or by exaggerating the effect of other speech differences. For example, Indian English is often spoken with a higher voice pitch than is American English. This difference in voice quality is part of a typical Indian English accent, and it is noticeable enough to add to a listener's processing load, especially if the listener is not familiar with or favorably disposed toward the accent.

Another feature that may play a role in judgments of comprehensibility is loudness (or its acoustic correlate, intensity). Loudness can play an obvious role if a speaker is excessively soft, or excessively loud, in that listeners will have to work harder to listen effectively. Loudness, however, has little role in linguistic categories. It is, perhaps, a component of stress in English (Zhang & Francis, 2010), but it is not as important as length or pitch. After all, one can identify stressed vowels whether they are whispered or bellowed. In one situation I am familiar with, a female Chinese teaching assistant (TA) was teaching American undergraduate students who had complained about her English, even though her language appeared to be highly comprehensible. However, she spoke very quietly. Upon being questioned, she said that she believed that, as a woman, she was supposed to speak quietly in public situations. This appeared to be a cultural difference (and perhaps an idiosyncratic one at that), but undeniably her lack of loudness harmed both her intelligibility and her comprehensibility. In another situation, a male TA from Sri Lanka was easy to understand when speaking one-on-one, but did not pass a test for TAs because he spoke so quietly. In this case, the quiet speech was not cultural but idiosyncratic.

Finally, another area of pronunciation that may affect comprehensibility has to do with energy or "liveliness." Hincks, in a series of articles (e.g., Hincks & Edlund, 2009), has advocated teaching spoken language through using computer-assisted feedback that measures "liveliness" of speech, a complex feature that appears to be most heavily connected to variations in pitch range throughout extended spoken discourse. Hincks has found that speakers who have livelier voices (with more variation in their pitch range) are heard as more effective. In contrast, speech that sounds more monotone, with flatter pitch over long stretches of speech, may require more work by listeners. The effect of pitch variation does not appear to be connected to linguistic categories of intonation (e.g., final intonation or focus placement), but is rather an effect of how animated voices are.

Error Gravity and Intelligibility

Language errors of any kind are likely to affect the ways that listeners understand a message. Even if the errors are not serious, they may be salient, and thus the errors become an extra part of the message being communicated. For example, children's speech is noted for its tendency to overgeneralize patterns to exceptions. English-speaking children may say "they flied" rather than "they flew" or "two mans" rather than "two men." Although this process may seem ubiquitous in children's speech production, one study that examined the speech of 83 children found that only a median of 2.5 percent of potential errors were actually regularized for all the children studied (Marcus et al., 1992). When I have asked students in introductory linguistics classes how often children make these kinds of errors, and given them options of 5, 25, 45, and 65 percent, they invariably choose 45 or 65 percent, and are shocked when they hear that 5 percent is closer to the actual occurrence. This finding regarding the perception of the frequency of L1 errors suggests a principle. When we consider our ability to understand a speaker with a foreign accent, we are likely to overstate the role of accent and to single-out errors that we know how to name, leading us to attribute to those errors an oversized role in intelligibility. Segmental errors, especially obvious ones like substitutions for /θ/, are noticeable and we can name them. While linguists know that such errors, even when they occur more than once in a sentence, rarely affect the most basic level of understanding – that is, intelligibility (Munro & Derwing, 2006) – the sounds continue to be taught first in many pronunciation classes. This is the equivalent of putting a bandage on a scratch when the accident victim is having trouble breathing.

Research into errors in written and spoken language has shown over and over again that certain errors are more serious than others. In an early study for English NSs, Hairston (1981) asked readers in various occupations to judge the seriousness of errors in grammar and usage that are typically addressed in college writing classes and writing handbooks. A surprising number of errors were not considered serious, while those that were considered most serious included those Hairston called status markers (i.e., glaring examples of nonstandard usage, such as double negatives) and errors that caused sentences to seem incompletely formed, such as sentence fragments. In addition, Hairston found differences between the judgments of male and female respondents. Females were stricter in their judgments.

Other studies have looked at judgments of spoken nonnative errors. Fayer and Krasinski (1987) asked English- and Spanish-speaking judges to evaluate the seriousness of errors from Puerto Rican speakers' speech. Spanish judges were stricter and more irritated than were native judges, suggesting that the intelligibility of spoken language is also dependent on the listeners and their connection to the language of the speakers. In another study, Derwing, Rossiter, and Ehrensberger-Dow (2002) found that NSs were better than nonnative speakers at identifying errors in aural than in written form, but that nonnative judges were stricter about the gravity of errors and were more annoyed by the errors.

Other Factors Affecting Judgments of Spoken Language

Judgments of speech may also be negatively influenced by factors unrelated to understanding. Some errors are more irritating than others, even though the message may be perfectly understood. For example, Hairston's (1981) status markers, her most negatively rated category, included errors such as "He don't" and "We was," both of which are well-known deviations from standard English found in nonstandard dialects. Lippi-Green (1997) described errors of native and nonnative speakers that are stigmatized even though the speech is perfectly understood. If speakers come from a social group that listeners consider less desirable, then the way they speak may also be considered less desirable.

There is also some evidence that accented speech may be more intelligible if the listeners become familiar with the features of the speech. Derwing, Rossiter, and Munro (2002) provided training for social work students who needed to interact with Vietnamese learners of English. The students were given training in the typical features of Vietnamese accents before interacting with Vietnamese immigrants to Canada. The training was minimal (20-minute sessions integrated with other classroom work over eight weeks). Their confidence increased and they reported being more successful in their interactions than those who did not do the training.

Firm answers about the differential effects of errors on understanding have been elusive. While we believe it is possible to identify which errors make a difference and which ones do not, even errors that are not usually harmful to intelligibility may sometimes be more serious, and errors that might be expected to cause difficulties may not. For example, errors in the pronunciation of /θ/ have been almost uniformly considered as not having a serious effect on intelligibility. Jenkins (2000) went so far as to include all consonants as important for international intelligibility except dark [ɫ] (as in *all*) and the two "th" sounds. The case of the "th" sounds is particularly interesting in making recommendations about how much effect errors have on communication. Jenkins (2000) and Jenner (1989) both say that these sounds are relatively unimportant. Brown (1988) found that errors involving "th" typically have a low functional load. However, Deterding (2005) found that the actual pronunciations of /θ/ as /f/ by Estuary English speakers was very harmful to intelligibility for Singaporean English listeners who listened to British English speakers. The lack of intelligibility was especially noticeable in the words *three* and *free*.

Similarly, word-stress errors can easily mask the identity of a word and cause serious difficulties in comprehension, but Cutler, Dahan, and van Donselaar (1997) found that NSs were rarely troubled by misstressing of words for which the stress was a key clue to lexical category. Word pairs like 'permit/per'mit and 'insult/in'sult differ only in stress, yet native listeners do not seem to rely on stress to interpret the words (Cutler, 1986).

These findings suggest that the gravity of errors in a language not only differ between categories, but that they also differ within categories. Thus, it is unlikely that suprasegmental errors are uniformly more serious than segmental errors or that consonant errors are uniformly more serious than vowel errors. Rather, it is likely that each subset of errors has members that are sometimes more serious and sometimes less so. While Gumperz's (1982) examination of Indian and Pakistani women's intonation shows that unexpected intonation can sometimes cause serious problems in intelligibility (as well as the consequent irritation), it is likely that the use of single-word utterances (*Gravy*↗ rather than *Would you like gravy*↘) also played a role in the depth of the misunderstanding. The same unexpected intonation in a syntactically complete question with the politeness marker "would" may be less likely to be considered rude than would the single-word utterance heard by the English NSs.

We need a nuanced approach to intelligibility, an approach that examines in detail what we know of intelligibility, an approach that specifies research priorities that will help tease apart those features that are important for those helping L2 students become more successful in communicating. While it is unlikely that we will ever know perfectly which errors always cause the greatest difficulty, we can know which are likely to do so. But we must examine pronunciation and other errors in greater detail before our language classes can truly reflect an approach that prioritizes intelligibility.

2 *Setting Priorities*

What Teachers and Researchers Say

Currently there is very little debate about whether intelligibility is an appropriate goal for teaching spoken language. At least since the late 1980s, a majority of knowledgeable teachers and researchers have advocated some version of the Intelligibility Principle for teaching pronunciation. This does not always affect how pronunciation is actually taught, or how published teaching materials are constructed, but the advocacy has influenced both implicit and explicit discussions of priorities.

The opposite of the Intelligibility Principle, the Nativeness Principle (Levis, 2005a), is now rarely put forth by teachers or researchers as a worthwhile goal, even though it remains vibrant, living on in popular beliefs about language learning, in spy novels (where effective spies always seem to become native-like in an unusually short time), and in accent-reduction advertising. The Nativeness Principle, by definition, says that learners have to completely match a native speaker's production of all pronunciation targets, segmental and suprasegmental, in order to have achieved the target pronunciation in a foreign language. A number of pronunciation class texts appear to follow the Nativeness Principle. Such books include a nearly exhaustive collection of exercises for teaching segmentals and segmental contrasts (e.g., Orion 2002), including sound contrasts that are rarely applicable, although often with a less than complete treatment of suprasegmentals. The advantage of such an approach to pronunciation teaching is that it defines what must be mastered and articulates a final objective – native-like speech. There is no obvious need to prioritize because the entire L2 sound system must be learned to mastery.

The power of the Nativeness Principle can be seen in the fact that it is not unusual to hear language learners themselves say they want to sound like a native speaker (NS). Every time I teach pronunciation, one or two students tell me unbidden that this is what they want. This is not surprising, as it shows that learners believe nativeness to be a desirable goal, and it shows that they understand that any deviation from that norm can mark them as being different or as being hard to understand. Their desire assumes a dichotomous state of affairs: native (and therefore unaccented and easy to understand) or nonnative (and therefore accented and harder to understand). Even though it is unlikely that they will ever reach their goal, their desire comes from a noble motive in that they want their spoken language to facilitate their communication. Not being language teachers, they do not realize that reaching a good-enough pronunciation is neither a sign of weakness nor of low standards, but is instead all that is really necessary (or all that is really possible, in most cases).

Unfortunately, few teachers or students have the time, aptitude, or the age necessary to achieve the kind of mastery needed for native-like pronunciation. An intelligibility-based approach, in contrast, requires prioritizing what is taught. Teaching to achieve intelligibility is challenging precisely because of this prioritized approach to errors. Such an approach is based on the assumption that some errors have a relatively large effect on understanding and others a relatively small effect. Judy Gilbert (personal communication) talks about priorities in terms of a battlefield medical image – triage. When faced with many people who are wounded, medics must prioritize treatment. Applied to pronunciation, the image suggests that certain errors (injuries to communication, to follow the metaphor) should be treated first because they are more likely to harm communication than are others. Other injuries to communication are far less problematic, and neither listeners nor speakers will be harmed by lack of accuracy in such cases.

What such an approach should look like in the classroom is not clear, however, partly because proposals based on the Intelligibility Principle conflict, and partly because the Nativeness Principle continues to strongly influence classroom practice and teachers' attitudes. Also, the Intelligibility Principle must be context-sensitive and connected to both speaking and listening – speakers need to be intelligible to listeners, and listeners need to be able to understand speakers. So decisions about priorities not only involve helping learners produce speech in an accessible way for listeners, but also involve teaching those same learners to understand the speech they hear.

What Is Involved in Pronunciation?

An intelligibility-based approach to teaching pronunciation requires a clear description of the key elements of pronunciation and how they relate to one another. This description is the goal of the following section.

When we use the term *pronunciation,* we are talking about an interrelated system of sounds and prosody that communicates meaning through categorical contrasts (e.g., phonemes), systematic variations (e.g., allophones), and individual variations that may mark gradient differences such as gender, age, origin, etc. As such, the system of pronunciation can be divided in a variety of ways, but the divisions are merely a way to understand pieces of the system, even though all parts of the system interact with each other in ways that often make it impossible to separate their effects upon understanding.

The classification of the features that I use here is somewhat unusual (Figure 2.1). Typically, pronunciation is divided into segmentals and suprasegmentals, but from the viewpoint of spoken language understanding, word-level features are those most likely to impact intelligibility at the lexical level, and discourse-level features are likely to affect intelligibility at the semantic and pragmatic levels, and they are also more likely to impact comprehensibility. There are also spoken language elements related to pronunciation that are nonetheless not included in my categories for pronunciation. Any of the categories (word-level, discourse-level, and related areas) may impact perceptions of speech. In addition, although Figure 2.1 divides features into separate categories, this is a failure of the visual in representing the ways in which the categories interact. For example, word stress and rhythm both affect the pronunciation of vowels, with unstressed syllables strongly leaning toward schwa. Schwa is clearly a frequent segmental, but it is not a phoneme of English, but rather a variant of other vowels when they occur in unstressed syllables (Ladefoged, 1980). Stressed syllables in any part of a word are also the location for aspirated voiceless stop consonants, as in *pill, repeat, till, return, kill,* and *acute,* creating a dependency of some consonant allophones

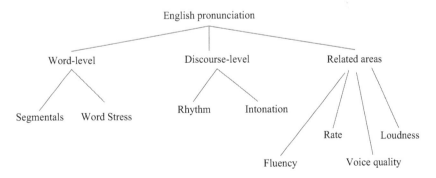

Figure 2.1 Pronunciation features related to intelligibility

and stress. The rhythm of the phrase level and the stress patterns of words affect the ways sounds change in connected speech (e.g., the phoneme /t/ as realized in *city, nature, button,* and *"can't you' "* are not the phonetic sound [t] in North American English). Pronunciation of the individual segments, in other words, is dependent upon where they occur in words, which are in turn affected by where they occur within a phrase. Prominence occurs on syllables that are emphasized through a combination of pitch, syllable duration (a rhythmic feature), and loudness. Prominence typically (but not always) occurs on the stressed syllable of the prominent word, connecting prominence to word stress. Prominence results in segments that are pronounced with particular clarity and precision. The prominent syllable in a phrase is often marked by pitch, and is the beginning of the final pitch contour in the phrase – that is, its intonation.

Word-Level Features

Word-level features include segmentals (vowels and consonants) and word stress (Figure 2.2). They also include consonant clusters, a type of segmental which may, when mispronounced, have an effect on syllable structure. This introduction is provided to define how segmentals and word stress are related to intelligibility and comprehensibility.

Segmentals include approximately forty phonemes for most varieties of English (around twenty-four consonant phonemes and fourteen or more vowel phonemes). The phonemes mask the number of sounds that English uses, since phonemes often have multiple well-known allophones that are important for pronunciation teaching. For example, English regularly employs a glottal stop ([ʔ]) before vowel initial words (e.g., *I* → [ʔaɪ]) or as an allophone for /t/ before a final nasal (e.g., button –[bʌʔn̩]). Other well-known allophones include

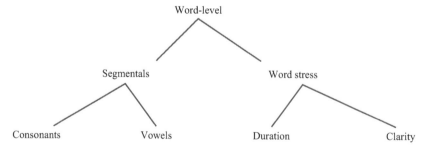

Figure 2.2 Word-based features important to intelligibility

aspirated voiceless stops and affricates in *pill/till/kill/chill*, the dark (velarized) /l/ in *all* (as opposed to the light /l/ in word initial position, e.g., *lap*), the flapped /t/ in *city*, the now increasingly rare voiceless labial-velar fricative [ʍ] in *which* (sounds like [hw]), and many others. For vowels, allophones are almost too numerous to count, as vowel quality often shifts noticeably in the presence of nasals, before /ɹ/ or dark /l/, before /g/, and in unstressed syllables.

Regarding word stress, English is a free-stress language in that stress is not fixed to a particular syllable. Stress can occur on first, second, or third syllables, but the placement is fixed for individual words. For example, the main stress for a word may fall on the first syllable (*COMfort*, *BEAUtiful*), the second (*caNOE*, *rePULsive*), the third (*referENdum*, *questionnAIRE*), etc. Stressed syllables typically have greater segmental clarity, greater syllable duration, and greater intensity than unstressed syllables. When they are in particular discourse contexts, they may also be marked with pitch movement (Ladd & Cutler, 1983)

Both segmentals and word stress are likely to impact intelligibility at the lexical level in that mispronunciations may lead listeners to fail to decode the intended words. This failure may come from identifying other possible words (as happens with minimal pairs) or failing to identify any word that matches the speech signal (as with segments that are distorted). Both consonants and vowels are affected by the stress patterns of words. Mis-stressed words may especially affect the ways that vowels are pronounced in English because of the ubiquity of the unstressed vowel schwa (33 percent of all vowels according to Woods, 2005). Schwa is a key perceptual clue to lack of stress in English, and listeners tend to classify full vowels, even in unstressed syllables, as stressed (Fear, Cutler, & Butterfield, 1995). Because of these interactions, word stress and segmentals are inseparable in their impact on intelligibility (Zielinski, 2008). An unexpected stress pattern on a word (e.g., *FORtune* → *forTUNE*) also may affect the ways that vowels and consonants are produced (e.g., [ˈfɔɹtʃən] versus [fɚˈtʰun]).

Discourse-Level Features

Discourse-level features (Figure 2.3) include suprasegmental features that carry categorical (i.e., phonological) meaning differences. In relation to how listeners may (mis)understand speakers, these suprasegmentals are not likely to cause listeners to misunderstand individual words (making words unintelligible) but are likely to cause listeners to process meaning with greater difficulty (making speech more effortful to understand). Another suprasegmental, word stress, as discussed

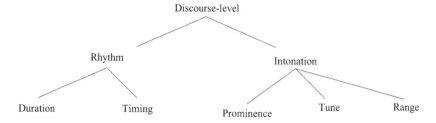

Figure 2.3 Discourse-based pronunciation features important to intelligibility

above, is included as a word-level feature because it is more likely to impact intelligibility (though it may also impact comprehensibility, or ability to process speech, even without a change in vowel quality, as in Slowiaczek [1990]).

Rhythm, the first discourse-level feature, involves at the very least the relative durations of syllables and the timing of syllabic beats. The constructed sentence in (2.1), made up of all single-syllable words, varies between longer, stressed syllables (in CAPS) and shorter, unstressed syllables (in lower case). The stressed words have a pronunciation that will be closer to the citation form, while the unstressed words are prone to simplification (e.g., *has* is likely to have the [h] deleted or even to be contracted with *John*).

(2.1)

JOHN has CLIMBED the TREE to GET the CAT that's been STUCK for a TIME.

In pronunciation teaching, rhythm has often been described in terms of stress timing and syllable timing (e.g., Pike, 1945). Stress-timed languages (like English) are asserted to have large durational differences between stressed and unstressed syllables, with relatively equal timing between stresses. Syllable-timed languages are considered to have quite similar durations between syllables and thus timing that is at the level of the syllable rather than at the level of stressed syllables. This well-known formulation is overly simplistic, however, and stress timing and syllable timing are tendencies rather than absolutes (Dauer, 1983). The rhythmic characteristics of many languages remain of interest to researchers, and a wide variety of rhythm metrics have been tested for different L1 speakers (e.g., Low, Grabe, & Nolan, 2000), L2 speakers (Yang & Chu, 2016), and L1–L2 comparisons (White & Mattys, 2007). However, there is great uncertainty about how well various rhythm metrics actually capture perceived rhythmic differences between languages (Arvaniti, 2012).

In English, rhythm and word stress are similar. The discourse level for rhythm in many ways mirrors the word-level rhythm of lexical stress. A major difference is that word stress typically is limited to multi-syllabic words, whereas rhythm includes stress for single-syllable words. In English, for example, content words (e.g., nouns, verbs, adjectives, adverbs, negatives), including those of one syllable, are normally stressed in discourse. Single-syllable function words (e.g., prepositions, auxiliary verbs, pronouns, determiners) are typically unstressed in discourse. Many single-syllable function words are also among the most frequent words in English, helping to contribute to the perception of stress timing.

Intonation, the second suprasegmental, includes at least three distinct ways in which meaning is communicated: prominence, tune, and range. The example in (2.2) illustrates these three. For context, imagine that the sentence is spoken in the middle of a lecture.

(2.2)

The initial extra-high pitch range in the example is meant to signal a topic shift, or what has been called a paratone (paragraph tone, see Wichmann, 2000). Pitch range may also signal gradient meanings related to emotional engagement. NEXT is a prominent syllable with a jump up in pitch to call attention to the importance of the information (in this case, NEXT is likely related to PREVIOUS, the topic(s) that came before.) The last use of pitch is the drop in pitch from NEXT to the end of the utterance. This is the tune. Each of these uses is part of how intonation works in English.

Intonation is the system that uses voice pitch changes to communicate meaning. However, intonation may include more than voice pitch. Prominent syllables are not only higher or lower in pitch than the syllables that precede them, they also have greater duration (a rhythmic feature) and more clearly enunciated segmentals. In addition, the varied intonational categories are closely related. The final prominent syllable in a phrase (the nucleus) is also the beginning of the tune, and both may be pronounced with greater or lesser pitch range.

In regard to comprehensibility, the specific contribution of these suprasegmental features is understudied and needs greater attention. Isaacs and Trofimovich (2012) found that more native-like vowel reduction and pitch contours correlated with better comprehensibility ratings, while pitch range was not significantly related to comprehensibility. Kang (2010) found that pitch range was instead associated with accentedness, but not comprehensibility. Tune, on the other hand, has also been suggested to have an effect on comprehensibility. Pickering (2001), for example, found that Koreans teaching in English used a greater number of falling tunes than would be expected, and that the relative numbers of rising and falling tunes made their speech more challenging for listeners. (This is an interpretation of Pickering, given that she worked within a model that considers tunes to communicate differences in information structure.)

Related Areas

Comprehensibility and intelligibility are not only associated with pronunciation, but also with other characteristics of spoken language (Figure 2.4) that have an indirect connection to pronunciation. These areas include fluency (Derwing, Munro, & Thomson, 2007), speech rate (Kang, 2010), loudness (not typically addressed for L2 pronunciation research), and voice quality (Esling & Wong, 1983; Ladd, Silverman, Tolkmitt, Bergmann, & Scherer, 1985; Munro, Derwing, & Burgess, 2010). Generally, this book will not address these characteristics in detail, because other than fluency and speech rate (which is a component of fluency), these things are more idiosyncratic than the other features.

In particular, research on fluency and speech rate seems to have significant effects on judgments of comprehensibility and accentedness. Pronunciation research on voice quality and its inclusion in teaching materials has never been common, despite its seeming promise in pedagogy (Jones & Evans, 1995; Pennington, 1989). Loudness is an especially important issue in regard to hearing loss, hearing in noise, and the intelligibility of speech for those with cochlear implants. Anecdotally, some L2 learners can become more intelligible simply by speaking at a volume more appropriate to the context (e.g., in a large classroom), but this has not been typically considered important for an L2 pronunciation syllabus.

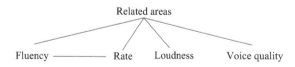

Figure 2.4 Spoken language features sometimes associated with pronunciation

Fluency is sometimes associated with general proficiency (Fillmore, 1979) or smoothness of speech (Lennon, 1990). I use fluency to refer to smoothness of speech. However, judgments of fluency are also closely tied to many discrete elements of speech, including the numbers of silent pauses and filled pauses, whether junctures in spoken phrases are grammatically logical, mean length of run, repetitions in speech, and more (Lennon, 1990), as well as the level of automaticity in speaking (Segalowitz, 2000), phonological memory (O'Brien, Segalowitz, Freed, & Collentine, 2007), and attention control (Segalowitz, 2007). Remedial attention to pronunciation is more likely to be successful when learners are relatively comfortable speaking and listening in the L2 – that is, when they are sufficiently fluent. The development of fluency is clearly an important part of the big picture of L2 speaking development and instruction (Firth, 1992), and comfortable fluency can help give a global structure to other elements of spoken language, but fluency is not, by itself, part of L2 pronunciation. The fact that it impacts comprehensibility and is critical in communicative language teaching (Rossiter, Derwing, Manimtim, & Thomson, 2010) means that, like pronunciation, it should be prioritized in teaching speaking and listening.

Speech rate is predictive of fluency judgments (Cucchiarini, Strik, & Boves, 2000; Kormos & Dénes, 2004). Fluent speakers can speak at different rates, so a fluent speaker could speak at a slower rate than a speaker who is judged less fluent. Speech rate is typically measured in syllables per second or words per minute. This rate may include all silences and filled pauses, or they may be removed, providing a measure of articulation rate. L2 speakers tend to speak more slowly than L1 natives, and their comprehensibility may be helped by faster speech. However, excessively fast or slow speech is more likely to be rated as less comprehensible and more accented (Derwing & Munro, 2001; Munro & Derwing, 1998).

Prioritizing: A Summary and Critique of Recommendations

Various writers have made recommendations about priorities for pronunciation teaching. These recommendations go from very general (learners should try for "listener-friendly pronunciation," in the words of Olle Kjellin) to more detailed descriptions of what might be included in instruction. Kenworthy's (1987) early approach to intelligibility was based on describing learner pronunciation issues that may result in unintelligibility. She lists both segmental and suprasegmental issues, including substituting one sound for another, deleting or adding sounds, connecting one word to another, mis-stressing words, not using stress-based rhythm, and the misuse of intonation or use of unfamiliar intonation. Kenworthy does not further prioritize these potential sources of unintelligibility.

In another early attempt to prioritize, Jenner described a "common core for pronunciation" that would "guarantee intelligibility and acceptability anywhere in the world" by specifying "what all native speakers of all native varieties have in common which enables them to communicate effectively with native speakers of varieties other than their own" (1989, p. 2). Rather than focusing on the differences between varieties, or indeed ruling out certain native varieties a priori while elevating others as models, Jenner thought it essential to look at commonalities, recognizing that speakers of native varieties have a better chance of being intelligible to each other because of what they share. Jenner suggested that the commonalities included vowel quantity (phonetic length differences), most consonants, syllable structure, stress-based rhythm, and varied commonalities of intonation, including tonic syllables and final movements of pitch. Jenner's recommendations refer to segmental and suprasegmental features, and they often distinguish between a category (e.g., consonants) and secondary features that are not essential in the category (e.g., distinctions between [l] and [ɬ]).

In another analysis focused on segmental pronunciation, Brown (1988) proposed functional load as a way to determine pronunciation priorities. Functional load, a topic that had been put forth long before Brown's application to pronunciation teaching, measures the "frequency with which two phonemes contrast in all environments" (Brown, 1988, p. 591). Functional load is therefore inherently contrastive and the use of minimal pairs gives a way to quantify priorities. Phoneme contrasts that have a higher functional load are more likely to cause confusion if mispronounced, and they should be given priority over those with lower functional loads (assuming, of course, that students have difficulty with the contrast). Brown's proposal for measuring functional load takes into account not only the number of minimal pairs for a contrast, but other issues such as the number of minimal pairs for the same part of speech, the extent to which a mispronunciation is stigmatized in native accents, and the acoustic similarity of the sounds involved in the contrast (not all minimal pairs are likely to be confused). For example, Brown's analysis lists contrasts such as /p, b/, /p, f/, /l, ɹ/, and /l, n/ as of the highest importance, and contrasts such as /f, θ/, /ð, d/, and /dʒ, j/ as very low-priority contrasts. The proposal quantifies importance, but Brown recognizes that quantification alone cannot completely determine priorities. In addition, functional load is a measure of segmental importance only and cannot be applied to suprasegmental features, even to relatively uncomplicated ones like word stress.

Firth prioritizes differently by proposing a "zoom principle" for teaching in which "a pronunciation syllabus should begin with the widest possible focus and move gradually in on specific problems" (1992, p. 173). By this, she means that pronunciation instruction should start with general speaking abilities and ability to communicate before moving on to phonetic details. This is put forth as the most likely way to promote comprehensible speech. Priorities beyond general speaking ability (including volume and clarity) include intonation and stress/rhythm (features that are more related to general speaking ability) before considering consonants and vowels. Interestingly, Firth's recommendations led to some paradoxical suggestions that seem to have little to do with communicative importance. Despite its not being seen as critically important for understanding, /θ/ is given high priority within the consonantal system because students perceive it to be important and because it is relatively easy to teach effectively, giving students confidence to try for more difficult sounds. Practically speaking, this may also be a feature to spend modest time on if it leads to greater commitment to features more likely to improve intelligibility (Derwing & Munro, 2015).

Evidence for Firth's recommendations comes from a recent study by Isaacs and Trofimovich (2012). With a goal of making explicit the issues involved in comprehensibility ratings used in a variety of spoken assessment tools, the researchers examined which factors were salient in ratings of comprehensibility. Using criteria collected from research studies, the researchers identified nineteen quantitatively scored speech measures, including segmentals, suprasegmentals, fluency, vocabulary, grammar, and discourse. Speech samples of forty French learners of English were analyzed, and the scores derived from the analysis were then correlated with naive NS raters' comprehensibility ratings (based on Munro & Derwing, 1995). Following this, three experienced ESL (English as a second language) teachers with minimal training in pronunciation listened to the speech samples and identified the factors they noticed when evaluating the speech of the French-speaking learners. Five factors were identified as important: fluency, breadth of vocabulary, grammatical control, construction of the discourse, and word-stress accuracy. Of these five measures, only one involves pronunciation in an explicit way, while the others are more global measures. The study concludes that expert raters do not focus overtly on pronunciation when evaluating speech comprehensibility, but that instead they take account of features that are not often included in pronunciation-oriented instruction. Other evidence for Firth's contention can be seen from the work of Derwing, Munro, and Wiebe (1998), who found that listeners rated L2 learners' comprehensibility higher after a pronunciation course focusing on global skills and suprasegmentals than after a course focusing on segmental improvement. Similar results for other groups of learners can be found in the work of Gordon and Darcy (2016).

McNerney and Mendelsohn (1992) argue for suprasegmentals to be given top priority in pronunciation instruction. Suprasegmentals control how information is related, and they also are said to have a special role in conveying attitudinal meaning (cf. Pike, 1945). McNerney and Mendelsohn say that "a short-term pronunciation course should focus first and foremost on suprasegmentals as they have the greatest impact on the comprehensibility of learners' English" and because through suprasegmentals "greater change can be effected in a short time" (1992, p. 186), although they provide no empirical evidence for their confident assertion. Suprasegmental features include:

- word stress and rhythm;
- major sentence stress (or focus);
- intonation;
- linking and pausing;
- palatalization in rhythmically related contexts such as "can't you" and "did you."

In another attempt to specify priorities for a short pronunciation course, Henderson (2008) identified pacing (stressed words per minute), speech rate (syllables per second), and word stress as important in promoting more comprehensible speech in spontaneous and prepared speaking tasks. The author argued that these three areas were most amenable to changes in the short term, and that learners of English in this university-level planned speaking course were most likely to be successful by learning to vary their pacing and speech rate. Word stress, which was asserted to be important in promoting understanding, was also presented as a feature that may not be easy to change in the short run. It may be significant that both Isaacs and Trofimovich (2012) and Henderson (2008) studied French learners of English, a group for whom word stress may be particularly important.

Gilbert (2001) suggests priorities for beginning learners based on her experience and repeated attempts to distill that experience into pronunciation features that are likely to be learnable and to make a difference in comprehensibility. She lists the following as essential: sound–symbol correspondences for the spelling of key vowel sounds, consonant sounds (mostly final) that serve as signals of grammatical meaning, linking between words, epenthesis and deletion of syllables, word stress, differences between weak and strong syllables (stress timing), and emphasis (prominence or nuclear stress). This set of priorities emphasizes suprasegmentals, but also says that certain segmental targets are both important enough to pay attention to and likely to be learnable even at the beginning levels of proficiency.

Not all writers who agree that a greater emphasis on suprasegmentals is important for pronunciation instruction prioritize what should be taught. Morley (1991), in her historical review of the evolution of pronunciation in TESOL (teaching English to speakers of other languages), described many of the changes from the traditional, segmental-based approach of the 1950s and 1960s to the more communicatively oriented approach becoming evident in the 1980s and 1990s. However, Morley's recommendations called for "an expanded concept of what constitutes the domain of pronunciation" (1991, p. 493) rather than setting clear priorities. This expanded domain saw pronunciation's proper sphere of influence as encompassing communication skills, suprasegmentals, segmentals, voice quality, body language, greater learner and teacher involvement in developing self-monitoring skills, contextualization, linking listening to speaking, greater attention to sound–spelling relationships, and attention to individual differences among ESL learners. These recommendations cannot be faulted in and of themselves, but taken together their approach to teaching pronunciation suggests that previous lack of success came not because of misplaced priorities or goals, but because the program of instruction was too limited to work. While Gilbert's triage metaphor suggests that certain pronunciation needs are medically critical, identifiable, and should be dealt with immediately, Morley's recommendations sound like an extended stay at a luxury pronunciation spa with personal accent trainers.

Prioritizing for Nonnative Speaker–Nonnative Speaker Communication

All these approaches assume that native listeners are the appropriate audience for determining what is intelligible and what is not. This assumption is called into question by Jenkins (2000) in her proposal for a prioritized set of features for pronunciation teaching, the Lingua Franca Core (LFC). Jenkins recognizes that most nonnative speakers (NNS) of English around the world interact in English not with NSs but with other NNSs. This difference in audience prompted Jenkins to consider changes in how priorities are determined, with mutual intelligibility being the standard by which pronunciation features are to be judged for importance. Jenkins studied the interactive interlanguage talk of NNS dyads doing communicative tasks. She analyzed where communication failed in these communicative tasks and determined the causes of the forty instances in which communication broke down. Of these, twenty-seven were related to pronunciation deviations. The deviations that caused loss of intelligibility were candidates for the LFC. Those features that did not cause a loss of intelligibility were typically excluded from the core. The core included most consonant sounds, some consonant cluster simplifications, vowel length, and nuclear stress (i.e., prominence). Consonants that were excluded were the interdental fricatives and [ɫ], the velarized, or dark, allophone of /l/. Consonant cluster deletions were included in the LFC because loss of sounds was argued to be more likely to impact intelligibility than was epenthesis. Perhaps the place in which the LFC departs from the other recommendations most radically is in its treatment of suprasegmentals. Only one, nuclear stress, is included in the core. Others, such as stress-based rhythm, intonation, and word stress are all excluded based on Jenkins' data, her appeal to teachability/learnability, and the impact of universals. Some of these decisions have been criticized, especially regarding word stress (Dauer, 2005; McCrocklin, 2012). In one description of pronunciation teaching in China that used the LFC as a rubric, Deterding (2010) showed what most experienced teachers know very well: Pronunciation difficulties are varied, and they include errors that reflect both core and non-core features.

In a replication of Jenkins' (2000) work, Kennedy (2012) found that the most common sources of unintelligibility were vowel and consonant segments, either individually or in combination. The only suprasegmental feature implicated in unintelligibility was word stress. Nuclear stress (prominence) was not a source of unintelligibility. Kennedy also suggested that learners may not always indicate that they do not understand a speaker and that researchers and teachers may not realize that pronunciation is a factor. This problem may be connected to the types of interactive tasks that are used to collect data, such that both listeners and speakers have to demonstrate understanding.

Walker (2010) applies the LFC extensively to pronunciation teaching, giving the original recommendations a classroom teacher's perspective. His defense of ELF (English as a lingua franca) priorities describes why he thinks the LFC is appropriate, including issues related to bottom-up rather than top-down processing, mutual intelligibility, speaker identity, and teachability. One of the benefits of the LFC, Walker argues, is that it recognizes that ELF speakers make greater use of bottom-up processing in their interactions. This means that they are much more reliant on the details of the acoustic signal in interactions, and thus more likely to be affected by unexpected pronunciations of segmentals. NSs, in contrast, make greater use of top-down processing, in that they can more easily guess at the content of a spoken message even when the segmentals deviate from what is expected. The LFC, however, remains controversial in many of its recommendations. It lacks robust empirical support, assumes that all NNS contexts are similar, and does not take into account the importance of stigma associated with otherwise intelligible pronunciations (LeVelle & Levis, 2014). The actual details of what should and should not be included thus have found uncertain acceptance despite its appeal, and influential researchers have criticized its consistency, calling for empirical verification of its recommendations (e.g., Szpyra-Kozłowska, 2015, pp. 77–84).

The second area discussed is mutual intelligibility. Intelligibility is a context-sensitive feature of spoken discourse, a characterization that will find little disagreement from almost anyone interested in teaching pronunciation. Walker is more nuanced than Jenkins, recognizing that the LFC may need to be adjusted in some ways because interlocutors may also include NSs. For example, the teaching of weak forms and vowel reduction may be strictly non-core as far as production, but mutual intelligibility suggests that it is a core feature for perception. NS interlocutors will reduce vowels, and it is important for ELF listeners to be able to understand such speech. For communication to happen, both speakers and listeners must be intelligible to each other, and learning materials typically make use of native speech.

The third positive aspect of an LFC approach is that it recognizes the importance of speaker identity. The LFC recognizes that achieving a native accent is not necessary, and that the influence of the speaker's L1 should be accepted, as long as intelligibility is not compromised. This is clearly not just part of NNS–NNS communication. Most people in inner-circle communities, especially in larger cities with significant immigrant communities, also think that an NS accent is not needed.

Finally, Walker discusses Jenkins' concept of teachability. Walker says that "many features that are essential in a traditional EFL syllabus are largely unteachable. This was the case with tone and stress-timing, and with the use of weak forms and certain connected speech changes. In contrast, most of the items in the LFC are teachable, with classroom teaching leading to learning" (2010, p. 63). While it makes little sense to teach things that our learners cannot learn, little evidence is provided regarding teachability. In fact, many of the features that are said to be unteachable are ones that Judy Gilbert (2001), who is a notorious stickler for teaching only those things that can be learned, provides as priorities for beginning learners: linking, word stress, and distinguishing strong and weak syllables.

What does it mean for a feature to be teachable? Walker (2010) says this about nuclear stress placement:

[It] is teachable in the sense that the rules are simple enough for learners to master in the classroom, although for some learners there may be a noticeable gap between receptive and productive competence. As a result, our primary aim in the classroom will be to make learners aware of the existence and importance of nuclear stress. This should make them more sensitive to its use by other speakers, and consequently more likely to acquire competence in its use.
                                                            (Walker, 2010, p. 64)

Teachability thus seems to mean a topic whose rules can be learned and applied by learners, leading to acquisition. It does not mean teachable. Any topic can be taught. What matters is the extent to which the teaching, the input, becomes learning, or intake. The principle of teachability/learnability will be discussed in detail in Principle 6 in Chapter 8.

Walker suggests ways the LFC might apply to speakers of different languages. Following Jenkins, he includes in the core rhotic /ɹ/ in all positions (characteristic of most North American English speakers), the non-flapped /t/ characteristic of British English, and word stress (an admitted gray area in Jenkins, 2000) because of its impact on the core feature of nuclear stress, as well as vowel reduction and weak forms for receptive competence. In addition, certain errors (such as final glottal stops) that are common among certain users of English should be addressed because they may cause loss of intelligibility by masking the character of final stop consonants (see Walker, 2010, p. 44; cf. Gilbert, 2001).

The LFC's recommendations have been used to examine features that promote the mutual intelligibility of emerging South-East Asian Englishes and the international intelligibility of Hong Kong English. Deterding and Kirkpatrick (2006) examined conversational interactions in English among speakers from ten South East Asian countries and identified features of speech that seem to form the basis of a developing regional variety. Features of this variety shared by speakers from at least four countries were the use of a stop for the voiceless dental fricative (*dis* for *this*), reduced initial aspiration of voiceless stops (*pill* sounds like *bill*), monophthongal mid-front and back vowels (*take* and *goat* do not have the extra glide typical of inner-circle varieties, so that they may sound like *tech* and *gut*), a lack of reduced vowels, stressed pronouns, and phrase-final discourse stress (e.g., *Give it to HIM*). Of these, several are features that Jenkins suggests should be treated as part of the LFC core (aspiration and nuclear stress) and others are part of her non-core features (dental fricatives and reduced vowels). Others are less obvious and may take finer analysis to determine whether they should be seen as core or non-core. Monophthongal vowels, however, may violate the quantity criterion for vowels while keeping the quality intact.

In the work of Kirkpatrick, Deterding, and Wong (2008), the intelligibility of the Hong Kong English of highly educated students was rated by university students in Singapore (a transitioning outer-circle country where English has an official role but is not the native language of all) and Australia (an inner-circle country in which English is the native language of most people). The students in Australia were both NSs and NNSs of English. Recordings of their speech were played for the subjects, who did a listening comprehension task about the content of the speech. In addition to this measure of intelligibility, raters considered the speakers in terms of intelligence and likeability, two concepts well-attested in other studies to be associated with speech, and in our terms, with the potential for irritation. In an interesting finding, the speakers who were the most intelligible were also seen as less intelligent and less likeable, often based on things they said, but sometimes on the basis of the speech being too good, suggesting that the raters thought the speaker was showy and proud. Clearly, intelligibility, a good thing in itself, may sometimes be judged negatively in some contexts based on unforeseen social values. Overall, Hong Kong English was widely intelligible in this area of the world, where it is likely to be a familiar variety of English. However, not all speakers were equally intelligible.

These different attempts to specify priorities for intelligibility-based instruction are interesting both in what they agree on and also in what they do not agree on. The variety found in the recommendations comes primarily from a heavy reliance on reasoning and a paucity of empirical evidence. Table 2.1 provides a summary of the recommendations.

Critiquing the Recommendations

The different attempts to specify priorities are a mishmash of incomplete and contradictory recommendations. Some of the studies offer recommendations based on experience (Firth, 1992; Gilbert, 2001; Kenworthy, 1987; McNerney & Mendelsohn, 1992), others provide priorities based on analysis of similarities and differences between English varieties (Jenner, 1989) or careful experimental evidence

Table 2.1 Pronunciation priority recommendations from various authors

Study	Recommended targets	Recommended for exclusion	Source of evidence
Studies related to ESL/EFL contexts			
Kenworthy (1987)	Sound substitutions, deletions, and additions; linking; word stress; rhythm; intonation		Reasoning based on experience
Jenner (1989)	Vowel length; most consonants; syllable structure; stress-based rhythm; prominence; movements of pitch	Vowel quality; [H]	Reasoning based on features shared by most NS varieties
Brown (1991)	High functional load contrasts, e.g., /p, b/, /p, f/, /l, r/, /l, n/, /æ, ɛ/	Low functional load contrasts, e.g., /f, θ/, /ð, d/, /dʒ, j/, /u, ʊ/	Functional load calculations based on minimal pair frequency modified by other criteria
Firth (1992)	In descending order: general speaking abilities; intonation; stress/rhythm; consonants and vowels	None specified	Based on a "Zoom Principle," a pedagogical approach that prioritizes general speaking habits over phonetic details
Isaacs and Trofimovich (2012)	Word stress; lexical richness; grammatical control; use of discourse features; fluency	Pitch range	Based on correlations between scalar comprehensibility ratings and careful quantitative analysis, informed by teacher's verbal protocols (one L1 only)
McNerney and Mendelsohn (1992)	Word-level stress/unstress; sentence-level stress/unstress; major sentence stress (or focus); intonation; linking and pausing; palatalization in rhythmically related contexts	None specified	Reasoning based on the belief that more change can be achieved by focusing on suprasegmentals in a short-term course

Gilbert (2001)	Key vowel sound/spelling correspondences; final consonants signaling grammatical meaning; linking; word stress; strong and weak syllables; emphasis (prominence)		Priorities for beginning learners based on experience as a teacher and textbook writer
Morley (1991)	An expanded domain for pronunciation, including (in no particular order): communication skills; suprasegmental; segmentals; voice quality; body language; greater learner and teacher involvement in developing self-monitoring skills; contextualization; linking; greater attention to sound–spelling relationships; attention to individual differences among learners	None specified	Reasoning based upon the asserted need for pronunciation to take on expanded roles in the language classroom
Henderson (2008)	Pacing of speech; rate of speech; word stress		A review of principles put forth by other writers. The choice of features for the short course are not clearly justified
Studies related to English as an international language (EIL)/ELF contexts			
Jenkins (2000)	Most consonant sounds; some consonant cluster simplifications involving deletions; vowel length,; nuclear stress (i.e., prominence)	Interdental fricatives; [ʰ]; consonant cluster epenthesis; stress-based rhythm; weak forms; intonation; lexical stress	Forty errors in NNS–NNS interaction, twenty-seven of which were directly related to pronunciation. Additional criteria of teachability and learnability *(continued)*

Table 2.1 (cont.)

Study	Recommended targets	Recommended for exclusion	Source of evidence
Walker (2010)	Same as Jenkins (2000), including rhotic [ɹ] in all positions; intervocalic [t] rather than flap in *city*, *beauty*; word stress as a basis for nuclear stress; weak forms and vowel reduction for receptive competence	Same as Jenkins (2000) with some modifications for specific language groups	Jenkins' (2000) findings modified by trying to implement the LFC. Other research findings also consulted
Deterding and Kirkpatrick (2006)	No priorities given		A descriptive study of the features that may be part of an emerging South-East Asian variety of English
Kirkpatrick et al. (2008)	No priorities given		A study of the intelligibility of Hong Kong English to listeners in Singapore and Australia. Hong Kong English speakers were generally highly intelligible, but high intelligibility did not guarantee perceptions of likeability or intelligence

(Isaacs & Trofimovich, 2012) or other objective analyses based on models of intelligibility (Brown, 1991; Jenkins, 2000); some study intelligibility without any intention of recommending pronunciation priorities (Deterding & Kirkpatrick, 2006; Kirkpatrick et al., 2008), and others describe not only what should be included but also what should be excluded (Brown, 1991; Jenkins, 2000; Jenner, 1989). Features such as word stress are seen to be essential in some research (Isaacs & Trofimovich, 2012), while they are seen as relatively unimportant in other recommendations (Jenkins, 2000) or potentially important in relation to other features (Walker, 2010). A focus on suprasegmentals is encouraged by some authors (McNerney & Mendelsohn, 1992), while it is largely bypassed in favor of segmentals in other accounts (Jenkins, 2000). Some writers seek to achieve quicker rates of improvement in intelligibility by focusing first and foremost on features that are not usually part of pronunciation instruction (Firth, 1992), while other recommendations read like a pronunciation wishlist with no attempts to prioritize (Morley, 1991). Sounds such as /θ/ are left off many lists, including Jenkins' influential LFC, but other writers long to keep /θ/ because its supposed teachability may make it easier for learners to feel success and thus try harder sounds (Firth, 1992) or because there are situations in which /θ/ can affect intelligibility (Deterding, 2005; Henderson, 2008). Some of these seemingly contradictory recommendations are likely due to different L1 learner groups, limited numbers in each study, and the context in which the study took place.

It is clear that there is a further need to examine principles that help teachers decide on priorities based on context, allowing a finer-grained analysis than any single study can provide. All teachers have to prioritize, and it is best to have explicit, research-based support for setting priorities (Derwing & Munro, 2005). Much that has been written about priorities cannot be called research-based, and the articles that are based on empirical data should therefore have greater weight. Jenkins (2000), for example, has been much discussed, much praised, and much derided, but her recommendations are valuable because they are based upon evidence. However, the amount of evidence is small and some of the recommendations have been called into question (Dauer, 2005; McCrocklin, 2012). Her twenty-seven pronunciation errors (of forty total errors impacting intelligibility) allow us to make suggestive recommendations about what should and should not be included in the core features. /θ/, for example, did not lead to loss of intelligibility in her data. Clearly, there must have been many other phonemes that likewise did not lead to loss of intelligibility, but Jenkins made recommendations against /θ/ as a core item, and for other sounds not only based on her evidence but also on her view of English's role in the world. This indicates that decisions about priorities must be made not only on explicit evidence, but on how implicit evidence is interpreted regarding pronunciation's role in communicative success or failure in particular communicative contexts.

Context and Intelligibility

Finally, intelligibility is sensitive to the context in which communication takes place. What this means is that the degree of accuracy that determines intelligibility changes from one situation to the next, depending on the type of language use required. Intelligibility can be seen as the lowest possible standard that a speaker has to meet in order to get by. Hinofotis and Bailey (1981), in a now famous phrase, talk about "an intelligibility threshold" that speakers must meet in order to communicate effectively. The intelligibility threshold, rather than being an objective criterion, is actually a moving target that includes much more than pronunciation (Tyler, 1992). Much of what causes the target to move is the context in which speech takes place. The influence of context is understudied, but it is likely to be an important determinant of how intelligible a particular speech sample is.

It should be obvious that certain contexts of use have higher stakes for both the speaker and the listener. For example, if your job involves staffing a cash register in an area in which ethnic shops are the norm (e.g., Chinatown), your needs for understandable pronunciation in English may be relatively low. Most of the customers are likely to either be from the same speech community or outsiders who have decided to take the extra step to shop there rather than somewhere else. The people the clerk interacts with are either sympathetic or are unlikely to come back regularly (tourists). Contrast this context with an instructor in a university class. Interactions are regular and required (students have to come to the lab or breakout session), high-stakes (performance in the class is highly dependent on being able to understand material through the mediation of the instructor), and subject to significant cross-cultural conflict (misunderstanding may be likely to be seen as caused by the inability of the other to play the expected role; cf. Rubin, 1992). High-stakes contexts include education, health, and translation, all areas in which speakers and listeners have to negotiate language and culture barriers and where the cost for failure is very real.

In North American higher education, many basic classes in the natural sciences, mathematics, and engineering are taught by NNSs of English. While some of these teachers are regular faculty, many are graduate teaching assistants who help fund their education through teaching. The classes they teach include not only majors in the field, but also students from other fields who are required to take courses that they may not feel comfortable with or enjoy. Their overall proficiency in English is very high. These NNSs have, after all, been admitted to demanding graduate degree programs in a foreign-language setting, and their needs for language support are targeted to specific areas such as speaking or writing.

Having these students teach sets up a natural context in which undergraduates' stress from learning that demands new content (e.g., organic chemistry) can interact with stress from the way the content is presented (which may be due to the graduate students being inexperienced teachers or due to cultural views of appropriate teacher and student behavior), mixed in with unfamiliar or hard-to-understand accents. Pedagogical effectiveness and unfamiliar or inadequate pronunciation or language skills may both be implicated in lack of achievement, but inadequate language skills are most likely to be blamed for ineffective teaching. Many international teaching assistants (ITAs) and faculty development programs recognize that working on teaching and presentation skills can lead to greater success (and presumably, a better perception of comprehensibility) even without extensive work on language skills.

Other studies also make clear that comprehensibility is not based only on pronunciation. Tyler (1992) asked raters to listen to two presentations, one given by an ITA and one by an NTA (native teaching assistant). Both presentations were then transcribed and read aloud by an NS of English so that pronunciation would not be a factor in how the presentations were rated. Raters evaluated the ITA as being less effective and less easy to follow than the NTA. The researcher argued that the ITA's use of unexpected, nonparallel discourse markers (e.g., "the first one" followed by "and then" and "after that"), not establishing clear synonyms or clearly linking pronominal forms to the original noun phrases, and overuse of coordination and underuse of subordination, caused a loss of understanding.

The use of discourse markers may also be involved in how easy it is to understand speech. Williams (1992) found that when discourse moves were explicitly marked, ITA presentations were rated as being more comprehensible. Tyler and Bro (1992), however, found that ITAs overused simple additive connectors that were ambiguous in the connections between ideas in the discourse. Liao (2009) examined Chinese ITAs' use of common English spoken discourse markers in interactions with an interviewer and found that the ITAs overused some (especially *yeah*) and underused others (e.g., *well, I mean*).

Overall, their markers were more restricted in range than for NTAs and included innovations that were not likely to be understood easily by NS interlocutors. At the level of grammatical competence, lexico-grammatical features may hamper ITAs' ability to communicate information clearly. Tyler, Jefferies, and Davies (1988) found that NTAs often used strategies to focus listener attention on information to be foregrounded and backgrounded, but ITAs did not.

In addition, even speech that is completely intelligible may be heard as heavily accented or take more effort to understand (Munro & Derwing, 1995). Expectations and implicit stereotypes may affect how well listeners understand a speaker, despite the speaker being intelligible. Rubin (1992) played a short lecture given by a female speaker of General American English to undergraduate students under two guises: a Caucasian guise and an Asian guise. In the study, some listeners heard the lecture while looking at a picture of a blond Caucasian woman, while other listeners heard the same lecture (spoken by the same voice) while looking at a picture of an equally attractive Asian woman. When asked to demonstrate their understanding of the lecture, the listeners who heard the lecture in the Asian guise understood significantly less well than those who heard the lecture in the Caucasian guise. Comprehension was measured via a cloze of the passage with every seventh word deleted. In addition, listeners completed a semantic differential instrument with scales measuring their attitudes, issues related to background, values, and appearance, as well as items related to accent, ethnicity, and teaching qualifications. While the Munro and Derwing (1995) study demonstrated that listeners can decode speech with 100 percent intelligibility yet find it heavily accented, this study suggests that lack of understanding can be affected by seemingly unrelated nonlanguage factors, in this case the unconscious biases that listeners bring with them to interactions. More recent research suggests that this bias may also be connected to congruence between the visual and the aural. McGowan (2015) used transcription accuracy in noise to examine whether listeners would be more accurate in transcribing Chinese-accented speech when presented with a Chinese face, a Caucasian face, or an unspecified silhouette. Listeners transcribed more successfully when presented with a congruent face (a Chinese face), a finding that was consistent despite differences in experience with listening to Chinese-accented English.

Conclusion

Many recommendations about priorities for pronunciation teaching are painted in broad brushstrokes that probably mask distinctions between important and unimportant features within the same category. For example, Isaacs and Trofimovich (2012) found that pitch movement correlated with comprehensibility ratings at a relatively high rate, whereas pitch range showed no correlation. Yet both are considered to be part of intonation. Levis (1999a) suggests that final intonation may be important for certain grammatical structures (e.g., declaratives), while the same pitch movements are relatively unimportant for others (e.g., yes–no questions). Syllable structure modifications are part of Jenner's (1989) core and Gilbert's (2001) recommendations, while Jenkins (2000) distinguishes between initial deletions (core) and some medial and final deletions and epenthesis (non-core).

It seems clear from the often conflicting, and sometimes contradictory, recommendations that the criteria we use to set priorities are often themselves unclear, based on (un)informed intuition, unsupported by research findings, perhaps because research findings themselves have many gaps. We are still trying to understand the picture in which too many elements are missing, like trying to understand the picture on a jigsaw puzzle with only half the pieces available. A first step toward understanding the bigger picture is to try to specify and justify guidelines that may help us describe what an intelligibility-based approach might look like in the classroom (as in Chapters 8 and 9). It may also be that we need a better picture of how pronunciation not only affects understanding in a vacuum (i.e., via the speech signal alone), but also how it affects understanding in social and communicative contexts.

Part II

Word-Based Errors and Intelligibility

3 *Segmentals and Intelligibility*

Vowel and consonant sounds are the heart of traditional pronunciation teaching, and they remain unavoidably important in an intelligibility-based approach to L2 pronunciation (Derwing & Munro, 2015; Derwing, Munro, & Wiebe, 1998). One cannot speak clearly without sufficient accuracy in pronouncing the sounds of a language. To be understood, the sounds a speaker produces must match what listeners expect to hear. This is why teaching materials typically have provided a great majority of practice exercises using segmental contrasts, usually through the use of minimal pairs (e.g., Dauer, 1993; Orion, 2002), and why the pronunciation of even challenging segmentals has been shown to improve through perceiving differences in L2 segmental contrasts (Thomson, 2011, 2012; Wang & Munro, 2004). In other words, the perception and production of vowels and consonants has to be sufficiently accurate to activate the speaker's intended vocabulary in the mind of the listener. Sufficiently accurate does not mean a perfect match to an ideal. This is unlikely for any speaker, since the realization of phonemes in any language varies according to linguistic environment, idiosyncrasies of individual speakers, and speech register, among other things.

Segmentals refer to the vowel and consonant sounds of a language. Segmentals are distinct from, yet overlap to some extent with, the suprasegmentals of the language. For example, [ə] in English is clearly a vowel, indeed the most common vowel in L1 English varieties. Yet, it is dependent on a suprasegmental, the non-realization of stress, for its pronunciation. Nonetheless, we typically treat schwa and other segmentals as different from stress, rhythm, and intonation. In some languages there may be a relatively equal distribution of vowel and consonant sounds in speech because the languages have a strong tendency toward CV (consonant–vowel) syllable structure, while other languages may have an unequal frequency of consonants and vowels, with more consonants than vowels. Some languages allow multiple consonants to cluster together, while consonant clusters are strongly restricted in other languages. Finally, all the phonemes of a language are unavoidable in speaking, and the extent to which these sounds are pronounced accurately is one factor that affects how well listeners understand speakers. However, it is also clear that different types of mispronunciations may be more or less serious in their impact.

This chapter looks at segmentals from the perspective of L2 intelligibility, primarily from the perspective of L2 English. The first part of the chapter looks at how sounds can be classified and what this means for L2 pronunciation. The second section classifies common L2 pronunciation errors. Following this, the chapter briefly recounts explanations for why errors occur in L2 speech, and what kind of improvement can be expected in the absence of instruction, and with instruction. The next section examines research on intelligibility as it relates to segmentals.

In doing this, the chapter will argue the following about segmentals in L2 pronunciation:

1. Segmentals are critical in judgments of intelligibility and comprehensibility, if for no other reason than they are unavoidable and determine whether we hear one word rather than another.
2. Although an error in any segmental can cause misunderstanding, some segmental errors are more likely to cause misunderstandings than others.
3. Segmentals are subject to different types of mispronunciations, and these different types of deviations (substitutions, deletions, distortions, insertions) are likely to have varied effects on intelligibility.
4. Individual mispronunciations may lead to loss of understanding, but words/phrases/sentences may also have a complex combination of deviations. In combination, these may cause difficulties in understanding that are hard to compute.
5. Naturalistic development of segmentals is likely to be fastest within the first year in the L2 environment, but this development will not apply equally to all segments.
6. Instruction on pronunciation results in improved segmental accuracy, but the short-term effect of improved segmentals on spontaneous speech intelligibility is less clear.

Segmentals are primarily a word-based feature when it comes to understanding. In other words, mispronunciations can lead listeners to hear different words entirely, and the overall effect of many small deviations can make it more challenging for listeners to understand the speaker's message. But human listeners, especially native speakers (NSs) of a language, can often interpret sounds in contexts that are not particularly ideal exemplars of the phonemes they represent. They may also be able to adjust to clearly wrong pronunciations because of the discourse context (e.g., *Thank you* pronounced as *Sank you* is unlikely to be misunderstood), perhaps because sound contrasts are relatively rare in the language (e.g., *stood* pronounced as *stewed*), or because a potential minimal pair does not exist (e.g., *value* pronounced as *balue*). Segmentals are also an important marker of accented speech, both for differences in native varieties (e.g., the New Zealand pronunciation of *left* sounding like *lift* to North American English speakers) and for nonnative speech.

Ways to Describe Segmentals

Segmentals can be described in various ways, and in pronunciation teaching these different classifications are important for different purposes. For example, segmentals can be classified quite broadly in their relationship to the way they are spelled, or they may be described according to the way they sound. Even though sound–spelling correspondences are important in the teaching of pronunciation, their connection to intelligibility is indirect at best, and this chapter will not address it, focusing instead on sound categories. In regard to sounds, segmentals can first be described phonologically. This means that all languages have sets of vowel and consonant sounds that distinguish meaning between words (that is, they have different sets of phonemes, signaled by the use of /forward slashes/). For example, English has three voiceless stops that distinguish meaning, /p/, /t/, and /k/ (*pick, tick, kick*). Languages such as German, Spanish, and French have the same three phonemes, whereas Arabic lacks /p/ but has /t/ and /k/, and Korean has three voiceless stop phonemes (/p/, /pʰ/, and /pp/) for the single category found for each voiceless stop in English. These phoneme categories are language-specific, and they affect how we perceive and produce spoken language.

We can also describe segmentals phonetically – that is, by the specific sounds that are pronounced for particular phonemes. Even though two languages may have some of the same phonemes, such as Spanish and English, this may not help language learners to pronounce the L2 accurately because of the language-specific variants (called allophones) that depend on the linguistic environment in which the vowel or consonant is pronounced. Thus, the /k/ allophones in English *kick* are different, with the first being spoken with aspiration, or [kʰ], and the second (typically) without aspiration, or [k]. (Note that when we are talking about actual sounds rather than phonemes, we use [square brackets].) Thus, *kick* can be narrowly transcribed in English as [kʰɪk]. The two /k/ sounds in *kick* include differences beyond aspiration, with the first /k/ being pronounced further forward in the mouth, toward the palatal region, and the second /k/ perhaps being pronounced with a closed mouth, that is, it is unreleased. For most pronunciation teachers, however, such details of articulation may seem irrelevant, and both allophones will be considered as examples of the phoneme /k/ even though they are quite different sounds. Indeed, most English speakers may not even notice these sound differences. A sampling of common allophones of English sounds are listed in Table 3.1. However, it must be emphasized that allophonic variation is far more common than any chart can show, as sounds vary in

Table 3.1 Some English phonemes and common allophones

Phonemes	Some common allophones and examples		
/p/, /t/, /k/	[pʰ] (pit, appear) [p] (spit, apple) [p̚] (top hat, lip)	[tʰ] (take, attain) [t̚] (stake) [ʔ] (button, certain) [ɾ] (city, beautiful) [tʃ] (train, nature)	[kʰ] (kit, accord) [k] (skit, acre) [k̚] (spoke, lockstep)
/m/, /n/, /ŋ/	[m] (input) [m̩] (emphasis) [m̥] (bottom)	[n] (onion) [n̩] (lemon) [n̥] (enthusiasm)	[ŋ] (bank, include)
/l/, /ɹ/, /w/	[l] (plate) [ɫ] (fall, hold) [l̩] (darling)	[ʋ] Some British English speakers [r] Scottish English [ɹ̥] (pray, tray)	[ʍ] (which, where)
/h/	[ç] (huge, human)		
/æ/	[ɛ] (bag – Minnesota)	[eɪə] (man, most American English) [iə] (man, New York)	
/e/	[eɪ] Most L1 English	[e] Nativized Englishes	Nasalization of vowels before nasals
/o/	[əʊ] Most L1 English	[o] Irish English	Note: /o/ is highly variable in different Englishes
/aɪ/, /aʊ/	[ʌɪ] Many varieties, including Canadian raising before voiceless consonants (night, skytrain)	[ʌʊ] Many varieties, including Canadian raising before voiceless consonants (house, about)	[a] (I, fine in Southern US English)

systematic ways depending on the sounds they are next to and according to the dialect of the speaker. In an intelligibility-based approach, it is important to recognize that an L2 learner's difficulties may stem from the production of allophones rather than phonemes.

Why is it important to distinguish between phonemes and allophones in teaching pronunciation? In L2 pronunciation learning, phonemes and allophones rarely match perfectly between the learner's native language and the second language. Sometimes two languages will have the same [sounds] but not associate them with the same /phonemes/. For example, speakers of North American English think [ɾ] (the alveolar flap) represents the medial /t/ in words like *city* and *beauty*, but the same sound represents consonants spelled with <r> in Spanish, as in *pero*. Another reason to distinguish between phonemes and allophones is that we all pronounce the phonemes of our native language in ways that are dependent on where they occur in a word or sentence, and sometimes in ways that are dependent on our dialects. The American English /t/ is pronounced in four different ways in the words *take, stake, city,* and *button* (see Table 3.1), but the same words in some varieties of British English will have different allophones. (For example, the flap allophone in *city* in American English will be pronounced as [t] in British English.) These differences not only affect intelligibility, especially for listening comprehension, but may also be important in social or regional identification. It is also important to determine whether an L2 learner is learning a sound that they already know how to pronounce, but in a different environment, or whether the sound is completely new. For example, American English speakers learning languages like Vietnamese need to learn how to pronounce a familiar sound [ŋ] (e.g., singer, long) at the beginning of words (e.g., Nguyen, a common Vietnamese name), an environment that is illegal in English. They also need to pronounce completely new sounds such as /ɨ/, which may involve a different level of challenge.

Segmentals in a language can also be described according to constraints on the linguistic environments in which they occur. The /ŋ/ phoneme of English, for example, distinguishes meaning in word-medial and word-final positions (*sin/sing, sinning/singing*), but not word initially (*net* but not **nget*). In another example, the [kʰ] allophone is pronounced at the beginning of stressed syllables in English (*kit*), but not after [s] (*skit*). These constraints are language-specific and may make pronunciation of even familiar sounds in a new language more difficult.

Finally, segmentals can be described according to how they fit into syllable structure, which is also a language-specific constraint. For example, Japanese maximally allows CV syllables (a shorthand description describing a syllable made of a *c*onsonant followed by a *v*owel), while English allows syllables that are far more complex. The word *strengths*, for example, can be spoken with three consonants before the vowel and four after, or CCCVCCCC [stɹɛŋkθs] (Cardoso, 2017). Japanese learners of English must learn to pronounce syllable structures that do not fit the syllabic structure of their native language. Japanese learners of English have a strong tendency toward creating "legal" syllables through vowel epenthesis so that borrowed English words in Japanese are modified to have a Japanese syllable structure (e.g., *strike* pronounced [su.tu.ɾaɪ.ku] rather than [stɹaɪk]). In contrast, Vietnamese only allows certain single-consonant sounds at the ends of syllables, while English allows many single and multiple consonants in syllable codas. For example, *lengths* has at least three consonant sounds at the end, [lɛŋθs] or [lɛŋks] in my speech, and [lɛŋkθs] in that of some speakers. As a result, Vietnamese learners of English must learn how to pronounce consonant clusters that are phonotactically restricted (i.e., illegal) in Vietnamese. Such a task is not impossible once a learner is aware of it, but pronouncing phonotactically restricted sounds in new environments can be challenging. Without instruction, improvement may be quite limited, as suggested by Osburne's (1996) case study of a Vietnamese speaker.

These four areas of classifying segmentals, according to the phonemes they represent, their allophones, phonotactic constraints, and syllable structure, influence the ways in which language learners pronounce their new language, but not always in obvious ways. Some of the errors of L2 learners can be predicted by contrasting the sounds of the L1 and the L2 (i.e., a contrastive analysis). But L2 learners also make errors that are not predicted by a contrastive analysis of the native and target language (Munro, 2018), or learners may be able to pronounce a sound well in one context but not in another. Sounds that are very similar yet different in the L1 and L2 are particularly difficult to hear and pronounce, while L2 sounds that are very different from anything in the L1 are often much easier to perceive and pronounce (Flege, 1995). A French friend talked about the difficulty of saying *Sushi shop* in English, even though French has both /s/ and /ʃ/. This suggests that what is difficult for a particular speaker is not always easy to predict.

Vowels and Consonants

Segmentals include, as mentioned, both vowel and consonant sounds, two categories that seem distinct yet often overlap. Glides (also called semi-vowels or semi-consonants) and English /ɹ/ have much in common with vowels in articulation, given that all of these sounds are made with an unobstructed vocal tract and full voicing. In addition, some sonorant consonants may carry the syllable nucleus when they are syllabic (e.g., the final consonant in *button, bottom, little*), making them behave like vowels.

The most intensively studied consonant contrast it the /l/–/ɹ/ contrast in English and (primarily) how Japanese L1 learners negotiate it. The short answer is, quite poorly. Japanese learners of English have tremendous difficulty hearing the differences between these two sounds, producing the differences between the two sounds, and experience does not always help. Japanese has one phonemic category (either the alveolar flap /ɾ/ or the retroflex flap /ɽ/, depending on the description), which Japanese learners map unsuccessfully to the two English phonemes. The important finding of research on this difficult contrast is that significant improvement is possible given experience and effective training. Perceptual and production changes are possible even for learners who start learning as adults. In what follows, I will review only a few of the myriad studies on the /l/–/ɹ/ contrast in order to show that improvement in pronunciation is possible for any contrasts, and especially for those that have a high functional load.

Cues present in the speech signal are sometimes ignored when they are unnecessary in the learner's L1. For non-experts in my undergraduate classes, roughly speaking, I explain that all speech sounds comprise a wide range of noise across a broad range of frequencies, and that what constitutes any given sound is how particular frequencies are amplified as a consequence of changes to the shape of the vocal tract. For efficiency, humans are very good at ignoring all frequencies that are irrelevant for discriminating between sounds. Unfortunately, what is efficiently ignored in an L1 may be important for the discrimination of sounds in an L2.

The /l/–/ɹ/ contrast in English is very common in all linguistic environments, and the contrast thus has the highest functional load possible, ten on the ten-point scale (Brown, 1988). Both sounds are difficult for Japanese learners to produce, and both are difficult to perceive (Goto, 1971). It appears that /l/ is perceived as more similar to the Japanese flap than /ɹ/, but /ɹ/ appears to be easier to learn, in line with predictions from models of speech learning (Bradlow, 2008; Riney, Takada, & Ota, 2000). The acoustic cues that distinguish /l/ from /ɹ/ are not important in Japanese, and Japanese learners of English find it difficult to attend to features in the speech signal that are habitually ignored in Japanese. Like any kind of speech learning, what is irrelevant in the L1 may be critical in the L2. All speakers are particularly good at attending to features that are important in the L1, but may also be particularly good at not hearing features that are critical for making distinctions in the L2. This process begins early in life, with infants demonstrating increasingly specific abilities in perception depending on the languages in their environment (Burns, Yoshida, Hill, & Werker, 2007; Vihman, 2015; Werker & Tees, 1984).

Experience with the L2 seems to help with improvement, at least to a point. Flege, Takagi, and Mann (1995) studied adult Japanese learners who differed in experience in the United States. The low-experience group had been in the United States an average of 1.6 years and the high-experience group an average of 20.8 years. The high-experience group produced both English sounds far more accurately (though not like NSs).

Research on the /l/–/ɹ/ contrast also demonstrates that perceptual training can not only improve the ability to hear difficult contrasts, but can also result in improved pronunciation of the sounds. Bradlow, Pisoni, Akahane-Yamada, and Tokhura (1997) trained eleven Japanese English learners on sixty-eight minimal pairs in which the /l/–/ɹ/ contrast appeared in varied linguistic environments. Production recordings before and after training showed a trend toward production improvement. McClelland, Fiez, and McCandliss (2002) found that feedback was especially important in improving perception, and Saito and Lyster (2012) found that feedback was also important in improving production of the sounds.

Although I am treating both vowels and consonants as having similar patterns as to their potential effects upon intelligibility, it is likely that they are also different in many ways. For example, Bent, Bradlow, and Smith (2007) examined the intelligibility of sentences produced by Mandarin speakers of English. They found that there was an overall correlation of segmental accuracy and intelligibility, but that overall accuracy of vowel pronunciation correlated with intelligibility judgments, while overall accuracy of consonant errors did not (although initial consonant production was correlated with intelligibility). This somewhat surprising finding suggests that vowels and consonants are not equal in their effects on intelligibility.

Similarly, Fogerty and Kewley-Port (2009) systematically examined the contributions of consonant and vowel units to intelligibility. Sentences had either consonant sections or vowel sections replaced by word-shaped noise. The results showed that intelligibility of the sentences was higher when the consonants were masked than when the vowels were. They explain these results by saying that "vowels as traditionally defined carry important perceptual cues that are not found in consonants. Furthermore, even truncated portions of vowels contribute strongly to sentence intelligibility despite providing much less of the overall sentence duration than consonants" (Fogerty & Kewley-Port, 2009, p. 855). This greater effect on intelligibility comes because vowels carry not only their own information but also the co-articulatory information about consonantal transitions into and out of the vowel. In other words, hearing the vowels more clearly in difficult listening situations (i.e., in noise) is more likely to lead to greater intelligibility than hearing consonants clearly. Vowels are essential to intelligibility. Consonants are less consistently so. This pattern holds only for sentences, however, not for words in isolation (Fogerty & Humes, 2012), and applies when younger normal-hearing listeners as well as older hearing-impaired listeners are the ones judging intelligibility (Miller et al., 2007).

Acquisition of Vowels

L2 learners show certain patterns when learning L2 vowels. Munro and Derwing (2008) examined the vowel production of recent immigrants to Canada from Chinese- and Slavic-language backgrounds. They found that learning was initially rapid, but that after the first six months in Canada, naturalistic learning of the vowel contrasts plateaued and showed inconsistent changes for the next six months. Both L1 groups showed similar trajectories in general, although not all vowels between groups were the same, indicating that there was also an effect of the L1. In a later study of vowel improvement after year one, Munro, Derwing, and Saito (2013) found that listeners heard improvements in Slavic pronunciation of /ɪ/, especially in bVC (*bit*) rather than pVC (*pit*) contexts. Mandarin speakers did not show the same improvements in this vowel, although both groups showed continued improvement on /u/ and /ʊ/.

Munro, Flege, and MacKay (1996) examined the perception and production of English vowels by Italian learners of English who had lived in Canada for decades. They found that accentedness of vowels could be predicted as a function of age of arrival (AOA), and that even long and extensive exposure to the L2 in the environment did not change accentedness. While some of these vowels were less accented than others, all were accented, but even the most accented vowels were highly intelligible. These results indicate that native-like production of L2 vowels is less likely with later AOA. The authors also suggest that the influence of the L1 on L2 vowels may be rooted in perception.

Relation of Perception and Production

The ability to perceive L2 vowel contrasts appears to increase with increasing L2 experience. Flege, Bohn, and Jang (1997) asked Korean and German L2 speakers of English to produce beat–bit and bat–bet vowels, as well as to perceive the vowels in synthetic tokens. Production of vowels was more accurate with more experienced speakers, and some vowels were more difficult than others (especially the bat vowel). More experienced speakers were also more likely to pay attention to vowel quality distinctions in perception, and less attention to durational differences.

In another study of vowel perception and production, Flege, MacKay, and Meador (1999) examined Italian L1 speakers of English. They found that the accuracy with which the Italian L1 speakers produced English vowels was connected to accuracy in perception, even when L2 experience was held consistent. In other words, "the accuracy with which L2 vowels are produced is limited by how accurately they are perceived" (Flege, MacKay, & Meador, 1999, p. 2973). Production and perception for early bilinguals (those who began learning English at an earlier age) was often indistinguishable from native English speakers, indicating that those who begin learning the L2 earlier are more likely to establish new perceptual categories that may be indistinguishable from those of NSs.

Hillenbrand and Clark (2000) examined how intelligible vowels were when their duration was modified in four different ways. In general, increased duration added very little to the intelligibility of vowels since they were all identified very successfully even at the original duration. However, duration had some effect in that vowels with relatively long durations tended to shift toward adjacent vowels (e.g., *beat* judgments shifted to *bit* when duration was shortened) and vowels with relatively short durations were judged as adjacent vowels when durations were lengthened (e.g., *bit* judgments shifted to *beat* when duration was lengthened). This suggests that duration is a cue to vowel intelligibility, albeit a minor one (Iverson & Evans, 2007).

So can vowel intelligibility be improved by manipulating duration or other features? Ferguson and Kewley-Port (2007) examined the clear and conversational speech of two sets of speakers that had been used in previous studies. Six of these had previously shown that they were more intelligible in noise, while six others were not. Acoustic analyses of the speakers found that those whose intelligibility was greater (the "Big-Benefit" speakers) were associated with an increased vowel space and greater duration, more than for the "No-Benefit" speakers. These patterns did not hold for all speakers, however, suggesting that clear speech benefits may include issues beyond vowels and duration.

Effect of Training on Vowel Perception

Cenoz and Lecumberri (1999) examined the effects of training on vowel perception. L1 Spanish and Basque learners of English received training on the discrimination of English monophthongs and diphthongs; they found that these learners, especially those whose perception was poor, learned to more successfully perceive even difficult vowel contrasts. Better improvement was also connected to learner desire to have a more native-like accent.

Computer-based perceptual training seems particularly effective in helping L2 learners to create new categories for difficult vowel contrasts (Thomson, 2011, 2012; Wang & Munro, 2004), which are more challenging to describe because of their less precise placement in the mouth. Thomson's studies employed high variability phonetic training (i.e., multiple voices) producing vowels in open syllables, even if those syllables do not represent actual words. Wang and Munro trained the *beat–bit*, *bat–bet*, and *Luke–look* contrasts, allowing L2 learners to control the type of practice they used from the computer-based program. This study also suggests that allowing learners to determine the kind of practice they have can be successful.

The kind of L1 vowel inventory that L2 learners have also seems to affect how well they can benefit from L2 vowel training. Iverson and Evans (2009) trained German and Spanish L2 learners on English vowels. German has a vowel inventory that is similar to English in size, while Spanish has a smaller five-vowel system. Given the same amount of training, German speakers improved more than Spanish speakers, suggesting that a larger vowel system may facilitate learning a larger L2 system. Spanish speakers also improved, but it took them three times longer to do so. Both groups retained their improvements over time. Despite suggestive evidence that vowels and consonants are different in regard to intelligibility, this chapter will largely collapse them because of the many places in which they seem to affect intelligibility similarly.

L2 Segmental Pronunciation Errors

One of the most noticeable things about pronunciation is that segmental errors are very common in L2 speech (Im & Levis, 2015) and are an important element in judgments of foreign accent, even if the errors made are hard to precisely identify. In some cases, errors may lead to loss of intelligibility in that the words are not understood at all (*watched* pronounced as *wat*) or are heard as a different word (as in hearing the word *watched* as *washed*). That most segmental errors do not cause loss of intelligibility is a testimony to the flexibility of human listeners, who hear effectively when words come at them in the stream of speech, even in speech that is degraded by noise and overlap (Scharenborg, 2007).

Some of the most common errors in L2 speech include substitutions of one phoneme for another, distorted pronunciations that do not match expected sounds, additions of extra sounds, and deletions of expected sounds. These four types of errors are called substitution, distortion, insertion or epenthesis, and deletion (Derwing & Munro, 2015).

Substitutions occur when the intended sound in the new language does not exist in the native language (such as English speakers pronouncing the high front rounded vowel [y] found in French or German) or when the allophonic patterns are different in the two languages. For example, Spanish speakers often substitute [d] for [ð] in English (*then* sounds like *den*), even though Spanish speakers use [ð] as an allophone of /d/ in Spanish, as in *nada* pronounced [naða]. Berlitz, a provider of language instruction, played on the potential of substitutions for unintelligibility with a distress call relayed from a sinking ship to a German Coast Guard operator: "We're sinking, we're sinking," says the crew member. "What are you sinking about?" responds the German L2 English speaker (www.youtube.com/watch? v=z78V_oo21Kc).

Across varieties of English, even categories of sounds may be different. Many American English speakers and Canadian English speakers have a merger of the low back vowels /ɑ/ and /ɒ/, leading to a different phonemic inventory from speakers of other varieties of North American English. Although the rounded vowel is typically referred to as open-o, or [ɔ], I will reserve that symbol for the more strongly rounded back vowel in the British English pronunciation of words like *caught*, *fall*, *taught*. Some varieties of American and British English also systematically realize the phonemes /θ/ and /ð/ as [f] and [v]. In other cases, speakers may use allophonic realizations in unexpected places. I have known several people who use [ɫ] as the only allophone of /l/, while most speakers use it only syllable-finally. Other speakers vocalize the [ɫ] so that it loses its /l/ quality altogether while retaining the velar co-articulation such that it sounds more like [w], e.g., *fill* as [fɪw]. These kinds of allophonic variations are often well known and stereotyped (such as the glottal stop for /t/ in some varieties of British English, even though [ʔ] is unremarkable as an allophone for /t/ in words like *button* and *cotton*).

Distortions occur when the pronunciation of a target sound cannot be classified as another L1 or L2 sound, although this is a relatively understudied type of error (Bent et al., 2007). The lack of classification may have as much to do with the listener as it does with the speaker. Language learners may substitute an L1 sound for an L2 target, but a listener from the L2 may not be able to classify the L1 sound. This is true for both untrained and phonetically trained listeners. To overcome this problem, it is possible to use trained listeners who share the native language of L2 learners. For example, Hong, Kim, and Chung (2014) used Korean L1 phonetically trained listeners to code Korean-influenced English and used a number of Korean sounds in their transcription that may not have been obvious even to phonetically trained native English listeners. Distortions are common in casual L1 speech (Cauldwell, 2013; Shockey, 2003), and in my experience L2 speech is full of these types of deviations. L2 learners approximate target sounds as closely as possible within their L1 perceptual system, but their pronunciations may not have the acoustic signature of a single sound category that listeners can classify as a native phoneme. Kaneko et al. (2015) examined the interdental productions of Japanese speakers and found that some started as [s] and ended as [θ], but that the productions as a whole were not easily identifiable as either sound.

Deletions or insertions, on the other hand, are likely to result from L1–L2 conflicts in syllable structure or from phonotactic constraints. Japanese speakers learning English, as noted above, may insert vowels between consonant clusters to make them more pronounceable, while Vietnamese speakers of English may delete consonants from consonant clusters. In San Francisco, under the Golden Gate Bridge, there is a gift shop for tourists. The historically large number of Japanese tourists in this area led to a sign being posted that adjusted the English words "Gift Shop" (CVCC CVC) to reflect Japanese syllable structure, or "Gifuto Shoppu" (CVCVCV CVCV). This same process is evident when Japanese borrows English words, so that the baseball terms such as *baseball* (CVCCVC) are pronounced in a Japanese way, *besuboru* (CVCVCVCV). Vietnamese speakers, on the other hand, whose native language also has strong restrictions against final consonant clusters, employ another strategy to pronounce English words. Rather than inserting vowels, they often delete consonant sounds in final clusters. This may come not only from the phonotactic constraints but also from Vietnamese being an isolating language with a largely monosyllabic vocabulary. Although varied learners of English speakers employ deletion and insertion, so do English L1 speakers. A study of American English and Korean speakers (Hong et al., 2014) showed that American English speakers were far more likely to employ deletion as a phonological strategy than insertion, although insertion is also evident for some speakers in words like *ath(e)lete* and *real(a)tor*. Advanced Korean speakers of English, in contrast, used insertion far more than deletion.

English speakers also demonstrate some of these processes in casual speech (Cauldwell, 2013; Shockey, 2003). Such distortions do not typically lead to loss of intelligibility during the course of conversational interaction even though they seem to distort sounds beyond recognition when looked at in phonetic detail or lead to elisions – that is, the loss of expected sounds in (casual) speech. For example, the word temperature on weather programs may not be pronounced in citation form with four syllables – that is, [tɛmpə˞ətʃə˞] – but rather as [tɛmpətʃə˞], or even with two syllables – [tɛmtʃə˞]. Johnson talks about this as "massive reduction," that is, "the phonetic realization of a word involves a large deviation from the citation form such that whole syllables are lost and/or a large proportion of the phones in the form are changed" (2004, p. 29). From the point of view of how learners produce the L2, these kinds of massive reductions are relatively unimportant. L2 learners do not need to try to imitate this kind of casual conversational speech. However, from the viewpoint of listening comprehension, learners must be able to negotiate massive reductions in the speech of NSs if they are to find normal conversational speech intelligible.

In terms of intelligibility and comprehensibility, these four types of deviations may have different effects. The effects of identifiable phonemic substitutions, for example, may be explained by the concept of functional load (FL) (Brown, 1988; Catford, 1987). Although FL includes more than minimal pairs (Sewell, 2017), substitutions that reflect greater numbers of minimal pairs (e.g., /p–b/, /p–f/) are likely to cause more serious intelligibility difficulties than those that have fewer minimal pairs (e.g., /ð–z/). The extent to which FL predicts intelligibility difficulties is unclear, given that few studies have examined this issue experimentally. Munro and Derwing (2006) examined the ways that high and low FL errors affected English-speaking listeners. They found that high FL errors had a greater impact on comprehensibility than low FL errors, and that multiple errors impacted judgments differently for the two areas. Multiple high FL errors led to significantly different judgments of accentedness, while multiple low FL errors did not. (Ratings for comprehensibility were not significantly affected for multiple high or low FL errors.) This suggests that substitutions are particularly sensitive to the potential for confusion, and that judgments of accent may be greater for increasing numbers of high FL errors. In a different approach, Kang and Moran (2014) classified the types of phonological errors in Cambridge ESOL (English for speakers of other languages) tests. They found that lower scores correlated with higher frequencies of high FL errors, and that higher scores had a much lower frequency of such vowel and consonant errors.

Distortions are, by definition, sounds that are hard to classify by a listener. As a result, they do not seem to be quantifiable in the same way that substitutions are. Unfamiliar distortions may not only affect intelligibility but may play a greater role in loss of comprehensibility because listeners need to work harder to get information from the speech stream, and they may face greater challenges in classifying the sounds that they hear as representative of particular phonemes. In other words, rather than sending listeners down the well-defined garden path of minimal pairs, unexpected distortions may defy straightforward interpretation. The effect of distortions is thus unclear on listener understanding.

Regarding deletions and insertions, both of these types of deviations can change the syllable structure of words and have the potential to affect intelligibility. Jenkins (2000) argues that insertions are less harmful to intelligibility precisely because the expected segments are present, though they may be masked by the presence of an extra vowel. Deletions, especially in initial consonant clusters, may affect intelligibility because the expected segments are not present. However, there is little empirical research examining this assertion.

This discussion about the effects of various types of pronunciation differences is overly simplistic, of course. L2 learners often do not make only one easily identified error of pronunciation, and computing the effects of multiple errors is especially difficult. For example, in some data I have examined from oral language proficiency tests, a student was teaching about satellites and how they are controlled. About ninety seconds into the talk, he began talking about "[zurɪst] power," a term he repeated multiple times. The raters (and the transcribers) found him unintelligible and the raters even asked him "What kind of power?" He replied, with great confidence, "[zurɪst]." One rater thought she heard "frost," to which he replied, "Yes, [zurɪst]." As I worked with another research assistant, we finally figured out that he was saying "thrust." The transcript shows that "[zurɪst]" was unintelligible more than ten times and that even when one of the raters tried the word "thrust" (the intended word) the confusion remained, both for the raters and later for the transcriber. Why was this word so difficult to understand? Minimally, the word had several phonetic differences from what was expected. First, [θ] was heard as [z], a difference of place and voicing. Second, this difference was at the beginning of the word, leading to immediate misclassification. Third, the word was spoken with two syllables rather than one. The cluster [θɹ] was broken up with the metathesized vowel [u], perhaps a spelling-influence pronunciation of the intended vowel [ʌ]. Finally, a second vowel was inserted into the word, leading to an ending pronunciation of [ɪst]. So there appear to have been two substitutions, metathesis, and an insertion, all relatively unexpected mispronunciations in a single word.

Naturalistic Development of Segmentals

The development of L2 segmentals has at least two aspects: how features develop normally in the learning of the new language, and the development that results from instruction. The first type of development can be referred to as naturalistic development, and the second as instructed development. Naturalistic development, or what other writers have called acquisition (e.g., Krashen, 1981), has been the focus of enough research to understand how L2 adult pronunciation develops in the absence of instruction. Questions about naturalistic development are always asked with a view to the observation that adults typically have noticeable foreign accents. This was originally seen as a reflection of having learned the L2 and its phonology outside the limits of a critical period (Scovel, 1969), but L2 learners continue to have the ability to acquire L2 sound systems throughout their lives (Piske, MacKay, & Flege, 2001). Some L2 learners are far more successful at this than others (Moyer, 2014), but there seems to be no obvious restriction related to age on acquiring a new sound system.

Studies on naturalistic development are closely related to questions about whether learners are able to associate L2 sound contrasts with separate phonemic categories, and whether they are able to produce such contrasts, even if the L1 does not have such categories. Baker, Trofimovich, Flege, Mack, and Halter (2008) looked at whether age was important in the ability to distinguish (both in hearing and production) unfamiliar sound contrasts in an L2. Using children and adults, the study included two experiments, the first testing whether children or adults were more likely to associate contrasting sounds with a single L1 sound category, and the second testing whether children and adults differed in producing sound differences. The sound contrasts were two pairs of vowels (*beat/bit, who'd/hood*). Both contrasts are difficult for L2 English learners from a wide variety of languages, with the first being relatively common in English words, and the second relatively uncommon. The results showed that younger L2 learners were better able to hear L2 contrasts that were not part of their L1 categories. They were also better able to produce the sound contrasts. This indicates an effect of age, which is influenced by the interaction of the L1 and L2 sound systems. The extent to which the two systems interact seems weaker for younger learners, and stronger for older learners, indicating a greater flexibility for younger learners in learning L2 pronunciation. The authors conclude:

> Both skills—being able to perceptually disassociate L2 sounds from L1 sound categories and being able to produce L2 sounds—appear to be associated with the age at which the children and the adults were first exposed to the L2, indicating that age may mediate the relationship between these two skills. Taken together, these findings suggest that children, perhaps due to the developmental state of their L1 at the time of their exposure to the L2, are able to perceptually distinguish L2 sounds from similar L1 sounds and to produce and (perhaps) perceive such L2 sounds more accurately than adults.   (Baker et al., 2008, pp. 337–8)

AOA is often used as a proxy for the effect of a critical period in pronunciation development. But it may also be the case that greater length of residence (LOR) influences phonological development. Baker and Trofimovich (2006) looked at whether AOA or LOR was more important in the relationship between perception and production by matching Korean learners of English in AOA and LOR. They found that perception and production depended on learners' AOA, not their LOR. They also found that the Korean speakers who showed the greatest self-awareness of their own production were also the most accurate producers of L2 sounds.

In a frequently cited study, Flege, Munro, and MacKay (1995) examined the accuracy of consonant production by Italian learners of English who had emigrated to Canada at different ages. All participants spoke English more than Italian, and all had lived in Canada for more than thirty years on average. The study found that there was a systematic effect of age on the accuracy of consonant production, with those who started earlier being more accurate. Accuracy was evaluated by native English listeners making forced choice judgments of how accurate the consonants were. In general, the subjects who learned English after five years of age became progressively less accurate in their pronunciation, but the decrease of accuracy was different for different sounds and for the linguistic environments in which the sounds occurred. For example, accuracy was greater for final stop consonants than for initial stops.

In a follow-up study (Flege, Frieda, & Nozawa, 1997), the effect of age on the accuracy of L2 pronunciation was influenced by the relative amount of use of the L2 and the L1. The L2 English accents of two groups of Italian English bilinguals who emigrated to Canada between the ages of five and six, and had spoken English for over thirty years on average, were differentiated by the amount that they used Italian. One group used Italian very little, while the other used it about one-third of the time. Both groups had detectable foreign accents, despite having begun learning English well within the expected critical period. The group that reported speaking Italian more, however, had significantly stronger foreign accents. The study suggests that the extent to which the L1 remains active influences the accuracy of L2 pronunciation in naturalistic development.

Particular periods of time seem to be especially influential for phonological development, what Derwing and Munro (2015) call the "Window of Maximal Opportunity" for changes in pronunciation. In one study of these changes, Munro and Derwing (2008) examined the acquisition of vowels within the first year in an English-speaking environment for L1 speakers of Mandarin ($n = 20$) and Slavic ($n = 24$, mostly Russians, but with Ukranians and a Croatian as well) languages. Both Mandarin and Slavic languages have smaller vowel inventories than English. Recordings for the ten vowel targets (in b_t and p_t frames in a delayed repetition task) were made at two-month intervals over the course of the first year in Canada. Tokens were evaluated by phonetically trained listeners. Production accuracy for the ten vowels for all learners increased from 64 percent to 74 percent. However, a large amount of variation from one speaker to another was evident in the pronunciation of different learners, with some learners showing changes in vowel production primarily in the categories that were familiar from their L1 (Thomson, 2011). For those vowels that learners improved on, improvement leveled off by the end of the study period, suggesting that naturalistic improvement reaches a plateau, and that continued exposure loses its effect even when the learners remain surrounded by the L2. Some patterns of improvement seemed also to depend on the L1 of the subjects, with Slavic-language participants showing greater improvement than Mandarin. Another experiment using phonetically untrained listeners found similar results, with greater improvement within the first six months of exposure, but learning for some vowels continued throughout the full year of data collection. In summary, naturalistic pronunciation development is strongest when learners are initially in the new environment, but such development does not occur for all sounds, and the sounds that show changes may also be dependent upon the L1 of the learner. The results led the authors to say that "phonetic learning remains possible in adults, even when they do not receive focused instruction" (Munro & Derwing, 1999, pp. 498–9).

Are certain sounds inherently easier to produce accurately? In a test of the Markedness Differential Hypothesis (a theory that says that certain sounds are inherently more difficult because they are more unusual across the world's languages – see Eckman, 1977), Chan (2007) looked at the accuracy with which Cantonese learners of English produced word-final consonants. She found that voiced obstruents and /l/ were the most difficult final consonants for the learners, but that voiceless obstruents and other sonorant consonants were generally produced accurately. The results suggested that markedness alone, while helpful in determining difficulty, was not an accurate predictor of difficulty, and that difficulty of sounds is also affected by the learner's L1 background.

Although there are many more studies looking at naturalistic development of L2 pronunciation, this small collection of studies suggests certain tentative conclusions about the development of pronunciation abilities for L2 learners.

1. The age at which L2 pronunciation learning starts is important but does not determine pronunciation accuracy.
2. The ability to develop new L2 sound categories continues throughout life, but this process may be more challenging the older a learner is.
3. The first 6–12 months living in the L2 environment is connected to the greatest amount of naturalistic pronunciation development, but then naturalistic development slows down greatly.
4. Pronunciation development is connected to the amount and quality of experience with the new language.
5. Sounds that are relatively difficult because of their rarity or markedness in the world's language may not be equally difficult for all learners. (Rarity refers to how frequently a sound occurs across languages.)
6. All L2 learners are not the same. Some will improve more than others even given similar demographic characteristics. Variation in development between learners is normal.

Instructed Development of Segmentals

Pronunciation is unusual in studies of second language speech because of its indirect connection to other measures of language proficiency, in that "a beginner can have excellent production and an individual with a superb grasp of L2 syntax and vocabulary can be difficult to understand" (Thomson & Derwing, 2015, p. 339). But learners can improve. The unambiguous findings of studies that have examined the effects of pronunciation instruction is that instruction is successful. Because most studies on instruction have focused on segmentals rather than suprasegmentals, the findings of improvement from one study are supported by findings from many others. Three recent summaries of previous research have looked at this issue: Saito (2012); Lee, Jang, and Plonsky (2015); and Thomson and Derwing (2015). Saito synthesized the results of fifteen quasi-experimental studies (five on segmentals alone); Lee et al. conducted a meta-analysis of eighty-six instructional studies (the majority teaching segmentals); and Thomson and Derwing conducted a narrative analysis of seventy-five studies from Lee et al. (again, with the majority having studied the teaching of segmentals).

Saito (2012) synthesized the results of fifteen pre- and post-test design quasi-experimental studies on the success of pronunciation instruction. He found that instruction that called explicit attention to pronunciation was typically successful in controlled contexts and sometimes in extemporaneous speech. Some of the fifteen studies employed control groups while others did not. Saito also examined results from the type of instruction (Focus on Form [FonF] versus Focus on FormS [FonFS] versus Focus on Meaning [FonM], i.e., form + meaning versus form alone versus meaning alone) and whether improvement showed up in relatively controlled or free speaking tasks.

Consistently, FonF instruction was most likely to lead to improvement, and FonM instruction (typically, the treatment for the control groups) did not lead to pronunciation improvement. FonFS led to improvement in controlled tasks but not extemporaneous speaking. Nine of the studies looked only at controlled speaking tasks, and most found pronunciation improvement. Only two studies showed improvement in spontaneous speech, which suggests that improvement in accentedness or comprehensibility that listeners can hear is a higher standard than simple improvement. However, the two studies also suggest that well-designed instruction over a sufficient length of time can lead to improvements in pronunciation that are audible in spontaneous speech.

In a meta-analysis of eighty-six studies, Lee et al. (2015) examined the success of pronunciation instruction. Their analysis showed an overall large effect of pronunciation instruction, meaning that instruction typically resulted in a relatively large degree of improvement, especially when done over a longer period of time, when learners received feedback on their pronunciation, and when improvement was measured using more controlled tasks (such as reading aloud or imitation). Such findings are encouraging on the one hand, in that pronunciation instruction seems to work, yet concerning on the other, in that the improvement largely shows up in more controlled types of tasks that allow learners to consciously attend to pronunciation form. The meta-analysis also shows that most studies looked at university students, which is not surprising but limits the generalizability of the findings.

Thomson and Derwing (2015), in a narrative analysis, analyzed most of the studies in the work of Lee et al. (2015), with attention to what makes an excellent pronunciation training study. In particular, they looked at the studies with respect to whether they were in line with the Nativeness Principle (that is, whether the goal was to improve features that contribute primarily to perceptions of accentedness) or the Intelligibility Principle (Levis, 2005a), meaning that the instruction helps learners become more understandable in less-controlled speaking. Studies of segmental improvement dominated the review, from as few as one segment to as many as fourteen. The nature of instruction was typically undefined, suggesting that improvement in controlled contexts resulted from all kinds of instructional interventions. A concern raised was that very few studies (9 percent) met what the authors call "the gold standard of enhanced comprehensibility and intelligibility" (Thomson & Derwing, 2015, pp. 332–3) – that is, global judgments of improvement that do not depend on phonetic analysis of changes. In other words, most studies looked at analyses of individual pronunciation features (including features with a low FL) without asking whether they lead to improvements in comprehensibility. This is a particularly problematic issue for the pronunciation of segmentals. The pronunciation of one segment in context may be noticed by a listener but is unlikely to affect intelligibility, and even instruction on a set of segments that are particularly difficult for L2 learners may not result in listeners hearing L2 learners as more comprehensible (Neri, Cucchiarini, & Strik, 2008).

Finally, few of the studies looked at the long-term effect of instruction, as few of them employed delayed post-tests. Such tests, when they occurred, showed that short-term improvement is subject to significant backsliding in the level of improvement (Hahn, 2002). To sum up, these analyses of previous studies suggest the following regarding improvement of segmentals based on instruction.

1. Instruction on pronunciation is typically successful, but certain types of instruction may lead to more robust improvement.
2. Improvement is more likely to show up in controlled tasks, but the ultimate goal of instruction is improvement that is evident in spontaneous speech.

3. It typically takes time for segmental improvement in controlled tasks to become evident in spontaneous speech.
4. Segments with a high FL are likely to impact comprehensibility more than those with low FL, but because comprehensibility is typically affected by multiple features, improvement for individual segments alone is unlikely to result in greater comprehensibility.
5. Longer treatments are more likely to lead to noticeable pronunciation improvement.

Segmental Errors and Intelligibility

Although suprasegmentals are often considered to have a greater impact on comprehensibility (Gordon & Darcy, 2016; Hahn, 2004; McNerney & Mendelsohn, 1992), segmentals are also critically important in how understandable speech is, and should not be ignored in instructional decisions (Derwing et al., 1998). Jenkins (2000) argued that consonants are essential for mutual intelligibility in English as lingua franca (ELF) communication, with certain exceptions (e.g., the interdental fricatives and the allophonic dark /l/), as are differences between lengthened and shortened vowels, so long as the vowel quality is within the range of a generally understood regional variety. Bent et al. (2007) found that vowel accuracy was the most important feature for intelligibility and that accuracy in initial consonants also corresponded with intelligibility in read sentences. Initial consonants show up regularly as important for intelligibility, perhaps because of their importance in leading listeners to expect one cohort rather than another.

While any error may cause some loss of intelligibility, in general, more frequent errors are more likely to affect intelligibility than less frequent ones (Prator & Robinett, 1985). But frequency of the errors alone is insufficient to measure the potential for loss of intelligibility. It also appears that the frequency of the words that sounds occur in correlate with how intelligible a particular error is (Thomson & Isaacs, 2009; also see Cole et al., 2010). The types of deviations also must be taken into account. It is well documented, for instance, that NS productions of segmentals may vary tremendously in casual or connected speech (Johnson, 2004). But if these deviations are expected by listeners, that is, if they reflect shared expectations of that speech register, the speech will be more intelligible.

Frequency may also be a factor in intelligibility, in that more frequent phonemes are likely to play a larger role in intelligibility than less frequent ones. Consonant phonemes, for example, are more frequent than vowels in English, accounting for nearly 60 percent of sounds (Hayden, 1950; Mines, Hanson, & Shoup, 1978), while vowel sounds are about 40 percent of phonemes, reflecting the syllable structure of English and the numbers of phonemes for each segmental category. Some segments are more or less frequent than others as well.

Frequency itself is affected by two moderating factors: the number of contrasts a phoneme has with other phonemes (its FL); and the degree to which a particular contrast is likely to be confused by L2 learners. In Table 3.2 (from Qian, Chukharev-Hudilainen, & Levis, 2018, based on Brown, 1988), the FLs of British English contrasts are shown, from ten (highest) to one (lowest). There is little disagreement that contrasts at the top end of the scale are more likely to affect intelligibility even if their raw frequencies are in the middle of phoneme frequency (e.g., /b/–/p/ are both slightly less than 2 percent in raw frequency but have many minimal pairs). Likewise, contrasts at the low end of the FL ordering are less likely to impact intelligibility because they are unlikely to be confused with other words when they are mispronounced. It is not clear, however, where the best division is between high and low FL.

The location of a sound in a word also has an important effect on the intelligibility of sounds. Zielinski (2008) explored sites of reduced intelligibility from the extended speech of three L2 speakers of English: Korean, Chinese, and Vietnamese. She found that non-standard syllable stress patterns and mispronounced segments both affected listeners' ability to successfully transcribe words. It was especially the case that initial consonants and vowels in stressed syllables were associated with incorrect transcriptions. Syllable-final consonants and unstressed vowels were much less frequently associated with loss of intelligibility. The one exception to this pattern was for the Vietnamese speaker, for whom mispronounced final consonants in strong syllables were more strongly associated with loss of intelligibility than was the case for the Korean and Chinese speakers. The Vietnamese speaker was more likely to delete final consonants than speakers of the other language backgrounds, suggesting that deletions of consonants are likely to impact intelligibility.

In a partial replication of Zielinski (2008), Im and Levis (2015) looked at the sites of reduced intelligibility for three Korean international teaching assistants (ITAs) in the United States. Each had been rated by NS raters at different levels (high, intermediate, and low) on a field-specific five-minute extemporaneous test of speaking. Five additional NS listeners with ESL (English as a second language) training listened to each of the speakers and stopped whenever they noticed something that either challenged them or where they noticed something unusual in the speaker's use of English. Using a

Table 3.2 Rank ordering of phoneme pairs commonly conflated by learners

	Vowels	Examples		Consonants	Examples
10	/ɛ–æ/	bet–bat	10	/p–b/	pat–bat
	/æ–ʌ/	bat–but		/p–f/	pat–fat
	/æ–ɒ/	cat–cot		/m–n/	home–hone
	/ʌ–ɒ/	cut–cot		/n–l/	night–light
	/ɔ–əʊ/	ought–oat		/l–r/	fall–fore
9	/ɛ–ɪ/	bet–bit	9	/f–h/	fat–hat
	/ɛ–eɪ/	bet–bait		/t–d/	tip–dip
	/ɑː–aɪ/	cart–kite		/k–g/	call–gall
	/ə–əʊ/	immersion–emotion	8	/w–v/	wet–vet
8	/i–ɪ/	beat–bit		/s–z/	singer–zinger
7	–		7	/b–v/	rebel–revel
				/f–v/	file–vial
6	/ɔː–ɚ/	form–firm		/ð–z/	clothing–closing
	/ɒ–əʊ/	cot–coat		/s–ʃ/	sea–she
5	/ɑː–ʌ/	bart–but	6	/v–ð/	van–than
	/ɔ–ɒ/	caught–cot		/s–ʒ/	person–Persian
	/ə–ʌ/	bird–bud	5	/θ–ð/	thigh–thy
4	/ɛ–eə/	shed–shared		/θ–s/	think–sink
	/æ–ɑː/	at–art		/ð–d/	though–dough
	/ɑː–ɒ/	cart–cot		/z–dʒ/	zoo–Jew
	/ɔ–ʊ/	bought–boot		/n–ŋ/	sin–sing
	/ə–ɛ/	further–feather	4	/θ–t/	thank–tank
3	/i–ɪə/	tea–tear			
	/ɑː–aʊ/	vase–vows	3	/tʃ–dʒ/	choke–joke
	/u–ʊ/	fool–full	2	/tʃ–ʃ/	chair–share
2	/ɪə–ɛə/	beer–bare		/ʃ–ʒ/	Confucian–confusion
1	/ɔ–ɔɪ/	saw–soy	1	/f–θ/	deaf–death
	/u–ʊə/	two–tour		/dʒ–j/	juice–use

Source: Adapted from Brown (1988, p. 604, table 2)

think-aloud protocol, they described to one of the researchers why they stopped. The reasons for stopping were then coded according to phonological and non-phonological issues in the speech. In agreement with Zielinski (2008), errors in stressed (strong) syllables had a greater impact on the listeners, but unlike Zielinski's findings, syllable-final consonants were more influential than syllable-initial, while stressed vowels also were regularly noticed. The highest rated speaker also had far fewer segmentals commented on than the middle and low speakers, and, paradoxically, had more comments on non-phonological features, a peculiar finding given that the lower rated speakers had far greater grammatical difficulties, but it appeared that the greater numbers of segmental errors for the intermediate and low speakers meant that the listeners were less able to comment on their grammar or other non-phonological features. The pronunciation dominated their attention.

Conclusions

Segmentals in any context are subject to misunderstanding if they are mispronounced. These mispronunciations may be heard as other phonemes by listeners, or they may not be identifiable as a target language sound. The gravity of segmental errors varies tremendously, but it is clear that the major factor in error gravity is the way sounds are presented in the speech signal rather than those that are dependent on the listener (Derwing & Munro, 2015). Measures of FL are one of the more promising predictors or relative gravity, but it is not clear whether substitution, deletions, additions, or distortions of segmentals are more serious. There is also little information on the cumulative effect of segmental errors, whether in individual words or across a sentence. Munro and Derwing (2006) found that low FL errors had no effect on frequency while high FL errors did. What might happen with a combination of high and low FL errors? We do not know.

4 Consonant Clusters and Intelligibility

Languages differ in the degree to which they permit multiple consonants to occur as the onset or coda in a syllable. In general, consonant clusters, like individual consonants, need to be produced and perceived accurately, or intelligibility may be reduced (Cardoso, 2017; Zielinski, 2006). L2 learners from languages that have less complex consonant onsets and codas may need to learn to produce and perceive more complex syllables when learning an L2 that has more complex syllable structures. The process of doing so may end in substitutions of sounds within the clusters (e.g., *play* pronounced as *pray*), deletions of sounds (e.g., *lapsed* pronounced as *lap* or *laps*), or insertions of vowels to make foreign words more pronounceable (e.g., *splash* pronounced as *esplash* by Spanish speakers, or as *siblash* by Arabic speakers [Al-Saidat, 2010, p. 129]).

Indeed, the issues surrounding the pronunciation of consonant clusters are primarily issues related to syllable structure. Syllable structure differences between the L1 and L2 may mean that L2 learners have to delete final sounds (such as the final consonant in *log*) or add a vowel (such as *age* being pronounced [eɪdʒi]) if the L1 does not sanction that sound in that position. When the syllable onset or coda becomes more complex, allowing multiple consonants or consonant clusters that are not found in the L1, the potential for perception and production difficulties multiplies. The nature of syllable structure is a matter of language-specific phonotactics (e.g., the English <pl> in *plume* is a cluster, but the <ps> in *psyche* is not, despite both being pronounceable onset clusters in French). Some otherwise illegal clusters may show up in fast speech, such as *Come here!* being pronounced as [kmiɹ]. In general, initial clusters are more restricted in English than are final clusters. For example, all CCC clusters start with [s], followed by a stop (p, t, k) and a liquid or glide ([l, w, j, ɹ]), as in *street*, *squelch*, *spew*, *splint*. It is also clear that the pronunciation of clusters, and therefore syllable structure, is far less commonly treated in pronunciation teaching than is the pronunciation of segmentals and other suprasegmentals (Cardoso, 2017), and when syllable structure is addressed, it is typically addressed in relation to the segmentals included in the clusters. It is likely that it should be addressed in its own right.

Two primary arguments will be made in this chapter. Both are important for onset (initial) and coda (final) clusters, and both are partially related to the information in Chapter 3.

1. Consonant clusters are important in word identification, and thus for intelligibility. But their effect on intelligibility is subject not only to substitutions of individual segments but to cluster simplifications, either through deletion or epenthesis. Some simplifications are unlikely to cause difficulties because native speakers (NSs) also simplify in certain linguistic environments, but many L2 simplifications will be unexpected for listeners and thus cause difficulties.
2. Final clusters also interact with morphophonological variants, in particular, inflectional endings (especially –ed, –s, –'s). Deletions of inflectional endings in clusters are unlikely for NSs, but are more likely to occur with nonnative speakers (NNSs) who may simplify clusters by deleting the last element of a cluster rather than the middle element. This may cause problems with intelligibility or comprehensibility because of the loss of grammatical information.

Consonant Clusters across Languages

Because languages differ in the degree to which they permit multiple consonants to occur as the onset or coda in a syllable, the pronunciation of syllables is a crucial aspect for intelligibility. In general, consonant clusters, like individual consonants, need to be produced and perceived accurately or intelligibility may be reduced (Zielinski, 2006). L2 learners from L1s that have less complex consonant onsets and codas may need to learn to produce and perceive more complex syllables when learning an L2 that has more complex syllable structures. L2 learners from L1s that have similarly complex syllable structures will find differences in the types of clusters that are used in the L2; L2 learners from L1s with complex syllable types are also likely to find less complex syllable types challenging, especially if the L2 is syllable-based in its pronunciation (Cutler, 2012). Pronouncing new syllable types may result in substitutions of sounds within the clusters (e.g., *play* pronounced as *pray*), deletions of sounds (e.g., *lapsed* pronounced as *lap* or *laps*), or insertions of vowels to make foreign words more pronounceable (e.g., the borrowed word *strike* pronounced as *suturaiku* in Japanese).

Consonant clusters are especially important in two environments in English: the beginning of a word (the syllable onset) and the end of a word (the syllable coda). In both cases, clusters may involve up to three consonant sounds (e.g., *strengths*). Consonant sequences in the middle of a word are also important, but they are also likely to be pronounced as parts of two syllables (Pierrehumbert, 2006). The number of possible clusters in onsets and in codas has been a subject of some debate (Algeo, 1978), with numbers subject to definitions of what is a consonant (e.g., whether *boards* ends in two or three consonant sounds) and a number of other factors. The acquisition of consonant clusters is an important developmental issue for child L1 learners. Kirk (2008) studied young children between the ages of seventeen months and thirty-one months. She found that the kinds of substitutions children made in clusters were not the same as substitutions for singleton consonants. She also found that the most common errors were cluster reduction or substitutions of one or more elements of the cluster (with the number of consonants in the cluster remaining the same).

For L2 learners, pronouncing consonant clusters is subject not only to the types of errors that are possible for singleton consonants (substitution or distortion), but also to simplification from deletions of part of the cluster, or epenthesis of a vowel. Both of these types of errors can change the syllable structure of the words. Accurate pronunciation of clusters is also subject to transfer from the L1 as well as errors that cannot be ascribed to L1 transfer. In addition to production of clusters, there is also evidence that L2 learners do not always perceive clusters in the way that L1 speakers do, and that they are subject to perceptual illusions (Davidson & Shaw, 2012) that may be a result of onset complexity or relative sonority of the cluster consonants.

Studies on L2 Consonant Clusters

The pronunciation of sC clusters has been especially studied. For example, a well-known difficulty with sC clusters in English is found with Spanish L1 speakers, who epenthesize the cluster (e.g., *eschool, esmoke, estop*). Many sC clusters (e.g., *speak, stay, skate*) are particularly problematic because they involve decreasing sonority in the cluster before reaching the peak sonority of the vowel ([s] is more sonorous than the stop following it). Other sC clusters (e.g., *snow, slow, smoke*) do not violate the sonority sequencing principle.

However, the sonority sequencing principle may not explain all L2-related problems. Cardoso, John, and French (2009) found that sC clusters seem to be acquired better if they are more frequent in the spoken input learners are exposed to.

L2 studies of consonant clusters have looked mostly at how errors can be explained by transfer or by development. Anderson-Hsieh, Riney, and Koehler (1994) examined the production of initial and final clusters for intermediate proficiency (IP) and high proficiency (HP) Japanese EFL (English as a foreign language) learners, and compared both groups to NSs. Japanese has a consonant–vowel (CV) syllable structure, so clusters are likely to be a challenge for learning English. The study found that IP learners had significantly more problems with English clusters than the other two groups. The IP groups also used epenthesis more than the HP learners, though both groups used deletion more than epenthesis in producing clusters. HP learners had more cluster errors than NSs, though not significantly more.

Hansen (2001) studied the acquisition of English coda singletons and clusters by three Mandarin speakers over six months. She found that the accuracy rate of coda production was relatively stable over the six months, but that the reasons for errors in codas with one, two, and three consonants were different. In single-consonant codas, errors involved substitutions of place or manner; in CC codas, most errors inserted a vowel before a pause; and in CCC codas, deletion of one or more segments was the most common mispronunciation.

Broselow and Finer (1991) tested the effect of the sonority hierarchy using mastery of onset clusters by Japanese, Korean, and Hindi learners of English. They especially looked at the accuracy with which six onset clusters, [pr, br, fr, pj, bj, fj], were produced in imitation and delayed production tasks. They found that pC clusters were produced with the greatest success, that [br] had a much higher error rate than [bj], and that both [fr] and [fj] were difficult. About two-thirds of the errors involved substitutions of another manner of articulation, while one-third involved deletion of one consonant in the cluster. The study, however, involved uneven numbers of subjects from each L1 (twenty-four Korean, eight Japanese, and eleven Hindi), which may have affected the accuracy rates reported.

Major (1994) studied the initial and final CC production in a four-week study with three data-collection points. Four beginning-level Brazilian learners of English produced the same words in word lists and in text. Major was looking for how transfer errors (including epenthesis and substitutions of Portuguese sounds) and developmental errors (deletions of sounds) were distributed over time and according to task. He found that transfer errors decreased over time but that there was no difference between the two tasks. Pedagogically, the decrease in transfer errors was unlikely to make a difference in how their speech would be heard, especially since developmental errors did not decrease over time.

Osburne (1996) used a case study of a single Vietnamese learner of English to look at final cluster reduction over time. Using recordings of two informal work meetings recorded six years apart, she found that the speaker's production of clusters improved over time but that errors remained in approximately 80 percent of final clusters. She claimed that cluster reduction could be largely predicted based on a variety of factors, including L1 influence and universal constraints.

In a study of initial cluster production that looked at the effects of style, gender, proficiency, and interlocutor type, Lin (2003) found that the relative amounts of deletion and epenthesis by Chinese EFL learners were affected by all four variables. Epenthesis was favored over deletion in more formal contexts, by HP learners, by female learners, and when speaking to NS teachers (for female learners only). When the task was informal, when learners were of a lower proficiency, were male, or when females spoke to classmates, deletion was favored as a strategy. This suggests that epenthesis is a strategy that involves more careful attention to speech.

Other studies have looked at the kinds of errors made, but have not examined how the errors were related to transfer or development. Anderson (1983), using a contrastive analysis framework, examined the types of cluster errors made by Arabic and Chinese English learners. Many of the errors were predicted because of the learners' L1s, but certain difficulties were shared between the two groups. Not all the clusters exhibited the same errors. Certain clusters seemed to encourage epenthesis, while others encouraged deletion. Overall, deletion was the more common strategy. In another study of Arabic, Ioup (1984) found that different dialects can use different patterns of epenthesis (vowels preceding and vowels in the middle) to simplify clusters. Even within English, different varieties may have different restrictions on acceptable clusters. Setter (2008) compared cluster production in an inner-circle and an outer-circle variety of English – British English and Hong Kong English. She found that Hong Kong English had a more limited set of syllable types than British English, both for onset and for coda clusters.

Consonant Clusters and Intelligibility

Few studies have explicitly examined the effect of cluster errors on the intelligibility and comprehensibility of L2 speech. Jenkins (2000) argues that speakers who are particularly concerned for intelligibility in their speech are more likely to use epenthesis rather than deletion, since epenthesis provides greater recoverability and is likely to be associated with higher proficiency learners (as in Lin, 2003). For this reason, Jenkins argues that "consonant deletion is more of a threat to intelligibility" (2000, p. 142), especially in onset clusters. She says that "addition is preferable to deletion; that sounds in initial clusters should never be deleted; that where elision occurs in a final cluster, it is preferable to opt for a /t/ or /d/ where this is possible" (2000, p. 143).

Zielinski (2006), in a study of reduced intelligibility in the English speech of a Korean, a Vietnamese, and a Chinese speaker, established that consonant errors in stressed syllables were more damaging to intelligibility than those in unstressed syllables, and that initial-consonant errors were worse than final-consonant errors (except for the Vietnamese speaker). Initial-consonant errors in stressed syllables were likely so damaging because they are likely to lead listeners to hear phantom vocabulary cohorts (Broersma & Cutler, 2008). But a more careful examination of Zielinski (2006) provides hints about consonant cluster errors and intelligibility. In general, Zielinski's examples indicate that errors in consonant clusters could also result in reduced intelligibility, and all types of errors (substitution, deletions, and epenthesis) were implicated in loss of intelligibility for clusters in all locations. For example, the words in (4.1)–(4.3) were identified as difficult to understand (Zielinski, 2006, p. 90). Note: The phonetic symbols underneath the word reflect how the word was pronounced, and the "s" and "w" mean strong (stressed) and weak (unstressed) syllables. The first example involves vowel epenthesis, the second deletion, and the third insertion of another consonant, leading to the interpretation of a cluster where none existed for the word.

(4.1)

Onset epenthesis error
"others degree" heard as "other stakary"

[deɪ][kə][reɪ]
  s   w   s

(4.2)

Onset deletion error
"proverb" heard as "problem"

[prɒ][bɒv]
 s   s

(4.3)

Consonant epenthesis error
"<u>sitting</u> for that kind of exam" heard as "<u>assisting</u> for that kind of exam"
[sɪs][tɪŋ]
  S   W

In another suggestive finding from Zielinski (2006), reduced intelligibility for cluster errors occurred less frequently than it did for single-consonant errors, perhaps leading to the conclusion that the multiple consonants in a cluster may provide a level of redundancy that single consonants do not. For the Vietnamese speaker, for example, for whom clusters were particularly a source of reduced intelligibility, there were twenty-six sites of reduced intelligibility for single consonants and sixteen for clusters.

Pedagogically, Zielinski recommends that

> any non-standard consonant or consonant cluster in the initial position of a strong syllable has the potential to mislead NSE listeners, as does any non-standard vowel in a strong syllable. In order to ensure that segments in strong syllables are a trustworthy source of information for NSE listeners, therefore, the standard production of any consonant or consonant cluster and any vowel that can occur in a strong syllable should be a priority. (Zielinski, 2006, pp. 154–5)

In other words, clusters should be treated like single consonants. Any deviation, especially in initial clusters involving high functional load sounds, is likely to be a threat to intelligibility. In addition, epenthesis, deletion, and substitution are all candidates for loss of intelligibility. Although initial and final clusters have different issues, final clusters cannot be ignored as unimportant, as research on Vietnamese learners of English shows. The relative importance of different types of cluster errors, especially epenthesis and deletion, is particularly ripe for research attention. We know that many L2 learners struggle with syllable structure in their new languages, but we do not know enough about which types of syllable structure errors matter and which do not.

Consonant Cluster and Morphophonological Variants

English has a wide variety of morphophonological variants. Morpho-phonology is the study of word forms (morphemes) that are pronounced differently within certain phonological environments. For example, *im/il/ir* are variants of the <in-> prefix, meaning "not." Thus we have words like <u>*im*</u>*probable,* <u>*il*</u>*legal,* and <u>*ir*</u>*relevant,* in which the pronounced (and spelled) forms anticipate the pronunciation of the following consonant sound. Many morphophonological forms are not noticed by listeners and are simply shortcuts in pronunciation to assimilate other sounds in their manner of articulation (e.g., emphasis → [ɛɱfəsɪs]), voicing (e.g., *have to* → *hafta*), or place of articulation (e.g., *input* → *imput*). There are three suffixes with variant pronunciations that are potentially relevant to pronunciation teaching: –ed, –s/'s, and –ing.

In most varieties of English, –ing has two variants, –ing [ŋ] and –in' [n]. The second variant is sometimes referred to as "dropping your 'g's," although there is no [g] in most varieties of English (this characterization is likely a consequence of English orthography). Instead the variants are two realizations of the final nasal, [ŋ] and [n]. These variant pronunciations are sociolinguistically marked and reflect choices made by speakers. All NSs typically use both variants, but [ɪn] is more commonly used in informal registers (e.g., Labov, 2001), by boys more than girls, and normal boys more than "model" boys (Fischer, 1958), by less educated speakers (Zahn & Hopper, 1985), and in lower socioeconomic classes (Shuy, Wolfram, & Riley, 1968), findings that have been replicated throughout the English-speaking world. It is also perceived to be more representative of straight than gay, and it intensifies the identification of southern US speech (Campbell-Kibler, 2007). It is also argued to be common in African-American speech (Wolfram, 1974). Differences in the proportional use of [ɪŋ] and [ɪn] marks differences in socioeconomic classes, with speakers from higher socioeconomic classes typically using more [ɪŋ] than lower socioeconomic groups in the same task. Speakers of each group will also use more [ɪŋ] in formal (monitored) than in informal (unmonitored) speech. From an L2 pronunciation perspective, learners should be made aware of sociolinguistic issues, but they almost invariably pronounce the –ing, a difference from both –ed and –s/'s endings, which are commonly subject to consonant deletion.

The other endings, the –ed and –s/'s suffixes, are commonly found in published pronunciation materials. Both sets of endings also contribute to final-consonant clusters (e.g., *slapped, slaps*), and may be subject to deletion and epenthesis. Further, I am treating variant forms similarly because their pronunciation regularities are such that they are consistent; however, the spelled forms are not completely regular (e.g., *jump* → *jumped; judge* → *judged*) and the pronunciation of each spelled form applies to multiple morphemes that function differently in English.

These morphemes and their phonological variants are also fundamentally different from phonemes because of their relationship to the morphological system of English. Each of these suffixes is connected to the English inflectional system, but they are not only inflections in modern English. For example, –ing endings are originally part of the verbal inflectional system, marking continuous states (e.g., *He is smoking*). In addition, –ing is used for gerunds (e.g., *Smoking is bad for health*) and adjectival forms (e.g., *a smoking gun*). The other inflections in English, the adjectival endings –er and –est (e.g., *funnier than I am, the funniest person*), are not typically issues for pronunciation.

Past Tense and Past Participle: The –ed Inflections

–ed is used for two verbal inflectional endings in English: regular past verbs (e.g., *loved, laughed, wanted*) and past participle forms (e.g., *has loved, have laughed, was wanted*). Like –ing endings, –ed is also used for adjectival forms (e.g., *a loved one, a laughed-at joke, a wanted child*). The regular past-tense ending is the dominant way to mark past tense in regard to the number of verbs it applies to, but it is not the only way to mark past tense in English. Suppletive forms (e.g., *go/ went*), ablaut forms (e.g., *come/came*), and other past forms that do not neatly fit the regular pattern (e.g., *bring/brought, can/could*) are used successfully by L2 learners at different rates (Bayley, 1994) and differently from the regular form. Indeed, Bayley found that saliency (defined as the difference in the number of sounds between present and past forms) predicted the number of correct forms. Regular forms of both kinds were low on his saliency hierarchy, and were less successfully produced than most other forms. The syllabic form [ɪd] was less accurately produced than the nonsyllabic forms ([t], [d]), but none were above 40 percent correct.

The rules for the production of –ed endings reflect an almost invariant set of sound/spelling connections, suggesting that L2 learners should be able to understand and apply the rules to unfamiliar forms. In contrast, irregular past and participle forms must be learned as independent lexical items because they do not follow a general rule. However, irregular past endings are more likely to be produced successfully under performance pressures (Bayley, 1994) precisely because they are stored as lexical items while regular past-tense forms have to be created by rule (Pinker & Ullman, 2002). Computing the rule creates an extra step that can lead to errors in phonological form while communicating or under other cognitive pressures. McDonald and Roussel (2010) found that artificially creating pressure through listening in noise made native English speakers significantly less accurate in judging whether regular past forms were actually used.

There is also some disagreement about whether the long ending (with the extra syllable) or the short endings ([d/t]) are more salient. Bayley (1994) found that the long ending was less successfully produced by both HP and LP Chinese learners, although HP speakers used both forms more frequently (but still below half of the time) than LP speakers. Both long and short regular forms were used less frequently than irregular forms. In contrast, Bell et al. (2015) found that the long ending was heard more successfully than the short endings. The two studies used different samples, with different age ranges and first languages, but the lack of agreement on such a basic issue means we have a lot to learn about the pronunciation of <ed> endings and their effects on intelligibility.

Verbal, Plural and Possessive Inflections: The –s/'s Endings

-s/'s refers to multiple spoken forms in English: regular plurals (e.g., *dogs, cats, matches*), possessives (e.g., *Jack's car*), third-person singular present verbs (e.g., *He walks* versus *I/We/You/They walk*), and the contracted auxiliaries "is" and "has" (e.g., *He's crazy, She's been sleeping*). The first three –s/'s endings are all inflectional suffixes, while the last is a spoken variant that has a grammatically equivalent full form (e.g., *She is crazy, She has been sleeping*). From a pronunciation point of view, all the forms are identical. From an acquisitional point of view, the forms are quite different in how early they are acquired (Brown, 1973; Krashen et al., 1977), a process that may be sensitive to L1 backgrounds. Luk and Shirai (2009) address acquisition orders of two of the three –s endings (possessives and plurals) and show that the orders are not universal but rather affected deeply by the L1 of the learner. In addition to looking at Spanish-speaker research, they compare them to similar research studies on Japanese, Chinese, and Korean learners. The article does not look at pronunciation issues, though primarily it refers to studies of spoken rather than written language. If the structure is subject to positive transfer, it tends to be acquired earlier; if not, it is acquired later. Thus, L2 learners of English may pronounce some –s endings well while pronouncing others poorly. For the noninflected form, learners often pronounce full forms rather than contractions. Such a pronunciation may be pragmatically quite different in effect from not pronouncing the auxiliary in any form.

The –ed and –s/'s morphemes are parallel in how their morpho-phonological variants are patterned. Each has three phonologically conditioned variants (Figure 4.1). One variant is pronounced with an

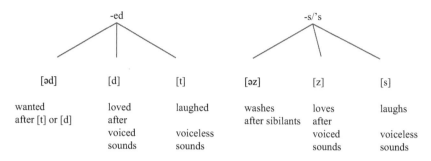

Figure 4.1 The three morphophonological variants of the suffixes spelled –ed and –s/'s

extra syllable (which for convenience I will call the long ending), and the other two are pronounced with voiced and voiceless sounds but without an extra syllable (the short endings). Each variant is environmentally conditioned by the sound that precedes it (i.e., progressive assimilation). The rules that describe which variant will occur are relatively straightforward. After accounting for the environment that creates the extra syllable (see Figure 4.1), the short endings assimilate in voicing to the preceding environments ([d/t] and [z/s]). These sound pairs are phonologically distinct in English (e.g., *den/ten, led/let; zip/sip, lose/loose*). Morphologically, however, the voicing distinction is less important and the two variants function more like allophones than phonemes. For example, final voiced variants may devoice in different environments. This can be important in how the morphemes should be treated in a pronunciation lesson (Dickerson, 1990).

These variant forms may often be a challenge for learners from different L1s, both in pronunciation and in acquisition. For pronunciation, learners may pronounce spelled forms invariantly (e.g., the –ed should always include a vowel because it is spelled that way). Alternatively, learners may delete sounds when the morphemes are part of final-consonant clusters. Deletion, especially of the [t/d] or [s/z], the carrier of the grammatical information, is likely to negatively affect intelligibility.

Regarding acquisition, pronunciation is not the only difficulty for L2 learners, nor may it even be the correct problem to address when learners mispronounce the endings. Morphologically diverse forms are not all acquired at the same rate (even for L1 English-speaking children), and indeed, some forms may be particularly resistant to being acquired by L2 learners. This is especially true of the verbal –s inflection (e.g., *He laughs a lot*), which often shows errors even in very advanced learners of English. Alternatively, mispronunciations of endings may continue to occur when advanced L2 users know the rules for the form and can produce the form almost perfectly in a written test (Hawkins & Liszka, 2003). Of course, pronunciation may also sometimes be the central issue. For example, some Spanish speakers, whose L1 shows a close correlation between pronunciation and the way sounds are spelled, may overgeneralize and pronounce most –ed endings in L2 English with an extra syllable. Their success in producing past forms shows that such learners have acquired the English past tense but are using the wrong phonological forms and would benefit from pronunciation practice.

To sum up, L2 learners' pronunciation of morphophonological variants in English may be affected by many causes. They may mispronounce because they:

1. have not yet fully acquired the form;
2. make a wrong guess about how the pronunciation system corresponds to the orthographic representation;
3. struggle to realize the form in a particular environment (e.g., as part of a consonant cluster);
4. are paying attention to other parts of their spoken language and do not prioritize this feature of English in their communication at that time.

Because morpheme mispronunciations are complicated in their causes, it is not enough to understand *what* learners do in pronouncing these forms. Instead, it is essential to understand *why* they are not pronouncing the forms correctly. It is not easy to tell the *why* and the *what* apart. We see only the surface performance, which may not give a clear picture of cause. Learners may seem to pronounce the forms invariantly, pronounce some forms more correctly while others are rarely correct, delete them in different environments from L1 users, delete –ed endings after voiced obstruents (begged) while pronouncing –ed endings with an extra syllable after voiceless obstruents (Koffi, 2010), and hear them at little above chance guessing in the absence of adverbial cues (Bell, Trofimovich, & Collins, 2015).

The results of the research on grammatical morphemes indicate that errors in how they are realized in speech are very common. Bayley's (1994) study of Chinese speakers showed that even the HP speakers (TOEFL [test of English as a foreign language] above 550) produced only 40 percent of nonsyllabic regular endings and 26 percent of syllabic endings correctly. Hawkins and Liszka (2003) found similar weakness in the pronunciation of regular endings, even though the subjects in their study demonstrated native-like knowledge of the rules in a written test of their grammatical knowledge. Such findings suggest that the way that –ed and –s/'s endings are taught in pronunciation materials must take into account acquisition issues, perception, and production. Being able to demonstrate knowledge of the morphophonological rules is not sufficient for spoken performance.

Perhaps more importantly, we do not know the extent to which errors in the spoken form of the endings affect intelligibility or comprehensibility. Past-tense forms in speech may be redundant because of the presence of time adverbs, and markers of possession, plurality, or present tense in verbs may also be redundant in speech, or listeners may be able to understand the meaning without clearly pronounced morphemes. The goal in this book is to address pronunciation as it affects intelligibility and comprehensibility, but we do not have any research that directly addresses the pronunciation of morphophonological variants. We can make some guesses by analogy to studies of final consonants. Deletions of word-final consonants (Im & Levis, 2015) or sounds at the end of consonant clusters seem to affect understanding (Zielinski, 2008), but we do not know if the same types of errors that are strictly phonological (pronouncing *cold* as *coal*) have the same effect when the errors affect morphosyntax (pronouncing *called* as *call*). One expects that morphological errors will be at least as serious as phonological, but the additional layer of meaning potential may have a different effect on understanding.

Jenkins (2002) also suggests that word-final insertion errors are less likely to impact intelligibility than deletion errors, but her proposal has not been systematically tested. It is alternatively possible that the addition of a syllable where it is unexpected could lead to loss of comprehensibility (e.g., *walked* pronounced as [wɔkəd] could be heard as *walk it*) when the surrounding linguistic context is not sufficiently redundant (e.g., with mismatching adverbial forms – see Bell et al., 2015). Even if such errors do not seriously impact intelligibility (that is, they do not cause complete loss of understanding), such errors in the use of grammatical morphemes may affect comprehensibility. Grammatical forms such as those expressing subject–verb agreement are among the most easily noticeable (Hopp, 2010), and inconsistent use of these inflections may slow language processing.

Researching the Pronunciation of Clusters and Grammatical Morphemes

The ways in which we teach the pronunciation of grammatical morphemes is badly in need of rethinking, and to do so we need targeted research. The amount of research done on the –ed endings (and other past-tense forms) far outstrips that done on the –s/'s endings, but very little of this has looked at how best to increase perception and production skills in L2 learners. We know that both production and perception skills are often impaired in L2 learners of English. We just don't seem to know what to do about it beyond giving them rules that look like they come from introductory linguistics textbooks. Some pedagogical research questions include:

1. What are the errors that L2 learners demonstrate for clusters and for different grammatical morphemes? How do they vary by proficiency level? By L1?
2. To what extent do various errors impact comprehensibility? Are errors in plurals, for example, equal to those of third-person singular verb endings?
3. To what extent do NNSs drop final morphemic endings in spontaneous speaking and in writing? What is the effect of planning time on production?
4. Do different –s/'s ending and –ed ending errors affect intelligibility and/or comprehensibility similarly? Do errors in clusters that do not have grammatical morphemes affect intelligibility differently?
5. What kinds of rule-based approaches are more effective in teaching the pronunciation of grammatical morphemes (as in Brutten, Mouw, & Perkins, 1986)? Do rule-based approaches work more effectively than approaches based on perception/production practice?

Conclusion

Consonant clusters share in some of the generalizations that are true of individual segmentals, but it is also clear that they may affect intelligibility in different ways because of their relationship to syllable structure, a vastly underexplored area in L2 pronunciation teaching and learning (Cardoso, 2017). It is not yet clear whether deletions or epenthesis in consonant clusters affect intelligibility more, or whether both are equally serious types of errors. One process removes sounds that may assist listeners in identifying the intended word (deletion), while the other most often preserves the segmentals in a word but by including an extra syllable or more than one. Until we know more, it would be a safe assumption that any change to the syllable structure is likely to impact intelligibility.

5 Word Stress and Intelligibility

Misplaced word stress in English can stop communication completely. When a word, especially a word central to the understanding of the message, cannot be recognized, listeners may stop all other processing to decode the word that was not understood. For instance, in a study I ran on the ways that teaching assistants (TAs) turned a written text into spoken language, TAs were given a paragraph from a basic physics text on the types of energy and how they were related. They were given a short time to prepare their spoken presentation, which was video-recorded. A research assistant (RA) transcribed each presentation. In one case the RA could not identify a word in the first sentence of a presentation from a speaker from India ("Well, we have a very good _____ today"). We knew the topic, and because the sentence was otherwise grammatical, we knew what the category of the word should be, but three of us could not decode the word over several days of listening. The three-syllable word was stressed on the middle syllable, which sounded like *most* or *must*. Finally, one of the researchers began to break down the segmentals, coming up with things like *at most here*, finally leading to the word *atmosphere*, a word identified by Bansal (1969, p. 227) as likely to be stressed on the middle syllable in Indian English.

There were multiple reasons for our difficulty in understanding, including the word choice itself. Instead of the more expected word *weather*, the speaker used a climate-related word that did not fit the expected collocation related to talking about the weather in an informal way. Also, because the first sentence was out of the blue, and we only knew the general topic of the presentation – energy – we had insufficient context to interpret the unexpected word. But our failure to recognize the word was primarily from its unexpected word stress. As listeners, we tried to decode it based on the stressed syllable, which led us down the wrong path. Indeed, there is a large amount of evidence that listeners use pronunciation characteristics of spoken words (the segmentals and the prosody) to identify the group of possible words that are likely before a word is fully articulated. The group of possible words changes as listeners are able to access more information about the utterance, including the information provided by the stressed syllables (e.g., van Donselaar, Köster, & Cutler, 2005). But if the wrong cohort is activated, intelligibility or comprehensibility will be compromised.

This chapter will build a case for why word stress is essential in an intelligibility-based approach to teaching pronunciation. It does not provide detailed recommendations for how to teach word stress, where to start, what to ignore and what to emphasize, or the types of activities that are most likely to be successful. Those decisions, while obviously important, will be addressed, at least to some extent, in later chapters and will depend on the L1 of the learners, their proficiency levels, the context in which they are learning, their age, and other factors (e.g., Murphy, 2004). The chapter will also argue that word stress is important for intelligibility in English as a second or foreign language (ESL or EFL) and ELF (English as a lingua franca) contexts because of the impossibility of separating stress and segmentals in regard to intelligibility (Zielinski, 2008), evidence that stress affects both native and nonnative listeners (e.g., Field, 2005; Richards, 2016), and findings that show how misplaced word stress can severely impact intelligibility for learners from particular L1s (e.g., Isaacs & Trofimovich, 2012).

The Role of Word Stress in Spoken Word Recognition

One of the strongest arguments for the importance of word stress in L2 pronunciation teaching is the evidence that stress patterns are critical for word recognition (Cutler, Dahan, & van Donselaar, 1997). That is, words spoken with expected stress patterns are recognized more quickly and accurately than those with unexpected stress patterns. In contrast, words spoken with incorrect stress patterns will not be recognized as quickly (that is, they will be less intelligible or comprehensible), will be heard as different real words (perhaps leading to loss of intelligibility or comprehensibility), or they will not be understood at all (a loss of intelligibility). Thus, mis-stressed words can lead to loss of understanding in multiple ways. For some words, however, it is possible that mis-stressing may not affect intelligibility or comprehensibility at all, such as with noun/verb stress pairs, e.g., *PERmit/perMIT* (Cutler, 1986).

Spoken language has no specified spaces between words, and from this continuous acoustic information listeners decode speech into its component meaningful units. This requires activation of the representation of intended words and the inhibition of words that were not spoken. In other words, possible words compete for recognition based on both segmental and suprasegmental information made available in real time. To take a simple example of a word spoken in isolation, *conjure*, the [k] will immediately bring to mind words starting with that sound, which will then be trimmed by the vowel [ɑ] to include only words starting with those two sounds. The [n] further narrows the possible words activated to *contact, constants, conjugate, converse*, etc., and the next sound, /dʒ/, will further limit the possible words to a set including *conjure, conjugal, conjugate*. The next sound [ɚ] will (in American English, at least), lead to recognition of the word *conjure* or one of its affixed forms (*conjured, conjures, conjuring*). This kind of high-speed decision-making in word recognition has been so convincingly demonstrated by a large number of research studies that "competition is an established component of human spoken-word recognition" (Cutler, 2012, p. 120). L1 listeners are not only superb at making these kinds of decisions for words in isolation, but also for words embedded in continuous speech, using not only phonemic and suprasegmental information but also phonetic co-articulatory information (for example, [k] will already sound different before [ɑ] than before [i] before the vowel is ever begun). One way of talking about what happens in recognition is that acoustic information activates a cohort (Marslen-Wilson & Welsh, 1978) of possible words, and that more information simultaneously facilitates certain words and inhibits others (e.g., a particular vowel immediately inhibits words with all other vowels that follow the onset). In word recognition, listeners use phonological information before they make use of semantic information.

The Problem(s) of Word Stress

Poldauf (1984) talks about the "problem of word stress" in English. By this he means that there are no simple rules or regularities to account for which syllable will receive word stress in a given word. Accounting for English word stress requires a hodgepodge of different patterns related to the length of the word, its lexical category, etymological origin, types of affixation, when the word became part of English, and which variety is being described (e.g., Berg, 1999).

English is a free-stress or variable-stress language. This means that, in principle, words of more than one syllable may be stressed on any syllable. Thus, four-syllable words may have their main stress on the first, second, third, or fourth syllables (e.g., *MARginally, moNOtonous, indePENdent, reappointEE*), although some patterns are more or less likely. Free-stress does not mean that the same word can be stressed on any syllable freely. Free-stress languages are typically contrasted with fixed-stress languages in which the same syllable is always stressed in every word, such as Finnish (the first syllable) and Polish (the next-to-last, or penultimate, syllable).

English has minimal pairs based on stress, such as *INsight/inCITE* or *REcord/reCORD*. In *INsight/inCITE*, the segmentals are identical while the stress is not. In *REcord/reCORD*, the difference in stress also leads to changes in how the vowels are pronounced (i.e., 'ɹɛkə-d /ɹə'kɔɹd). Such stress minimal pairs are actually relatively uncommon, especially when the segmentals are identical (Cutler, 1986). There are perhaps as many as 100 in English, most of which involve two-syllable words.

Stress also operates in English as a reliable cue to word identification in spoken discourse. About 90 percent of stressed syllables in discourse are onsets to words (Cutler & Carter, 1987), and stress is important for identifying both single- and multi-syllabic words in the stream of speech. This is true for single-syllable words because content words in English are typically stressed, whereas single-syllable function words are unstressed and are marked by the presence of reduced vowels in their normal spoken forms (e.g., *go for* sounds like *gopher*). Multi-syllable words of all sorts, in contrast, always have at least one stressed syllable with a full vowel. When stress is not word initial, the placement of the stressed syllable is often related to affixation; etymologically related words may be distinguished by the placement of the main stress, as in (5.1). Likewise, unrelated words may share similar stressed syllables and segmentals, as in (5.2).

(5.1)

PHOto, PHOtograph, phoTOgraphy, photoGRAphic

(5.2)

DIStant, DIStaff, DIStal

Lexical stress is thus often important for word identification, but not always so, and it can be manipulated by speakers in relation to other levels of prosody (such as in phrases like *KNOWN and UNknown* in which the normal stress of the second word is changed to show a discourse contrast). Stress information is almost always preserved in slips of the tongue (Fromkin, 1971) and slips of the ear such as mondegreens (Content, Dumay, & Frauenfelder, 2000).

Acoustic Cues to Word Stress

Acoustic information is central to word recognition. In free-stress languages, stress may be marked by duration, pitch, intensity, vowel reduction, or a combination of these features. Spanish, for example, does not make use of vowel reduction (Flege & Bohn, 1989), whereas Dutch and English do. English, however, has far more pervasive use of vowel reduction than Dutch. For English, then, there are four features that are associated with stress. Which features do English speakers pay the greatest attention to?

In terms of importance, it appears that English speakers first listen for segmental cues to stress, followed by duration, pitch, and intensity. In other words, listeners privilege segmental cues because they are so reliable in English; prosodic cues are not as consistently consulted because of the reliability of segmental cues. Segmental cues are immediately available and can thus be used by listeners to begin identifying words before prosodic cues become apparent. Van Donselaar et al. conclude that "in word recognition ... listeners are unlikely to rely on any dimension of variation that yields little in the way of crucially distinctive information regarding word identity" (2005, p. 269). Because English segmentals yield so much information about stress patterns, English-speaking listeners rely on them more than on prosodic information.

Prosodic cues can be consulted, of course, and they can help listeners with word recognition. Durational cues to stress are noticed by listeners and used as a guide to stress, but though they are often redundant with vowel quality in English, they are less redundant in other stress languages. In fact, speakers of Dutch have been shown to be better at identifying stress in English words based on duration than native English speakers (Cooper, Cutler, & Wales, 2002; Cutler, 2009).

Pitch is often cited as a marker of lexical stress as well, but it is much less reliably used except when a stressed syllable is also accented (Cutler, 1984), that is, when it receives a pitch accent because of its placement in a phrase, as in (5.3). The word *conversation* in the first line has primary lexical stress on the SA syllable, but in the sentence it would also be marked with pitch because it is the nucleus of the sentence. In the second sentence, the same syllable is much less likely to be marked by pitch, even though it is still stressed – that is, its first and third syllables have longer durations and full vowel quality, while the second and fourth syllables are reduced in vowel quality, with a shorter duration.

(5.3)

It was a boring converSAtion.
But conversations with her are ALways boring.

Intensity appears to be the weakest cue to stress in English. Zhang and Francis (2010) showed that English listeners are able to identify stress from intensity differences, but that intensity is much less useful than vowel quality and the other prosodic cues. They also demonstrated that listeners could make use of all four cues when they were isolated.

Native Speaker Knowledge of Word Stress

There are two primary roles for stress in word recognition. The first involves the way that listeners use stress to identify individual words that differ prosodically. The second is the way that stress allows listeners to segment continuous speech. In English, the second use is critical for lexical access, while the first use of stress is important in some cases but not others.

In the second use of stress, English listeners rely on stress information to identify words in the stream of speech. Cutler and Norris (1988) examined the effect of strong syllables (those with full vowels) on the identification of embedded words in nonsense syllables (e.g., recognizing the word *mint* in *mintayf*, with the second syllable being strong, in contrast to *mintef*, where the second syllable had a reduced vowel). They found that listeners were significantly less efficient at recognizing *mint* when the second syllable was strong. They argued that this required segmentation across boundaries (min-tayf → mint + ayf), whereas the initial strong syllable in *mintef* required no such re-segmentation. This led them to propose that English listeners treated strong syllables as likely onsets to words in speech.

Fear, Cutler, and Butterfield (1995) further examined how listeners interpreted the distinction between strong and weak syllables, especially how listeners classify unstressed, unreduced vowels (e.g., the first vowel in *audition*). They used five sets of four words that differed in stress and in vowel quality and examined the acoustic characteristics of the vowels and how listeners judged their acceptability when the vowels in each word were extracted and spliced onto another word in the set. For example, the set of words 'audiences, audi'toria, au'dition, ad'dition includes initial vowels with primary and secondary stress as well as unstressed vowels with full and reduced vowels. The third category, unstressed unreduced vowels, formed an acoustically distinct category in its duration, F0, intensity, and spectral characteristics. However, in listener perception, unstressed unreduced vowels were grouped more consistently with strong (full) vowels than with weak (reduced) vowels. The authors suggested that the results indicated that listeners make decisions in a binary manner between strong and weak syllables, and that unstressed unreduced vowels are more often classified as strong, presumably leading to more efficient processing of continuous speech. In their words:

> Why should listeners make use of a binary distinction between strong and weak syllables? We suggest that listeners will in general prefer to make discriminations which are absolute rather than relational in nature. Absolute judgments can be made immediately; relational judgments require comparison between at least two instances (in this case, two syllables), and hence may involve a delay in making the decision. Studies of spoken word recognition suggest above all that recognition is fast and efficient; recognition decisions are not delayed. If this is indeed the case, then spectral characteristics offer the best basis for an absolute discrimination, on the grounds that category judgments about vowel identity draw upon spectral information.
> (Fear et al., 1995, p. 1902)

The pervasiveness of vowel reduction in English means that a large number of spoken words (the great majority of the 100 most frequent words) are function words with reduced vowels (e.g., *a, an, in, on, the, can*, etc.). Non-initial stressed words are much less frequently used, with the effect that stress is an extraordinarily reliable cue to the beginning of content words in continuous speech.

The less consistent use of stress is that which allows listeners to use prosody to identify one word in contrast to another. For example, the three words *octopus*, *October*, and *occur* all begin with the same spelling, *oc-*. The first word has the primary stress on *oc-*, the second has secondary stress on *oc-*, while the third *oc-* is unstressed. The first two vowels are pronounced similarly while the third has a reduced vowel [ə]. Using stress to identify these words means that listeners need to distinguish degrees of stress reliably in the kinds of words that are in an activated cohort of possible words beginning with *oc-*. In English, there is little evidence that this kind of activation happens as a result of prosodic information.

The relative importance of acoustic cues in word recognition means that English speakers will use segmentals to make decisions about word identification before using prosodic information, but that both may be useful. As Cutler says, "activation will be affected by whatever aspects of the incoming signal serve usefully to identify the spoken word form" (2012, p. 97). In a language like Spanish that does not mark stress differences segmentally, listeners rely on prosodic features to distinguish stress. In Dutch, which relies less on vowel quality changes than English, prosodic information is also important in word recognition. Research has demonstrated that English speakers can use a variety of prosodic features in word recognition (Zhang & Francis, 2010), but in general, English listeners do not have to use prosody because vowel quality is a highly reliable marker of stress differences. Cutler puts it this way: "English listeners do not seem to bother much with suprasegmental information in lexical activation and selection. For them, segmental differences ... are far more important than suprasegmental differences" (2012, p. 120).

Features that Influence Native Judgments of Word Stress

What kinds of word-stress features help listeners make decisions about the correct identification of a word? Research has examined this question for both L1 and L2 users of English. Three characteristics have been particularly evident: *syllabic structure*, *word class*, and *phonological similarity*.

Syllabic structure, the first parameter, signifying the stress-attracting properties of different syllable types, especially the propensity of long vowels to attract stress more than short vowels and coda consonant clusters to attract stress more than coda consonant singletons (e.g., *append* versus *open*). The second parameter, word class, is seen in the strong tendency of two-syllable nouns to have initial stress in English (e.g., *cable*) and the lesser tendency of two-syllable verbs to have final stress (e.g., *reveal*). A variety of studies (e.g., Davis & Kelly, 1997) have shown that English speakers are sensitive to this statistical regularity and that whether the word is used as a noun or verb influences their choice of stress pattern (when faced with nonsense words). The final factor, phonological similarity, appeals to analogy as a factor in stressing unknown words. For example, if someone knows the word *a carton* and is faced with the unknown word *a varton*, then similarities in the phonological (and orthographic) structure of the words may influence the choice of initial stress on the new word.

Guion, Clark, Harada, and Wayland (2003) examined the relationship of these three features on stress placement decisions made by speakers of English. They found that all three parameters helped to explain how English speakers made decisions about how to stress two-syllable nonsense words. (Nonsense words are made-up words that speakers cannot, by definition, be familiar with. They are used to make sure that subjects cannot be making decisions based on prior knowledge of the word.)

To determine the influence of these three possible parameters for word stress in English, the researchers created forty two-syllable nonsense words in four combinations based on syllables that differed in structure (i.e., CV–CVCC, CVV–CVCC, CV–CVC, CV–CVVC) to test the effect of syllabic structure. Each syllabic structure combination was represented by ten nonsense words. Both perception and production were tested. In the production task, subjects were presented with the syllables spoken in isolation and asked to repeat them together (e.g., they heard "dɛ" then "kɪps" and were asked to repeat the two syllables in the same order as one word). For syllabic structure, they said the nonsense words in a neutral frame ("Now I say _____").

To test for the effect of word class, the study used a perception task. Subjects were presented with the nonsense words with different stress patterns (read by a trained phonetician) in both noun and verb frames ("I'd like a _____" and "I'd like to _____"). They were asked to listen to two readings of a single frame (e.g., I'd like a ˈdɛkɪps versus I'd like a dɛˈkɪps; I'd like to ˈdɛkɪps versus I'd like to dɛˈkɪps) and decide which of the two readings sounded more like a real English sentence. Each stress pattern was presented in both noun and verb frames.

Phonological similarity was determined by asking subjects if the nonsense word reminded them of any real words. This open-ended task asked subjects to write down real words they thought of when they heard the syllable pairs from the syllabic structure task.

Guion et al. (2003) found that all three of these factors were active in the decisions made by native English speakers in stressing nonsense words, with phonological similarity being the strongest influence. This confirmed previous research, and they reported that "analogical predictions won over rule-based predictions for cases in which analogical stress predicted first syllable stress on nouns or second syllable stress on verbs. While analogical effects were seen for all word lengths, longer words were more likely to receive the stress of phonologically similar words" (2003, p. 407).

Features that Influence Nonnative Judgments of Word Stress

Does L1 background influence the way listeners perceive stress in the L2? This question has a complicated answer, given the wide variety of L1 sound systems and the way they do or do not use stress or its acoustic correlates. Speakers of languages like Dutch, in which stress is similar to English, seem able to transfer their ability with stress to their use of English. They even seem better than English speakers in attending to prosodic features in judgments of stress placement, while also showing evidence of being able to attend to segmental correlates of stress such as vowel quality (Cooper, Cutler, & Wales, 2002). Speakers of Spanish, another free-stress language, make effective use of prosodic features for word stress in English but not segmental ones since Spanish does not use vowel reduction (Flege & Bohn, 1989). French speakers, in contrast, are said to be stress-deaf in learning Spanish (e.g., Dupoux, Sebastián-Gallés, Navarrete, & Peperkamp, 2008), leading the researchers to suggest that it is extremely difficult for French speakers to encode free-stress patterns into their representation of L2 vocabulary. Another study by Peperkamp and Dupoux (2002) indicates that not all fixed-stress languages behave in the same way. While they found evidence that Hungarian and Finnish speakers also exhibit a degree of stress-deafness in perception, speakers of Polish do not. Archibald (1998) argues that interlanguage differences result from differences in the ways that languages use different prosodic parameters.

Speakers of non-stress languages like Japanese and Chinese present a different case. Stress is an unfamiliar feature in their L1 representations, but some of the same acoustic correlates used for stress in English are also present in the L1 (such as pitch in Chinese and Japanese and duration in Japanese). Archibald (1997a) found that one Japanese and three Chinese subjects seemed to be successful with stress in English, but the study was limited by the small number of subjects. Archibald's other studies (e.g., 1992, 1993a, 1993b, 1997b) hypothesized that L2 learners transferred the metrical parameters of their L1 to the production and perception of English word stress. Specific metrical parameters included syllable weight (heavy syllables such as CVV and CVC[C] are more likely to attract stress than CV, which are called light syllables), lexical class (e.g., nouns and verbs are treated differently in regard to stress placement), and potential affixation (e.g., deciding that a spelling in the L2 should be treated as a look-alike suffix in the L1).

Zhang and Francis (2010) examined whether Mandarin-speaking subjects made use of vowel reduction, duration, pitch, and intensity as clues to stress perception in English. Using synthesized tokens of the word pair *DEsert/deSERT*, the study systematically varied vowel quality, duration, intensity, and pitch to isolate the contribution of each feature to stress recognition. Because Mandarin uses pitch for lexical tones but does not use vowel reduction, their hypothesis was that Mandarin L1 listeners should find it difficult to use vowel quality as a cue to stress placement. This hypothesis was not upheld.

Mandarin listeners and English listeners both showed strong sensitivity to vowel quality as a marker of stress. In each experiment, vowel quality was at least equally important in perception of stress for both Mandarin and English-speaking listeners. The study argued that even though the Mandarin speakers were not able to consistently produce reduced vowels, they were able to perceive and use them in identifying stressed syllables. The results must be qualified somewhat in that the task itself used only one word pair in perception, and listening was done in the most advantageous conditions possible, but the evidence still suggests that lack of experience with prosodic correlates of stress does not mean they cannot be used by L2 learners.

Tremblay and Owens (2010) examined the production of lexical stress in two- and three-syllable words by L2 French learners of English and English speakers. The L2 learners were divided by English proficiency level (intermediate, low-advanced, and high-advanced). The study in particular examined how well the French L2 learners attended to heavy syllables in trochaic (non-initial) stress patterns. All data were collected in nonsense word productions in which two or three syllables had to be spoken together in a noun frame.

In two-syllable words, all groups preferred initial stress, with the intermediate group preferring it significantly less frequently than the other three groups. The three-syllable words, however, showed differences across all groups. Native English speakers almost always stressed the middle (heavy) syllable and avoided the final syllable. The French L2 learners of every proficiency, in contrast, produced initial stress around half the time. The use of middle stress increased as proficiency increased and only the highest-level L2 learners were similar to the English speakers in avoiding final stress. The L2 learners who were more successful in producing English stress patterns used duration as their primary cue, whereas those who were less successful seemed to attend to pitch as a primary cue. However, none were fully successful, given the dominance of initial stress even on three-syllable nonsense words. English speakers, in comparison, stressed the penultimate heavy syllable. These learners also seemed insensitive to syllable weight as a cue to stress placement.

A series of production studies replicating the work of Guion et al. (2003) looked at whether L2 learners attended to the same features in choosing which syllable to stress. Guion, Harada, and Clark (2004) examined how two groups of Spanish speakers made stress placements. Participants included early Spanish English bilinguals (those who learned English before age six) and late bilinguals (those who learned in their teens or later). Spanish, like English, is a free-stress language, but it does not have the same connections of stress to vowel reduction since Spanish is a five-vowel language without vowel reduction. Early bilinguals behaved like NSs of English in almost every way. They showed the same sensitivity to lexical class and syllabic structure (except that they showed no preference for long vowels in final syllables). Late bilinguals, on the other hand, behaved quite differently. The noun–verb effect was restricted to one of the four syllabic structures (CVCVC nonsense words, e.g., *demip*). In addition, the late bilinguals used a higher level of initial stresses for nouns than either of the other two groups. This suggests a hypersensitivity to noun initial stress. This also shows that age of acquisition (AOA) may be important in the ultimate success of bilinguals being able to use English stress for unknown words.

Guion (2005) extended this work to Korean English bilinguals. Korean, unlike Spanish, does not use word stress as a phonological parameter (using phrasal accents instead that are not tied to lexical items), and thus the question is whether Korean English bilinguals make use of any of the same cues that NSs of English are sensitive to. Early Korean bilinguals (EKBs) and late Korean English bilinguals (LKBs) were examined and compared to NSs of English. Results showed that syllabic structure was a significant predictor for NSs, EKBs, and LKBs, but with reduced effects in that order. In other words, NSs showed the strongest sensitivity to syllabic structure, followed by somewhat reduced effects for EKBs and greatly reduced (but still present) effects for LKBs. In syllabic structure, long vowels were the strongest predictor of stress placement for all groups. The LKB group did not connect to any other clue, while the EKBs also showed connections to coda clusters as a clue to stress placement. All three groups also showed a relationship between phonological similarity and pronunciation of nonsense words. In regard to lexical class, LKBs were not sensitive to the tendency of nouns to have initial stress and verbs final. This is a striking difference to the late Spanish English bilinguals in Guion et al. (2004), who showed a hypersensitivity to initial stress for nouns. This is evidence that L1 background may have an effect on what learners notice about the English stress system.

The methodology pioneered by Guion et al. (2003) was also used by Wayland, Landfair, Li, and Guion (2006), who looked at intermediate Thai learners' acquisition of English word stress following the same study procedures as earlier studies. Thai, unlike Spanish and Korean, is a tone language. Like Korean, word stress is not phonological in Thai. This study did not look at the effect of AOA on acquisition, instead looking at a single group of learners who were all at the same general level of proficiency with an average stay in the United States of 1.4 years. In regard to the effect of long vowels (e.g., heavy syllables) to attract stress, Thai learners' syllable structure awareness in production of English non-words was native-like (p. 298), a finding interpreted as a transfer from Thai since long vowels also have associations with tones in Thai. However, for perception in general, there was no connection between lexical class, syllabic structure, and stress placement. Only the effect of phonologically similar real words had a significant connection to how Thai learners stressed non-words, leading the researchers to argue that "native Thai speakers relied heavily on the stress patterns of already known words" (p. 298).

Chen (2013) adapted Guion et al.'s (2003) methodology for Chinese learners from Hong Kong. These learners come from a tonal (non-stress) language but learn English in a social context in which English has a long history. Thus, they provide a different view of the influence of these three factors. In addition to the use of the same syllables/nonsense words used in the earlier study, Chen also included perception and production of real English words, eighteen that followed regular stress patterns and eighteen that did not. Subjects performed at around 90 percent accuracy on the real words, suggesting that they had internalized the stress patterns of words that they already knew. For the nonsense words, however, there was evidence only for the effect of lexical class. Syllabic structure and phonologically similar words did not seem to influence Chinese L2 subjects' stress decisions. Chen argued that this may have been due to Chinese learners storing stress on a word-by-word basis rather than according to rule.

These findings can be summarized in the words of Wayland et al. (2006):

results ... strongly suggest that aspects of knowledge influencing the assignment of stress patterns in English can be acquired by adult L2 learners to a varying degree of success depending on such factors as differences between English and the learners' L1 prosodic system, age of acquisition, and perhaps English proficiency.   (2006, pp. 298–9)

It is important to point out that these studies are talking about acquisition. In none of these studies is there evidence that any of these learners were taught about these regularities in English word stress. Although it may be the case that teaching these patterns would result in improved perception and production, there is currently no evidence for how learners would improve as a result of instruction.

The acquisition of stress may also be affected by higher-level prosodic constraints. Visceglia, Tseng, Su, and Huang (2010) looked at the production by Taiwanese L2 learners of English word stress in two-, three-, and four-syllable words under two conditions: when word stress alone was targeted (in carrier sentences) and when word stress was embedded within higher-level prosody demands (at phrase boundaries and in contexts requiring narrow focus – e.g., *It's in JANuary that I need it*). They measured F0, duration, and intensity by NSs of American English and Taiwanese learners in both conditions. While the L2 learners approximated native controls in carrier sentences, their production diverged when higher-level prosody was required. Whereas native speakers continued to make word-stress differentiations in higher-level prosodic contexts, lexical stress markers were no longer evident for L2 learners when they had to pay attention to phrase boundaries or narrow focus.

Another study by Tseng and Su (2014) examined how Taiwanese learners used F0 and duration as cues to lexical stress production in English, again compared to NS controls. There was little difference between the two groups in how they used duration, but Taiwanese learners did not use F0 to distinguish primary, secondary, and tertiary stresses. A third study by Tseng, Su, and Visceglia (2013) employed Pairwise Variability Index measures to examine word-stress parameters (F0, duration, and intensity) by Taiwanese and English speakers. The Taiwanese L2 learners were most different from the English speakers in F0 contrasts, and the contrasts between stressed and unstressed vowels for all parameters were greater for English speakers than for the L2 learners.

Clearly, there is much that remains to be done in understanding how different groups of L2 learners perceive stress, but Cutler suggests possible challenges with such research (2015, pp. 120–1):

In perception, non-native listeners ... may or may not match to the listening strategies encouraged by the probabilities of English; where they do not match, they will generate speech perception difficulty unless listeners can succeed in inhibiting their use. At the word recognition level, such perceptual problems fall into three principal groups: pseudo-homophony, spurious word activation, and temporary ambiguity ... Pseudo-homophones are not a serious problem for the non-native listener (or indeed for native listeners processing non-native pronunciation), simply because ... every language contains many homophones and all listeners have to be able to understand them by choosing the interpretation appropriate to the context.

Spurious lexical activation and prolonged ambiguity are more serious problems. The first occurs when embedded "phantom words" are activated for the non-native listener and produce competition that native listeners are not troubled by. Remaining with the /r/–/l/ phonemic contrast, an example is competition from *leg* in *regular*. Such extra activation and competition has been abundantly demonstrated in non-native listening (Broersma, 2012; Broersma & Cutler, 2008, 2011). The second occurs when competition is resolved later for the non-native than for the native listener (e.g., register is distinguished from legislate only on the sixth phoneme, rather than on the first). This phenomenon too has been extensively documented (Cutler, Weber & Otake, 2006; Weber & Cutler, 2004).

Addressing these challenges will make it more possible to connect findings from native listening studies (e.g., Cutler, 2012), to L2 problems with lexical access, to studies of intelligibility, especially in regard to how L2 listeners process speech from L1 and other L2 speakers.

Word Stress, Intelligibility, and Comprehensibility

As argued at the beginning of this chapter, stressing an unexpected syllable can impair intelligibility and comprehensibility. But misunderstanding is not inevitable. Unexpected stress can also signal regional or social accent (such as saying *INsurance* rather than *inSURance*, or *FRUStrate* instead of *frusTRATE*). However, it is clear that misplaced word stress can lead to loss of intelligibility – that is, the word will not be recognized at all, as in the *atMOSphere* example at the beginning of this chapter. In other cases, misplaced word stress may lead to greater difficulty in processing speech (that is, loss of comprehensibility). It appears that there is also a middle ground between intelligibility and comprehensibility (perhaps what Zielinski [2008] calls reduced intelligibility) in which words are initially not recognized but then are decoded within a short time. It is also possible that some misplaced word stress will not cause serious processing difficulties, such as some noun–verb minimal pairs like *INsult/inSULT* (Cutler, 1986) or words like *'ESti,mate* pronounced by learners as *,esti'MATE*, in which the major and secondary stress switch locations but both retain their full vowel quality (Slowiaczek, 1990).

In general, loss of intelligibility also leads to loss of comprehensibility, but loss of comprehensibility does not mean that speech will be unintelligible. Indeed, this situation often occurs when we listen to things we do not have the background knowledge to understand (for me, a lecture on physics would qualify). I may be able to understand the words being spoken and even write them down, but not be able to process the message easily. Listening to the same lecture in German, however, will for me result in loss of intelligibility at both the lexical and message level.

Mis-stressed Words and Loss of Intelligibility or Comprehensibility

Misplaced stress in English words can include movement of primary stress to a less stressed syllable or a change of stress from an unstressed to a stressed syllable (involving a change in vowel quality as well). These variations affect understanding in different ways. When stress changes from one full vowel to another, it seems at most to slow down processing.

In one study involving primary and secondary stressed vowels (that is, with no reduced vowels), Slowiaczek (1990) conducted a series of experiments to examine the effect of correct and incorrect stress placement on spoken word recognition for two-, three-, four-, and five-syllable words. Some of the experiments included noise as a variable. All experiments examined words that had two stressed syllables (one primary and one secondary). Incorrectly stressed words involved putting primary stress on the secondary stressed syllable (e.g., *REScue* → *resCUE*). Subjects listened to the words and typed them out.

Results showed that noise affected the accuracy of word recognition, with greater noise leading to less accurate recognition, but there was no effect of noise on the level of recognition for correctly and incorrectly stressed words. That is, for the same level of noise, subjects typed out the intended words at the same rate regardless of stress placement. Further experiments employed shadowing tasks in which subjects repeated words as quickly as possible when they were presented over loudspeakers. In three experiments, correctly stressed words were repeated more quickly than incorrectly stressed words, which participants responded to more quickly than nonsense words. A final response-time experiment asked subjects to classify auditory stimuli as words or nonsense words. The study employed eighty-eight words (half correctly and half incorrectly stressed) to create eighty-eight equivalent nonsense words by changing one phoneme but keeping the same stress patterns (e.g., *ANGuish/anGUISH/ANGlish/angLISH*). Subjects were instructed to classify each stimulus as a word or nonsense word. Results showed that real words were identified more quickly than nonsense words and that correctly stressed words were identified more quickly than incorrectly stressed ones.

In agreement with such findings, Cutler (2015, pp. 118–19) states that changes in stress involving only full vowels are not likely to lead to loss of intelligibility:

Mis-stressing can cause similar difficulty for the listener whenever it affects the segments that make up the word – that is, whenever a vowel is changed. Mis-stressing will NOT cause difficulty if it involves suprasegmentals only, e.g., when secondary and primary stress are interchanged; as the early research already mentioned has shown, mis-stressed words where vowels are unchanged (e.g., *stampede* pronounced as *STAMpede*) are recognized easily.

Another type of mis-stressing seems not to affect intelligibility or comprehensibility. This is evident in one of the most commonly taught areas of word stress, noun–verb pairs such as *CONtract/conTRACT*, *REcord/reCORD*. Word pairs like this are often used to demonstrate to learners that stress makes a difference in English word categories (it changes a word from a noun to a verb or vice versa) or meaning (*proDUCE* is a verb that means *to make* while *PROduce* refers to fruits or vegetables). These word pairs may have very similar vowel quality in both syllables (*PERmit/perMIT*, *INsult/inSULT*) or the change in stress may lead to a change in vowel quality (*REcord/reCORD*). Two studies indicate that these stress differences are unimportant for native listeners.

Cutler (1986) examined pairs of stress homophones in English (e.g., *FOREbear/forBEAR*; *TRUSTy/trusTEE*) to determine whether English listeners used stress differences alone to access these words. Results showed that there was no significant difference in the time it took to access the competing word in a cross-modal priming task: "lexical prosody, i.e., the fact that *FORbear* is stressed on the first syllable and *forBEAR* on the second, would appear, from the results of the present experiments, to be irrelevant in the lexical access process" (Cutler, 1986, p. 217). This may not be a great problem given that these true stress homophones are rare in English and Dutch, with fewer than twenty such pairs in each language (van Donselaar et al., 2005).

Small, Simon, and Goldberg (1988) also examined the effect of homographs on listening. Their words included those that differed both in stress and vowel quality (e.g., *CONvert/conVERT*) in contrast to those that differed in stress alone. They found that "changes in vowel quality, when stress was shifted, appeared to have no effect on lexical access of the homographs" (1988, p. 277). This result was different from the lexical access for non-homographs, in which stress changes affected lexical access. In summary, there is evidence that word pairs like this are processed by speakers of English as homophones, whether they have the same segmentals (Cutler, 1986) or whether their segmentals vary with stress changes (Small et al., 1988). While interesting from a linguistic point of view in demonstrating how stress can distinguish one word from another, these stress pairs are less useful as teaching tools since they do not impact intelligibility.

When Misplaced Word Stress Affects Intelligibility

In successful communication, speech has words that are identifiable (intelligible) and easily processed in the stream of speech (comprehensible). Word stress is thus one factor influencing the intelligibility and comprehensibility of speech. When misplaced stress results in segmental deviations or when misplaced stress is to the right rather than the left (Field, 2005; Richards, 2016), there is a greater likelihood of unintelligible or incomprehensible speech. According to Cutler (1986), full versus reduced vowels may be the most important factor involved in the intelligibility of multi-syllabic words in English.

Benrabah (1997) argues that word stress is highly likely to be a source of unintelligibility in English. Benrabah presented stress errors within sentences from three speakers (from Algeria, Nigeria, and India) for British English listeners who transcribed what they heard (a typical intelligibility task). The transcriptions of the words showed how mis-stressings misled the listeners (e.g., *suiTAble* heard as *the level*, *interVAL* as *only trouble*, *cheMIStry* as *community*) into trying to make sense of what they heard by writing down real words or phrases that matched the stress patterns they heard. Benrabah argued that "natives as listeners tend to impose their interpretation based on their 'aural expectancies,' relying heavily on the stress pattern produced and totally disregarding segmental information" (1997, p. 161). The words that were written down mostly matched the stress patterns the listeners heard, and listeners tried to create sense out of the speech signal, heavily relying on the stress pattern to do so (despite the transcriptions sometimes not making sense).

Benrabah's study also hints at the importance of the listener in interpreting word-stress deviations. English is spoken in a wide variety of contexts throughout the world, involving not only NSs (inner-circle countries) and nonnative speakers (NNSs) (expanding-circle countries), but also speakers in countries where English has an official status and is almost universally a language of wider communication (outer-circle countries). The speakers in the study were from the outer circle (India, Nigeria) and expanding circle (Algeria), but the listeners were from the inner circle (Kachru, 1992). We do not know what types of transcriptions would result if they were heard by listeners from other L1 backgrounds.

Stress and Sites of Reduced Intelligibility

Stress and segmental information often work together in impacting intelligibility. Zielinski (2008) sought to make the effect of misplaced stress on unintelligibility explicit. She examined the intelligibility of utterances spoken by three NNSs of English, one each from Korea, Vietnam, and China. Each NNS was interviewed for between ninety minutes and two hours, then their interviews were transcribed and individual utterances were extracted from the overall interview and saved in separate sound files. The individual utterances were then played for five NS listeners who rated them for how difficult they were to understand. The most difficult to understand utterances numbered fifty-one for the Korean speaker, fifty-eight for the Chinese speaker, and sixty-eight for the Vietnamese speaker.

These utterances were the input for the next part of her study, in which three female NSs of Australian English listened to the target utterances (usually twice), and transcribed them orthographically. They then were asked to comment on the problems they had in identifying the words. Each NS listener individually listened to one speaker at a time, with at least two weeks separating listening sessions (a total of nine sessions in all). These "sites of reduced intelligibility" (Zielinski, 2008, p. 73) were analyzed for syllable strength by the researcher and phonetically transcribed by another phonetician. The phonetic analysis was then compared to the orthographic transcriptions (enhanced by the listeners' comments about what they heard), allowing the researcher to identify whether difficulties were caused by suprasegmental or segmental features.

The results showed that "the listeners always relied to some extent on the speakers' syllable stress pattern and the segments in the speech signal to identify the intended words at sites of reduced intelligibility" but that their "reliance on segments ... was not as consistent as their reliance on the speakers' syllable stress pattern" (Zielinski, 2008, p. 76). When they did rely on segments, they were segments in strong (i.e., stressed) syllables, especially initial consonants and vowels. This general pattern, however, did not hold for the Vietnamese speaker, for whom non-standard syllable-final consonants were a source of difficulty for the listeners. This is likely due to the tendency of Vietnamese speakers to simplify or delete syllable-final consonants and consonant clusters in English.

Although the ways that segmentals and suprasegmentals interact may be different for other languages, the two are frequently connected in stress languages. In one examination of Chinese and French learners of Dutch as a second language (DSL), there was no difference in loss of intelligibility based on stress versus segmental errors, but the combination of stress and segmental errors created a much larger loss than either error alone (Caspers & Horloza, 2012), especially for the Chinese DSL speakers.

The L1 background of raters and the context of instruction may also affect the ways that the relative contributions of stress and segmental factors are evaluated. Kashiwagi and Snyder (2010) found that NS and NNS teachers in Japan paid attention to different features of speech in evaluations of intelligibility and accentedness. Whereas NS (i.e., American) teachers were more attentive to vowel and consonant errors, Japanese L1 teachers paid more attention to consonant and stress errors. This finding is similar to Riney, Takagi, and Inutsuka's results that Japanese and American non-teachers also paid attention to different features of speech in judging accent, in which "American listeners relied more on segmentals (especially /ɹ/ and /l/), [but] NNS Japanese listeners relied more on intonation, fluency, and rate of speech" (2005, p. 460).

Word-Stress Errors Are Not All Created Equal

Discussions of word stress as a source of unintelligibility sometimes make an assumption that is not warranted – namely, that any word-stress error is equal to any other stress error in its effect. We've already seen some evidence that this assumption is wrong. As Poldauf (1984) points out, word stress is not a unitary concept in English. But what is the evidence that word-stress errors differ in their impact?

Field (2005) showed that not all word-stress errors have similar effects on NS and NNS listeners. He examined the intelligibility of word stress with two-syllable words in which mis-stressings were shifted leftward (e.g., laGOON → LAgoon) or rightward (e.g., WAllet → waLLET). Field used twenty-four relatively frequent (based on a corpus) two-syllable words (twelve with first-syllable stress and twelve with second-syllable stress) as the listening input in three conditions: standard stress and pronunciation (all twenty-four words), stress shifted (all twenty-four words), and stress shifted with vowel quality changes (eleven words, e.g., *conTAIN* → *CONtain*). The last group was smaller since it only used stress shifts likely to create a change in vowel quality. An additional distractor word was included to give sixty items, which were divided into three groups of twenty for the listening task. Each set of twenty included eight words with standard stress, eight with stress shifting, and three or four with stress shifting plus vowel quality changes. No word was repeated within each set.

The words were played for both NS and NNS listeners in intact classes. Each group of listeners heard only one set of words. For the NS listeners, transcription accuracy was significantly affected for both stress shifting and for stress shifting with vowel quality changes. Stress shifting plus vowel quality changes did not affect intelligibility as much as stress shifting alone. This result is paradoxical since the presence of two errors made the word more intelligible. Further analysis showed that rightward shifts impaired identification more than leftward shifts, a result mirrored in the stress-shifting condition without a change in vowel quality. NNS listeners showed the same patterns that NSs did despite starting "from a lower baseline in that their recognition of items in the standard form was less accurate" (Field, 2005, p. 413) in comparison with the NS listeners.

Field also connected intelligibility (his goal) to comprehensibility, saying that the loss of intelligibility in connected speech may also lead to greater processing demands that lead the listener to try to access other words that fit the phonetic form they have heard. As Field (2005) says,

> stressing the second syllable in *foLLOW* will lead the listener toward a cohort ... that includes *low, local,* possibly *below,* and away from the target word. The consequent increase in processing demands [i.e., affecting comprehensibility] might well limit the listener's ability to perform under the pressures of a conversational context.   (2005, p. 418)

Richards (2016) examined some of the same issues as Field, but for words of two, three, and four or more syllables. Richards tested an English Word Stress Error Gravity Hierarchy based on vowel quality changes and direction of stress shift as predictors of the effect of word-stress errors on comprehensibility and intelligibility. Results indicated that both features predicted the impact of English word-stress errors, with rightward mis-stressing being more serious than leftward, stress errors that changed vowel quality being more serious than stress shifts that do not, and multiple vowel quality errors being more serious than one error. Finally, like Field (2005), Richards found that these errors in stress placement and vowel quality affected both native and non-native listeners similarly, albeit from different baseline performances for words with no errors.

Field's and Richards' results show that some errors in word stress are more serious than others, that errors may affect NS and NNS listeners similarly, and that greater access to context may not help listeners. Second, their results suggest that NS and NNS listeners may not be very different in how they respond to mis-stressed words. Both groups showed similar effects in transcribing, even though both groups started from a different baseline. Third, Field (2005) may have something to say about the effects of context on intelligibility. The listening task used by Field was not complicated in that it involved frequent words in citation form, thus lowering the processing load in comparison to what would be faced in normal conversational speech. While conversational speech may also provide greater access to contextual clues, Field also argued that the belief that "listeners can compensate for [stress errors] by drawing on information provided by context" is flawed because it is based on "how much of the previous input the listener has been able to decode accurately" (2005, p. 418). As a result, the results may underestimate the contribution of lexical stress to overall intelligibility. Listening to NNS speech in an authentic communicative context, whether by NSs or NNSs, will place much greater demands on processing of speech. In addition, NNS listeners listening to NS speakers in normal communication (Lecumberri, Cooke, & Cutler, 2010) will also face much greater demands in identifying where words begin and end and in identifying phantom cohorts of potential words that are activated not only by stress perception but also by inability to perceive phonemic contrasts in the L2 (Broersma & Cutler, 2008).

Word Stress in Relation to Other Phonological Features

It is impossible to separate word stress from segmentals as a source of unintelligibility or loss of comprehensibility, but it is also impossible to separate word stress from other elements of discourse regarding its effect upon understanding. Spoken language does not work this way. Kang and Moran (2014) examined the effect of functional load in the ratings of Cambridge English Proficiency testing for four different levels corresponding to four Common European Framework of References (CEFR) levels. They found that high functional load (FL) errors for consonants and vowels were significantly related to differences in ratings across the levels (in general, the higher the level of proficiency, the fewer high FL errors were made, a pattern that did not hold for low FL errors). In addition, an equally significant feature was incorrect stress patterns, but the authors did not discuss this finding in accounting for the variance in ratings across the CEFR levels.

In a more explicit discussion of the importance of word stress in relation to other factors, Isaacs and Trofimovich (2012) examined the contribution of phonological and non-phonological factors to comprehensibility ratings. In research studies, comprehensibility is sometimes connected only to phonological factors, but this study expanded the scope of factors considered to create rating scales that could be used by teachers in evaluating the spoken production of learners. The spontaneous spoken production of forty French learners of English of varying spoken proficiency levels was analyzed for nineteen quantitative speech measures divided into four categories: phonology (e.g., word-stress error ratio), fluency (e.g., mean length of run), linguistic resources (e.g., grammatical accuracy), and discourse factors (e.g., story breadth). Next, sixty raters rated the French learners' production for comprehensibility on a nine-point scale. Correlations between the comprehensibility ratings and the nineteen quantitative measures were calculated to determine which objective measures were most strongly associated with intuitive comprehensibility judgments.

To develop a usable rating scale, the researchers asked three experienced ESL teachers to listen to the spoken presentations and rate them for comprehensibility and give reasons for their ratings in written teacher reports. The final rating guidelines included those features that showed the highest correlations and also overlapped with teacher comments. The final rating categories were type frequency (a measure of vocabulary richness), mean length of run, story breadth, grammatical accuracy, and the only phonology-related measure, word-stress error ratio.

Word stress was the most sensitive measure of the five included in the final rating scale, and was the only factor to reliably distinguish between the three proficiency levels rated by the scale. In relation to comprehensibility judgments, the results suggest that word stress plays a central role in how teachers rated oral proficiency. It may be that this is a particularly important issue for Francophone learners of English, given that word stress is not distinctive in French, but the authors argue that because of "the sheer number of learners from other L1 backgrounds for whom English word stress (and rhythm) generally pose a problem (e.g., Spanish, Polish), English stress patterns could be a much more global feature in distinguishing between different L2 comprehensibility levels" (Isaacs & Trofimovich, 2012, pp. 497–8).

A summary of what we know about stress shifts is presented in Table 5.1. Some cells are not completed because it is impossible to have a word in which the primary stress is replaced by a primary stress (there is only one primary stress in each word). Also, there is no research suggesting what would happen if a secondary stressed vowel were replaced with another secondary stressed vowel (in effect, this is a segmental not a stress error). However, there is a suggestion about what could happen when an unstressed vowel is replaced with another unstressed vowel (e.g., delight pronounced as [diˈlaɪt] rather than [dəˈlaɪt]). In addition, there is the possibility that an unstressed vowel is given full quality even though the stressed vowel remains as it is. Cutler says:

if the word *target* is uttered with correctly placed stress on the initial syllable, but with the second syllable unreduced – so that it sounds like *get* – it is liable to be perceived as two words rather than one; the same will happen if in correctly stressed *utterance* either its second or third syllable is not reduced.   (2015, p. 118)

Table 5.1 Likelihood of unintelligibility when stress patterns are changed

		Realized stress		
		Primary	Secondary	Unstressed
Expected stress	Primary	* * * * *	NS recognition unaffected with some slowdown in processing (Slowiaczek, 1990)	Disruption of recognition (Richards, 2016) especially when stress is shifted rightward (Field, 2005). True for NS and NNS listeners.
	Secondary	Recognition unaffected, with some slowdown in processing (Slowiaczek, 1990)	* * * * *	Disruption of recognition (Richards, 2016) or not (Field, 2005)
	Unstressed	Disruption of recognition for NS and NNS listeners (Richards, 2016)	Disruption of recognition (Richards, 2016)	Full vowels from unstressed syllables can sound acceptable to NSs when spliced into words where the same vowel is primary or secondary stressed (Fear et al., 1995)

Conclusions

The research on the contribution of word stress to intelligibility is compelling: misplaced word stress can cause loss of understanding. Caspers and Horłoza (2012) found that for Dutch (a closely related language to English), word-stress errors impaired intelligibility (even for words spoken by native Dutch speakers), though no more than segmental errors. They also showed that pronunciation of words with both stress and segment errors was associated with a significantly greater loss of intelligibility than either type of error alone. Zielinski (2008) and Benrabah (1997) provide evidence that NS listeners pay attention to stress patterns in trying to interpret accented speech, and that stress may be a greater source of reliability for word recognition than segmental information. Nor can the interaction of segmental and prosodic features be ignored.

What does this mean for teaching? Clearly, in an ESL context, word stress should be a high-priority feature because of its salience and the possibility that it is important for NS listeners in trying to access the words spoken by L2 learners. Even where intelligibility is not completely lost, mis-stressings often impair comprehensibility (cf. Cutler & Clifton, 1984). What about EIL/ELF contexts? Jenkins (2000, 2002) places word stress outside the Lingua Franca Core (LFC), even though Dauer (2005) and McCrocklin (2012) criticize this decision. Walker (2010) is also less certain about the place of word stress in his pedagogical application of the LFC. However, Lewis and Deterding (2018) found that word stress did cause loss of intelligibility in South Asian ELF. Thus, it seems that Jenkins' decision is unwarranted on the basis of the available evidence. We do not know how nonnative listeners react to errors in word stress made by interlocutors from a range of L1s, whether those speakers come from outer or expanding circles. In addition, the near-impossibility of dividing segmental and prosodic features involved with English word stress means that it is wise to advocate a role for word stress in ELF communication. It may be that in ELF communication, listeners pay greater attention to segmentals than stress, but it may also be that stress information remains essential to lexical access, as suggested by Field (2005) and Richards (2016). It is also likely that the first languages of the interlocutors will provide different results on the relative contribution of stress and segmentals to intelligibility. But until we know more, the compelling evidence for the salience of word stress indicates that it should be considered a priority for pronunciation teaching in all L2 contexts.

Part III

Discourse-Based Errors and Intelligibility

6 *Rhythm and Intelligibility*

In current approaches to pronunciation teaching, rhythm has peripheral status, especially in regard to English as a lingua franca approaches (Jenkins, 2000; Walker, 2010). Even before discussions of the Lingua Franca Core (LFC), when rhythm was considered to "be one of the most important phonetic aspects for the auditory comprehension and intelligible oral production of English" (Chela-Flores, 1998, p. 13), it was nonetheless neglected in pronunciation teaching. Nonetheless, this peripheral status has typically applied only to production, not perception. The evidence for rhythm's direct effect on intelligibility is scarce (though not missing). This is likely because the primary function of rhythm in language understanding is different than for related prosodic features like word stress. Rather than affecting intelligibility, rhythm is more likely to affect comprehensibility, that is, the amount of work listeners have to do to understand a speaker. Mismatches of rhythmic structure will make processing of speech more challenging, regardless of whether the mismatches of rhythmic structure involves native speakers (NSs) and nonnative speakers (NNSs), or two NNSs.

Although the connection of rhythmic differences to loss of intelligibility appears to be indirect, there are times when it is less indirect, at least for production. Recently, I analyzed the teaching presentation of an Indian speaker of English (his presentation took place in the United States and was given to an audience used to interacting in American English). Later, his presentation was transcribed by native English-speaking undergraduate students, who struggled in doing so. He spoke with a fluency that matched typical fluent American speakers of English (about five syllables/second), but his speech was frequently unintelligible to the transcribers, who had the luxury of playing back his speech as often as they desired. Some loss of intelligibility was caused by segmental realizations, some by unexpected word-stress patterns, but there were often stretches of five or six words that were unsuccessfully transcribed because of, in my opinion, the speaker's rhythm. If this had been only a matter of comprehensibility (i.e., effort), multiple listenings would have led to success. Instead, the transcribers regularly could not understand, suggesting that rhythm cannot be cast aside as irrelevant to intelligibility.

Rhythmic differences can cause difficulties for native listeners, as my example suggests, but rhythmic differences can also cause difficulties for nonnative listeners. In another example from my work, Chinese students in computer science at my university complained to me about how hard Indian professors and graduate students were to understand, even though both Indian English and Chinese can be classified as having a rhythm that is syllable-based. Indeed, one of the primary challenges to teasing out the effect of rhythm on understanding is the implicit assumption that there are two kinds of rhythm: native and nonnative. This cannot be true, of course, as many L2 learners of English come from widely different languages that have rhythmic peculiarities every bit as distinct as English. Such L2 English speakers bring their own rhythmic patterns into how they speak and hear English.

Rhythm is also essential to how listeners process speech and segment the stream of speech into identifiable words and messages, both key elements of intelligibility (see Cutler, 2012). This, then, indicates that rhythm is likely to be critical for intelligibility, but that its role will also overlap with other features of speech. Rhythm underlies the stream of speech and influences the shapes of vowels and consonants in different linguistic environments. Rhythm also affects how listeners access words and messages, and the different rhythmic structures across languages almost guarantee that rhythm will affect how listeners and speakers understand each other.

What Is Rhythm?

Rhythm is a general suprasegmental category that describes the timing patterns associated with a language. It is based on the regular occurrence of similar events, such as strong and weak beats (Low, 2014). Because it is based on a regular occurrence of events, rhythm is not tied to a single syllable but is a measure of how syllables occur in groups called feet. In the examples in (6.1) S refers to a strong or stressed syllable, and W refers to a weak or less stressed syllable.

(6.1)

S W	W S W	S W W	W S	S W
| o – ver |	| a – ma – zing |	| beau – ti –ful |	| the man |	| liked it |

All languages have a rhythmic structure that is unique yet similar to other languages. In learning a language, we learn its rhythm. Infants can distinguish between different types of rhythms. Infants surrounded by French, for example, react differently to English (stress-based) and Japanese (mora-based) rhythm. The sensitivity, however, does not extend to two rhythmically related languages, such as Dutch and English (Ramus, Nespor, & Mehler, 1999).

In learning a new language, the native rhythm, like other aspects of L1 pronunciation, will transfer to the production of the new language. As L2 learners become more proficient in the new language, their rhythm will become more like that of L2 speakers, but the extent of change may be limited by the rhythmic differences between their L1 and the L2. For example, French and German speakers learning English will both become more English-like in their rhythm, but German speakers are likely to become more native-like in their production (Ordin & Polanskaya, 2015a,b)

In general, rhythm is the patterns created by relative differences between syllable durations. Syllable differences may also be connected to variations in the pronunciation of segmentals, especially vowel quality (this is especially true of English rhythm). One of the best-known characterizations of rhythm is the distinction between syllable-timed and stress-timed rhythm (Abercrombie, 1967; Pike, 1945). This indicates that languages can largely be divided into two camps. The first camp includes languages that have relatively even timing between syllables, such that most syllables of similar structure take about the same amount of time to pronounce. In the second camp, the regular timing of the language is thought to be relatively equal between stressed syllables (not all syllables are equally stressed), and the number of syllables between the stresses are squeezed to fit the speech duration between them. For example, the two sentences, *John would like the cars*, and *John would have liked some of the cars*, would each have three stresses, *John*, *like*, and *car*, as in (6.2) and (6.3). In the first sentence, there would be one syllable between each stress with reduced vowels in each, but in the second, there would be two and three stresses. In theory, these multiple syllables would fit into the same timing unit that the single syllables did, leading to greater reduction in the pronunciation of the unstressed syllables, including making the reduced vowels shorter, sound or syllable deletions (e.g., *would have* as **woulda*), coalescent sounds (e.g., *not your → notcher*), contractions, etc.

Figure 6.1 Stress-timed rhythm

(6.2)

<u>John</u> would   <u>like</u>   the <u>cars</u>.

(6.3)

<u>John</u> would have <u>liked</u> some of the <u>cars</u>.

Stress-timed and syllable-timed rhythm have been visually represented in pedagogical treatments by changes in the size of people walking along a path (Prator & Robinett, 1985, p. 29) or other images, such as a stick moving on a fence (Grant, 1993, pp. 97–8), as in Figures 6.1 and 6.2. Such views of rhythm have been used for decades to teach English pronunciation to foreign learners from syllable-timed languages (e.g., Spanish).

This attractive view of rhythm, unfortunately, is uncertain at best, and untenable at worst. Rebecca Dauer (1983), a phonetician and pronunciation teacher, established that the difference between stress- and syllable-timing was more perceived than real, and that the perceived rhythm of different languages did not fit into two categories but rather on a continuum. The evidence that languages were not divided into stress-timed and syllable-timed has not stopped researchers and teachers from using these terms as a shorthand for dominant tendencies among the world's languages, but subsequent attempts to find measurements to validate the perceptual categories, including the durations between consonants and the durations between vowels, has been largely unsatisfactory (Arvaniti, 2009).

Features Associated with Rhythm

Rhythm does not refer to a unitary feature. At the very least, it involves both syllable length and vowel quality, but rhythm also overlaps with speech rate, measures of fluency, and realizations of

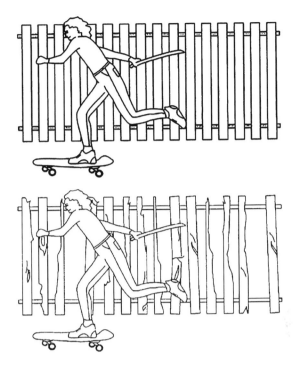

Figure 6.2 Syllable-timed and stress-timed rhythm

sounds in connected speech. There is also evidence that measurements of rhythm differ from one spoken register to another. The traditional treatment of stress-timed rhythm in pronunciation teaching includes, at a minimum, two features: durational difference between strong and weak syllables, with stressed (strong) syllables taking longer to say and unstressed (weak) syllables taking less time; and the effect of stress on vowel quality. Stressed syllables have full, stable vowel pronunciations, while unstressed syllables have a strong tendency toward being pronounced with a centralized, less stable vowel called schwa [ə]. Schwa usually varies between being realized as [ɪ] and [ə], depending on the linguistic environment of the vowel and the speaker. These are the primary characteristics of stress-timed rhythm as presented in most L2 pronunciation materials for learning English. Cauldwell (2002) argues that the stress-timed and syllable-timed paradigm may create a self-fulfilling prophecy, causing listeners to hear a particular rhythm while ignoring evidence to the contrary.

Nonetheless, English rhythm is closely tied to word classes (Table 6.1), with content words being almost invariably stressed and

Table 6.1 Content words and function words and how they affect rhythm

Content words (stressed syllables)	One-syllable function words (typically unstressed)
Nouns (e.g., friend, dog, sound)	Personal pronouns (e.g., him, them, your)
Verbs (e.g., go, fall, swim)	Articles (e.g., the, a/an, some)
Adjectives (e.g., best, high, hard)	Auxiliary verbs (e.g., can, could, should, will)
Adverbs (e.g., fast, quick)	
Possessive and demonstrative pronouns (e.g., hers, theirs, that)	Conjugated "be" verb (e.g., is, are, been)
	Possessive and demonstrative determiners (e.g., her, their, that)
Negative words (e.g., no, not, can't)	Conjunctions (e.g., but, and, or)
Interrogatives (e.g., which, what, why)	Prepositions (e.g., in, at, on, for, from)
	Contractions (you're, he'll, I'd)

carrying at least one full vowel, and one-syllable function words heavily tending toward lack of stress and schwa-like vowel pronunciations (for more, see Celce-Murcia, Brinton, Goodwin, & Griner, 2010). This strong tendency in English provides the overall image of stress-timing, with much greater reductions associated with unstressed words and syllables. Note that words of more than one syllable will always have one stressed syllable.)

Besides the effects of lack of stress on reduced vowels, at least in inner-circle Englishes, there are also effects on the clarity of words when they are repeated in discourse. The same stressed word when it is new information and in a prominent position, may later be pronounced quite differently when it falls into the category of given information and is not prominent. Cauldwell (2013) gives the example of the word *student* in a spoken text. The first time it was said, it sounded like [studənt], but the second time it sounded like [stunt], showing that rhythm even of stressed words can be influenced by other aspects of prosodic structure. Again, this is a consequence of fluent speech, and is likely important at least for perception. These kinds of variations have been discussed in regard to inner-circle Englishes, but they may also be important for English and lingua franca (ELF) communication, where they have not been described.

In addition, the difference between strong and weak syllables also affects the way that sounds change in connected speech. The palatal glide [j] is found in the word *annual* ['ænjuəɬ] but not in *nudity* ['nudɪti]. This difference comes from the stress patterns of the two words, with the [n] before an unstressed syllable in *annual* and before a stressed syllable in *nudity*. Rhythm is associated with a wide variety

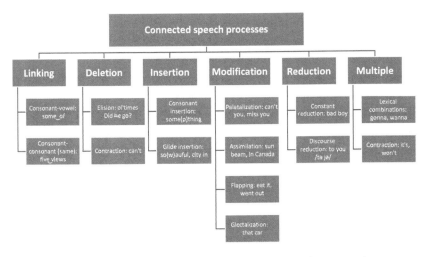

Figure 6.3 Connected speech processes as categorized by Alameen and Levis (2015)

of connected speech modifications, from the way that words are linked together (Alameen, 2014) to changes in segments (e.g., *Would you* → *Wouja*), features that are so common in pronunciation teaching that they have even had books published. The best known of these is *Whaddaya say* (Weinstein, 1982). These types of connected speech are important for perception.

Connected speech features are ubiquitous in inner-circle Englishes, and different researchers categorize them differently. Alameen and Levis (2015) proposed a taxonomy (Figure 6.3) of connected speech features which may be useful for future research into intelligibility, perhaps helping researchers and teachers to decide which of these features should be taught or not taught.

Finally, rhythm is closely connected to spoken fluency, phrasing, speech rate, and speech register. Spoken fluency includes not only the ability to speak smoothly, but to also speak without excessive pauses, either silent or filled (e.g., umm). Pauses may also affect perceptions of fluency when they break up linguistic constituents and thus make speech harder to follow. Phrasing may be signaled by pitch movement and final lengthening (Katz, Beach, Jenouri, & Verma, 1996), and poorly constructed phrases create a sense of poor fluency (Nakatani & Hirschberg, 1994) and make an expected rhythm almost impossible to achieve. Phrases may also be logical but too short, affecting the mean length of run (the number of words between pauses) and creating a possible impression of a rhythm that never quite gets going and a speech rate that is slower than expected. Indeed, most L2 learners tend to speak considerably more slowly than their L1 counterparts, and comprehensibility improves when their speech is made somewhat faster (Munro & Derwing, 2001). Finally, fluency can be smooth yet too fast (too fast for the listeners to process, that is). This is a common situation with speakers of English from nativized varieties (e.g., India, Nigeria, Singapore), whose normal rhythm in English may not easily be processed by listeners from inner-circle and expanding-circle countries. This effect is unevenly distributed, however, and may not be wholly associated with rhythmic features.

Listeners may not be able to tell the difference between rhythm and speech rate when making judgments about L2 speech rhythm. Dellwo (2008) found that speech rate is an important correlate for cross-linguistic rhythm identification. In a study of German learners learning English, English listeners struggled to use rhythmic measures in classifying the proficiency of German learners, relying instead on speech rate. In other words, German learners were heard as more English-like in rhythm when they spoke more quickly, and less English-like when they spoke more slowly (Ordin & Polanskaya, 2015a). This suggests that speech rate is a salient cue for rhythm and may be conflated with concepts of rhythm.

Finally, the type of spoken text affects the measurements of rhythm, and any cross-language measurements of rhythm must keep the text consistent. In one study of rhythm measurements for the speech of NSs, Wiget et al. (2010) looked at how five sentences produced by six speakers differed in rhythmic measures. Even though all the sentences were read aloud, there was substantial variation in the rhythm measurements, but the greatest amount of variation appeared to be related to the linguistic content of the sentences. The variation between speech that is read aloud and speech that is spontaneously produced is that some of the more obvious markers of stress-timing seem more likely to be neutralized in casual speech (Cauldwell, 2002).

How Is Rhythm Measured?

Attempts to measure rhythm have largely failed to distinguish between syllable-timed and stress-timed languages (Dauer, 1983; Roach, 1982). The work on mora-timed languages such as Japanese found the same uncertain support for rhythm being able to accurately characterize rhythm classes (e.g., Port, Dalby, & O'Dell, 1987). Despite ever more intricate measurements, such as the vowel intervals, consonant intervals, and successive duration of vowels in an utterance (see Low, 2014), the accurate measurement of rhythm remains somewhat uncertain, leading to combinations of measurements to tease out the differences that listeners are sure of. Although the vast amount of research has found certain measures that are useful for distinguishing languages from each other, rhythm remains somewhat elusive. At the same time, its psychological reality seems well founded.

The acoustic measurement of rhythm today is primarily related to a variety of rhythm metrics that measure the variations of vowel and consonant timing in both raw and adjusted forms. The overall finding of studies using rhythm metrics suggest that while rhythm is psychologically salient, it is acoustically challenging to measure, and dividing languages on the basis of timing has met with unsatisfactory success (Arvaniti, 2009). (Those who are interested in the use of rhythm metrics, see Low [2006]. A detailed overview of metrics is not directly relevant to the importance of rhythm for intelligibility or for pronunciation teaching.) In a study of the usefulness of rhythm metrics to distinguish between classes of languages as well as between languages in the same class, White and Mattys (2007) applied metrics to the analysis of rhythm in four languages: Dutch, Spanish, English, and French. The different measurements successfully classified the four languages into two general rhythmic classes, the first including Dutch and English, and the second French and Spanish. However, within the two general classes, variations were large, indicating that even general classes have significant differences.

The study of L2 rhythm has shown that L2 rhythm differs from L1 rhythm, but that L2 learners appear to learn some aspects of the L2's rhythm. Again, White and Mattys (2007) hypothesized that speakers who shifted between rhythmic classes (e.g., Dutch speakers speaking French, or Spanish speakers speaking English) would show tendencies toward the L2 in rhythm measurements. Such shifts occurred but were only approximate, and the authors cautioned that "rhythm is primarily a perceptual property ... and more work is required to ascertain how these [rhythm] metrics relate to the subjective experience of linguistic rhythm" (White & Mattys, 2007, p. 520).

In a study of nonnative rhythm in German (a stress-timed language related to English), Gut (2003) used a prosodically annotated corpus to examine how nonnative rhythm differed from native German-speaker rhythm in vowel reduction, deletion of inflectional endings, and the durational differences between reduced and unreduced syllables. The results showed differences in L1 and L2 rhythm, especially in read speech, suggesting that formal tasks are more likely to show the effects of native language influence.

In another examination of L2 rhythm of German learners learning English, Ordin and Polanskaya (2015a) found that German speakers learning English spoke with a less stress-based rhythm at lower levels of proficiency, but that their speech became more stress-based as they became more proficient. In a related study (Ordin & Polanskaya, 2015b), these authors found that French learners of English followed a similar trajectory to the German learners, becoming more stress-based in their rhythm at higher levels of proficiency, yet did not achieve the rhythmic abilities of German learners at higher levels.

Tortel and Hirst (2010) used rhythm metrics to examine rhythm from the ANGLISH corpus of native (English L1) and nonnative (French L1) speakers. They found that a combination of rhythm metrics effectively defined three groups from the spoken data: two French groups differing in proficiency, and one English group, with overlap (sometimes substantial) between the groups.

Such uncertainty about the acoustic measurement of rhythm does not inspire confidence for the teaching of L2 rhythm. A feature that is psychologically salient but acoustically slippery may be especially challenging, both for teacher and for learners. However, a pedagogy that builds on the psychological reality of rhythm may also be as effective as one that is based on quantitative measurements.

A different approach to studying rhythm is found in psycholinguistic research on native listening. This research indicates that rhythm fulfills a critical role in helping listeners segment the speech stream into identifiable words, and subsequently into identifiable messages (Cutler, 2012). Rhythm in English, that is, the alternations of strong (S) and weak (W) syllables, is a primary clue used by native listeners in identifying the beginnings of words in speech. This was first demonstrated by Cutler and Carter (1987) in an examination of the spoken London–Lund Corpus. The stressed syllables in the corpus included about 60 percent monosyllabic words (e.g., *dog*, *desk*), 31 percent initial stresses on multi-syllabic words (e.g., *beautiful*, *conversation*), and less than 10 percent where the stress was non-initial after an unstressed syllable (e.g., *deliberate*, *amazing*). In other words, around 90 percent of the time a stressed syllable (primary or secondary) signaled the beginning of a word, a number that was so high that the authors said that English listeners would typically be correct if they assumed that every stressed syllable was the beginning of a new word.

This also suggests that the stress-based rhythmic system in English is exploited by listeners in listening comprehension. In other words, listeners pay attention to strong syllables with the assumption that they begin a new word. This also assumes that function words do not get segmented in the first run through, but are fit into the segmentation of continuous speech later. The findings also suggest that differences in rhythm are exploited by L1 listeners in ways that are most appropriate to the rhythm of each language.

The Purpose of Rhythm

Rhythm is the "organizational principle [of speech] which has its roots in the coordination of complex action and its effect in the realm of prosodic structure" (Cummins & Port, 1998, p. 145). Its primary purpose is to help listeners segment continuous speech and identify the beginnings of actual words while ruling out possible words that were not actually spoken. This primary purpose suggests that rhythm may affect both intelligibility and comprehensibility in a second language.

There is strong evidence that rhythmic structure is essential in understanding how speakers of a language segment continuous speech. Different languages with different rhythmic patterns also have different poetic structures that reflect rhythmic preferences (Cutler, 2012). These rhythmic patterns guide the way the language is acquired, and they are exploited by listeners for the purposes of speech processing (Ordin & Polanskaya, 2015b).

Cutler (2012), in discussing segmentation by native English speakers, says that rhythm assists them in segmenting words. They pay attention to strong syllables and make decisions about the lexical consequence of those strong syllables. In English (and in other stress-based languages), research indicates that strong syllables are likely to be the beginning of a word. The strong–weak character of English rhythm privileges this segmentation strategy. Mishearings, slips of the ear, and mondegreens (e.g., "she's a must to avoid" heard as "she's a muscular boy" in Cutler 2012, p. 123) provide evidence that English listeners privilege stressed syllables in segmenting speech.

Reporting on research examining speech segmentation, Cutler showed that French and English listeners have different procedures for segmenting speech into words. French listeners applied syllable-based segmentation strategies even to English words, and the English listeners applied stress-based segmentation strategies even to French words. "French listeners were apparently inclined to apply syllabic segmentation to whatever spoken input they received, whereas English listeners did not apply it, whatever the input" (Cutler, 2012, p. 129)

Cutler argues that these two segmentation strategies demonstrate the essential use of rhythm: how native listeners find words in continuous speech. The rhythm of different languages varies in the segmentation strategies that are most effective. The use of full and reduced vowels in English, differing in vowel quality reflects a system in which a full vowel is heard as stressed, creates the right conditions for successful segmentation for English. The rhythmic system of French has no direct reflection of this English strategy (Cutler, 2012).

This research (for a fuller account, see chapter 4 in Cutler, 2012) indicates that attending to the rhythmic cues of the native language makes finding real words and ruling out phantom words in continuous speech efficient. Cutler, suggesting that the difficulties in acoustic measurement do not negate the psychological reality of rhythm, says that "rhythm is not a concrete property that lends itself to simple measurement...It concerns the level of structure that is most involved in expressing regularity in utterances. In French and Romance languages, that is syllables. In English and Dutch, it is stress. Because the basis of rhythm differs across languages, so does the way listeners segment speech" in different languages (2012, p. 132).

The kind of rhythm that reflects the phonological regularities in a language is the kind that native listeners will exploit. This also suggests that L2 listeners, especially those who come from a language that privileges different segmentation strategies, will have difficulties in segmenting speech in the L2, perhaps resulting in the belief that NSs speak too quickly. The effects of rhythmic mismatches also raise the question of whether L2 learners can be taught to segment speech with different cues. If so, instruction would improve their abilities to understand normal L2 speech. It is also an open question whether slowing down speech would provide extra processing time as learners try to hear the rhythmic clues in the nonnative language.

Rhythm in Spoken Language Understanding

ACCENTEDNESS

Nonnative rhythm in a second language affects the ways listeners evaluate speech in relation to accentedness, intelligibility, and comprehensibility. While accentedness is not in itself essential to an intelligibility-based approach, rhythm's connection to judgments of accent indicate that listeners (typically L1 listeners in most of the studies) notice differences in rhythm and evaluate speech as different, primarily based on phonological factors (Saito, Trofimovich, & Isaacs, 2016) and on speaking rate (Munro & Derwing, 2001). In a study of content-masked speech (in which the speech was played backward), Munro, Derwing, and Burgess (2010) found that foreign accents were identified as foreign when segmental, grammatical, and lexical features were made unidentifiable. This suggested that judgments of accentedness were, when other features were removed, still affected by voice pitch, voice quality, and elements of prosody.

Although accentedness is not directly related to intelligibility or comprehensibility, foreign-accented speech creates challenges for listeners because foreign-accented speech is systematic yet has greater variability across speakers. This variability is partly due to variations in second-language proficiency, but in regard to pronunciation it is also due to variations in spoken performance that may be quite unrelated to proficiency in other areas of language. The net effect of accent is that listeners may face more "difficulty in interpreting phonemic categories and consequently in lexical access" (Bent, Bradlow, & Smith, 2007, p. 332). An unfamiliar rhythm or rhythm-related feature is likely to compound the difficulties. Contributors to variability in intelligibility across speakers included errors in word stress, intonation, non-reduction of function words, and lack of relative stress on function words. The last two are directly part of rhythm in English, and indicate that, at least when inner-circle speakers are involved, rhythm is tied to intelligibility because of its impact on lexical access – that is, to the listener's ability to understand what words are being said.

Speech rate seems to be implicated in the way speech is understood, perhaps because of the way that faster speech changes and flattens the overall shape of the speech stream and therefore affects the ways that segments are pronounced, especially in the rate of deletions, insertions, and reductions. For example, accented speech that is faster can result in greater challenges for comprehension when accentedness is greater, making speech rate a factor in how well listeners comprehend speech (Anderson-Hsieh & Koehler, 1988). In the same study, speech that was evaluated as more accented was also judged as being faster (even when it was not).

Accentedness is related to many factors, but unexpected speech rhythm may be one of the reasons for perception of a foreign accent (Fuchs & Wunder, 2015; Kolly & Dellwo, 2014). This marker of accent remains even for very advanced EFL (English as a foreign language) learners. Certain aspects associated with native rhythm seemed more evident in nonnative rhythm, such as differences in vowel length. This suggests that different aspects of speech timing associated with rhythm may be more or less salient to learners, and more or less salient for teaching.

INTELLIGIBILITY

The connection of rhythm and intelligibility has sometimes been taken for granted. Taylor (1981) says that rhythm provides a critical set of cues for listeners, allowing them to chunk spoken language and thus understand a speaker's meaning. For this reason, Taylor argued that "correct rhythm is thus an essential ingredient of intelligibility"

(1981, p. 242). Taylor's assertion that rhythm may affect how listeners understand speech is borne out in other studies. In a study of the effect of timing (i.e., rhythmic timing) on the intelligibility of deaf children's speech, Osberger and Levitt (1979) found that listeners who were unfamiliar with the character of deaf speech understood sentences better when relative timing (i.e., correction of vowel duration only) was corrected. Intelligibility did not increase when the durations of all segments were corrected (that is, uniformly slowed speech), nor when pauses were corrected. In fact, correcting pauses had a negative effect on intelligibility, a finding that was interpreted as creating an increased processing load for listeners who were not used to the speech of the deaf. Pauses seemed to give listeners more time to listen. Correcting pauses took away this time.

In a study of the effect of nonnative rhythm on the ability of native listeners to understand, Tajima, Port, and Dalby (1994) examined the effect of temporal corrections (largely rhythmic and rate corrections) on the intelligibility of a Chinese speaker, with NSs of English as listeners. The original phrases spoken by the Chinese speaker of English were edited to make the segments agree with the way the same segments were produced by a native speaker of English. The quality of the segments, however, was not modified. While a forced-choice, two-choice listening task resulted in chance accuracy, the temporally modified utterances were much more successfully understood, at around 80 percent accuracy. A follow-up study (Tajima, Port, & Dalby, 1997) with three choices found similar results, with chance identification accuracy on unmodified speech and nearly 65% accuracy with temporal correction. The combined results suggest that disruptions in speech timing (i.e., rhythm) reduced the intelligibility of the utterances, and that explicit training in temporal features of speech result in a noticeable increase in intelligibility.

Quené and van Delft (2010) examined the effect of deviant durational patterns on intelligibility of Dutch sentences. As in English, duration patterns in Dutch are a key element of stress-based rhythm. The research transplanted nonnative durational patterns onto native sentences and vice versa, and further masked the signal with white noise. Listeners listened to the sentences in a soundproof booth and immediately repeated the sentence they heard. The results showed a relationship between nonnative segmentals and duration patterns. Intelligibility seemed to be compromised by rhythm when segmental features were relatively good, but when there were more segmental errors, listeners paid less attention to rhythm. In other words, segments were heard and processed first, followed by the rhythm. As the researchers say,

If the speech contains more non-native speech segments, then durations are apparently less relevant for intelligibility … this suggests that hearing a native-like speech sound in an inappropriate durational pattern may be relatively worse than hearing a non-native-like sound in an appropriate duration pattern. (Quené and van Delft, 2010, p. 917)

Additionally, segmental errors had a relatively greater effect on intelligibility, but rhythm was also a significant factor for intelligibility and "targeted attention to linguistically important duration patterns … may well be worthwhile when learning to speak a foreign language" (p. 919).

When L2 listeners are given control over the speech rate, they perform better on a test of listening comprehension (a type of intelligibility) and their listening comprehension improves more quickly. Zhao (1997) argues that slower speeds can help leaners improve and that slowed speech for teaching and learning will not make them want to listen to slower speeds only. This kind of learner-controlled speech rate may make different aspects of prosody, including rhythm, easier to negotiate.

COMPREHENSIBILITY

Rhythm may also affect the ease with which listeners can process speech. This seems to be at the heart of long-standing recommendations that L2 English learners be taught to listen to natural speech if they are to progress in the new language, even if they do not need to produce English rhythm to be understood (Brown, 1977). Even the proponents of the LFC make this type of recommendation (e.g., Walker, 2010), recognizing that the ability to perceive the rhythm of others' speech is an essential part of intelligibility-based teaching.

In a study that suggests an effect of rhythm on comprehensibility, Pisoni, Manous, and Dedina (1987) matched natural and high-quality synthetic sentences for segmental intelligibility, yet found that listeners were slower in understanding synthetic speech, indicating that a change in suprasegmental quality was likely to be the cause. In addition, they found that highly predictable sentences were understood more quickly while sentences with low predictability were responded to more slowly.

Derwing and Munro (2001) examined the speaking rates (a feature related to rhythm; see Ordin & Polanskaya, 2015b) preferred by English-L1, Mandarin L1, and mixed L1 users of English when listening to texts read by NSs of English and Mandarin learners of English. The listeners evaluated the texts at their unmodified rate and three modified rates (the average of all English speakers, the average of all Mandarin readers, and 90 percent of the mean Mandarin rate). Results showed that the listeners typically preferred a faster rate than was provided by the slow (3.4 syll/second) Mandarin speech, though not as fast as the typical NS of English (4.9 syll/second). In other words, listeners did not want speech that was too slow, nor speech that was too fast. In the researchers' words, "for advanced L2 listeners, unmodified rates are preferable to slowed rates and slightly speeded rates are preferred" when the speaker's rate is very slow (Derwing & Munro, 2001, p. 333). Rate, in other words, seemed to play a minor role in listeners' preferences, but it may be that rate in natural conditions also leads to other modifications that affect comprehensibility. Saito et al. (2016) also found that comprehensibility ratings were related to speech rate, especially up to an intermediate level of proficiency.

Moving from production to perception, it may be that clearly articulated speech is helpful to nonnative listeners in helping them process L2 speech more easily. Building on research that shows that clear speech is helpful for hearing-impaired listeners and for listeners with normal hearing when the conditions are less than ideal, Bradlow and Bent (2002) examined how clear speech helped high-proficiency nonnative listeners (average TOEFL [test of English as a foreign language] of 626) who heard naturally produced sentences varying in clarity and speaker gender. Clear speech involved speakers reading the sentences "as if speaking to a listener with a hearing loss or from a different language background," while conversational style included instructions "to read at their normal pace without any particular attention to clarity" (2002, p. 275).

While nonnative listeners benefited from the clear speech effect, the benefit was relatively small. It may be that the "decreased speech rate, longer and more frequent pauses, less alveolar stop flapping, more final stop releasing, greater consonant to vowel intensity rations, a higher mean pitch, a wider pitch range, and an expanded vowel space" (2002, p. 281) used by the speakers changed the rhythmic structure of the speech in a way that was harder for the listeners to take advantage of. The nonnative listeners in general found the enhancements of the female speaker more helpful, though not invariably so. This may be partly because the amount of reduction and expansion of pitch range used by the male speaker was greater, perhaps leading to less effective enhancement of intelligibility (2002, p. 281). The researchers had predicted that many of these clear speech processes were likely to enhance intelligibility greatly for all listeners, including rhythm-oriented features, but the modifications helped nonnative listeners far less than expected.

In summary, rhythm and related features, especially speech rate (a correlate of spoken fluency), appear to affect judgments of accentedness and comprehensibility, as well as impacting intelligibility. We do not know the extent to which these findings apply to interactions that do not involve NSs. However, it seems clear that the perception side of the intelligibility equation is essential when it comes to rhythm.

Rhythm in the Teaching and Learning of Pronunciation

Rhythm in Traditional Teaching and in ELF

The teaching of rhythm in English pronunciation has long been a mainstay, and along with intonation, rhythm has been thought to highlight the centers of attention in speech (Wong, 1987). Even before the current attention to suprasegmentals, rhythm was an important part of pronunciation teaching (e.g., Pike, 1945) because it was seen as a common problem for learners of English from a wide variety of language backgrounds (Taylor, 1981). Like so much in relation to intelligibility in pronunciation teaching today, the claims of Jenkins (2000) that stress-timed rhythm does not affect the intelligibility of ELF communication have deeply influenced how many teachers look at rhythm.

Not only are L2 learners likely to carry the rhythmic structure of their L1 into their language learning (White & Mattys, 2007), different Englishes throughout the world are likely to have different rhythms in the way their English is typically spoken (Coniam, 2002; Low, 2014). The ability of speakers from one variety to understand another depends on the ability to process information quickly by processing the rhythmic packaging of the speech. In much of the English-speaking world, NNSs have a great advantage in negotiating different rhythms because of their familiarity with the inner-circle Englishes used in classroom instruction and across the internet.

Jenkins (2000) suggests, in effect, that in ELF communication, the rhythm of inner-circle English can be replaced by a different kind of rhythm and that no loss in intelligibility will result. Although Jenkins clearly argues for the importance of rhythm and weak forms in perception, the blanket statement against teaching the production of rhythm and weak forms is strikingly sweeping in regard to intelligibility, especially in light of noticeably weak evidence and because rhythm is crucial in regard to perception, even in Jenkins' own recommendations. There are three reasons to question the certainty of the ELF view on rhythm in pronunciation teaching.

The first is that rhythm is not as simple as stress-timing and the presence of reduced vowels in weak forms. Instead, rhythm in English is a complex combination of interrelated features and of their effects on understanding. Not all of these features are likely to affect intelligibility in the same way, and we should consider that different elements may affect understanding in different ways. Just as the dichotomy of stress-timing and syllable-timing does not adequately describe English versus other languages, so it does not adequately describe all Englishes, and there is little evidence about the effect of these rhythmic differences between varieties of English in contact. Such differences may be much ado about nothing, but until we know this, it is best to keep an open mind.

The second is that the non-teaching of rhythm may put teachers, both native and nonnative, in a somewhat contradictory position "of having to teach their students about suprasegmentals, employed by the instructors themselves, and at the same time discouraging learners from using such features" (Szpyra-Kowłowska, 2015, p. 83). This may be addressed in regard to perception, to be sure, especially when the L2 speakers are also language teachers (Coniam, 2002). But there is also the possibility that learning to produce elements of rhythm may make those elements more salient in perception.

The third is that rhythm may be more likely to affect comprehensibility, making the job of the listener more challenging, even if there is intelligibility at the level of both words and messages. Because unfamiliar rhythmic patterning in speech is distributed over long stretches of speech, listeners may find that they need to work harder to understand the speaker's message. In this, speakers of English from both inner, outer, and expanding circles may share difficulties in processing speech spoken with unfamiliar rhythmic structures, especially if the rhythm carries segmental and stress differences. Interlocutors may ultimately understand each other, but the effort will be greater than with a familiar rhythm they are used to hearing, making speech less comprehensible. Findings from research on word stress (e.g., Field, 2005; Richards, 2016) suggest that rhythm may also impair intelligibility by causing listeners to not be able to identify words or meaning, but there is at this time little evidence for such an effect. However, we have not really looked yet.

Even if the production of inner-circle English rhythm is not critical for production, it remains critical for perception, the other unavoidable half of spoken intelligibility. In ELF contexts, where NSs may rarely be part of communication in English, listeners need to be able to negotiate different ways of speaking English, both nonnative and native. The omnipresence of UK and US language teaching materials throughout the world, and the extensive reach of the global entertainment industry, guarantees that, at least for the near future, native Englishes will remain influential even in communicative contexts where NSs are rare. This means that the recommendation that L2 learners be exposed to input from a wide variety of English speakers (e.g., Lindemann, Campbell, Lindenberg, & Subtirelu, 2016; Sung, 2016) can improve pronunciation instruction related to perception. It goes without saying that using a wide range of Englishes would be valuable for all teachers, native or otherwise, and in all contexts. English is becoming not only a lingua franca across the world, but is also increasingly the language of higher education in countries where English is not the language of daily life (Hincks & Edlund, 2009).

Teaching Issues

Because of the influence of rhythmic structure on the ability to identify words, and thus to understand messages (both aspects of intelligibility), it is difficult to argue that rhythm and vowel quality are not part of the core of pronunciation teaching. One cannot speak without some type of rhythm, and one cannot listen successfully and access the words and messages in speech without negotiating rhythm.

Description, Analysis, and Awareness

Dauer (1983) was instrumental in showing that accounts of stress-timed and syllable-timed rhythm were more apparent than real, but in her later pronunciation teaching book (Dauer, 1993), she appealed to many of the same features that were used to characterize English as a stress-timed language. She did not, however, use "stress-timed" to describe the language. In this she perhaps is a model for how to describe English rhythm when teaching L2 learners of English. She was careful to name features and tendencies, such as "The rhythm of English involves an alternation of strong or stressed syllables and weak or unstressed syllables. The stressed syllables are longer, clearer, and sometimes higher pitched; the unstressed syllables tend to be shortened and reduced" (1993, p. 84). She also appealed to the content/function word distinction in English rhythm, insisting that "good rhythm in English" had to demonstrate both longer content words and shortened function words, but she refrained from insisting that content words were always stressed and function words always unstressed.

Teaching L2 learners to produce an unfamiliar L2 rhythm may be effective in reducing judgments of accentedness. Gluhareva and Prieto

(2017) examined whether watching the use of native physical beat gestures (e.g., the use of hand or body gestures aligned with the rhythmic beats of speech) would promote more native-like rhythm in English among Catalan learners. Learners watched a video of an NS with or without beat gestures. The L2 learners were recorded before and after the video prompts. Afterward the L2 learners provided a similar answer to that produced by the English speaker on the video. The answers that were a response to the beat gesture videos were rated as less accented, although intelligibility was not measured.

Implicit in the teaching of L2 rhythm is the assumption of a native model. In second language contexts, with multilingual classes, learners from different L1s presumably will converge toward the native model in their production, while simultaneously communicating with class-mates who have imperfect models of the same rhythm. The target language (TL) model of rhythm will likely include prosodic features that are and are not salient to different learners, and that therefore are and are not equally learnable. Most of these elements may require explicit teaching. But these same types of multilingual classrooms may also provide a way to raise learner awareness of prosodic differences between the TL, the native language, and other L1 systems, including rhythm (Gabriel, Stahnke, & Thulke, 2015).

Production

To improve production of rhythm, teachers and learners may focus on lengthening the stressed vowels sounds to create a timing distinction between stress and unstress (Chela-Flores, 1998; Jenkins, 2000), or they may also try to learn to reduce unstressed syllables, especially those in frequent forms (Dalton & Seidlhofer, 1994). The first strategy focuses on timing issues, while the second attends to segmental conse-quences of rhythm and timing. Brown says that "it is more useful to distinguish between 'strong' stressed syllable initial consonants and 'weak' consonants" (1977, p. 75), attending to the segmental conse-quences of stress. Because English stress and rhythm are most profit-ably interpreted by listeners according to their segmentals rather than their prosody (Cutler, 2015), perception improvement is likely to be more successful in attending to schwa, whereas the clear speech effect (Derwing & Munro, 2001; Munro & Derwing, 2001) suggests that attention to duration may be a more effective strategy for production.

In the teaching of rhythm, there may be a conflict between a strict application of stress-timing (with highly regular variation of stressed and unstressed syllables), and attention to the consequences of stress in English, especially at the segmental and lexical levels (Barrera-Pardo,

2008). The consequences of stress in English include the ways that consonants and vowels are realized, the differences in the way that content and function words are realized (this is the issue of weak forms, but also the fact that even content words may be pronounced in a somewhat reduced form, and the interaction of stress and prominence (sometimes called sentence stress or nuclear stress). In other words, the rhythm of English, no matter how challenging it may be to measure, affects the relative clarity of segments, words, and phrases. These effects are challenging for L2 learners to produce (especially in the production of unstress) and to perceive (especially in successful lexical access for weak forms or linked speech in context). Encouraging L2 learners to notice a different timing pattern in L2 English may be the place to start. Chela-Flores (1998), for example, teaches English rhythm to Spanish speakers by substituting *TAA* for stressed syllables and *ti* for unstressed, with *TAA* being longer and *ti* shorter.

It should be noted, however, that pronouncing words and phrases like an NS may not lead to greater intelligibility. As Jenkins says, "too many pronunciation courses are based on the premise that learners will increase their speed through the acquisition of these [connected speech] processes rather than vice versa" (2000, p. 149). The push for production practice to improve intelligibility is nowhere more evident than with connected speech, where it is sometimes argued that students need to be able to adjust their speech styles, and that connected speech features are ubiquitous even in the most formal type of speech (Brown & Kondo-Brown, 2006). Melenca (2001) argued that failure to link words together in connected speech can cause communicative difficulties when speaking to NSs. The nature of these difficulties does not necessarily seem to be connected to intelligibility, but rather to judgments of speakers as being aggressive or abrupt in their communicative intent. Such judgments may be seen as a type of intelligibility (interpretability in Smith & Nelson, 1985), in which speakers' intent is misinterpreted. It is evident, however, that much of the work on connected speech does not explicitly refer to intelligibility.

Perception

The greatest challenge of rhythm for L2 learners may not be the production of a particular tempo. After all, research on the utility of rhythm metrics finds a strong effect of speech register, with read-aloud speech differing from spontaneous speech for the same speakers (White, Wiget, Rauch, & Mattys, 2010). Nevertheless, English has a strong tendency in all speech registers for the effects of rhythm to be seen in segmental variations, especially in the use of reduced vowels in lexically unstressed syllables and in the weak forms of very frequent, one-syllable function words (e.g., *in, and, on, of, the, a*). The occurrence of schwa in normal speech is far more frequent than any other vowel, up to 33 percent of all vowels (Woods, 2005), making the recognition of unstressed segments an unavoidable feature of English speech.

There is no question that rhythm should be taught in regard to perception, both for inner-circle and ELF contexts (e.g., Walker, 2010). Although the modifications of segments and the ways that segments in context connect to each other may not be critical for intelligibility in production, there is general agreement that they are important for perception. Brown stated this principle four decades ago, saying that "it cannot be too strongly urged that students should not be required to produce the [connected speech forms], only to recognize them and understand utterances in which they occur … The teacher's aim here should be to make the student aware of the simplified forms so that he can understand them" (1977, p. 55). All fluent speakers of a language modify their pronunciation unknowingly and naturally, and NSs most of all (Brown, 2014). Such modifications are a natural outcome of the rhythm of English (Szpyra-Kowłowska, 2015). Barrera-Pardo similarly argues that "the main challenge for most EFL learners is to decode the unstressed, weak function words contained in natural spoken English, a listening strategy that must be rehearsed" (2008, p. 14), giving primacy to perception of rhythm in classroom practice. According to Setter and Jenkins (2005), L2 users of English need to learn how to successfully process the speech of other speakers of English. This means explicit instruction on the kinds of connected speech modifications that are likely to occur. Although this generally means the speech of NSs, it also means the speech of other proficient users of English who are likely to be interlocutors. The availability of authentic speech via the internet, along with the easy availability of transcripts, make it far easier to develop materials for this kind of perception practice.

Conclusions

Like any aspect of pronunciation teaching, teaching rhythm may not lead to a close approximation of native performance, nor will improvement of features associated with rhythm be equally effective in improving intelligibility. But there is evidence to suggest that instruction may result in improved intelligibility. Lima (2015) found a sizable increase in intelligibility (39 percent to 58 percent) after computer-assisted instruction on suprasegmentals. Lima taught several suprasegmental features, including prominence, word stress, and rhythm, so it is not clear that rhythm instruction alone was related to the change in intelligibility. But in the short run, it appears that instruction on rhythm may be helpful in promoting greater intelligibility. There is some evidence also that work on production may lead to improved perception (Catford & Pisoni, 1970) and that the production of language with respect to declarative knowledge can result in the ability to use that knowledge in fluent speech, the so-called output hypothesis (de Bot, 1996; Swain, 1993).

It is also critically important to consider the perception side of intelligibility when talking about the core status of rhythm. L2 learners of English, and indeed any language, have as much of a need to understand the speech of others as they do to be understood. The importance of teaching listening comprehension skills, and the perception skills related to rhythm underlying comprehension, has been noted for many years (Rivers, 1981). Even among pronunciation writers who argue about whether the production of rhythm, connected speech, and weak forms should be taught for production, there is no argument about whether rhythm should be taught for perception, although there is equally little attention to it in the classroom.

7 Intonation and Intelligibility
The Roles of Prominence and Tune

Intonation is the use of voice pitch to communicate meaning at the phrasal level. The meaning communicated may be categorical in nature, or it may be gradient. Categorical means that native speakers (NSs) largely will agree on the nature of that meaning, such as a question or statement, and gradient differences reflect much more varied and subjective perceptions of meaning, such as emotions or attitudes. It is almost impossible to talk about intonation's effect on intelligibility in the narrow sense of the word because variations in intonation for a given utterance almost never mean that listeners cannot decode individual words. This is quite different from vowel, consonant, cluster, and word-stress deviations, which can cause loss of intelligibility at the word level.

Intonation, then, is rarely the cause of unintelligibility at the word level because intonation variations are not right or wrong in the way that deviations in segmentals and word stress are. However, intonation is important in other types of misunderstanding such as difficulties with comprehensibility (Isaacs & Trofimovich, 2012), comprehension of the content of speech (Hahn, 2004), or interpretability (the intention of the utterance; Smith & Nelson, 1985), which may be also thought of as the pragmatic force of an utterance (Cummins & Rohde, 2015), depending on whether the speaker's intention is being considered or the listener's interpretation. For this reason, the kinds of misunderstandings that are related to misuse of intonation will often not be immediately evident.

This chapter looks at several aspects of intonation and how they can affect intelligibility in English. Specifically, the chapter describes three important aspects of intonation (prominence, tune, and pitch range) followed by a specific examination of two aspects of intonation that are clearly relevant to questions of intelligibility: prominence and tune.

What Do We Mean by Intonation?

Intonation is one of the most elusive features of pronunciation for many teachers, who may be uncertain not only about how to teach it but also about what it includes and does not include (Sonsaat, 2017). Sometimes it has been used to mean prosody, that is, an umbrella term for variations in pitch, duration, voice quality, and loudness. And sometimes it refers primarily to variations in pitch. It is this meaning that is used in this chapter. This does not make intonation in English simple, but it does help to limit the description of its forms and functions. Intonation involves, at the very least, multiple linguistic and gradient ways that speakers use pitch to communicate meaning. This chapter looks at three of these because of their relationship to intelligibility: relative prominence, tune, and pitch range (Figure 7.1).

The two best-known features, tune and relative prominence (Ladd, 1996), are also known by many other terms (e.g., nuclear stress, sentence stress, and tonic for relative prominence; intonation, tone, and contour for tune). Both tune and relative prominence are categorical (e.g., rising versus falling final pitch signify meanings that most speakers agree on) in English, that is, they both independently communicate meaning. As an example of these two features, following Ladd (1996, pp. 8–9), Figure 7.2 shows how the two can change with the same utterance. Consider the phrase *three days* as representing a response to a question. Option (a) would be the typical answer to a general, broad-focus question such as "How long did it take?" This default answer includes relative prominence on the last content word, DAYS. It also uses a falling tune to assert its answer. In contrast, (b) has the same relative prominence, but the use of a rising tune expresses uncertainty about the answer. Options (c) and (d) both have a marked relative prominence that is not on the final content word. Option (c) might be the response to a question such as "Why did it take two days?" where prominence on THREE corrects the error in the

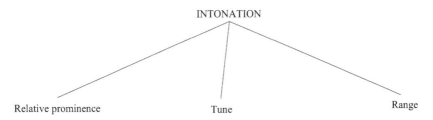

Figure 7.1 Three aspects of intonation that are important for intelligibility

		Relative prominence	
		Weak–strong	Strong–weak
Tune	Falling	*(a) three DAYS*	*(c) THREE days*
	Rising	*(b) three DAYS*	*(d) THREE days*

Figure 7.2 Tune and relative prominence in English

question. Finally, (d) again questions the number of days. As a response to a question like "Why did it take three days?" the rising tune on *THREE days* questions the assertion implied by the question. These examples show that in English, both tune and relative prominence contribute to meaning independently and should be treated separately in regard to spoken intelligibility.

Both tune and relative prominence are also related. The prominent syllable is the beginning of the tune, and together they may be called an intonation contour. As a result, the combination of the two aspects of communicating meaning may cause confusion for those who are not experts. More generally, the ways in which intonation has been described by different writers reflects the lack of long-term consensus among researchers and teachers regarding the status, importance, and interrelatedness of these features. Such differences in how to describe intonation reflect, and have always reflected, variations in orientation toward the topic (Levis, 2013). For example, there is a strong divide today between pedagogical and theoretical orientations. Autosegmental (theoretical) approaches to intonation that have developed from the work of Pierrehumbert (1980), Liberman (1975), and Ladd (1980), among many others, are attempts to establish the phonology of intonation – in other words, the system that underlies the phonetic variations in voice pitch. Some speakers speak with higher pitch, some with lower, but all NSs of a language share an implicit agreement on how systematic variations in pitch communicate meaning. In this, intonation is not any different from segmentals, in which allophonic variations of phonemes are heard in terms of categorical meanings. In other words, some variations, at certain parts of the utterance, are part of the system, or the "grammar" of intonation, while other uses of pitch can be idiosyncratic in the kinds of meaning they carry.

In contrast, pedagogical approaches to intonation usually reflect earlier eras in intonational description. For example, Pike (1945) pioneered a four-pitch level phonological/phonetic model that continues to be used in a well-known teacher-training book (Celce-Murcia, Brinton, Goodwin, & Griner, 2010), and modern British tonetic approaches to teaching still reflect those in Kingdon (1958) and O'Connor and Arnold (1961). Although it would be desirable to have closer connections between theory and pedagogy, theoretical and pedagogical approaches are each appropriate for their own purposes. The autosegmental model is not meant for teaching L2 learners, and researchers such as Pike (1945), or Wells (2006) for British English, may be pedagogically more useful in helping L2 learners visualize intonation, despite being theoretically limited. Differences in how intonation is approached also reflect differences in how intonation has been described in British and American approaches (Levis, 2005b), not to mention the wide variety of descriptive apparatuses that have been used for other languages (e.g., Hirst & Di Cristo, 1998). More recent treatments have been more successful in using a consistent descriptive approach in describing varied languages (Jun, 2006).

Intonation is often referred to in terms of contours, especially in the British tradition (e.g., O'Connor & Arnold, 1961; Wells, 2006). In this tradition, (a) in Figure 7.2 would likely be a rising–falling contour (rising on the prominent syllable, and falling to the end of the phrase). In this tradition, and in other treatments, relative prominence sometimes seems to have been neglected, being seen primarily as the beginning of the intonation contour. Thus, in Brazil's (1997) approach to discourse intonation, information structure in English is connected to generally rising tunes (a referring meaning, related to given or shared information) and falling tunes (a proclaiming meaning, related to new information). Brazil's approach to intonation has been widely used to account for how English speakers convey meaning, but because it somewhat conflates two independent sources of meaning, I will not address its underpinnings in this book. For recent explications of its uses in description and teaching, see Pickering (2018). Pronunciation teaching textbooks based on Brazil's model include Bradford (1988) and Brazil (1997).

Prominence and tune have meanings that must be understood as connected to a spoken phrase and often to the ways that phrases are connected. This also means that the kinds of meanings that intonation contributes is typically context-dependent rather than right or wrong in and of itself. In addition, prominence and tune are closely connected in that the final prominent syllable in a phrase is also the beginning of the final pitch movement, as in (7.1), which is represented using the moving typeface format used by Bolinger (1986). The prominent syllables IN and VI (in CAPS) include a move up in pitch to make the syllable noticeable; the pitch movement then extends from the prominent syllable to the end of the phrase. In the first phrase, the pitch falls and rises (a fall–rise contour), while in the second, it falls (a falling contour). Figure 7.3 shows the same constructed sentence analyzed using Praat, a widely used acoustic speech analysis program that can show relative pitch movement in spoken language (Boersma & Weenink, 2009). The different ways of representing intonation also seem to have different effects upon learnability for L2 speakers, with more iconic representations, such as stylized lines drawn over an utterance, being more successful than more abstract representations, such as autosegmental approaches (Niebuhr, Schümchen, Fiscer, & Alm, 2017).

(7.1)

The ^{un}ion's   ^{IN}   divi _{sib} ^{le} le / not di ^{VI} si _{ble}

Intonation in English also involves variations in pitch range. These variations in pitch range may be categorical, especially in topic changes in which speakers use an extra-high initial pitch to signal a new spoken "paragraph," that is, a paratone (Wennerstrom, 2001;

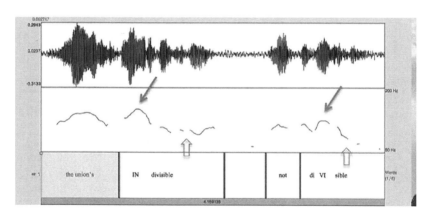

Figure 7.3 Pitch movement for two phrases: "The union's indivisible/not divisible." Downward-pointing arrows show the prominent syllables IN and VI. Upward-pointing block arrows indicate the final pitch movement (the tune) for each phrase. The first is falling–rising, while the second is falling

Wichmann, 2000). Earlier researchers such as Pike (1945) suggested that range differences invariably created categorical differences, but such treatments of pitch range seriously over-predicted the number of possible contours in English (Liberman, 1975). Today, most researchers believe that pitch range does not usually have the kind of categorical status that relative prominence and tune have. For example, the syllables <IN> and <VI> above could be pronounced with greater or lesser prominence (that is, the pitch excursion could be higher or lower), but as long as the syllables are heard as being prominent relative to the other syllables in the phrase, their categorical meanings will not change. Instead, increased pitch range may cause a listener to evaluate the speaker as being more emotionally engaged in some way (Levis, 1994), while lesser changes in prominence may suggest some lesser level of engagement with the message. Emotion and attitude (e.g., Pike, 1945) have often been cited as part of the special meaning contributed by intonation in research and in teaching materials, but agreement on the nature of emotional meanings has always been problematic, even when speakers are asked to evaluate their own utterances that were previously spoken to reflect some type of meaning (Crystal, 1969). Generally, variations in pitch are register-sensitive, with fewer pitch-prominent syllables in casual than careful speech (Kochanski, Grabe, Coleman, & Rosner, 2005). Pitch range may also be different for different speakers, so that there are no clear meanings to range variations that will hold true across speakers. Differences in how range variations are evaluated may also be language-specific, with speakers of related languages interpreting pitch range differences in different ways (Chen, Gussenhoven, & Rietveld, 2004). For these reasons, range in English is largely considered a paralinguistic feature of intonation, even though some researchers have encouraged students to exaggerate pitch range as a way to improve speaking skills (Hincks & Edlund, 2009).

Prominence

Prominence is probably the most important intonational feature in terms of intelligibility; this is frequently asserted and is supported by research findings. Prominence is also relatively straightforward in its acoustics, at least in careful speech, and its form (with either a movement down or up in pitch) appears to be learnable by L2 learners. But prominence is also complex in the various functions it is used for in English, so it is important to clarify both the terminology surrounding prominence and the kinds of functions it serves. This section looks at several of these areas: the relationship between prominence and focus; how prominence is related to other aspects of intonation; and the relationship of prominence and information structure. In relation to teaching, the chapter then moves on to the perception of prominence, the effect of prominence on intelligibility, the teaching of prominence, and the role of prominence in the Lingua Franca Core (LFC).

Relative Prominence and Focus

Prominence refers to the acoustic marking of syllables to make them salient. Prominence is marked by a combination of features, including pitch, greater duration, greater intensity, and segmental clarity. The most prominent syllable typically falls on the last content word within a linguistic unit (typically, a spoken phrase). Historically, prominence was thought to occur only once within each phrase, and this syllable was called the nucleus. This remains the most common pattern in English, and I will call it the default pattern. This most prominent syllable in a phrase has also been referred to in the literature by a variety of names, such as sentence stress (Schmerling, 1976), nuclear stress (Jenkins, 2000), tonic (Halliday, 1967), accent (Bolinger, 1986), highlighting (Bradford, 1988), focus (Levis, 2001), and primary phrase stress (Hahn, 2004). In general, all of these names refer to the same feature of English speech though different names reflect different theoretical and practical orientations. Although a single prominent syllable is the norm, phrases in spoken language may have more than one prominent syllable (Pierrehumbert, 1980), and some phrases may have no prominent syllables, especially in structures like parentheticals (Slater, Levis, & Muller Levis, 2015).

Prominence is sometimes used synonymously with focus (e.g., Gilbert, 2012; Levis & Grant, 2003), especially with reference to languages like English, in which focus is primarily marked through acoustic prominence. The two terms refer to different features of language, however, and should be considered separately. Prominence is an acoustic feature – a form – and focus is a semantic feature – a function that is associated with prominence. The position of a prominent syllable is a semantic feature of an utterance in context. For example, in response to a question, the answer would be in focus (Cutler & Fodor, 1979). In a broadly worded question (e.g., "What happened?"), the entire response may be in focus (e.g., "A tree fell on my car"). In a more precisely worded question (e.g., "Did something fall on your car?"), only part of the response would be in focus (e.g., "A TREE fell on it"). All languages have strategies to call attention to particular parts of an utterance in particular discourse contexts. Some languages, especially those with grammatical redundancy such as inflections, may primarily use syntactic changes to achieve focus (e.g., clefting, changes in word order), while others may primarily use acoustic cues without changes in word order. The latter is the main strategy used by English speakers, since English has limited resources to mark grammatical relationships because of its relatively fixed word order.

Prominence and Intonation

Relative prominence has not always been seen as important in its own right, and thus has had an inconsistent history in pronunciation teaching. Pike (1945), for example, in one of the first pedagogical and theoretical models of American English intonation, barely mentioned prominence, considering it a function of stress with either an innate placement or a special placement; he therefore called it sentence stress (1945, p. 85), having "the superimposed meaning of SPECIAL ATTENTION" (p. 86). Instead of analyzing prominence separately, Pike analyzed intonation primarily in terms of inherently or specially stressed syllables that began contours. Thus, stressed syllables were merely the beginning of contours, and contours may or may not have been equal to spoken phrases. Hockett (1947) also recognized nuclear stress as the beginning of intonational movement, but he also did not seem to give it special attention. This was not uncommon in that era, nor afterwards. Brown (1950), for example, used a tadpole-type notation but did not accord nuclear stress a special status. Similar treatment of prominence is given by Clarey and Dixson (1947), for whom the prominent syllable is associated with a high pitch, but given no other special status.

By the 1960s, prominence was beginning to be treated differently. One set of materials (English Language Services, 1961) provided most of its content on varied uses of phrase stress, including prominence for typical and emphatic/contrastive uses, with only a small amount of practice provided for other uses of intonation. In another approach, Bolinger described prominence in terms of particular functions such as contrast, in which "two or more members of a group are counterbalanced and a preference indicated for some member or members of a group" (1961, p. 83). He also argued that prominence placement was largely unpredictable and that its placement was primarily controlled by the mind of the speaker (Bolinger, 1972). The functions of prominence were most notably expanded by Halliday (1967) to include the marking of information structure, particularly new and given information.

This then indicates that the function of prominence can be explained in English in at least three major ways. The first is the default placement (the last content word or lexical item in a phrase), which helps shape the characteristic prosody of English speech. This is the most common use of prominence. This default accent structure, tied to broad focus (Ladd, 1980), occurs when English speakers place prominence on the last content word of a phrase in spoken English. This regularity means that up to 90 percent of prominent syllables in normal spoken English occur on the last content word of the phrase (Crystal, 1969).

In the great majority of teaching materials, the default use is also the most neglected, though this is changing. For example, Gilbert (2012) starts her presentation of prominence (which she calls "focus") by talking about the beginnings of conversations (the out-of-the-blue usage) and Grant (2012) starts with normal focus. Other writers, however, say things like "you can stress any word in a sentence you want, depending on the meaning (intent) you want to convey" (Reed & Michaud, 2005, p. 103) or that prominence is the way of "showing what is important" (Miller, 2000, p. 49). These types of statements are not likely to be particularly helpful in leading L2 learners toward producing prominence in the 90 percent of times it occurs on the final content word, since learners may have unusual interpretations of what is important.

The second major use of prominence is to select member(s) of a group in some kind of comparison or contrast to other members of a group, members that may or may not be spoken aloud. This is often referred to as contrastive accent/stress/focus, and is common in many teaching materials (e.g., Reed & Michaud, 2005, p. 104 – "*John* has lived here for *two* years, but *Susan* for *four*"). It is likely that there would be two phrases in this sentence, each marking contrastive items with prominence. Contrast has been studied in regard to teaching, with strong evidence that it is learnable in perception (Pennington & Ellis, 2000) and production (M. Hahn, 2002; Muller Levis & Levis, 2012; Muller Levis, Levis, & Benner, 2014). There is also evidence that contrastive uses of prominence may be acoustically distinct from uses that do not mark contrasts (e.g., Chafe & Li, 1976; Katz & Selkirk, 2011).

Third, prominence is used to highlight new information in spoken discourse, and lack of prominence can be used, among other linguistic features, to signal given or shared information between speaker and listeners. This use of prominence is the most commonly presented function in teaching materials (e.g., Gilbert, 2012, p. 60 – "A: I lost my **hat**. B: What **kind** of hat? A: It was a **rain** hat."), though the explanations of what makes information new or given may be confusing.

In addition, pronunciation teaching materials for L2 learners may include other uses, such as correcting misinformation (Gilbert, 2012; Grant, 2012; Kenworthy, 1987), emphasizing agreement (e.g., Grant, 2012, p. 116 – "X: This chapter's EAsy! Y: It IS easy."), checking (Gilbert, 2012, p. 66 – "A: They got here at one o'<u>clock</u>. B: <u>**When**</u> did they get here?"), and emphasizing function words while de-accenting content words (Gilbert, 2012, p. 69 – "A: You'll have to wait till you're **old** enough. B: But I **am** old enough.") or syllables that are typically unstressed (Chan, 1987, p. 147 – "I'm en<u>cou</u>raged. Did you say en<u>cou</u>raged or di<u>scou</u>raged?") Note: Font usage in the examples here match those in each textbook cited.

However, a number of well-documented prominence placements are not easily explained by any of these categories. (For many of these, see Dickerson, 1989). Allerton and Cruttenden (1979), for example, discuss utterances in which English speakers place prominence on subjects that are not the final content word of a phrase, and cannot be argued to meet the criteria for reflecting contrasts or new information. An example is given in (7.2), where the normal prominence placement is *kettle*. Prominence on *boiling*, the last content word, far from sounding unmarked, would likely sound contrastive even though it is the last content word. A variety of other special domains for relative prominence placement have also been studied (e.g., M. Hahn, 2002).

(7.2)

The KETTle's boiling.

Prominence and Information Structure: New, Given, and Accessible

As the most commonly included function of prominence in teaching materials and the most researched function as well, information structure requires exploration. Information structure refers to the differential weight given by speakers and listeners to parts of an utterance. In any speech context, not all lexical items are equally informative. Words (and the concepts they represent) that are especially informative when introduced at one point in time (when they are "new," or not identifiable from the discourse context) may not be equally informative at another point in time. This is true even when the words remain present in the discourse (that is, when they are "given," or likely to be recoverable from the developing discourse). (Although *new* and *given* are commonly used terms for analyzing information structure, other terms such as background–focus or theme–rheme have also been used, depending on the theoretical model.) Information structure "defines how the information conveyed by a sentence is related to the knowledge of the interlocutors and the structure of their discourse" (Prevost, 1996, pp. 294–5). Information structure cannot be talked about in relation to only a speaker or a listener, but is based on what both speaker and listener know, and, more importantly, what each thinks the other knows. This knowledge includes information that they bring to the discourse and information that is co-constructed within the development of the discourse.

New and given are best understood as part of a continuum, and given information may be considered actively recoverable by listeners, or only partly recoverable (*accessible*). Accessible information includes textual accessibility, i.e., something that was already mentioned, but that has receded from consciousness because it has not been part of the discourse for several clauses. Accessible information may also be situational (e.g., *Look at that RAINbow over the mountains*), where the mountains are presumably part of the physical context, or inferentially accessible (e.g., *I was supposed to go to the CLInic, but I couldn't FIND the place*), in which "the place" is inferred on the basis of the mention of a clinic (see Baumann and Grice [2006] for more on types of accessibility). The difference between given and accessible information is that given information is more likely to be de-accented, whereas accessible information may be accented in order to reactivate it. Information structure is thus used to convey information about "the discourse status of discourse referents, modifiers, predicates, and relationships specified by accented lexical items" (Pierrehumbert & Hirschberg, 1990, p. 271). Whether information is new, given, or accessible is anything but straightforward, and teaching materials often present information structure in ways that quickly become untenable in authentic speech.

Perceptions of Prominence

Perception of prominence is affected by bottom-up features of the speech signal and by top-down features related to expectations of the discourse structure. Regarding the speech signal, the acoustic features of intensity, F0, and duration, along with the relative effects they have on the clarity or reduction of segmentals, help create a perception of prominence. Syllables that are perceived as prominent may be marked by any of these features, and none are invariantly present in all prominent syllables.

For example, even though prominent syllables in English are typically thought to be marked by pitch accents, intensity and duration have been found to strongly correlate with perceptions of prominence in spontaneous speech (Kochanski et al., 2005). This may be because faster or more casual speech is associated with more limited cues to prominence. More carefully produced speech (e.g., speech that is read aloud) is more likely to have all acoustic cues for prominent syllables.

What types of words are heard as prominent? The first generalization is that content words are more likely than function words to be heard as prominent. This may be because function words in general are more frequent or predictable, while content words are less frequent and predictable, and "less probable words are produced with greater acoustic prominence" (Turnbull, Royer, Ito, & Speer, 2017, p. 125). Higher-frequency words are also likely to undergo greater reduction in all registers of speech. Prominence is also strongly correlated with the stressed syllable of the final content word of a phrase. This final content word may also be new information because of the ways that previously mentioned content words are represented by pro-forms. For words that are likely to be more prominent, the first mention is likely to be more prominent than the second mention, but prominence may increase again by the fourth mention (Cole, Mo, & Hasegawa-Johnson, 2010). The phonological reductions associated with second mentions are not just because of a previously accented syllable being subsequently de-accented, but is instead a more general pattern in English, with even previously mentioned but not accented items undergoing reduction when they are mentioned again (Baker & Bradlow, 2009). This means that on the other side of prominence, de-accenting occurs with words that were recently prominent. As a result, there is not a rigid connection between the given/new status of words and whether they are prominent or de-accented.

The perception of prominence, however, requires taking a listener's viewpoint, and research suggests that features such as word frequency and expectations can affect perceptions of prominence even when acoustic cues are ambiguous. It is well-known, for example, that pre-nuclear accents in an utterance tend to be more pitch-prominent in an absolute sense than the nuclear accents, but nuclear accents are likely to be perceived as equally or more prominent. Also, words that are less frequent in the language are more likely to be perceived as prominent than are more frequent words, and this can lead to listeners perceiving words as prominent even when speakers have not produced them that way (Cole et al., 2010).

The role of expectations is seen strongly in the work of Bishop (2012), which examined the perceptions of relative prominence for two syllables in an SVO (subject–verb–object) answer to a question. Each syllable was marked by pitch accents. Listeners rated their relative prominence on a five-point scale under three conditions, the sentence-focus, verb phrase (VP)-focus, and object-focus conditions, as in (7.3). In the example, *bought* and *motorcycle* were marked by the same pitch accents in each answer rated by the listeners.

(7.3)

Answer: I *bought* a *motorcycle.*

Questions: What happened? (Sentence-focus – I bought a motorcycle)
What did you do? (VP-focus – bought a motorcycle)
What did you buy? (Object-focus – motorcycle)

In the sentence-focus and VP-focus conditions, verbs and objects were heard as similar in relative prominence. However, in the object-focus, or narrow focus, condition, the object (*motorcycle*) was heard as significantly more prominent than the verb even though the answer was acoustically identical to the answer in the other conditions. As Bishop says,

listeners' judgments of prosodic prominence are significantly and independently affected by their interpretation of the utterances' information structure . . . the pattern was such that the object was made prominent relative to the prenuclear verb. The significant interaction between word and focus indicated that objects were not simply heard as more prominent, but also that verbs were heard as less prominent.   (Bishop, 2012, p. 12)

In other words, listeners expected a particular word to be more prominent because it was in focus, and so they heard it as more prominent.

Prominence and Intelligibility

Besides its important role in models of prosodic phonology, prominence has a central place in pronunciation teaching. This central role is justified by compelling empirical evidence for the importance of prominence in relation to intelligibility.

As mentioned earlier, intelligibility at the word level is unlikely to be compromised by accenting the wrong word, or indeed, not using appropriate cues to accent at all. However, prominence does affect how well listeners process information in extended text. Hahn (2004) found that a lack of prominence led to lower comprehension scores on a short lecture. Unexpected placements of accented words are likely to compromise intelligibility in a more general sense. (A detailed discussion of this study can be found later in this chapter.) Misplaced prominence can cause listeners to work harder to make connections, to have poorer comprehension of content (Hahn, 2004), and to misinterpret the intent of what is said (Low, 2006). Comprehension times can be significantly slower when information status and accent placement are incompatible (Birch & Clifton, 1995). In contrast, compatible accent placements can aid comprehension. Appropriately prominent words can evoke anticipation of a coming contrast (Bock & Mazella, 1983) and so aid in comprehension (Cutler & Foss, 1977). Even less intelligible words, if appropriately de-accented, can help listeners to connect to previous referents and identify information that is given (Cutler, Dahan, & van Donselaar, 1997). In other words, prominence in English builds coherence by signaling a hierarchy of information for understanding. This appeal to understanding assumes NSs are involved in the interaction, and it is an unanswered question as to how what we know about new and given information applies to the use of English by nonnative or nativized speakers when they are not interacting with NSs.

There are some generalizations about the relative seriousness of errors in prominence use. First, given information that is re-accented does not seem to seriously impair understanding as much as new information that is not accented (Birch & Clifton, 1995). Second, L2 learners who do not use nuclear stress in the way that English speakers expect are likely to still be understood, and may be perceived to be accenting particular words, because English speakers expect particular words to be accented. Third, L2 learners, in order to aid their own comprehension of native English speech, must understand how prominence works, and how unexpected prominence placements can signal implied meanings (such as for contrasts). The types of meaning communicated by prominence cannot always be understood without instruction.

The importance of prominence in relation to how listeners understand discourse-level messages is seen in Hahn (2004), in a study that bears detailed discussion. In a mixed-guise study on the effect of prominence placement on understanding, Hahn created a short (4.5 minute) spoken lecture with three conditions: with expected prominence patterns, with unexpected prominence patterns, and with no clearly marked prominence patterns. The same lecture was recorded three times by a bilingual Korean English speaker who was able to read the lecture with all three prominence conditions. (Korean does not use prominence, so the no-prominence condition was read with a Korean-like prosody.)

The lecture was played to three randomly assigned groups of thirty native English-speaking undergraduates (ninety in total). After the lecture, each group took a comprehension test that involved two tasks: writing down all the things they remembered, in which their comprehension was evaluated on the number of major and minor ideas they recalled; and a short multiple-choice test. They also rated the speaker for likeability using scalar questions related to teaching. The findings showed that listeners in the correct-prominence condition recalled significantly more ideas than the other two conditions, and that listeners in the no-prominence condition recalled more ideas than those in the unexpected-prominence condition, though the difference between these last two groups was not significant. All three groups had non-significant differences on the multiple-choice quiz. However, the listeners in the no-prominence condition commented more frequently that they thought the speaker spoke too quickly. It appears that lack of identifiable prominence caused listeners to feel they had greater difficulty processing the information because it was not familiarly packaged by the speaker. Finally, the affective evaluations of the speaker were highest in the correct-prominence condition, less positive in the unexpected-prominence and no-prominence conditions, and included the largest number of comments critical of the speaker for the no-prominence condition.

A clear result of the work of Hahn (2004) is that NSs of American English (and likely by extension of any version of inner-circle English) recalled significantly more information when the information was spoken with expected prominence patterns. Incorrect prominence placement or lack of English prominence cues led to poorer recall of main ideas, and may even have led to a sense that the speaker was a bad communicator, especially when prominence cues were not present. Prominence placement was correlated with recall of information, and this suggests that nonnative speakers (NNSs), even with no change in accent, can become more intelligible to NS listeners with improvement only in this feature. This also suggests that prominence is a critical feature for pronunciation teaching, especially when NSs of English are likely interlocutors.

The Teaching of Prominence

There is compelling evidence to indicate that prominence influences the ways NSs of English process information, and that expected prominence placements lead to greater recall than unexpected placement or lack of prominence. The uses of prominence are also salient for NNS learners of English. Pennington and Ellis (2000) found that the perception of contrastive prominence seemed to be more noticeable by learners after a short amount of instruction, whereas the subjects did not improve with the other intonational features in the study (none of which involved prominence). Two other studies showed that modest amounts of instruction on contrastive prominence led to improved production for more advanced (Muller Levis & Levis, 2012) and less advanced ESL (English as a second language) learners (Muller Levis, Levis, & Benner, 2014), and that this also led to improvements in comprehensibility (Levis & Muller Levis, 2018).

Like almost all other pronunciation features, it appears that not all types of prominence patterns are equally learnable. In an extensive study of the effect of instruction on prominence patterns, M. Hahn (2002) examined the improvement in producing prominence for nine different patterns (Table 7.1). Subjects were thirty-six university L2 learners who took part in a pronunciation course. The course focused on identifying and predicting prominence patterns and then producing them, primarily from reading aloud. (All tests involved reading aloud

Table 7.1 Prominence learning persistence for nine prominence patterns

Patterns of improvement for prominence patterns	T1	T2	T3
Learning persisted but with decreases from T2 to T3			
1. Contrasts in choice questions (e.g., Do you want STEAK or CHICKen?)	15.28	70.83	56.25
2. Contrast either (e.g., I can meet you either DOWNtown or at the AIRport)	30.56	75.00	51.39
3. Parentheticals (e.g., I'll TRY, I suppose)	30.55	78.70	56.02
4. Context-setting time adverbials (e.g., I've got a MEETing tonight)	9.72	51.39	28.47
Performance improved at T3			
5. Return questions (What do you want? What do YOU want?)	8.33	22.22	33.33
No persistence of learning at T3 from T1			
6. Last new content word with following (e.g., How was the PARty? It was a GREAT party.)	29.76	71.82	29.37
7. Last new function word (e.g., Where WERE you?)	54.17	75.00	47.92
8. Noun-highlighting structure that is not the final content word (e.g., I've got WORK to do)	25.00	69.44	13.89
9. Double final time adverbials (e.g., The meeting's at SEVen tonight)	50.00	77.78	25.00

T1 = pretest percentage correct; T2 = posttest percentage correct; T3 = delayed posttest percentage correct. N = 36 subjects.
Source: M. Hahn (2002)

rather than spontaneous speech.) Subjects took a pretest, a posttest at the end of the fifteen-week course (three hours per week), and a delayed posttest between six and thirty-six months later (the timing of the delayed test depended on when the subjects had taken the course). Results included improvement from pretest to posttest for all nine patterns. Often, this improvement was large, moving from around one of four correct placements to three of four correct. In the delayed posttest, however, the patterns of improvement changed. First, eight of the nine patterns showed backsliding, which was often significant. Only one pattern, the lowest in initial accuracy at pretest, showed continued improvement (from 8 percent pretest to 22 percent posttest to 33 percent delayed posttest). Second, four of the delayed posttest patterns remained significantly greater than pretest levels (learning was retained to some extent), while scores for four others fell back to initial levels or lower (i.e., the learning demonstrated at posttest did not stick).

Several lessons are evident in the results shown in Table 7.1. First, some patterns seemed more learnable than others, in that they persisted. Of the first five, three involved contrasts of some sort that were easily identifiable in written texts because of their connections to other features of spoken language (choice questions, the use of other, and the use of return questions, a common routine in small talk). Another pattern, parentheticals, is typically set off by punctuation in written language, and thus may be more noticeable. Finally, the last item, context-setting time adverbials (see also Cruttenden, 1990), has a similar pattern in the no-persistence category, in which two time adverbials appear at the end of an utterance. This suggests that patterns with less complexity are likely to be more persistent in the improvement demonstrated by learners.

The four patterns with no persistence of learning all had non-final prominent words, sometimes having no content words included in the utterances. This indicates that these types of patterns, especially isolated from a larger context, are not likely to be learnable in the long run. In addition, the nine patterns did not include the default pattern (final content word) and most did not have patterns (except for #9) reflecting new and given information, which need more than one utterance to be evident, so generalizations about learning other functions of prominence are limited.

It is possible that the way that the patterns were taught by Hahn (2002), with a highly cognitive approach to instruction, did not promote long-term retention, despite the success of the instructional approach in the short term. This is an important question to explore for pronunciation teaching in general, and for prominence placement in particular.

Learnability of prominence is also important in terms of the needs of the learners. For those who will interact regularly with NS of English, it seems likely that understanding the uses of prominence and being able to use high-value uses to communicate will be particularly important. Reed and Michaud (2005) discuss the receptive importance of prominence with examples like (7.4).

(7.4)

The TEACHer didn't grade the papers.

When students hear this prominence placement, and are asked "Were the papers graded?" they almost invariably said "No." They were reported to be quite surprised to find that the answer was "Yes," showing that they did not understand the way that prominence, negation, and the use of a fall–rise tune are used to select one item from a group, with the implication that the papers were graded by someone else. Even if learners cannot produce this kind of pattern, learning to interpret it is important in participating successfully in interactions with NSs.

Prominence in the Lingua Franca Core

Because of its unusual role, it is important to discuss the role of prominence in the work of Jenkins (2000) and later discussions of the LFC. Prominence (called nuclear stress by Jenkins) holds an unusual place of honor in the LFC, the list of features put forth as critical for intelligibility in NNS–NNS interactions. Prominence is the only suprasegmental feature in the LFC; other suprasegmental features were either evaluated by Jenkins as not mattering to intelligibility (e.g., intonation, p. 153) or as being a gray area as regards intelligibility (e.g., word stress, pp. 150–1). Prominence holds a place midway between intonation and word stress: intonation and prominence both make use of pitch movement, while word stress and prominence both make use of duration and other cues, and the prominent syllable in a phrase typically is on the stressed syllable of multi-syllabic words. In other words, if word stress on the last content word is misplaced, prominence is also misplaced. The evidence for the effect of prominence on intelligibility seems clear when NSs are involved, but the evidence is much more modest for LFC contexts, even in the work of Jenkins (2000).

The place of prominence in the LFC has not been questioned, largely because it is included while other suprasegmentals are not, and not because the evidence in Jenkins (2000) is unassailable. It is easier to question the exclusion of a feature than its inclusion, as its exclusion typically requires more explicit reasons. Indeed, given the evidence she presents, Jenkins could also have made a solid case for word stress in the LFC, while leaving prominence as a gray area. But there are at least three reasons to question the evidence for nuclear stress in the LFC:

- it did not by itself lead to misunderstanding (indeed, it doesn't seem to be documented in the phonological errors upon which the LFC is built; 2000, pp. 85–6);
- there is a lack of evidence that the learners in the study productively exploited nuclear stress in their speech;
- there is a lack of evidence that the learners perceived the meaning of nuclear stress placement in the way that NSs of English would perceive it.

Rather, much of the evidence presented suggests that misunderstandings with nuclear stress involved an NS (i.e., Jenkins) or that misunderstandings may have come from some cause other than nuclear stress, such as word stress or perhaps a source that is as yet unidentified.

Three examples in Jenkins (2000, p. 42) are provided to build the case for including prominence in the LFC. Each involves a judgment of an error for prominence, but each also involves misplaced word stress on the final content word, the default placement for prominence. In addition, the last example includes [p] for each [f] in the last word, adding a high functional load error to the mix.

- *Does anyone know where is CarRIbbean?* (Note: This stress pattern is acceptable in American English).
- *Do you think the advertisers exaggerate subject about something that is UNreal?*
- *To undertake more than you can FULfil.*

In each example, the placement of the prominence was correct (assuming that the final word was pronounced with prominence cues), while the word stress, and in one case the consonant, was not. This suggests that even though "advanced learners of English make frequent intonation errors, particularly with the placement of nuclear stress" (Jenkins, 2000, p. 43), their correct placement of nuclear stress cannot be blamed for any misunderstanding. Instead, this is a matter of lexical stress rather than nucleus placement.

The second reason to question whether Jenkins (2000) provides sufficient reason for including prominence in the LFC is that there is no evidence that the learners productively exploited prominence to communicate their intended meaning. Jenkins indicates that these speakers do not use nuclear stress well. The English use of nuclear stress, along with the relatively flexible ability to place prominence on any syllable in a phrase, is not shared by many other languages, which may call attention to particular words using other strategies, and thus affects their production. Jenkins argues that productive use of prominence may take more than a year to show up, and that these students "fail to recognize the communicative value of prominence in English" (2000, p. 51). Even though this feature may be "the most important key to the speaker's intended meaning" (p. 53), this can only be said if the language learner productively uses it to communicate such nuances in meaning (p. 153). If they do not, they may use other strategies to focus a listener's attention, which may confuse NS listeners or other NNSs. Indeed, there is almost no evidence that the presence or absence of prominence by NNSs will confuse other NNSs, nor the ways that NNSs from varied L1s realize prominence, or even if they do so.

The final reason to question the inclusion of prominence in the LFC has to do with perception. Jenkins argues that students had acquired the receptive use of prominence based on a small-scale study that examined their ability to both produce and perceive prominence in unmarked and contrastive contexts. But other research suggests that when learners come from a language that does not use contrastive prominence in the way English does (e.g., Pennington & Ellis, 2000 for Cantonese learners), they may not even recognize that prominence or other prosodic parameters contribute meaning independently to an utterance. Reed and Michaud (2015) also indicate that the perception of prominence may have less to do with hearing the acoustic cues than it does with understanding the messages prominence communicates. Some learners will likely learn this faster (e.g., the Swiss German speakers in her study, whose L1 is typologically close to English) than others (the Japanese speakers, with a typologically distant language). But it is difficult to say whether the more abstract meanings communicated by prominence are perceived by NNSs better than the relatively concrete differences communicated by word stress.

In summary, it seems that Jenkins, who so compellingly argues for intelligibility apart from NS viewpoints for other features, falls into an NS mindset for nuclear stress. When she defines nuclear stress as the prominent syllable "which the speaker has chosen to highlight (by means of length and loudness, and a change in pitch level) as carrying the most salient part of his or her message, and thus the part on which he or she wishes to focus the listener's attention" (2000, p. 42), it seems that she uses the NS as her model listener/speaker, not the NNS whose production and perception of prominence is suspect. None of her examples of misplaced prominence (e.g., pp. 42, 43, 50) are represented in her list of phonologically caused unintelligibility (pp. 85–7), an odd omission since she states multiple times that nuclear stress was implicated in unintelligibility.

I do not mean to say that prominence should not be part of the LFC. I think it should be taught, especially because it is a powerful strategy for communicating meaning in L1 varieties. For this reason alone, prominence should be presented receptively at the very least, since many NNSs will have to listen to NSs of English, even if only online or in the classroom. It is also likely that prominence is used in nativized varieties of English, though perhaps with other patterns of use (e.g., Levis, 2005a; Low, 2006). But without knowing whether outer- or expanding-circle speakers are productively and receptively using prominence to communicate messages in the same ways that NSs do, we cannot say that we have empirical evidence that misplaced prominence is the cause of unintelligibility in NNS–NNS interactions. Deviations in prominence may trip up NSs, but they may also go unnoticed by other NNSs.

Summary

Prominence, and its inverse, de-accenting, are critical elements of English pronunciation for L2 learners. All inner-circle varieties of English use prominence in similar ways, making prominence a feature of spoken English that English speakers use to package their speech so that it is easy to follow, to call attention to categorical contrasts, and to communicate the relative importance of information in speech. Although prominence is unlikely to compromise listeners' ability to decode words (the narrow sense of intelligibility), learners' intended messages are likely to be misunderstood if they do not use prominence in expected ways (Hahn, 2004). In addition, L2 learners are unlikely to understand the messages being communicated by NSs of English if they are not attentive to the ways in which prominence communicates meaning. Thus, prominence is important both for production and perception, and is essential if learners are to do anything more than communicate surface meaning through speaking and listening.

Prominence also seems to be unusually learnable. Pennington and Ellis (2000) found that contrastive prominence was the only one of four intonational features that Cantonese learners could begin to recognize after brief instruction. Muller Levis and Levis (2012) found that contrasts were also learnable for production. M. Hahn (2002) showed that a number of special uses of prominence showed long-term learning, although several others did not demonstrate persistence in learning. We do not have a large amount of information about how prominence is learned in relation to the default placement – on the last content word – nor in relation to the marking of new and given information. We also do not know whether the marking of prominent syllables or the de-accenting of subsequent given information is more challenging. This suggests many avenues for pedagogically valuable research.

Tune and Intelligibility

In addition to prominence, the intonation system of English includes the contributions of tune and pitch range. This section will address the meanings associated with tune (the pitch movement from the nuclear syllable to the end of the phrase) and pitch range. Although tune and pitch range are sometimes considered peripheral to an intelligibility-based approach (e.g., Jenkins, 2000), there is abundant evidence that intonation variations are associated with a wide variety of important meanings in English. These meanings rarely impact intelligibility at the word level (the type of intelligibility described by Jenkins), but regularly affect intelligibility at the level of the message and how those messages are interpreted (called interpretability by Smith & Nelson, 1985). It is also likely that unexpected intonation patterns can make messages or intentions more challenging to follow – that is, it can affect the ways that information is heard as being connected across phrases. In this way, intonation is also likely to influence the way information is processed – that is, comprehensibility.

Wichmann (2000) speaks of intonation in discourse as functioning at beginnings, middles, and ends. Thus intonation is a phrase-edge phenomenon, and its general purpose is to connect the message(s) being communicated by a phrase to other phrases, looking backward and forward and connecting the meaning of one phrase to another. This is reflected by the ways that other researchers talk about the functions of intonation as well. According to Pierrehumbert and Hirschberg (1990), the relationship of the information within successive intermediate and final phrases is marked by pitch movement at the ends of the phrases (phrasal and boundary tones). Nolan (2002) says that intonation "helps to demarcate … phrases, it conveys information structure by highlighting certain words in an utterance, it contributes a separate attitudinal layer of meaning to the words used and it helps to regulate turn taking in conversation" (p. 1). At least three of Nolan's four general functions have to do with beginnings and ends, indicating that these communicative functions signaled by intonation variations connect messages and intentions both within a speaker's turn and across turns with other speakers.

Intonation Patterns: Forms and Functions

Although intonation is primarily a discourse-based pronunciation feature that creates meaning across and between phrases (e.g., Couper-Kuhlen, 1996, 2001), it has primarily been described in regard to its forms and functions at the phrase and sentence level. A brief overview of this sentence-level description tradition is presented next.

The most common patterns for final intonation in English are the falling and rising tunes in (7.5) and (7.6) – that is, the pitch movement from a relatively high pitch to a relatively low one (falling, or HL) and its opposite (rising, or LH).

(7.5)

So, are you ^{GO}i$_{ng?}$ So, are you$_{GO}$ i $^{ng?}$

(7.6)

So, you're ^{GO}i$_{ng.}$ So, you're $_{GO}$ i $^{ng?}$

Rising and falling tunes occur on all kinds of complete and incomplete grammatical structures, and sometimes have clear difference in meaning, as in (7.6), and sometimes a more subtle difference, as in (7.5), as described in Thompson (1995).

In addition, the fall–rise final intonation (HLH) is also well studied, and comes with a meaning of incompletion, as in (7.7) and (7.8). In (7.7), the fall–rise signals that the speaker is not finished, as evidenced by the succeeding phrase. In (7.8), when the speaker says nothing more, the listener is likely to interpret the seemingly positive response as leaving something undesirable unsaid, or as Halliday (1967, p. 41) says, "There's a but about it."

(7.7)

I'd like to ^{HELP} y$_o$u; Let me check my schedule.

(7.8)

$$\text{I'd like to }^{\text{HELP}}\text{ y}_{\text{o}}{}^{\text{u...}}$$

A wide variety of other tunes have been described for English, such as the calling contour (Liberman, 1975), the children's chant (Liberman, 1975), the O-contour (Bing, 1985), rise–fall and level contours (Bradford, 1988; Brazil, 1997), as in the examples in (7.9)–(7.13). Examples (7.9) and (7.10) are known for a series of level pitches (low, mid, high) and are highly stylized. Example (7.11) is an intonation that is relatively flat and has no prominent syllables. It may or may not have a slight rise at the end. It is used, among other things, for epithets, as in the example, some names in introductions, and narrative reports (e.g., "I can't, he said"). Example (7.12) begins its move toward a high pitch before the stressed syllable, and may sound more emotionally engaged. Finally, (7.13) is an intonation with very little movement. Brazil (1997) talks of it as the intonation that is used when treating language as an object, such as when flight attendants have given the same presentation so many times that the announcement is simply a task to get through.

(7.9)

$$\text{Alex }^{\text{AN}}\text{ }_{\text{der!}}\text{ }^{\text{JO}}\text{ }_{\text{hn!}}\text{ Ra}^{\text{MO}}\text{ }_{\text{na!}}\text{ Come to dinner!}$$

(7.10)

$$\text{Johnny }_{\text{has a}}{}^{\text{GIRL}}\text{ }_{\text{friend!}}$$

(7.11)

$$\text{He did it, }_{\text{the jer}}{}^{\text{k!}}$$

(7.12)

$$\text{It was e}^{\text{xTRE}}\text{ }_{\text{M}}{}_{\text{E}}{}_{\text{ly difficult!}}$$

(7.13)

It was very interesting. (It doesn't sound like it)

Over many years, there has been little agreement on the numbers of distinct tunes in English. Pike (1945), for example, hypothesized that intonation contours (i.e., tunes) were built from four pitch levels (with one being highest and four lowest), and that each different configuration was a contour with distinct attitudinal meanings. The system predicted that 1–4, 1–3, 1–2, 2–4, 2–3, and 3–4 were all distinctive falling contours. Pike's system, elegant in its simplicity, over-generated the numbers of contours that seemed justifiable in English. On the British side, intonation also had a large number of contours, with O'Connor and Arnold (1961) providing more distinct contours than are likely to exist. Both of these descriptions had a theoretical and pedagogical purpose, and L2 speakers who learned to pronounce English learned (or at least were taught) to hear and pronounce a wide variety of contours.

Current pedagogical treatments reflect sentence-level descriptions, but they present intonation as a far simpler system than theoretical researchers have described. Many contours that are well attested have minor relevance for most L2 speakers (e.g., the children's chant), and the majority of teaching materials spend most of their attention on falling and rising final intonation. Other materials include falling–rising intonation, especially for utterances that are not complete (Levis & Muller Levis, n.d.). Most materials also make connections between intonation and grammatical structures. For example, yes–no questions are said to be spoken with rising intonation, and statements and WH questions with falling intonation. These connections are made despite it being well established that intonational and grammatical meaning are independent (Levis, 1997). Yes–no questions can be, and are, spoken with both rising and falling .intonation (Lee, 1980), and meaning differences based on intonation are not easy to categorize on yes–no questions. Thompson (1995) called the rising intonation on yes–no questions "polite" and the falling "businesslike," admitting that neither meaning could be said to be unmarked.

Some pedagogical approaches (e.g., Brazil, 1997) expand rising and falling categories to include rising and falling–rising as generally rising, and falling and rising–falling as generally falling; this approach also includes level tunes as a separate category, treating different contours as having a connection to whether the proposition expressed in the phrase is new or given information, or perhaps uncommitted to the information status of the proposition (i.e., level tunes).

Despite these pedagogical simplifications of a more complex intonational system, teachers report being uncomfortable teaching intonation (Sonsaat, 2017). Part of this comes from confusion related to intonation terminology. Even cursory familiarity with pedagogical approaches to intonation makes it clear that the same phenomena have as many names as characters in a Russian novel. British and American pedagogical traditions to intonation use different terms and different formalisms (Levis, 2005b), and teachers who eclectically consult various sources cannot help but be confused.

Tune and Intelligibility

The effect of tune on intelligibility and comprehensibility seems implicitly clear from many research studies. For example, Hirschberg and Litman (1987), in examining the cue phrase "Now," argued that "now had two uses, one which made specific reference to the structure of the discourse (the cue phrase 'Now,' e.g., 'Now what about Pennsylvania state tax' [p. 164]) and another use which refers deictically to time (e.g., 'You know, I see more coupons now' [p. 164])." They demonstrated that the cue phrase "Now" is distinguished from the deictic use because of its intonational and phrasal characteristics. In this study, intonation affects the interpretation of the discourse, not the word intelligibility of "now." Indeed, while intonation rarely affects word intelligibility, it does affect the intelligibility of messages and intentions, and the ease with which speech is processed. This can be seen in research demonstrating how intonation is used to create cohesive discourse, how speakers use intonation to signal topic changes (i.e., paratones), how intonation is used to signal pragmatic meanings, and how it influences listeners' perceptions of speakers' social convergence. These are only some of the ways in which intonation functions in English, and an important future direction in pedagogical approaches to intonation must be how to teach intonation's communicative functions beyond the constraints of grammatical forms and the level of the sentence. This next section will describe some ways in which tune is associated with different types of discourse meaning in English. The goal of the examples is to provide evidence that, far from being irrelevant to an intelligibility-based approach, tunes are critical to how speakers construct discourse and communicate connections between and among utterances. Looked at in this way, it is almost certain that tune is essential for intelligibility. Teaching materials may not reflect this kind of intelligibility, but that is a reflection of the limitations of the ways we teach intonation, not a reflection of the lack of importance for intonation in an intelligibility-based approach.

Tune, Cohesion, and Speaker Evaluation

Pierrehumbert and Hirschberg's (1990) insight that propositions are related in speech by the intonation of successive intermediate and final phrases indicates that intonation in discourse plays a role in creating cohesion and coherence – that is, in tying together the messages and functions of utterances with those preceding and succeeding them. In a study of Mandarin-speaking international teaching assistant (ITA) lecture effectiveness, Wennerstrom (1998) explicitly tested whether intonation played such a role in signaling cohesion, employing functions found by Halliday and Hasan (1976). Wennerstrom recorded and analyzed the ways that ITAs used paratones at topic boundaries, distinguished content from function words, used high phrasal boundary tones (i.e., rising intonation) to signal a connection between the phrase and the one following it, and the use of pitch to mark contrasts. Each intonational feature was hypothesized to reflect different elements of cohesion. The study hypothesized that ITAs who made more effective use of the features would also score higher on a test of oral proficiency. The results affirmed this for the use of paratones to mark topic shifts, but not for any of the other variables. This suggests two things. Not all uses of intonation correlate with test scores, but some do, and greater proficiency is also associated with more native-like use of at least one intonational feature. It also indicates that greater intelligibility and comprehensibility may be likely to result from better use of some aspects of intonation.

In Pickering (2001), the classroom teaching presentations of six native and six nonnative teaching assistants with similar training in teaching were recorded and their use of intonation was analyzed in regard to how well the intonation choices made the content of the teaching accessible to listeners. As Pickering points out, the cumulative uses of rising and falling intonation are largely subconscious, but they affect how the propositions of the developing spoken discourse are related to one another. The two groups used rising and falling intonation very differently in their presentations. Pickering argued that the way that NSs used intonation made the material more understandable and made their students rate them higher in rapport. NNSs, in contrast, were seen as distant and their lectures were seen as relatively confusing.

Regarding communication convergence with their students, Pickering said that the differences in the ways NSs and NNSs used rising tones affected two aspects of their speech: the social connections made with the students and the ease with which lecture content was understood. This was especially the case for the number of rising, or converging, tones used. NNSs used these far less than NSs, and the functions reflected by rising tones were thus more severely limited for NNSs. For this reason, Pickering recommended that attention to these discourse meanings of intonation be required in programs for NNS teaching assistants because of their effects upon comprehensibility and the ways that intonation is used to create social connections.

A third study of intonation's effects upon the organization of spoken academic discourse looked at how intonation is represented in academic listening materials intended for academic training for NNSs. Thompson (2003) argued that awareness of how intonation is used helps nonnative listeners perceive a mental map of the information being presented, including the relative importance of propositions and the way the propositions are related to each other. These hierarchical relationships may be quite complex, but from a listener's point of view, this is a clear place where intonation contributes both to intelligibility (message content) and comprehensibility (the ease with which complex relationships among ideas can be processed).

Paratones: The Signal for Topic Changes

Paratones (intonation paragraphs) are intonational markings of topic changes. They are a 'beginning' use of intonation (Wichmann, 2000), in that they signal the start of a major new section of spoken text, divide larger discourse units in speech, and are used as one type of organizational tool in the construction of informational importance in spoken discourse. Yule describes a paratone as "the first stressed syllable to be raised high in the pitch range, followed by a descending order of pitch height on subsequent stressed syllables until the final stressed syllable, which is realised as a fall from high to low" (1980, p. 36). Wichmann (2000) argues that the readings in a news corpus (from Brown, Currie, & Kenworthy, 1980) include a default pitch range, a low and a raised range, and an extra-high range for topic onsets (i.e., paratones), defined by their place at a beginning boundary. Levis and Pickering (2004), in showing how paratones can be taught in marking topic boundaries, used sentence-level and discourse-level readings from male and female readers to demonstrate how readers mark discourse boundaries with high-pitch resets. In (7.14), a pitch reset was noticeable at the word "second" (p. 522), indicating to listeners a change that was consistent with the paragraph structure of the written text.

(7.14)

Let us look at the competition. Our main competitor – Benton – entered the market 10 years later than us. But since then they have grown more rapidly and are now the biggest in terms of market share. Why? Their products are better, sold at lower prices and presented more attractively.

Now, our **second** major competitor is Zecron.

Other studies have shown the use of paratones in read and spontaneous speech, in academic presentations, and in spontaneous non-academic narratives. In a study of native and nonnative graduate students, Wennerstrom (1994) found that native English speakers made use of pitch variation in free and read speech, according to their roles at beginnings (paratones), middles, and ends; they also highlighted prominent syllables. Spanish, Thai, and Japanese NNSs did not consistently make use of intonational cues that are typical of English. The use of paratones is not limited to academic language, but is also essential to how stories progress, signaling important shifts in speakers' arrangement of spontaneous narratives (Wennerstrom, 2001). In an authentic study of classroom speech by native and international teaching assistants, Pickering (2004) similarly found that native TAs created a hierarchy of information by employing high initial pitch (i.e., paratones marking topic shifts), variations in intonation patterns in the middle of a spoken test (to mark propositions as belonging to a topic), and finally ended at a lower pitch level (to indicate that the topic was finished). These kinds of signals were not consistently used by the ITAs, resulting in a "disturbance in prosodic composition that materially affects the comprehensibility of the discourse for native speaker hearers" (2004, p. 19). Thus, inadequate command of intonation cues, including paratones (and likely a lack of awareness of the functions of those cues) resulted in speech that was more challenging for listeners to process. In other words, the speech was more challenging to comprehensibility.

Paratones are one way that intonation creates a hierarchical structure to spoken language, both in more formal academic language and in less formal speech events. The sampling of research presented in this section is evidence that intonation provides ways to understand speakers' messages (intelligibility at the semantic level) and in processing speech (that is, comprehensibility). Most importantly, this kind of meaning cannot be found in decontextualized sentences, which have been the traditional vehicle for teaching L2 intonation. Only by moving beyond the sentence can the effect of intonation on intelligibility be seen clearly.

Tune and Pragmatic Meanings

Pragmatics is the study of meaning in context. In spoken language, intonation is an important part of how meaning is communicated in different spoken contexts, and is thus a critical element in how messages are communicated and interpreted. The example already discussed (see Chapter 1) about offering "Gravy," with falling rather than rising intonation (Gumperz, 1982) is a striking example not only of how intonation communicates meaning, but also of how the message being communicated is dependent on the sociolinguistics of the context of communication as well as the linguistic context. By itself, "Gravy" with falling intonation could be perfectly appropriate. If asked to name the food (e.g., "What's that?"), it would be the appropriate answer, whereas a rising tune to the same question would indicate an uncertainty that might be interpreted as humorous. But in the context that Gumperz describes, a falling tune was interpreted through a cultural lens that included expectations based on class, race, and speech act realization on the part of the British Airways aviation workers. The same falling tune from the Indian and Pakistani servers was intended as the appropriate way to serve food based on the conventions of their L1s. Because of the cross-cultural context of the interaction, they delivered an unintended insult through a single word spoken with an unexpected tune. This reflects the way that intonational tunes help communicate messages and intentions, and why tunes are likely to be important for intelligibility. The intelligibility is dependent upon the use of intonation in context, however, and any type of pronunciation teaching that depends on teaching intonation apart from context is likely to miss out on the ways that intonation influences intelligibility.

This section examines some examples in which intonation is connected to pragmatic meanings. Wichmann (2004), using a spoken corpus, demonstrated how intonational differences can distinguish the ways that "Please" requests are interpreted. "Please" is traditionally described as a politeness marker, but it also can be associated with different intonations that may reinforce or undermine the politeness it communicates. Wichmann examined the intonation differences for "please" in its own phrase (not as part of a larger phrase); she argues that while "please" has a basic meaning in English, the intonation used with "please" is constrained by context. Public uses (where social distance is greater) were spoken with falling intonation to signal indirect requests or to soften imperatives. In private speech, however, where social relations are more equal, rising intonation was more common, with indirect requests dominating the corpus. Wichmann argues that these intonations depend on whether the requests and imperatives are speaker- or listener-oriented. From an intelligibility perspective, "please" requests send different messages depending on their intonation in context. Although "please" has a basic obligation-related meaning, the way the obligation is discharged (its interpretability) is dependent on its intonation. Wichmann (2004, p. 1546) gives the example of *please* spoken with a falling tune as being used by more powerful speakers in asymmetrical interactions (e.g., a lecturer speaking to an assistant: "Could I have the slides on please?"). Rising tunes on *please*, in contrast, are more common in symmetrical, intimate interactions (e.g., "Could I have a glass of water please?").

A second type of pragmatic meaning is proposed by Ward and Hirschberg (1985), who analyze the fall–rise intonation as expressing uncertainty, which is interpreted as a type of implicature. The fall–rise intonation, as described earlier, is the intonation that "has a but about it" (Halliday, 1967, p. 41). Thus, "I'd like to help you" with a fall–rise indicates an unsaid "but" that indicates some kind of reservation about what was said, an "uncertainty of the appropriateness of some utterance in a given context" (Ward & Hirschberg, 1985, p. 756), specifically with regard to some kind of implicit scale (e.g., chapters in a book, fractions of chapters, people that could be invited to a party, etc.). The implicature of uncertainty can be used to express true uncertainty, but it may also be used to express politeness or irony, as in the example "Did any linguists come to the colloquium yesterday?" "Well, \X / did." In this example, where the fall–rise is marked by a backslash and a forward slash on the person's name ("X"), the reply is interpreted as an ironic comment about whether "X" (who is a linguist) should really be considered a linguist" (p. 773). Other cross-language research on how NSs and NNSs express uncertainty and how intonation is used to do so is found in the work of Verdugo (2005), in which NSs expressed uncertainty with the phrase "I think so" with a strong falling–rising tune, while NNSs used a falling tune (pp. 2100–1).

Tune and Social Interaction

Intonation is highly conventional in the kinds of meanings it conveys in speech. Unlike vowels and consonants, intonation is unlikely to be heard as right or wrong, and unexpected use of intonation is much more likely to be judged not as a pronunciation error but a social failing. Tannen says that all participants in gatekeeping encounters tend to *look through* language, petitioners assuming they are being judged on their qualifications and interviewers believing they are making decisions based on the petitioners' qualifications; in fact, the speakers' mutual judgments of abilities and intentions are profoundly influenced, if not determined, by automatic uses of the nuts and bolts of language-pitch and amplitude; intonational patterns; pacing and pausing; the structuring, foregrounding or backgrounding of information; and so on.   (2005, p. 206)

Tannen goes on to say that intonation's link to social meaning lurks in the background of any cross-cultural interaction, playing a significant role in how relationships and beliefs about each other are subconsciously negotiated, and in the ways that intonation (and other linguistic features) differ in the conventional meanings assigned to them. Thus, we may interpret intonation variations in terms of rudeness and politeness rather than accent.

Conclusions

According to Jenkins (2000), intonation, apart from nuclear stress, is not part of the core for NNS–NNS interaction because it is not implicated in unintelligibility. She suggests that the best that L2 users of English can hope for with intonation is to live where they can use it and hope that it will be acquired. Pickering (2009), however, finds that both final intonation and the relative pitch of speech help to orient NNSs in interactions with other NNSs, leading to successful repair of spoken misunderstandings. For this reason, she argues that "pitch movement clearly has a role in the production of intelligible and successful interaction in ELF discourse" (2009, p. 251). This makes sense in that intonation is conventionalized differently in different languages (Gumperz, 1982; Tannen, 2005), and English speakers with different L1s are likely to use pitch in ways that may be similar in form but not necessarily similar in function. Some of these uses (the use of pitch to indicate trouble) may be more common across L1s, but other uses are likely to have different connections between form and meaning in different L1s, and thus, in the ways that those speakers communicate meaning using English.

Because so little research has directly examined the effects of tune on intelligibility, it is likely that the examples of tune and meaning only scratch the surface of the ways in which intonation impacts intelligibility and comprehensibility. Intonation may be important in communicating sarcasm (Pincus, 2016), in how interactional strategies and turn-taking are accomplished (Chun, 1988), in expressing implicatures, especially with falling–rising contours (Ladd 1980; Ward & Hirschberg, 1985), and in improving the intelligibility of utterances in noisy conditions (Watson & Schlauch, 2008). When L2 listeners do not use intonation like NSs, NSs are likely to misunderstand what the speakers intended to communicate. When L2 listeners hear different uses of intonation produced by L1 speakers, they are also likely to miss out on the types of meanings that are being communicated. As a result, intonation is more than likely to be critical for intelligibility. When L2 speakers and listeners from different L1s interact with each other, conventionalized yet different forms and functions of intonation in their L1s may affect intelligibility in much the same manner. Intonation has been argued to be unimportant for intelligibility, however, most research on intelligibility has focused on the intelligibility of words, precisely the area that is unlikely to be affected by intonation.

Part IV

Teaching and Research Approaches to Intelligibility

8 *Teaching for Intelligibility*
Guidelines for Setting Priorities

The evidence for how pedagogical priorities should be determined is sketchy and sometimes contradictory, but there is enough evidence to suggest guidelines for a way forward in determining priorities. The guidelines presented in this chapter do not offer an unambiguous way to mechanically determine priorities for instruction. Indeed, the argument of this chapter is that no category of sounds is a priori either to be included or to be excluded in an intelligibility-oriented curriculum. Each general category (e.g., consonants), and likely each individual category (e.g., /p/), includes more and less important features. In other words, there appear to be more important and less important consonant and vowel sounds, just as there appear to be more and less important elements of intonation or word stress.

The guidelines serve several purposes. First, they are an explicit attempt to define parameters by which informed intuition can be described and examined. In arguing for pronunciation needs, even the best teachers and researchers display a combination of informed intuition and linguistic prejudices. My goal is to offer more explicit reasons for setting priorities. Second, the guidelines are an attempt to argue for a nuanced approach to priorities that takes into account the context of instruction. It seems clear that pronunciation needs are different for learners who live in ESL (English as a second language) contexts (Derwing & Munro, 2005) as opposed to those who use English primarily for English as a lingua franca (ELF) communication (Jenkins, 2000). Within these general contexts of language use, of course, it is likely that priorities fit into several categories as well: critical, advisable, desirable, and unnecessary, each of which may differ depending on the particular country in which English is taught. Finally, the guidelines are meant to have an impact upon classroom practice, to assist in making better decisions, and in so doing, to make more effective use of the time that is available for pronunciation work. The guidelines are listed below and will be discussed in turn.

Six Guidelines for Intelligibility-Based Teaching

1. Features that have an explicit connection to communication and to other areas of language should be prioritized.
2. Mispronunciations that cause difficulties in processing should be given priority.
3. The pronunciation of important lexical items should be given priority over less important items.
4. Errors that carry a high FL should be given priority over those that do not.
5. More frequent errors are more important than less frequent errors.
6. Features that are learnable should be prioritized over those that are not.

Guideline 1: Features that have an explicit connection to communication and to other areas of language should be prioritized.

From research evidence and anecdotal evidence, pronunciation errors are consistently implicated in loss of intelligibility, whether in communication between native speakers (NSs), as happens when speakers of unfamiliar dialects come into contact, between NSs and nonnative speakers (NNSs) (Munro & Derwing, 1995), or between NNSs (Jenkins, 2000). This is a strong argument for working on pronunciation in learning English as an additional language. Nevertheless, working on pronunciation by itself is only a first step in creating the conditions for intelligibility. While pronunciation is an unavoidable element of communication, by itself it is not enough to make communication happen. Pronunciation, like grammar, is a servant skill that speakers exploit for communicative purposes. In Murphy's words, "pronunciation encompasses subsets of both listening and speaking skill development," with its subskills being "slices of a significantly larger pie" (1991, pp. 52, 66) of listening and speaking. This means intelligibility cannot be fully addressed by working on pronunciation alone, but only in relation to whether *speak*ers are intelligible when they speak, and in relation to whether *listen*ers find the speech of others intelligible. Goodwin reflects this larger view of intelligibility when she describes it "not simply as acceptable spoken *production* but as successful spoken *interaction*" (2005, p. 225, emphasis in original). Good pronunciation is the initial gateway for communication to take place, in that pronunciation that deviates too much from what is expected can make communication almost impossible.

While intelligibility is typically considered to be a function of pronunciation, the actual scope has to be broader. Largely, calls for intelligibility have been made for classrooms in which pronunciation plays a central role, but listening and speaking materials rarely mention intelligibility as an objective. Murphy (1991) asserted that oral communication courses involve two competing yet complementary strands: fluency and accuracy. Typical instructional techniques for listening and speaking attend to the fluency strand, while pronunciation is most important for accuracy. In communicative language teaching, Murphy says, pronunciation was expected to take care of itself when the bigger-picture skills were addressed, an expectation that was not adequately met for many learners. Murphy talks of the fluency/accuracy goals as reflecting the same "necessary and pivotal tension" (1991, p. 61) found in writing instruction, where teachers must weigh competing demands to teach composing and accuracy of expression. While an obvious way to relieve the tension is to focus on speaking/listening or on pronunciation, this misses Murphy's key point that "phonological accuracy need not be sacrificed at the expense of conversational fluency, nor should the opposite be the case" (p. 66).

Communicative approaches to pronunciation teaching have been described for more than three decades. Celce-Murcia (1987) describes a variety of techniques that, at the time of her writing, did not exist for teaching pronunciation. The exercises she describes (primarily for segmentals) are those that focus on meaning and form. These types of activities always stop short of real communication, acting as bridging activities (Levis, 2000) that are somewhere between very controlled exercises and real communication, and they give practice both to fluency and accuracy. Celce-Murcia foreshadows the importance of form-focused instruction for acquisition, in which meaning-oriented tasks promote noticing and acquisition of linguistic forms, an accuracy-oriented goal. Morley (1991) also implies a focus on the big picture when she says that pronunciation instruction should include greater attention to communication skills, suprasegmentals, body language, self-monitoring skills, contextualization, and linking listening to speaking. The difficulty with including pronunciation in communicative teaching, however, is the temptation to focus only on accuracy, but then to leave off attention to accuracy within communication. Even suprasegmental teaching can go for the quick fix, such as connecting intonation to grammatical form rather than promoting intonation as a separate system of meaning that is only loosely correlated with grammatical forms (Levis, 1999b).

The principle that we should prioritize pronunciation features that explicitly connect to other areas of language is suggested by many of the writers reviewed earlier. Firth (1992), with her Zoom Principle, says that we need to start with ability to communicate, leaving the details of phonetic accuracy until the overall framework of communication is in place. Suprasegmentals by their very nature are features that should have communicative ends. Much of the supporting language that we use in discussing the importance of pronunciation's role in language teaching entails a focus on communication. For example, when we talk of discourse intonation (Brazil, 1997; Pickering, 2002), we assume communication is taking place beyond sentence level. Discourse involves language and communicative decisions beyond the word and sentence levels, and it involves a communicative context that can be described. It also involves interlocutors, whether they are receptively listening to a formal talk or whether they are involved in co-constructing the discourse. This co-construction leads to accommodation and adjustments in pronunciation (Jenkins, 2000; Walker, 2010) to promote communication. Hardison (2005), using another term that gives attention to communication while recognizing the need for accuracy, talks about helping learners improve pronunciation in a "multifaceted contextualized [speech] event" by using techniques related to theater voice training and making use of feedback techniques connected to use of technology (2005, p. 594).

Bridging the gap between accuracy and fluency is always challenging, and it is always easier to focus on accuracy at the expense of fluency when teaching pronunciation. Hardison (2005) provides one way in which such bridging may take place, using techniques from a context (theater) in which focus on form and focus on fluency naturally interact (Cerreta, 2016; Galante & Thomson, 2017). Goodwin (2005) employs similar techniques (without the use of technology for feedback) in asking learners to reenact movie scenes in which two people interact. Rather than simply working off of a script, learners try to imitate the voice quality, gestures, and interaction styles of the actors. The result is improvement in both accuracy and fluency. Levis (2001) suggests a variety of activities that promote the use of sentence focus in conversation, especially in relation to question–answer adjacency pairs, a basic routine in conversational speech. Levis and Grant (2003) suggest ways in which pronunciation can be integrated into oral presentations, through attention to word clarity, narration (thought groups), conversational back-channeling (intonation), and discussing comparisons and contrasts for a pre-writing exercise (focus). In each case, pronunciation is essential to effective completion of the task.

There is evidence that focusing on the big picture can lead to great improvement in how speakers are understood. This is because perceptions of a speaker's comprehensibility are tied to more than pronunciation alone. In one study, Derwing, Moulton, and Campbell (2005) found remarkable progress through a focus on teaching skills and minimal attention to pronunciation, with one instructor going from receiving very poor teaching evaluations to winning a teaching award after ten weeks of intervention. As Derwing reports, "our participants' own undergraduate students had blamed L2 accent in their course evaluations, because accent was so salient, and it blinded them to what the real problems were" (2010, p. 32). In another study, Derwing, Munro, and Wiebe (1998) studied changes in comprehensibility for two sets of learners who received pronunciation instruction. One group received instruction on global skills (presumably including general speaking skills) and suprasegmentals, while the other group received instruction with a traditional pronunciation approach focusing on segmentals. Both groups improved when their pretest and posttest speech was analyzed. However, only the group that received global and suprasegmental instruction was judged as having better comprehensibility. The segmental group's improvement, while quite real, did not lead to a change in how easily listeners understood them.

Most of these suggestions are linked to spoken language skills, but accuracy is also important for listening. Communication is a two-way street, and it is just as important for listeners to find speakers intelligible as it is for speakers to work to be intelligible. Yet listening is relatively ignored in relation to intelligibility research, and it is also neglected in teaching. Listening comprehension, like reading comprehension, is usually taught from the perspective of getting the main idea first before looking at the details. These two aspects of listening are called "bricks and mortar" by Field (2008). The main ideas, largely represented by the content words, are the bricks of the communicative wall. The mortar, represented by the function words, is what helps the wall stay together. Unfortunately, it is the mortar that NNSs are least likely to hear well and least likely to be able to guess. Field says that the strategy used by the L2 listeners he studied was to "go for the bricks and let the mortar look after itself" in listening to English (2008, p. 427). NSs can use their far more developed grammatical competence to "exploit the connection between vowel quality and membership of the two classes" (p. 415). This helps them make good guesses about the nature of the mortar (the function words), which specifies the grammatical and semantic relationships between the bricks.

A second type of low-level error in listening is the lack of accuracy in identifying words in connected speech, called the "commonest perceptual cause of breakdown in understanding" (Field, 2003, p. 327). Partly, this error is one of lexical segmentation from incorrect interpretations of the phonetic signal, a decidedly bottom-up error in processing. This error comes, in part, from learners' inability to identify words that they know in isolation when they occur in connected speech. Field (2003) argues that L2 listeners can best be helped through traditional bottom-up exercises such as dictation, in which close attention to phonetic form is supplemented by analysis and discussion. Likewise, Wilson (2003) suggests explicit attention to bottom-up processes (which are largely phonetic in nature) as a way to improve noticing of features in L2 input, and therefore to improve overall listening comprehension abilities.

Listening and speaking are the most obvious areas of language that interface with pronunciation, but they are not the only ones. Some L2 reading teachers I have talked to tell me that they often notice pronunciation difficulties more in their reading classes than in oral communication instruction, likely because L2 learners encounter vocabulary and sentence structures that they do not use in speech. Their skills with sound–spelling correspondence are exposed as relatively shallow, as is their ability to orally interpret groupings of words on the page. Walter (2008) finds that reading comprehension can be improved through attention to phonological form, and that better readers also have better understanding of how words and sentences are likely to sound. Vocabulary, another important area of language in many classrooms, calls for attention not only to spelling and meaning, but to the way words sound when met in discourse. And even grammar has connections to phonological form, not only in the allomorphs of –s and –ed endings, but also in the connections to contracted forms (Gilbert, 2001) and the ways in which pronunciation carries social significance, such as with the different pronunciations of the –ing morpheme or the social meanings of dialect differences.

Connecting pronunciation to other areas of language and communication makes sense not only for pronouncing, but also because the pronunciation is doubly purposeful. It addresses the common objection to teaching pronunciation by many teachers, that they don't have time to do something extra. In integrating pronunciation into the teaching of other skills, teachers may end up teaching other skills more effectively.

Guideline 2: *Mispronunciations that cause difficulties in intelligibility or in processing should be given priority.*

John Field, in a 2005 article, examined whether rightward mis-stressing (e.g., *COMfort* pronounced as *comFORT*) or leftward mis-stressing (e.g., *deLETE* pronounced as *DElete*) in two-syllable words led to a greater loss of intelligibility. Field found that rightward mis-stressing caused more "cases where intelligibility is entirely lost" (Field, 2005, p. 415). However, the kind of understanding he measured was quite narrow, and may not be the type of understanding that is most important for being able to understand normal speech. While he measured total loss of understanding, he did not test whether the speech was perceived as more difficult. As Field says,

The transcription gave participants time after hearing the recording to form conclusions about what they had heard. A further study is needed that investigates the extent to which misplacing lexical stress increases the listener's processing load at the moment of hearing. Let us accept, for the sake of argument, the notion that the stressed syllable of a word provides an access code or, at the very least, a reliable signpost to its identity. Shifts in stress will then clearly create *garden path* situations: For example, stressing the second syllable in *foLLOW* will lead the listener toward a cohort (Marslen-Wilson, 1987) that includes *low*, *local*, and possibly *below* and away from the target word. The consequent increase in processing demands might well limit the listener's ability to perform under the pressures of a conversational context.   (2005, p. 418)

In Field's study, processing demands were not measured and the pressure to understand over longer stretches of speech did not exist for the listeners. This kind of listening demand, in which words can be understood, but only with extra work on the part of the listener, may be particularly relevant for pronunciation instruction. Munro and Derwing (1999) suggest a reason why perfectly *intelligible* speech (that is, it can be written down with complete accuracy, though perhaps not with complete confidence) can also be rated as highly accented as well as perceived as being difficult to understand (that is, less *comprehensible*). Listeners have to work harder with speech that is unfamiliar in some way because of segmental errors, unexpected prosody, or other unexpected features. Listeners have more trouble processing the speech signal with an unfamiliar accent than with a familiar one. They have more trouble when the listening context is not ideal, and they struggle more if they cannot easily connect new information to what is already known. All of these conditions, which are often connected to pronunciation features or conditions related to the listener or environment, impair comprehensibility, making listeners work much harder than in ideal conditions. Munro and Derwing's research shows that loss of comprehensibility is common and serious for communication. Loss of comprehensibility is likely connected to greater demands on listeners in processing speech, and as such has social implications for how willingly interlocutors will interact with someone.

There is a large body of research demonstrating how varied language input can affect the speed at which listeners process spoken language. Anne Cutler and colleagues have carried out many studies with a wide variety of findings. For example, native English-speaking listeners use anticipated stress locations to comprehend more quickly (Cutler, 1976). Listening for stress is particularly important, whether it is lexical stress (Cutler & Clifton, 1984) or sentence stress, i.e., prominence (Cutler & Foss, 1977). Stressed syllables/words are processed faster than are unstressed ones. Even though the dominant pattern in English is for content words to be stressed and function words unstressed, stressed function words are processed just as quickly as stressed content words (Cutler & Foss, 1977), although lexical stress is not always a critical cue by itself. Cutler (1986) examined word pairs in English that are distinguished only by stress (e.g., *FOREbear* versus *forbear*) without any corresponding change in vowel quality or consonant articulation (e.g., *REcord* and *reCORD* have not only a stress difference but differences in vowel quality). In the study, she found that prosodic mispronunciations alone did not slow processing if segmental phonology was not changed.

In another finding, phonemes are identified more quickly when they occur in words that are the semantic focus in a spoken sentence (Cutler & Fodor, 1979). Even though semantic focus is usually marked by prosodic accent – the redundancy of prosodic cues in English (e.g., stop closure duration, vowel duration, fundamental frequency variation) – listeners seem remarkably flexible in making use of multiple cues to identify semantic focus and sentence stress. As Cutler and Darwin (1981, p. 221) put it,

What seems to be most likely is that the human sentence processor can make extremely flexible use of prosodic information. It may be the case that no single source of prosodic variation will prove to be a necessary cue to where sentence stress will fall, whereas variation along any prosodic dimension will prove sufficiently effective.

What this suggests is that listeners sample all kinds of spoken language cues in order to extract and interpret meaning. When the cues come in expected ways, listeners can make use of many different cues. Not all cues are equally effective in promoting comprehensibility, however. Some spoken words may provide more complex cues in that they evoke a larger cohort of possible words (Cutler, 1983); word beginnings whose acoustic identity are unclear are more likely to lead to misunderstandings than are those whose word endings or word middles are unclear (Cutler, Hawkins, & Gilligan, 1985).

A recent study suggests that nonnative listeners may be at an unexpected disadvantage when listening to speech in their second language. Broersma and Cutler (2011) examined how Dutch learners of English and NSs of British English processed near-words. Focusing on the vowel sounds /æ/ and /ɛ/, the study demonstrated that Dutch learners' relative lack of ability to hear /æ/ and /ɛ/ differences in English led them to activate words that were not relevant to the listening task. For example, the first syllable of *daffodil* activated words related to the English word *deaf* for the learners, but not for the native English speakers. Similarly, Weber and Cutler (2004) found that the word *panda* helped to activate the word *pencil* for Dutch listeners. Related to processing, Broersma and Cutler say that "such extended availability of alternative interpretations of speech may not irreversibly disrupt L2 listeners' processing, but it could certainly slow it down" (2011, p. 75).

These findings from Broersma and Cutler (2011) and Weber and Cutler (2004) call to mind one of the most commonly cited examples from Jenkins (2000, pp. 85–6). In one communicative task, a Japanese and a Swiss German-speaking student get confused over understanding the other person's speech. The German speaker was trying to identify one of six pictures being described by the Japanese speaker. The picture in question had a red car. The Japanese speaker, who had difficulty producing the distinction between /l/ and /ɹ/, is heard to say [l]. The German speaker, who perceives final voiced obstruents as voiceless, hears the /d/ as /t/ and creates the interpretation of a "let" (hired) car. The confusion is one both of perception and production. In another example, the Japanese speaker hears "gray house" as "clay house." This mishearing shows the same effect, in that mishearing a phoneme can lead to the activation of other words and, at a minimum, delays in processing and loss of comprehensibility. In ELF contexts, in which two NNSs of English communicate through the filter of their own perceptual systems, the potential for processing difficulties is enormous and will likely result in surprising difficulties, depending on who the speakers are, since there are so many possible L1–L1 combinations.

NOISE

Another factor that impacts both intelligibility and comprehensibility is the presence of noise, that is, an imperfect listening environment. In ideal conditions, NSs of a language can get much of what is said as long as they are listening to familiar dialects. When listening to unfamiliar dialects, however, there may be some differences in perception of segments such as vowels (Cutler, Smits, & Cooper, 2005), in the ability to write down words or utterances accurately, or in the ability to identify dialects (Clopper & Bradlow, 2009). Native speech is also likely to be more intelligible than nonnative speech for native listeners, and there is mixed evidence about whether nonnative listeners benefit from listening to speech of speakers who share their L1.

In laboratory conditions connected to research on intelligibility, degradation of the signal may be a problem for NSs when listening in adverse conditions as part of the experimental design. In addition, in normal listening contexts (such as telephones, classrooms, and contexts in which other speech or non-speech noise compete for a listener's attention), noise may affect both the ability to hear accurately and the ability to process a message quickly.

A large body of research has demonstrated that noise affects the comprehension of NSs when listening to native speech (see Bronkhorst, 2000 for a review). There is also evidence that listening to nonnative speech results in greater difficulties with understanding. In one study of listening to native and nonnative English speech, Munro (1998) examined how native Canadian English listeners assessed the truth-value of sentences (verification) and transcribed them (transcription) in quiet and noisy conditions. He found that Mandarin-accented speech was less successfully verified and transcribed than native speech. Even when the Mandarin-accented speech was verified and transcribed perfectly in quiet conditions, this result did not hold for noisy conditions. As Munro says, "the noise added ... made the utterances significantly harder to verify than did the presence of a Mandarin accent alone" (1998, p. 146). The study also found that being more or less intelligible in quiet conditions was no guarantee that the same level of intelligibility would hold in noisy conditions. The effect of noise was to render transcriptions completely wrong at a higher rate than was expected: "Although the number of mistranscriptions of Mandarin-accented speech did not increase when noise was added, the frequency of completely unintelligible utterances doubled from the quiet to the noisy conditions" (1998, p. 151). Related to the focus on processing, what was interesting was that the verification task took about 50 milliseconds longer for Mandarin-accented utterances.

Intelligibility and comprehensibility involve both a speaker and a listener. The research discussed so far focuses on the NS listener, as is most common in research on intelligibility. However, it is just as important to examine the difficulties faced by nonnative listeners when listening to native speech. Nonnative listeners invariably face two difficulties that affect both intelligibility and comprehensibility of speech: *"imperfect signals and imperfect knowledge"* (Lecumberri, Cooke, & Cutler, 2010, p. 864). As the authors state, even if the same spoken word recognition system is available in the L2 as in the L1, this may not help; indeed, it may hinder the nonnative listener. They point out that nonnative listeners may suffer from inaccurate phonemic perception, an impoverished vocabulary in the L2, the presence of competing words from the L1, and the inability of higher-level listening processes to resolve the lower-level inputs in the most efficient way (see also Field, 2008). Lecumberri et al. describe how this cascading set of difficulties leads to a set of difficulties for the L2 listener (2010, p. 7):

> If the L2 listener's phonemic processing is inaccurate, more alternatives are passed on to the word recognition stage, and if the word recognition stage involves more competition than it should, sentence-level context has more work to do to sort it out. In other words, at all levels there will be more uncertainty to be resolved for the L2 than for the L1 listener. Yet the higher-level processes that are here called upon to do more work than is in principle necessary are also themselves less efficient in the case of the L2 listener. L2 listeners do not have the extensive experience with lexical and syntactic transitional probabilities that an L1 listener can call upon, they do not have as fine a sensitivity to the subtle syntactic and pragmatic differences that choice of words can convey, and so on.

In adverse conditions of masking or reverberating noise, these difficulties become far more serious. Lecumberri et al. (2010, pp. 12ff.) describe a series of consequences to listening in adverse conditions. L2 listeners show greater difficulties than L1 listeners in word- and sentence-recognition tasks and in identification of consonant sounds. In addition, competing background speech makes it harder to process the informational importance of utterances, and utterances that are of lower acoustic quality (e.g., the speaker mumbles or does not articulate clearly) are likely to result in greater degradations in adverse listening conditions. If the cognitive load of the listening task increases, then L2 listeners show a greater tendency to use bottom-up listening strategies to make sense of the speech signal, with weaker comprehension being the likely result.

Targeting pronunciation issues related to processing needs is crucial, but this is unlikely to be perceived by many teachers as being as important as segmentals or word stress. When we speak of loss of intelligibility, especially word-based intelligibility, the errors are more likely to be obvious. One word sounds like another and is misinterpreted, another word is mis-stressed and is unrecognizable, or sentences make no sense even though it seems like we may understand individual words. In loss of comprehensibility, understanding may come, but it will be slowed down. Or a listener and speaker may think the message has been understood, only to find later that the intended meaning was never communicated. Processing issues may also be connected to problems with segmentals or word stress (which can be identified as right or wrong), but they are more likely to involve suprasegmental issues of rhythm, focus, intonation, and speech features related to fluency. In contrast to segments and word stress, deviations in these areas are less likely to be heard as right or wrong, but instead are likely to be heard as strange or impolite or emotion-laden or to send messages that are unexpected or unclear. These higher levels of meaning making are subtler than low-level errors that lead to loss of intelligibility, but they are likely more important. Even the most pronunciation-impaired learners typically produce some words that are intelligible, but their communication may still be successful. Many research studies examine misunderstandings in constrained contexts such as syllables, vowels, word recognition, or sentence meaning. Processing difficulties may show up in these contexts, but their real impact is to be found in extended discourse, where weariness in interpreting unfamiliar speech may lead to increasing difficulty in following the message being communicated. All foreign-language learners speak in ways that can lead to slower processing, and all NSs speak in ways that may make them hard to understand for even the most advanced nonnative listener.

Guideline 3: Important lexical items should be given priority over less important items.

Communication in English is not just a matter of the right sounds but of the right words being understood, either in isolation or in context. This means that the pronunciation of vocabulary is central to an intelligibility-based approach. This especially involves the stress/unstress distinction and the teaching of key vocabulary.

In English, stress is an important factor in word recognition, although it does not always seem to be an essential clue, given that stress also affects vowel quality and the clear articulation of other segments (Cutler, 1986). Stress applies both to single-syllable and multi-syllable words. Cutler, Dahan, and van Donselaar, in a review of the role of prosody in spoken word recognition, say that English's "strong/weak syllable distinction is based primarily on a segmental property (vowel quality) rather than on a stress distinction" (1997, p. 148). Their review of the role of prosody in spoken word recognition states that, at a general level, listeners rely on strong and weak syllables to help them segment incoming speech. Listeners recognize unstressed words more slowly when the words are stressed incorrectly, puns based on stress shifts are typically less successful (presumably because they do not process quickly enough), and mis-stressed words that affect vowel quality are far more likely to inhibit word recognition. For example, mis-stressing *e'valu,ate* as *e,valu'ate* (typical of many L2 speakers) is unlikely to cause difficulty for listeners because both vowels are stressed anyway. Mis-stressing *e'valu‚ate* as *'eval‚uate*, on the other hand, is more likely to cause problems.

Word stress is important in measures of intelligibility because intelligibility is frequently a word-based phenomenon. The traditional approach to teaching the accurate pronunciation of words is to teach the accurate pronunciation of sounds, on the assumption that a collection of accurate sounds in the right order will lead to a recognizable word. Another approach is to teach the accurate pronunciation of words through prosodic features such as word stress, usually through predictive rules that have identifiable suffixes (e.g., Dauer, 1993; Grant, 2007; Kreidler, 2004), through rules that deal with groups of words that follow similar stress patterns (Murphy & Kandil, 2004), or through spelling patterns that go beyond recognizable suffixes (Dickerson, 1989; Hahn & Dickerson, 1999). Whatever the approach, all these approaches recognize the importance of pronouncing key vocabulary for intelligibility.

Probably the most common approach to teaching word-based pronunciation, especially of multi-syllabic words, is to use suffixes as clues to stress placement. Suffixes such as *–ic*, *–ion*, *–ate*, *–ity*, and others can be found in many textbooks. It is well known that English word stress is not fixed, always occurring on the same syllable, but is rather variable, so that the syllable that is stressed can be predicted by the suffixes on the word (Chomsky & Halle, 1968). Thus, the related words in (8.1) shift their stress because of their suffixes.

(8.1)

'SPEcify, spe'CIfic, speci'FICity

An example of this approach in Figure 8.1 can be seen in the excerpt from Dauer (1993, p. 79). Dauer gives seven rules for stressing words in English, some of which have up to four sub-rules. She also provides a table of forty-three suffixes and their pronunciations that can help determine the stress of multi-syllabic words. Clearly, using suffixes in English can be useful, but it is not hard to see that it also could place students under an enormous cognitive burden if the whole system is taught. This is another example of the need for priorities.

Murphy (2004) and Murphy and Kandil (2004) describe an approach to teaching the stress of words from the Academic Word List (AWL) (Coxhead, 2000). Since many words on the AWL are multi-syllabic, the approach employs syllable counts and numbers of stressed syllables to classify words. For example, *photograph* would be classified as 31 (three syllables, major stress on the first),

Stress the syllables in **boldface** type and reduce the underlined vowels.

1.	phot<u>o</u>graph	ph<u>o</u>t<u>o</u>graphy	phot<u>o</u>**graph**ic
3.	**dem**<u>o</u>crat	d<u>e</u>**mo**cr<u>a</u>cy	dem<u>o</u>**crat**<u>i</u>c
5.	**pol**<u>i</u>tics	p<u>o</u>**lit**<u>i</u>c<u>a</u>l	pol<u>i</u>**tic**<u>ia</u>n
7.	**comp**<u>e</u>t<u>e</u>nt	c<u>o</u>m**pet**it<u>o</u>r	comp<u>e</u>**tit**<u>io</u>n

Figure 8.1 Word-stress practice
Source: Adapted from Dauer (1993, p. 79)

photography would be classified 42, and *photographic* as 43. The approach assumes that acquiring the stress patterns of some words will provide a hook for learning words with the same stress patterns. The authors report that thirty-nine patterns are needed to cover all the AWL words, but that a smaller set of fourteen patterns gives more than 90 percent coverage. Anecdotally, the approach was reported to be successful with advanced learners taught to use it.

Teaching students to predict word stress from suffixes is one approach, but Dickerson (1989) provides rules that capture generalizations from final spelling patterns that not only include suffixes but also non-suffix spellings. These are used to predict stress of unknown words in the same way as the suffix approach. For example, the *–ion* suffix in English is easily identifiable for most literate learners, but other words without suffixes also have similar spelling patterns consisting of the letter i + another vowel, as in (8.2).

(8.2)

infla<u>ti</u>on, ra<u>di</u>o, fol<u>io</u>s, ra<u>di</u>um, soc<u>ia</u>l

Pronouncing words perfectly does not mean that a speaker will be understood, but not pronouncing important words intelligibly almost guarantees that connected speech will be less understandable. Key vocabulary has to be recognizable for the overall message to be understood. Nation (2002) says that listeners need to be able to understand at least 95 percent of words in a spoken text in order to be able to successfully navigate the words that are not understood. This suggests a reason why language learners, even at a very advanced level, often do not understand what is said. From a production point of view, learners who do not pronounce key vocabulary correctly cause listeners to work very hard to process the content of their speech.

One of the areas that the pronunciation of key vocabulary has been most emphasized is in the training of international teaching assistants (ITAs) at North American universities. In perhaps the most widely used book for training ITAs, Smith, Meyers, and Burkhalter (1992) provide extensive lists of field-specific vocabulary for a variety of academic fields, including biology, chemistry, electrical engineering, economics, computer science, and others. Their training materials assume that these field-specific terms, along with general academic terms that cut across fields (words such as *develop*) will comprise a large part of the content to help make ITAs more easily intelligible in their classroom teaching duties.

While this discussion has focused mostly on multi-syllabic vocabulary, the principle of importance applies to other key vocabulary. The word *usually*, for example, is commonly mispronounced by Chinese learners of English who produce something like *urally*. One way to teach such a word would be to teach learners how to say [ʒ] (this would be the traditional, sound-oriented approach). Alternatively, one could teach learners to recognize the spelling pattern that promotes the palatalization of the [z] into [ʒ], because of the following <u> vowel, following the pattern of words like *measure* and *casual*. Or, we can simply teach learners to pronounce the single high-frequency word *usually*, ignoring the more general patterns that may not be particularly learnable and still leave the learners saying *urally*. David Deterding (2009) reported on teaching Chinese learners in a study to say the words *you Shirley* (with an r-less British accent) and that the learners in the study improved greatly with what otherwise seemed like an intractable problem. The same principle applies to words like *months* and *clothes*, words frequently mispronounced as *monthes* and *closes* by learners who are valiantly trying to say a sounds that NSs do not.

One final set of important vocabulary should be mentioned. Although it is a small set of words, it has the potential for an oversized effect on how listeners react to NNSs. Mispronunciations sometimes lead listeners to hear taboo words rather than the intended word. From counting items of paper (where *piece* and *sheet* can sound like *piss* and *shit*) to words that would never enter my head as dangerous (such as *focus*), certain mispronunciations can cause embarrassment or can cause listeners to ignore the message. In one particularly mortifying situation, I once was taking a first-year French class that met right after lunch. I was the only graduate student in a class full of first- and second-year undergraduates. The instructor's native language was neither French nor English. Although she was supposed to teach only in French, she didn't always do so, especially when frustrated by the lack of enthusiastic response. One day, we were working on the vocabulary for a unit on the kitchen and meal preparation, and the students were more lethargic and less engaged than usual. She went from French to English to encourage responses, but when none were forthcoming about the utensils for eating, she blurted out in frustration: "A fork! Haven't you ever had a fork?" Her pronunciation of the word, with no /r/ and a somewhat centralized vowel, was electrifying. The sleepy football players sat up straight with a "What??" and the students all asked each other "What did she say?" At least five minutes later, when the students finally understood what she meant (though the teacher never learned what she had actually said, at least to my knowledge), the class finally began to calm down. I have never forgotten the uproar caused by that one unexpected pronunciation error. I have ever since believed that we do a service to our students when we call attention to these kinds of errors and offer ways around the problem, if at all possible.

Taboo words or sound-alikes are rarely causes of unintelligibility. Few situations have the extended explosive value seen in my French class. Nevertheless, these kinds of word-based errors are important because of a related concept: irritation. There are many situations in which someone can be perfectly intelligible yet express themselves in ways that are irritating to listeners. Irritation can come from the kind of shock we experience, but it can come from things that are much more mundane, such as any type of speech that is understandable yet unpleasant for some reason. Any kind of noticeable accent can lead to feelings of irritation, especially if the accent is associated with a group that the listener does not value. For words, the kinds of things that can cause irritation may include somewhat familiar yet unusual pronunciations that may be known (such as *dance* pronounced [dɑns] or *laugh* as [lɑf] for general American speakers, or r-ful pronunciations in an r-less area (e.g., *farm* said with the <r> rather than without), especially if the accent markers are socially salient (Preston, 1996). One difficulty with irritation is that the factors that irritate a listener are hard to predict beyond obvious cases like taboo sound-alikes. Another difficulty is that teaching to lessen a listener's irritation rather than teaching to promote communication places the burden for success back on the language learner. It also looks suspiciously like linguistic bigotry despite being clothed in well-meaning concern for another person's welfare. There is plenty of evidence that this kind of prejudice is not far from the surface in NS interactions with other NSs (Lippi-Green 1997), with NNSs (Munro, 2003), or even in perceptions of understanding where one expects someone to be accented (Rubin, 1992). Bias is pervasive, and teachers should be careful not to give it more importance than it deserves. However, it should not be ignored either.

Guideline 4: Contrasts with a high functional load are more important than those with low functional load.

FL attempts to quantify the likelihood of confusion from mispronunciations of particular sounds in a language. The principle is based on the fact that different phonemes in a language do different amounts of work in distinguishing one sound from another. Not all sounds are equally frequent, and not all sounds distinguish meaning among words to the same extent. Thus, FL is an attempt to measure the way different phonemes in a language distinguish one word from another, and by extension, the likelihood that mispronunciations of particular sounds will lead to misunderstandings. It is not a measure that can be applied to a particular phoneme in isolation, but rather, "it is only the contrasts between pairs of phonemes that can carry functional loads" (Brown, 1988, p. 594). In other words, FL "is a measure of the work two phonemes do in keeping utterances apart" (King, 1967, as cited by Munro & Derwing 2006, p. 522).

FL can be estimated by a number of factors, three of which are central. First, how many initial minimal pairs do two phonemes have? For example, the phonemes /p/ and /b/ have many minimal pairs in English, whereas the phonemes /θ/ and /ð/ have very few (*thigh–thy*), neither of which is very common or even necessarily present in any given variety of English. Applied to English spelling, the principle of FL suggests a reason why the two "th" sounds in English are represented by the same digraph. There is little likelihood of confusion between the two sounds, and thus there is little necessity to reflect the differences in orthography (Wells, 1986, as cited by Brown, 1988).

The second factor is the number of final minimal pairs that two sounds have. Phonemes in English, especially consonant phonemes, are highly contrastive at word ends, and two sounds that have many potential misunderstandings at word ends will have a higher FL than those that do not. The phonemes /l/ and /ɹ/, for example, constitute a contrast with the highest FL rating in the work of Brown (1988). At word ends, these two sounds not only occur in words like *feel/fear*, but also in contractions such as *we'll/we're* and *you'll/you're*. Mispronunciations of these sounds can thus not only mask the identity of a word but also the meaning of the grammar.

The final influence on FL is the likelihood that a distinction exists and is enforced in all varieties of English. While /p/–/b/ is a contrast that is universally enforced, other contrasts like /θ/–/f/ are not. The use of /f/ for /θ/ is widespread in British English and in African American English in the United States (e.g., *think* sounds like *fink*). While many speakers of English think such a substitution sounds uneducated or undesirable, this is not the same as intelligibility. Brown (1988) says that it is possible that "listeners are accustomed to making the perceptual adjustment necessary" (p. 598) for these incompletely enforced contrasts, and as a result, not producing the contrast is unlikely to be a great enough surprise to cause loss of intelligibility.

The small amount of empirical research done indicates that using FL to determine importance may be a useful way to classify potential errors. In the only study of its kind, Munro and Derwing (2006) tested both high FL and low FL contrasts from Catford's (1987) taxonomy. The high FL errors included /l/–/n/ (*light–night*), /s/–/ʃ/(*sell–shell*), and /d/–/z/ (*ride–rise*). The low FL errors included /ð/–/d/ (then–den) and /θ/–/f/ (three–free). Both high and low FL errors were selected from a database of sentences read by NNSs of English. Each sentence was rated by listeners who judged them for accentedness and perceived comprehensibility. The results confirmed the prediction that high FL errors are more serious than low FL errors. While the presence of even one low FL error resulted in a worse accentedness rating and perceived loss of comprehensibility than sentences with no errors at all, "high FL errors had a significantly greater effect on the listeners' ratings [for comprehensibility] than did low FL errors. Even sentences that contained only one high FL error were rated significantly worse for comprehensibility than sentences containing three low FL errors" (Munro & Derwing, 2006, p. 527). These results suggest that errors in phoneme contrasts that are higher in FL are more likely to be those errors that are classified as serious by listeners – that is, they are more likely to affect the comprehensibility of speech. Low FL errors, on the other hand, will result in a perception of accentedness and minor loss of comprehensibility, as would any deviation from what is expected, but it is unlikely that they would, by themselves, be serious enough to warrant instruction.

These results do not answer a number of other questions that are of interest. Because the sentences used in the study included only high FL errors or low FL errors, there is no information about the interaction between the errors. For example, if a sentence contains a high FL error and a low FL error, will it be rated significantly worse than a sentence with only a single high FL error? Errors rarely come in tidy packages of only high FL or only low FL, and while we can guess that the sentences with only high FL errors will correspond to the greatest loss in comprehensibility, we do not know this is so. A second question has to do with the effect of these types of errors on listeners over a longer stretch of discourse. Will the relative seriousness of the low FL errors continue to hold after reaching a limit, or will it eventually increase to a point where it becomes a serious barrier? The /θ/–/f/ contrast studied by Munro and Derwing (2006), for example, occupies the lowest spot on Brown's FL hierarchy, a rating of 1 on a 1–10 scale. If a hypothetical learner has only this kind of error, using /f/ for /θ/, will listeners simply get used to it and process the speech as quickly as if the expected sound was used? Or, will the error begin to carry a larger burden? Will the same pattern hold for errors that are higher in the FL hierarchy? The few errors tested do not give an answer.

Third, the errors examined in this study all involved consonant phonemes. Consonants are much more precisely articulated than vowels, which have a much less precisely defined perceptual space in which they may or may not be acceptably pronounced. Vowels also show greater variation between varieties of English, such that the connections between written form and the pronunciation associated with it can be quite different from one variety to the next. Brown's (1988) FL hierarchy is set up for the received pronunciation (RP) accent of British English, and while it is not clear how accurate the hierarchy is for other varieties, especially for vowels, it is likely to be similar. It would also be important to test the theory for other languages, since using multiple languages can often tell us interesting things about how listeners perceive language (Cutler, 2012).

Finally, a fourth question is raised by the research. Brown's FL hierarchy has ten steps. Munro and Derwing tested the extremes, and it is not clear at which point in the hierarchy errors move from low FL to high FL. Indeed, it is even possible that there is a category of mid-FL errors that behave differently than the two categories tested. To make the hierarchy more useful, we need to know more about the practical boundaries of the hierarchy and what factors may interact with FL (such as word frequency and the likelihood that minimal pairs will actually occur in the same contexts).

These four issues, as important as they are in making FL useful in determining priorities, miss perhaps a more crucial issue. FL is a system that measures the relative contribution of segmentals. Suprasegmentals have no place in the FL hierarchy. Derwing and Rossiter (2003) indicate that instruction in global and suprasegmental features is more likely to lead to improvements in comprehensibility than is instruction in segmentals. Even instruction in critical segmentals may not be effective in improving comprehensibility, especially in the short run. Neri, Cucchiarini, and Strik (2006) studied L2 learners of Dutch who received instruction in critical Dutch errors. Even though the learners improved their pronunciation of these highly noticeable Dutch phonemes, their comprehensibility did not improve. As important as high FL errors may be, it seems that improvement of segmentals alone, even critically important segmentals, may not be enough to provide an improvement that listeners actually notice in connected speech.

Word stress may also be related to the kinds of issues related to FL, given that problems with stress lead to word-based comprehension problems, as do vowel and consonant errors. FL, however, is measured in relation to contrast. Word stress has few examples of obvious contrasts, such as 'record versus re'cord. Most word-stress errors only show a contrast between correct and incorrect stress. As such, it is not clear how one could adapt the FL hierarchy to such a feature as word stress. Field (2005) shows that rightward mis-stressing of two-syllable words does not have an equal effect to leftward mis-stressing, so it is likely that word-stress errors have their own equivalent of an FL hierarchy (but see Richards, 2016). However, we do not know. If we wish to quantify the relative contributions of other suprasegmental features, such as rhythm, focus, and intonation, we have no equivalent system to the FL hierarchy. This makes it important that we examine other principles to help determine priorities.

Guideline 5: Errors that are frequent are more important than those that are infrequent.

This guideline says that the relative frequency of errors is related to how those errors impact comprehensibility. The base belief of this principle is that speech that contains a greater number of errors will be less understandable than speech that contains fewer errors. In other words, all things being equal, speech with many errors is more likely to cause difficulties for listeners than speech with fewer errors. Applied to segmentals, speech with a larger number of phonetic and phonemic errors will cause listeners more trouble than speech with fewer errors. Prator and Robinett state this principle when they assert that "unintelligibility ... [is] the cumulative effect of many little departures from the phonetic norms of the language. A great many of these may be phonemic – many others are not. Under certain circumstances any abnormality of speech may contribute to unintelligibility" (1985, p. xxii). There are two elements to Prator and Robinett's statement that are notable. The first is that any error can affect a listener's ability to understand at some level. The second is that a larger number of errors per number of words is likely to lead to a greater loss of intelligibility.

Applied to suprasegmentals, frequency may be a reason why deviations in this part of a language's pronunciation can be so serious, leading to loss of understanding both of the meaning and processing of speech (comprehensibility) and understanding the intent of an utterance in discourse, or interpretability (Low, 2006). One cannot speak without suprasegmentals, yet it appears that perception of language-specific suprasegmental patterns may not always be noticeable to L2 learners (Pennington & Ellis, 2000). As a result, L2 learners are likely to use suprasegmentals that are unfamiliar to NS listeners. Like a familiar musical theme heard in an unexpected context, language with unexpected suprasegmentals can take longer to recognize.

What studies have examined frequency? Very few have actually controlled frequency as a variable, but the Munro and Derwing (2006) study on FL offers some evidence that frequency may sometimes cause greater problems with understanding while at other times there is no cumulative effect. In the sentences used in the study, Munro and Derwing included sentences with one, two, and three errors, all within either the high FL or low FL categories. Low FL errors did not seem to show any effect of frequency in accentedness ratings. As the authors say

the presence of one, two or three low FL errors resulted in significantly worse judgments of accent than the presence of no errors. However, sentences with two or three low FL errors were not rated as more accented than sentences that contained a single FL error. In other words, there was no evidence of a cumulative effect of low FL errors on accentedness.   (Munro & Derwing, 2006, p. 527)

The same pattern held for comprehensibility ratings. Sentences with more than one low FL error were no less comprehensible than sentences with two or three. Whether such a frequency effect would hold for longer stretches of speech is unknown, but it appears that frequency by itself may not always be a critical factor in listener judgments.

There is a different pattern for high FL errors, especially with regard to accentedness, where more than one error led to significantly lower ratings:

Although ... the presence of one or two high FL errors led to a significant increase in the perception of accentedness over the no-error condition, sentences containing two high FL errors were rated as significantly more accented than sentences containing only one high FL error. In other words, a cumulative effect of high FL errors was seen.   (Munro & Derwing, 2006, p. 527)

Comprehensibility ratings did not show the same effect, with two high FL errors being rated as being just as comprehensible as one. There were no sentences with three high FL errors, so we do not know if an extra increase in frequency would lead to a change in comprehensibility ratings. The authors conclude that "it may be … that numbers of segmental errors alone do not account fully for variability in accentedness or comprehensibility. Rather, the nature of the errors may affect their performance" (2006, p. 530). In other words, some errors show an effect of frequency while others do not. Does accentedness matter? It is clear from earlier research that speakers can be seen as heavily accented yet be completely intelligible (Munro & Derwing, 1999). It was also clear that accentedness ratings positively correlated with comprehensibility, although the strength of the correlation varied widely. While this particular study does not show a significant connection between accentedness and comprehensibility, listeners may feel that greater accentedness (difference) in speech takes more effort to understand, leading to a loss of comprehensibility.

Another study suggests a link between numbers of errors and spoken proficiency ratings. Im and Levis (2015) studied how raters stopped while listening to a videotaped presentation by three different Korean speakers giving a professional presentation in English. All three had independently been rated at different spoken proficiency levels. Raters were instructed in using verbal protocols (think aloud) and told to stop every time they heard a language error and then to explain what the error was. A major goal of the study was to examine whether proficiency was related to frequency of segmental errors. The authors found that raters stopped significantly less often for the presenter who had already been rated at the highest proficiency level than for the other two presenters, for whom there was no difference. There was no independent count of errors, but the different number of think-aloud stops suggests that proficiency may be related to the number of easily identifiable errors. This study is a little bit of a chicken-and-egg quandary. Are the lower-proficiency speakers rated that way because they make more pronunciation errors or do they simply make more errors because they are lower in proficiency?

Another element of frequency relates to the frequency of particular phonemes. This is partially connected to issues of FL, but this frequency count does not require contrasts. Certain phonemes in English simply are not very common, such as the [ʊ] in words like *cook* and *pull* or the [ʒ] in words like *usually* and *measure*. They do not have many minimal pairs with easily confused phonemes because there are simply not many words that contain the sound. For example, /ʊ/ is a very difficult sound for many learners of English, who typically substitute the [u] for it and find it a difficult sound to hear and produce. Thus, *cook* may be pronounced like *kook* and *pull* like *pool*. Frequency suggests that the sound is not terribly important, even though it is present in a large number of common words (such as the auxiliaries *should, could, would*). [ʒ] is also often mispronounced, yet its rarity in English words means that it will almost never be confused with other words. In an examination of the word frequency of minimal pairs from pronunciation course books, I found that a minority of the words used could be counted among the 2,000 most frequent words in English, and even fewer minimal pairs had both words that frequent.

The same frequency issues relate to the words in which the problematic phonemes are said. Many words that are used to teach pronunciation are rare in corpora of spoken and written English. Examining minimal pairs for /i–ɪ/ and /θ–s, t, f/, Levis and Cortes (2008) found that books typically present minimal pairs in which at least one item is rare, suggesting that the kinds of problems learners have may be more profitably addressed by attending to particular words rather than the sounds they encompass. As mentioned in Guideline 3, the [ʒ] in *usually* is important because the word is common in spoken language. Other words containing [ʒ] are much less commonly used and so are less likely to cause problems with understanding.

The evidence for frequency being a primary determinant of intelligibility is mixed. While there is evidence that one error in a sentence leads to some loss of comprehensibility, there is less evidence that more than one error adds to the listener's burden. Unfortunately, we do not know how true this is at the discourse level, and whether one or more errors per sentence over many sentences will show the same kind of effect.

The effects of frequency on spoken intelligibility are connected to how speakers of a language understand and process language. According to Ellis (2002), unconscious and largely accurate judgments of whether a string of sounds is a word are based on language users' knowledge of frequency effects – that is, whether that string of phonemes is more or less likely to be a word. Frequency is the principle by which language users access possible words, using phonological and phonotactic knowledge to access likely words in their internal lexicons. High-frequency words are more quickly recognized in speech than are low-frequency words. The research that Ellis reports involves NS listeners' processes of recognition. In listening to NNS speech, one can guess that the processing effects would be much greater, and that greater numbers of errors in spoken language would limit the usefulness of the frequency patterns that allow NS listeners to quickly recognize language spoken by other NSs. These frequency effects on spoken word recognition suggest that errors in beginning sounds in a word may be more critical than errors in later sounds because of a cohort effect that can activate the wrong cohort of possible words. The cohort effect is based on the fact that

> our implicit knowledge of phonotactics is found in cohort effects in spoken-word recognition. We seem to handle this by using the initial phoneme of a word to activate the set of all words in the lexicon that have this same phoneme. Then, as the speech signal unfolds over time and more information is received, we narrow the set down. In the cohort model of speech recognition ... activation in the cohort varies so that items are not simply "in" or "out." Rather, higher frequency words get more activation from the same evidence than do low-frequency words. This assumption provides a means for accounting for lexical similarity effects whereby a whole neighborhood of words is activated but the higher frequency words get more activation. The result is that listeners are slower to recognize low-frequency words with high-frequency neighbors because the competitors are harder to eliminate ... These effects demonstrate that our language-processing system is sensitive both to the frequency of individual words and to the number of words that share the same beginnings.   (Ellis, 2002, p. 150)

Guideline 6: Features that are learnable should be prioritized over those that are not.

This guideline is one that is intuitively appealing but also can lead to a great deal of misunderstanding. The principle is sometimes stated in terms of teachability and sometimes learnability, even though teachability and learnability refer to very different concepts. Teachability seems to refer to whether a teacher can successfully present and practice particular pronunciation features in a classroom context. Learnability is whether input and practice, whether from a teacher or another source, results in successful learning. I do not intend to revisit Krashen's (1985) division between learning (whether learners can consciously learn language and make use of it when thinking about their production) and acquisition (whether learners can use language unconsciously because of how they have learned it). There have been many debates about this concept of learning and whether learning can become acquisition. Instead, I will assume that any language feature that is learned consciously can at some point become automatic in most contexts.

In her groundbreaking recommendations for EIL/ELF pronunciation, Jenkins (2000) makes the argument that certain features should not be included in the Lingua Franca Core because they are not essential for mutual international intelligibility. Among these are word stress and intonation. Her exclusion of these features comes from two considerations. First, they did not unambiguously lead to loss of intelligibility in her interactional data. Word stress was indirectly connected to some loss of intelligibility, but segmental features seemed to cause the greatest loss of intelligibility. Intonation, on the other hand, was never implicated in loss of intelligibility, not a surprising finding given intonation's connection to higher-level processing rather than simple loss of lexical intelligibility (Low, 2006).

Second, the non-core features are said to be unteachable. Jenkins asserts that "as many pronunciation teachers are aware, some of these features seem to be unteachable. That is, no matter how much classroom time is spent on them, learners do not acquire them" (2002, p. 97). For word stress, Jenkins cites the variability in multi-syllabic word stress in native varieties of English and the complexity of the rules put forth to teach word stress. For intonation, Jenkins suggests that the best a teacher can hope for is to raise awareness of the relevant patterns that are possible and then leave acquisition to learners who are immersed in English-speaking environments. Walker (2010) takes up this notion of teachability, suggesting, in agreement with Jenkins, that stress timing, the use of weak forms, certain connected speech changes, and vowel quality distinctions are also unteachable.

The main problem with using teachability as a criterion for any pronunciation feature (indeed for almost anything) is that it is a specious argument. Anything is teachable. For example, Pike (1945) and O'Connor and Arnold (1961) both had great success teaching intonation in American and British English. Dickerson (1989) has found success over many years in teaching word stress using complex rules based partly on Chomsky and Halle's (1968) research. All teachers have had students, often many students, who learn features that other students do not learn. Saying something is not teachable says little more than that the teacher does not think teaching a feature is worth it. This says a lot about the teacher, but little about the pronunciation feature or the learner.

My arguments, however, somewhat misrepresent Jenkins' idea of teachability and suggest that describing certain features as teachable and others as unteachable is an unfortunate choice of terms. Teachability for features like nuclear stress, for example, comes because of "the clear-cut, generative nature of their rules" (Jenkins, 2002, p. 2). Features that "can only be acquired through extensive (and probably non-pedagogic) exposure to the second language" (p. 107) are by definition not teachable. Other features may be unteachable "in the sense that learning will not follow classroom teaching" (p. 119) because of the strength of L1 transfer or the power of developmental sequences. However, even if features are not teachable, learners may be able to acquire them over time through exposure to the L2, especially if teachers draw attention to them, priming learners "for future learning by being made explicitly aware of features in the spoken output in receptive pronunciation work, without focusing on these features in productive work" (p. 133). This characterization looks suspiciously like teaching using perception practice, in which learning may follow teaching, albeit at a greater distance. Items that are unteachable may, in fact, become teachable if learners are motivated to learn something that they see as improving their own intelligibility. Suspiciously, items that are core to EIL intelligibility are all teachable, while those that are non-core all fall into the unteachable category (see, for example, p. 133), an oddly circular definition, given the paucity of persuasive evidence available.

Jenkins also bases her concepts of teachability and learnability on a well-known fact: What we teach does not invariably relate to what learners learn. So only those features that clearly lead to learning in the classroom are said to be teachable, even though "we cannot guarantee that all learners will make an effort to learn the core or, subsequent to learning, will actually use it at all times in all appropriate interactions" (Jenkins, 2002, p. 165). One reason that features may not be teachable (and therefore not learnable) is that learners see no relevance in them and no need to put forth sufficient effort to change (p. 133). Her conclusion is that we must distinguish between learning that can occur within a classroom context and that which cannot, in that it can only be acquired through exposure.

How do we identify unteachable and teachable items? Jenkins says that "the identification of unteachable items is, to some extent, a matter of common sense and experience, It is also predictable from a knowledge of transfer effects" (p. 133) and an understanding of marked and unmarked sounds, although "it is by no means clear that *marked* equals *unteachable* " (p. 134, italics in original).

Teachability and learnability are put forth as being intimately connected. Learnability suggests that we know that there are things that L2 learners of a particular L1 background or L2 learners in general simply cannot succeed with, a kind of built-in fossilization factor. If this were true, it would be very helpful for a teacher to know which features fall into the category of non-learnable. However, this assertion is as suspect as teachability because there is no list of items that are not learnable. Some features may be harder, or more marked, but even Jenkins says that these features may still be important for intelligibility or may be quite learnable. But almost anything is learnable, even in foreign-language pronunciation. Learners may not be perfect, but that is not the goal. A person may not be a professional player when playing basketball, but can still play and perhaps even play well.

We all have had learners who are hard to understand yet produce perfect [θ] and [ð] sounds. Learning a new sound or sound pattern may take time, it may be difficult, it may be subject to a mixture of correct and incorrect forms before mastery, and it may even be subject to significant backsliding in more demanding communicative contexts (such as Eliza Doolittle's trip to the races at Ascot in *My Fair Lady*), but this does not mean that the feature is not learnable. It simply means that features do not move from fully monitored to fully automatic with no in-between stages.

Some evidence that certain features may be less learnable than others come from Pennington and Ellis (2000), who examined Cantonese learners' ability to recognize several aspects of English intonation/stress. The four features they examined were

- contrastive sentence focus (*Is HE driving the bus?* versus *Is he driving the BUS?*);
- final pitch movement on tags (*He's going, isn't he?* rising versus falling);
- phrasing (*The fight is over, Fred* versus *The fight is over Fred*); and
- internal phrase structure (*She's a lighthouse keeper* versus *She's a light housekeeper*).

The researchers examined recognition tasks when there was no previous instruction, and when there was previous instruction. They found that subjects performed well in terms of recognizing the words and grammar of previously heard sentences when prosodic form was not tested, but that they performed poorly on recognizing previously heard sentences if the prosodic form was included. This was especially so when there was not previous explicit focus on form.

Next, Pennington and Ellis trained learners by explicitly focusing on the prosodic form for each of the four areas. The training increased recognition ability only for contrastive sentence focus. The other aspects of intonation/stress did not improve, suggesting that only contrastive focus was learnable, *given the amount and type of instruction and given the time involved in the study's treatment*. This caveat is critical in discussions of learnability.

Why did only contrastive sentence focus show improvement? The researchers said that "... certain aspects of prosody – such as the relatively universal relationship of enhanced prosody and marked meaning, as contrasted with neutral prosody and unmarked meaning – can be more readily taught than some other more language-specific aspects [of prosody]" (Pennington & Ellis, 2000, p. 387). This is the crux of the learnability arguments. Some features are more amenable to instruction than others.

It should also be evident that some features may not be worth teaching for other reasons or for all learners. Levis (1999a) argued that pitch movement differences on certain types of grammatical forms (e.g., yes–no questions) are not important to teach because the differences between rising and falling do not reflect easily understood categorical changes in meaning. In contrast, the difference between rising and falling pitch on declaratives or on phrases would be crucial because of the obvious differences in meaning. Thompson (1995) analyzed the differences between rising and falling pitch for yes–no questions as well, describing how pitch choices could lead to pragmatic differences in how the questions were interpreted (that is, whether they were polite or business-like). It is possible that this information could be of use to some learners while being too much for others. In either case, it does not mean the information is not learnable.

Other studies show that learning for L2 pronunciation does occur for a wide variety of features. Some of these findings come from classrooms, while others come from laboratory conditions. Wang and Munro (2004) found that learners of English improved their perception of three English vowel pairs. Learners were Mandarin and Cantonese L1 speakers and had a large amount of control over how much they worked on computer-presented stimuli. Their perception not only improved, but the improvement was sustained for three months and transferred to novel stimuli. Hardison (2004) studied the computer-assisted improvement of learners of French who were given training in French prosody (specifically, intonation). Their productions of French sentences were rated for prosodic appropriateness and showed improvement and extension to novel utterances. In addition, as learners became more familiar with the exemplar sentences used to focus attention on prosody, they also began to notice and make improvements in segmental features and liaison, which were not taught during the training. In another study of a particularly difficult segmental contrast, Bradlow, Pisoni, Akahane-Yamada, and Tohkura (1997) found that training Japanese L1 learners to recognize English /l/ and /ɹ/ with high-variability input (i.e., multiple voices) led to improvements in their being able to recognize these sounds, as well as improvement in their accurate production of the two sounds. Follow-up research (Bradlow, Akahane-Yamada, Pisoni, & Tohkura, 1999) showed that these improvements persisted over time. Similar findings of improvement have been documented by Hirata (2004) for American English L1 learners learning Japanese vowels and consonant length distinctions. Learners who were trained both at the word and sentence level showed improvement in Japanese length distinctions, but the ability to generalize length distinctions was greater for those who learned in the sentence context. In a further study, Hirata (2004) found that computer training was effective for English speakers learning pitch accent and duration contrasts in Japanese. In this study, training in production led to improvements in both production and perception, an interesting counterpoint to Bradlow et al. (1997), in which perceptual training led to improvements in both perception and production. Many other studies show that disparate features of pronunciation are learnable, and that computer-assisted and human-led instruction can be successful. As a result, while learners do not always learn what we teach, neither do they learn something quite different. Teaching can lead to learning.

The teachability/learnability issue has greater importance if we see it as an argument that certain features are not acquirable in the long run, no matter what we do to teach effectively or no matter how much effort learners put into learning. This is a far more serious issue, and indeed may be the only one we need to pay attention to when looking at whether a feature is learnable. If learning will not last, then no one should waste time on such a pronunciation feature, no matter how interesting it may be to teachers or how interesting to learners. Unfortunately, we have very little evidence that any features fit into this category. Partly, this comes from the paucity of longitudinal studies of pronunciation development. Partly, it comes from our own inability to determine where a valid achievement point would be between zero mastery and complete automaticity. Jenkins (2000) suggests that many of the items that are not teachable can still be ultimately acquired, given sufficient exposure, and presumably, a learner who is primed, either through instruction or through exposure, to notice the features.

There is some evidence that certain features may be acquirable over the long run, both as the result of instruction and through exposure. M. Hahn (2002) studied the acquisition of prominence (i.e., nuclear stress) by advanced learners in the United States. Subjects had been placed into a pronunciation class through a placement test, and as part of the class had learned nine rules describing patterns for primary stress placement in English. Subjects were given a pretest (T1) and a posttest (T2) during the class, at the beginning and end of a fifteen-week term of study. They were then given a delayed posttest (T3) at various times after they had taken the course, up to three years later. Improvement from T1 to T2 was significantly higher. However, the percentage correct decreased at T3, indicating that improvement did not last for all patterns.

Other research carried out by Munro and Derwing (2008), Derwing, Thomson, and Munro (2006) and Derwing, Munro, and

Thomson (2007) examined the acquisition of English vowels and fluency for Mandarin and Slavic learners of English who were immigrants to Canada. In the first study, the researchers demonstrated that recent arrivals to Canada acquired some English vowels without instruction, but that initial acquisition plateaued within the first year and that different vowels were acquired at different rates. The results suggested that certain features could be acquired without instruction. Regarding fluency, the research found that Slavic speakers' perceived fluency improved over time more than the fluency of the Mandarin speakers, even though both groups had started at the same levels. This improvement in fluency and perceived comprehensibility may have occurred because Slavic speakers reported greater interactions with those outside their own communities compared to Mandarin speakers, leading to greater opportunities both to notice English speakers' speech and to use English in interaction. This research suggests that greater exposure can lead to greater improvement, but it also suggests that exposure alone is not sufficient for most learners. Other research on pronunciation teaching is discussed in greater detail in Chapters 9 and 10.

The jury is still out as to the ultimate value of teachability/learnability as a guideline whose goals cannot be met by other guidelines. Whether something is learnable within the confines of a class and whether that learning can be sustained and built on in later learning outside the classroom would be very important in setting priorities for intelligibility-based instruction. Teaching priorities should be based on both short-term and long-term learning of pronunciation. While it seems clear that any pronunciation target can be learned in the short run, we need greater information about what kinds of teaching techniques make learning stick, and what types of features are most learnable for certain types of learners. The more information we have, the greater will be our ability to make teachability and learnability part of our decisions.

Conclusion

Teaching for intelligibility means setting priorities for what is taught. Teachers do this all the time whenever they teach. There are always decisions to be made about what to teach and what to leave out, about which chapters in a course book to emphasize and which to skip over, and about how to use the limited time we have with our students. We can give homework, send students to language labs for extra practice, or work on making them autonomous learners who can take charge of their own learning more successfully. But there is no teaching context in which we do not have to set priorities. In this, pronunciation is no different from any other language-teaching topic or skill area. However, there are ways in which pronunciation is different. We know that teachers often do not teach it in spite of their stated beliefs that it is important. Even when it is taught, it may take up only a small portion of available teaching time, making it even more important that the topics and skills that are taught are critical both in potential for listening and speaking improvement and in likelihood of being successfully taught and learned.

The six guidelines proposed here are an attempt to provide context-sensitive principles that can help teachers determine what is more or less important. They are also call for researchers to provide evidence for or against the guidelines. Derwing and Munro (2005) appealed for more research upon which pedagogical decisions can be based. In the years since their appeal, we have seen more and more research that fits their recommendations, but the research remains a trickle. We need a torrent. Until that happens, guidelines such as those presented here will necessarily be based on an overly shaky foundation and overly subject to the best intuitions we can make use of.

All of the guidelines are based on certain beliefs that are rarely addressed explicitly within pronunciation-teaching materials. First, pronunciation only makes sense in relation to a bigger picture of listening and speaking skills. Pronunciation is, and must be, a necessary but subservient skill. We cannot speak without pronouncing, and accented and error-laden pronunciation can get in the way of successful communication. When it does, it needs to be addressed wisely and explicitly. In listening, many of the difficulties that learners face are pronunciation-based and cannot be quickly learned without explicitly addressing the phonetic details of the spoken language. Words in context frequently do not sound like words in isolation because pronunciation changes and varies according to context and register.

Second, pronunciation should not be addressed as an ad hoc part of language teaching, but instead it should be incorporated in substantial ways that are critical to communication. In most integrated texts, pronunciation is included in the same way that salt and pepper are included with meals, that is, it is ok in small doses. Pronunciation is thus included by many teachers for lesson-plan seasoning, but if it is skipped, teachers may feel that they are still giving students the meat of the lesson. In contrast, I am arguing that pronunciation is not just seasoning, but rather essential for the development of listening and speaking skills. We would never teach basic listening and speaking only as problems come up. Instead, we determine what students' needs are and then plan for them. Such planning must make reference to pronunciation as well. We cannot afford to wait until learners are advanced in other areas before we go back and fix entrenched pronunciation errors. Pronunciation is appropriate even at the beginning of learning (Zielinski & Yates, 2014).

Finally, the guidelines are meant to be interpreted differently by teachers in different contexts or when they are teaching students with differing levels of proficiency. In other words, priorities will vary with the teaching context and the types of learners and learner goals. They will also vary with the comfort level of the teacher with various topics and the teacher's level of training. We have seen that pronunciation priorities must be nuanced – that is, they must be determined not with regard to large categories of goals but with regard to critical student needs for communication. Some consonant sounds may be critical, but not all. Some word-stress issues will pay off with great improvement, but others may be a waste of time. The guidelines do not offer a quick fix, but a starting point for teaching specific learners in specific contexts. This is as it should be. No single set of targets will be right for all learners and all teachers. Rather than providing such a set of targets, the guidelines recognize that teachers are professionals who make such decisions about priorities for other language skills every day. Their ability to make decisions about pronunciation should be no different than any other area of language teaching.

9 *The Intelligibility-Based Classroom*

Introduction

A long-desired goal among pronunciation practitioners has been to see pronunciation overcome its Cinderella status in language teaching (Celce-Murcia, Brinton, Goodwin, & Griner, 2010; Dalton & Seidl-hofer, 1994; Kelly, 1969). The Cinderella metaphor suggests that pronunciation has been denied its proper and equal place in the language-teaching household, made instead to labor unseen while other skills receive adulation and recognition.

The first use of the Cinderella metaphor (Kelly, 1969), oddly enough, indicated the exact opposite of how the metaphor is often used today. Instead, it stated that pronunciation had finally achieved its proper place through a recognition of its importance in language teaching. Kelly's metaphor should be read in the context of the time, starting with the close connections between language teaching and the establishment of the International Phonetic Association in the late 1800s, to the development of new oral language-teaching methods in the early 1900s and the dominance of Audiolingual teaching in the United States and Oral-Situational teaching in the United Kingdom during the 1940s to 1960s. So by the time of Kelly (1969), pronunciation was presented as no longer being Cinderella (Levis & Sonsaat, 2017).

But why has the Cinderella metaphor endured? At the time Kelly wrote, language teaching was in the midst of a revolution that only became evident with time. The dominant language-teaching approaches, Audiolingualism and Oral-Situational teaching, were already being challenged by paradigm changes in linguistics, psychology, and learning theory rooted in biology. The Structural approach that had dominated linguistics for decades had been upended by the Generative-Transformational approach of Noam Chomsky (e.g., Chomsky, 1965), Skinner's Behaviorist paradigm was called into question by new paradigms in psychology (Krasner, 1978), and Chomsky's challenge (1959) from generative linguistics, while research into biological systems and critical periods (e.g., Lenneberg, 1967; Scovel, 1969) raised serious questions about the assumption that second-language learners could ever become native in their second language, a claim that was especially consequential for second-language pronunciation attainment.

The Changing Role of Pronunciation

A consequence of the cognitive revolutions in linguistics, psychology, biology, and language teaching was that the 1970s saw a related revolution in language-teaching approaches. Comprehension-based approaches to teaching such as Total Physical Response (Asher, 1969) and the Natural Approach (Krashen & Terrell, 1983; Terrell, 1977), psychology-based approaches such as Curran's Counseling Learning (Curran, 1961, 1976), Gattegno's Silent Way (Stevick, 1976), and Lozanov's Suggestopedia (Bancroft, 1976); and the ever-changing Communicative Approaches (e.g., Widdowson, 1972; Wilkins, 1976) that ultimately came to dominate language teaching all had their beginnings in the churning language-teaching world following the changes of the 1960s.

Each of these approaches to language teaching had a different view of how instruction affected the development of pronunciation skills. At the risk of simplifying the great variations of that time, comprehension-based approaches largely expected pronunciation to take care of itself (i.e., it largely wasn't taught, though see Terrell, 1989) as long as the learners went through appropriate learning procedures (with comprehension preceding production). Psychology-based approaches focused on the learners, and assumed learning could be most effective if the learners were attended to appropriately using counseling techniques, in settings that made them less anxious, and with techniques that engaged them in learning. In most of these approaches, pronunciation continued to hold a central place. But in the communicative approaches, pronunciation found itself once again shut out of the language-teaching ball, partly because of the research that suggested native pronunciation to be unattainable by adult language learners, and partly because the approach itself focused on the development of communicative ability ("use") rather than the form of the language ("usage"). Pronunciation was usage, not use. Cinderella had been invited to the ball by the late 1960s, but the nature of the ball changed in the communicative era, and Cinderella was once again on the outside looking in.

As in all revolutions, the role of pronunciation greatly changed, at least in how it was viewed, though actual practice sometimes took much longer to change. In the short run, because native accents were highly unlikely, an assumption was made by many that pronunciation was not worth teaching. Pronunciation experts still existed and in some ESL (English as a second language) programs in the 1970s and beyond, they influenced many teachers; however, there was no in-between. Either pronunciation was still considered important, or it largely disappeared from language-teacher training. Many researchers and teachers, especially in the growing field of TESOL (teaching English to speakers of other languages), objected to this disappearance, and argued for a continuing role for pronunciation during the 1970s (e.g., Parish, 1977; Stevick, 1978; Stevick, Morley, & Robinett, 1975; Strevens, 1974). Pronunciation continued to be written about and researched, despite the ascendancy of the communicative approach (Levis & Sonsaat, 2017), but it was not until pronunciation itself adjusted to the new paradigm that its role began to change in the wider field (see Morley [1991], for an early take on the changing paradigm).

An early article with long-lasting impact was that of Hinofotis and Bailey (1981), which documented the importance of pronunciation that was *good enough* – that is, intelligible. The article examined the communication skills of international teaching assistants (ITAs) in the United States. (It is hard to underestimate the importance of ITA work in the changing role of pronunciation, and the research done with ITAs went hand in hand with many of the changes in L2 pronunciation teaching.) These nonnative speakers (NNSs) of English were mostly graduate students in what we today call STEM (science, technology, engineering, mathematics) fields. Their graduate education was funded by their working as teaching assistants, sometimes lecturing to beginning college students, sometimes grading for professors, sometimes supervising laboratory sessions, etc. The fact that they were admitted to graduate programs taught in a foreign language demonstrates the high proficiency of their English language skills. But many, despite high proficiency in academic English, could not speak in such a way that they were easily understood. Hinofotis and Bailey argued that their primary need was for pronunciation instruction to improve intelligibility.

Because nativeness was a binary distinction, nonnative pronouncers could not by definition become native. Furthermore, the assertion that pronunciation was particularly prone to fossilization (Selinker, 1972), with all that metaphor implies, suggested that changes in pronunciation were unlikely. The proposal that the learners who could not become native-like could become more intelligible was part of a broader change in how pronunciation became relevant again. Because intelligibility was not binary, language learners could be more intelligible without becoming native. And the assumption of fossilization was called into question by Acton (1984), who described how fossilized pronunciation could become unfossilized – that is, how seemingly stuck learners could still improve their pronunciation.

Besides the growing importance of intelligibility, pronunciation's relevance in other areas of language teaching and learning became central to communicative approaches. One of the most important of these was a greater importance placed on suprasegmentals (stress, rhythm, intonation) and voice quality (Esling & Wong, 1983; Kenworthy, 1987) for speaking. Unlike segmentals, suprasegmentals were an easier fit with approaches that placed importance on fluent productions of longer stretches of speech (discourse). This is because, by their very nature, they applied to discourse and communicated meaning about the relative importance of information (Brazil, Coulthard, & Johns, 1980; Halliday, 1967) and the pragmatic appropriateness of a message (Thompson, 1995). In addition, pronunciation was asserted to be relevant to almost every other language and learning-related area, including self-monitoring, speech awareness, new ways of thinking about the roles of teachers and learners, connections to sound–spelling relationships, listening skills, and real-life communication skills (Morley, 1991).

The Nativeness Principle and the Intelligibility Principle

Underneath all of these changes regarding the role of pronunciation in language learning was a continuing tension about teaching pronunciation. Although pronunciation was important for intelligibility, and intelligibility did not mean nativeness, the assumption of native-like attainment continued to be influential if only because it allowed for a clear sense of the end goal. Intelligibility had no easily specified level of attainment. These contrasting principles, the "Intelligibility Principle" and the "Nativeness Principle" (Levis, 2005a), have continued to vie for supremacy in pronunciation pedagogy. The Nativeness Principle is well-established and has been at the heart of most L2 pronunciation teaching. It assumes that the goal of pronunciation teaching is to achieve an accent that is virtually indistinguishable from that of an educated native speaker (NS), and that instruction should be based on those features that mark a speaker as nonnative. The Intelligibility Principle, in contrast, is advocated in some form by most researchers and many teachers. It assumes that accents are a normal part of speaking a foreign language, and that instruction should target primarily those features that will impact understanding, whether that is in understanding others or in being understood. The Intelligibility Principle also assumes that not all features of a foreign accent are equally important in promoting understanding of the speaker's message. In addition, these two principles make other assumptions about other elements of the teaching and learning process, as in Table 9.1.

Table 9.1 Differences implied by the Nativeness Principle and the Intelligibility Principle

	Nativeness	Intelligibility
Overall goal	Speak with a native accent.	Speak so that your message is understood, and listen to others so that you are able to understand.
Targets	All deviant pronunciations.	Primarily deviations that affect understanding.
Teachers	Native speakers, preferably trained.	Any intelligible speaker with training.
Learners	Learners of any age can (and should) become native-like if they are taught correctly.	Age of onset affects how native-like one can become, but intelligibility can always be improved.
Model	Native prestige models, especially those of the United Kingdom (received pronunciation, or RP) and the United States (general American, or GA).	Any intelligible model of English. Intelligibility is a complex interaction of speakers, listeners, and context.
Perception/ production	Native-like production is the primary goal of teaching pronunciation.	Perception and production are both important for intelligibility.
Who are the listeners (and therefore judges of intelligibility)?	Native speakers	Native and nonnative speakers
What are the evaluations of speaking with a foreign accent?	L2 learners are deficient when they continue to have an accent. Comments like "heavy accent" suggest the extent of the deficiency.	Accents are normal and expected. Accents are not directly related to intelligibility.

There is a challenge in implementing these two principles in that they are not always easy to distinguish in practice. Most teachers of pronunciation who believe that intelligibility is important may also defend the teaching of sounds that are primarily markers of nativeness. Take, for example, /θ/, as in *think, nothing*, and *both*. This sound is relatively rare in the world's languages and is therefore a distinctive marker in many varieties of English, and especially in the reference accents of RP and GA. It is also a sound that is extremely salient to many native listeners, who criticize errors with it, and to learners of English, who frequently request instruction for it. And it is a relatively teachable sound, given that it is visible and easy to feel (with the tongue tip at or between the teeth). But there is very little evidence that mispronunciations of /θ/ are likely to lead to misunderstanding of the speaker's message because of a number of factors. First, /θ/ has a number of well-known variations used by NSs of English, such as [f] and [t]. African American speakers in the United States and many speakers in the United Kingdom use [f], as in *fink, nuffing*, and *bof* (for *think, nothing*, and *both*). Social class pronunciations of /θ/ as [t] are widely known. /θ/ pronounced as [s] is not a typical native variation, but it is a stereotyped nonnative pronunciation (e.g., "I sink so" for "I think so"). When /θ/ is pronounced as [t], [f], or [s], its functional load is almost always low to moderate. Brown (1988) lists /θ-s/ as five on a ten-point scale, /θ-t/ as four, and /θ-f/ as one, the lowest likelihood of confusion. Jenkins (2000, 2002), one of the more influential researchers on this topic, argues that /θ/ is one of the few consonants that should not be taught in English as a lingua franca (ELF) contexts.

Why, then, do teachers who advocate intelligibility continue to teach /θ/, often early in their instructional routines? Teachers I have talked to do so for several reasons. First, they say that students want instruction on this sound. In teaching it, they are being learner-centered. Second, they do it because they think it is a good place to start instruction. Since many learners have trouble with /θ/, and many want to work on it, the sound is as good any other sound to start instruction to whole classes on features such as place, manner, and voicing. Third, the mispronunciation of /θ/ is a key marker of a foreign accent in English, and as such, its absence may be so annoying to many teachers that they find it hard to ignore. So they teach it.

What Does an Intelligibility-Based Approach Look Like?

The nativeness approach to pronunciation teaching and learning assumes certain things, often unstated (see also Grant, 2014 for a similar view). For example, it assumes at least the following:

1. It is possible for all learners to achieve a native accent.
2. It is desirable for all learners to achieve a native accent.
3. Some native accents are good and others are not.
4. Foreign-accented speech results in misunderstandings. Native accents will ensure understanding.
5. L2 pronunciation difficulties can be predicted from the interaction of the L1 and L2.
6. Native accents can be achieved apart from social interaction, especially from habit formation developed by listening and repeating.
7. All difficult sounds and suprasegmentals are learnable with sufficient effort.
8. Effort put into perfecting the new accent in controlled contexts will transfer to normal speaking.
9. Pronunciation can be improved when teachers and learners understand the principles of phonetics.

These assumptions – regarding the types of models that are desirable, ultimate attainment, how speakers and listeners understand each other, how transfer from controlled practice to normal speech takes place, and the role of expertise in learning – are at best questionable and out of step with years of research. They are also in stark contrast to the assumptions of the Intelligibility Principle.

Basic Assumptions of the Intelligibility Principle

There are a number of assumptions that form the basis of intelligibility-based instruction. These are:

1. Pronunciation can improve, no matter the age of the learner (Derwing, Munro, Foote, Waugh, & Fleming, 2014).
2. A small number of L2 learners may achieve a native-like accent, especially those who are deeply involved in social networks within the L2 (Levis & Moyer, 2014; Lybeck, 2002; Piller, 2002).
3. Intelligibility and accent are not the same thing. Intelligibility can improve whether or not accent is perceived to improve (Munro & Derwing, 1995).
4. Learning without instruction is most likely within the first year in the L2 environment, the so-called window of maximal opportunity (Derwing & Munro, 2015).
5. Improvement in intelligibility is most likely to occur with instruction, especially instruction on certain features (Derwing & Munro, 2015).
6. Intelligibility may improve more quickly with instruction on suprasegmentals, but segmentals are also important for improvements in

intelligiblity (Derwing, Munro, & Wiebe, 1997, 1998; Gordon & Darcy, 2016).
7. Intelligibility involves both production and perception (Levis, 2005a).
8. It is possible to define the targets that are most likely to impact intelligibility (Brinton, 2014).
9. Instruction can be more or less effective, depending on the teachers, the learners, and the practices employed in instruction (Thomson & Derwing, 2015).

First, we know that pronunciation can improve, no matter the age of the learner. In the absence of instruction, pronunciation is likely to improve rapidly within the first year in the L2 environment and then plateau (Munro & Derwing, 2008). Further improvement may be affected by the amount of experience with the target language (Moyer, 2004), but nativeness in accent is likely to correlate with the age of acquisition (AOA) (Flege, Yeni-Komshian, & Liu, 1999), with younger learners more likely to become native-like in accent than those who start learning the foreign language later in life. It may also be the case that learners whose first language (L1) is more similar to the target language (e.g., Dutch speakers learning English) will achieve better pronunciation than those whose L1 is quite different (e.g., Japanese learners of English). Pronunciation improvement is especially amenable to instruction (Lee, Jang, & Plonsky, 2015; Saito, 2012), and even older learners who have spent many years in a "fossilized" state may show significant improvement with instruction (Derwing et al., 2014). Most studies on improvement have focused attention on accuracy (more critical to the Nativeness Principle), but research has also demonstrated improvements in intelligibility with instruction (e.g., Derwing, Munro, & Wiebe, 1998; Thomson & Derwing, 2015) or in some cases, in the absence of instruction (Derwing, Mouton, & Campbell, 2005).

Second, there has always been evidence that some learners become native-like in pronunciation, even when they learn the L2 as adults. For example, Coppieters (1987) studied a large number of French L2 speakers who started the study of French as adults yet were native-like in their speaking (including their pronunciation), even though their grammatical intuitions were anything but native. These good language learners (Naiman, 1978) have been studied throughout the years. They seem to make use of both social interaction and metacognitive strategies in their pronunciation attainment (Moyer, 2014). Social interaction may be especially important in exceptional attainment. Lybeck (2002) found that American women married to Norwegians had better pronunciation when they were part of social networks (family and friends) and worse pronunciation when they continued to feel like outsiders. Piller (2002) found that the nonnative half of bilingual couples in Germany were more likely to pass as NSs, at least in limited contexts, when they could also make use of marked dialect features. And some learners seem to be better equipped to take on new accents than others. This individual variation is partially related to the proximity of the L1 and L2, but even when two languages have many similarities, individual variation in pronunciation attainment is the norm even for otherwise advanced proficiency learners.

Third, measures of intelligibility and measures of accent are not equivalent. We know that intelligibility can improve whether or not accent improves. Research by Munro and Derwing (1995) first demonstrated that intelligibility, comprehensibility, and accentedness are only partially related, and that changes in one measure do not necessarily entail changes in another. For example, subjects could be judged as having a strong accent yet be completely intelligible. Other studies show that perceptions of accentedness (as rated by listeners using a scale) do not change very much as a result of instruction or over time despite improvement in targeted pronunciation features (Neri, Cucchiarini, & Strik, 2008). Comprehensibility ratings can change based on lexical, syntactic, fluency, phonological, and discourse-related factors, so that even if pronunciation does not change, comprehensibility ratings may change because of other factors (Isaacs & Trofimovich, 2012).

Fourth, there is evidence that pronunciation improvement occurs rapidly within the first 6–12 months in the L2 environment, but after that levels off and may continue to improve, albeit more slowly when the target language is in regular use as opposed to when the L1 continues to dominate (Flege et al., 1995). This window of maximal opportunity (Derwing et al., 2014) may be even greater if pronunciation instruction is included during this time, but we don't know the extent to which changes can be maximized.

Fifth, instruction works. Recent analyses of large numbers of published studies (Lee, Jang, & Plonsky, 2015; Thomson & Derwing, 2015) show consistent improvement is the normal outcome of instruction, often with a large effect size. It can be more or less effective, depending on the teachers, learners, and the way pronunciation is taught. Regarding teachers, they should be well-trained to teach pronunciation (Derwing & Munro, 2015), and there are no obvious advantages of NSs as teachers over NNSs, assuming equal levels of skill and the same materials (Levis, Sonsaat, Link, & Barriuso, 2016).

Sixth, even though instruction works, learners still show variable outcomes. Learners who seem quite similar may show very different trajectories in improvement (e.g., Nagle, 2017). These differences in improvement are well-documented throughout language-learning research and may be a result of aptitude (Hu et al., 2013), social engagement and metacognitive abilities (Moyer, 2014), experience with the L2 (Derwing, Munro, & Thomson, 2007), motivation (Smit, 2002), practice (Ingels, 2011; Sardegna, 2009), phonological awareness (Venkatagiri & Levis, 2007) and a host of other factors. Learners are different, and the ways they improve their L2 pronunciation are also different. Some are exceptional learners (Moyer, 2014), while others may show very high levels of general language proficiency yet remain hard to understand (Bongaerts, Planken, & Schils, 1995; Hinofotis & Bailey, 1981).

Seventh, it is possible to define, at least partially, the targets that are most likely to impact intelligibility. The enormous appeal of the Lingua Franca Core (LFC) in the work of Jenkins (2000) was precisely her willingness to define what was, and was not, likely to affect intelligibility. Jenner (1989), a precursor to Jenkins, tried to define critical pronunciation features that were likely to hold across varieties of English. The concept of functional load (see Chapter 2) also offers evidence for why some segmental features are important and others are less so (Brown, 1988; Munro & Derwing, 2006; Sewell, 2017). Some features may be especially critical for learners from some L1 backgrounds (e.g., word stress for French learners of English), but this is not surprising, since the L1 of learners is always likely to affect the features of the L2 that can cause loss of intelligibility.

Eighth, intelligibility involves both perception and production. Pronunciation is typically thought of as involving production (i.e., the L2 learner should be intelligible to the native listener). But it is equally important for the L1 or L2 speaker to be intelligible to the L2 learner. Communication involves both L2 speakers and native/nonnative speakers playing both roles, as speaker and listener, and both are crucial to intelligibility (Levis, 2006). This also means that intelligibility instruction must include perception work for L2 learners so they can better negotiate interactions with NSs. However, this does not go far enough, especially in relation to languages like English (Levis, 2005a). Most English interactions in today's world involve nonnative speakers and nonnative listeners (Crystal, 2008; Jenkins, 2000), and listener–speaker interactions cannot be assumed to be successful without familiarity with the speech of others. L2 speakers are affected by their L1s both in pronouncing and in perceiving, and the

L1-influenced speech of others may cause loss of intelligibility on many unexpected levels.

Ninth, focusing instruction on prosody/suprasegmentals seems more likely to lead to comprehensibility improvement for spontaneous speech, at least in the short run (Gordon & Darcy, 2016), while focusing on segmentals may not result in the same type of improvement in spontaneous speech despite similar improvement for controlled speech (Derwing, Munro, & Wiebe, 1998). This focus on suprasegmentals has long been advocated (e.g., McNerney & Mendelsohn, 1992; Morley, 1991; Wong, 1987), but the next steps are clearly to determine what types of suprasegmental features are most effective at improving intelligibility (e.g., primary phrase stress in Hahn, 2004; contrastive stress in Levis & Muller Levis, 2018), and which are less effective. Like segmentals, suprasegmentals are not all equal in their effects, and some should be taught while others should not. (Despite these arguments about the use of suprasegmentals, it is also clear that instruction on segmentals is important, and that improvement in segmentals may simply take longer to show up in judgments of spontaneous speech. Advocating for the importance of suprasegmentals does not mean that segmentals are not important.)

Finally, there is increasing evidence that different types of pedagogical practices lead to different types of outcomes. High-variability phonetic training, for example, in which listeners improve their ability to hear difficult sounds through listening to the sounds spoken by multiple voices and in different linguistic environments, seems to lead to more robust changes in phonological perception than training using a single voice (Thomson, 2011, 2012, 2018; Wang & Munro, 2004; Wong, 2013). And well-designed teaching using techniques like shadowing (Foote & McDonough, 2017), the use of focus-on-form feedback (Saito & Lyster, 2012), and prosodic features in context rather than isolation (Hirata, 2004), seem to promote greater improvement. It remains important to determine, however, what kind of improvement is being measured. While most studies have shown that pronunciation instruction leads to improvement (see Lee et al., 2015), fewer studies of improvement have focused on whether listeners judge the speaker as being more intelligible (Thomson & Derwing, 2015). This gold standard of improvement (Derwing & Munro, 2009) has not been typically addressed in studies of pronunciation improvement, but it should be. Ultimately, we should be concerned more with improvement in communicative effectiveness than just with improvement on discrete features.

Why We Need a Different Approach to Teaching

The nativeness approach to pronunciation teaching is sometimes presented as upholding high standards. Language learners are being asked to model their speech in all details on NSs, a standard they seem all too happy to take on (Levis, 2015), despite the unlikelihood that their attempt to match this standard will be successful. Unfortunately, the call for native-like pronunciation is likely to lead to general failure because of how pronunciation is typically addressed. Teachers do not typically teach pronunciation consistently or well, language-learning materials do not consistently include pronunciation, pronunciation is usually ignored in standardized language tests, there is almost never systematic coverage of pronunciation, and by and large, learners' needs are not being addressed. Each of these problems is unlikely to be solved in the short run, which means that we need a different solution if pronunciation is to be relevant beyond a limited group of teachers and teacher trainers. This means we need a solution that works; one that is good enough to improve learners' communicative effectiveness to the extent that is possible through pronunciation training.

So what are the problems with the nativeness approach to pronunciation teaching? First, teachers are undertrained and lack confidence in their understanding of pronunciation and their ability to teach it (for a review of studies on this, see Murphy, 2014). A long-term solution to this problem is better training for pre-service teachers, but such a solution is too long term to make a reasonable difference in the short run, where in-service teachers need to be reached. Second, better examples of materials and curricula need to be available and usable. Teachers need to see pronunciation as essential to teaching listening, speaking, reading, grammar, etc., if they are to make a place for it in their classes (Jones, 2016; Levis & Grant, 2003). Third, even though pronunciation is clearly a factor in spoken language tests (Levis, 2006), making it an explicit factor will encourage teachers to pay attention to it. Greater attention to pronunciation in spoken language tests offers an important opportunity for washback from testing to instruction (Isaacs & Trofimovich, 2017). Fourth, pronunciation is rarely covered in systematic ways because of its marginalized status in L2 teaching. The influence of Jenkins' (2000) LFC suggests that teachers may be waiting for authoritative assertions of what to do and not do. Finally, the problems in other areas mean that learners' needs are not being met. Learners care about pronunciation (Derwing & Rossiter, 2002) because they know that it affects not only communication but also because they believe it affects how others perceive them (Gluszek & Dovidio, 2010).

Potential solutions to these problems, unfortunately, may not lead to improvements in the overall place of pronunciation in language teaching. For example, pronunciation is now widely integrated into four-skills books (reading, writing. listening, speaking) but the exercises are often printed in smaller type or placed in such a way that they are ignored (Levis & Sonsaat, 2016). We provide training for teachers in workshops at conferences or in webinars, but there is little follow-up. We propose lists of features to be taught, but we do not offer help for how they can be flexibly interpreted. And we continue not meeting the needs of teachers and learners. So what might a different approach that emphasizes intelligibility look like?

Intelligibility-Based Instruction: A Proposal

It would be easy to see intelligibility-based teaching as reductive, a deficient nativeness approach. In this view, teaching for intelligibility means not teaching certain things (e.g., /ð/, /θ/, /ɫ/ in Jenner, 1989) because they do not impact intelligibility or because they are considered unimportant for other reasons, despite their importance as markers of what it means to sound like an English speaker. It also means not teaching other features because of variability across varieties of English (e.g., word stress in Jenkins, 2000) or because they are "unteachable" (e.g., intonation in Walker, 2010, p. 39).

However, an intelligibility-based approach is actually the only reasonable approach to teaching pronunciation, given that the traditional approach (full coverage of all features following a widely accepted native model) is both unrealistic and doomed to failure. It is unrealistic because it simply does not happen. Teachers who can follow the traditional approach are few and far between, and language study rarely offers the luxury of long-term pronunciation study. Instead, language study is based upon textbooks that treat pronunciation, if they treat it at all, as a garnish for the real language meal made up of other skills. The traditional approach is also doomed to failure because the numbers of learners who can become native-like in pronunciation is limited by age, context of learning, and sociolinguistic constraints on accent (LeVelle & Levis, 2014; Lybeck, 2002). Some learners are exceptional and become native-like (Moyer, 2014), but even the best or most motivated learners may be limited in their ability to pass as native to situations like brief service encounters (Marx, 2002; Piller, 2002).

Finally, an intelligibility-based approach explicitly recognizes that pronunciation features are not equal in their impact upon understanding. Some word-stress errors seem to affect understanding while others do not (e.g., Cutler, 1986; Field, 2005; Richards, 2016). Consonant errors in stressed word-initial position seem particularly problematic, while the same errors in medial position are less so (Zielinski, 2008). Some variations may also be differentially important depending on the sentences they occur in. The difference between rising and falling intonation, for example, is more important in declarative and elliptical utterances than in inverted yes–no questions, where any difference in meaning is subtle and hard to explain (Levis, 1999a). The traditional approach, in contrast, assumes that all pronunciation features are equally important, perhaps even giving greater emphasis to segmental features that affect perceptions of accent while ignoring suprasegmental features that are more challenging to describe and teach.

Perhaps a better way to consider the differences between the traditional and intelligibility approaches to pronunciation teaching is to use the metaphor of a house. The traditional approach presents a show house as the model, with just the right pictures on the wall and the right colors of paint. It looks like no one's house in particular but gives an idea of what a house could look like. The intelligibility approach, on the other hand, has everything important that any acceptable house has: Heating and cooling, plumbing, electrical, a roof and walls, etc., but this kind of house reflects how the owners have accented the variable elements and made it their own in how the house is decorated, painted, and furnished. NSs largely accept this kind of individuality from each other in regard to accent, even if they comment on or criticize particular ways of speaking. An intelligibility approach advocates extending this courtesy to language learners.

Intelligibility-based teaching involves three things: the features that are likely to promote intelligibility; the needs of the learners, both collectively and individually; and the use of techniques that are most likely to promote learning. An intelligibility-based approach assumes teachers that are sufficiently knowledgeable and willing to teach pronunciation, and that, like any other language skill, they will teach pronunciation as well as they are able. An intelligibility-based approach advocates that pronunciation instruction should be

- selective rather than complete;
- individualized rather than collective;
- multi-modal rather than mono-modal;
- communicative rather than isolated;
- correct rather than incorrect;
- socially significant rather than insignificant.

Selectivity

As already argued, instruction should be selective, focusing only on those features that are likely to impact understanding. For example, segmental contrasts that have high functional load are far more likely to cause loss of understanding than segmental contrasts that have low functional load (Munro & Derwing, 2006). Thus, those with high functional load are relatively important while those with low functional load are not. For example, the /i/–/ɪ/ contrast in English, as in *leave–live*, has many potential minimal pairs, while the /u/–/ʊ/ contrast, as in *stewed–stood*, has very few. Both sound contrasts are challenging for many L2 learners, but in normal speech listeners have a much greater opportunity to misunderstand when speakers do not make a clear distinction between /i/–/ɪ/, and L2 learners have a much smaller likelihood of misunderstanding others when /u/–/ʊ/ are in contrast. In addition, each general pronunciation feature (in any L2) likely includes elements that have a high chance of making a difference to intelligibility and elements that do not.

Individualization

An intelligibility-based approach recognizes that learners are individuals, even when they are also parts of a group. Just as pair or group work on pronunciation is essential, so is individualization. While Korean speakers or Spanish speakers or any other group of learners may have certain difficulties in common because of their first language, they will vary greatly as well. Not all Spanish speakers, for example, will pronounce –ed endings with an epenthetic vowel. Instead, some may pronounce them correctly, while others may delete complex consonant clusters. This kind of variation may be a result of linguistic environment (Koffi, 2010), proficiency level, or individual variation (Qian, Chukharev-Hudalainen, & Levis, 2018). Ultimately, however, an intelligibility-based approach means that we teach students, not groups.

This criterion implicitly indicates that teachers will take note of each student's challenges either through diagnosing the student's speech or through noticing difficulties during class. In some contexts in which pronunciation is an important component of teacher education programs (e.g., in Poland), this kind of deliberate attention is part of established programs. This criterion also implies that the teacher or students will have access to materials and sound files that can be used independently. Because teachers in many contexts only teach pronunciation if they see a need, access to high-quality materials is critically important in addressing pronunciation needs.

Multi-modality

An intelligibility-based approach is multi-modal rather than mono-modal. This means that pronunciation is connected to other means of communication, such as body language, and that pronunciation addresses productive, visual, auditory, and embodied elements of communication. When I was a new teacher, I was taught to cover my mouth or ask students to look down when teaching the interdental fricatives. Supposedly, this would help them to focus on perception and thus learn better. However, because the interdental fricatives are acoustically quiet in relation to other confusable sounds, an important clue is the visibility of the tongue tip. In noise (e.g., normal conversation in a group), the visibility of the tongue tip or the lip–teeth interaction may be the only reliable clue to the difference between *thought* and *fought*. Additionally, features such as syllable length and pitch movement may be more effectively learned through the use of kazoos, rubberbands, or movement (Acton, Baker, Burri, & Teaman, 2013; Gilbert, 1991). Finally, because better production is tied to better perception, especially for sounds that are very similar in the L1 and L2 (e.g., /l/ and /ɹ/ for Japanese learners of English), carefully designed perception practice using multiple voices can be particularly effective in helping L2 learners create new phonological categories (e.g., Bradlow, Akahane-Yamada, Pisoni, & Tohkura, 1999; Thomson, 2018).

Multi-modality also means that pronunciation teaching and learning must recognize not only the essential nature of spoken language, in which sounds vary according to linguistic context and register, but also that written language is an essential component in how we teach spoken language and how learners learn it. Because of this, learners must be helped in connecting orthography and pronunciation (Dickerson, 2015; Gilbert, 2001). Although exceptions to sound–spelling patterns in English exist, spelling is largely regular and rule-guided in English, even if it is not phonetically transparent (Chomsky & Halle, 1968), and many of these regularities can be profitably taught (Dickerson, 1989). Most learners frequently have to connect written representations to spoken ones, and it is important for teachers and materials writers to call attention to obvious regularities when needed.

Communicative Rather than Isolated

An intelligibility-based approach should emphasize the end goals of being able to speak intelligibly and understand the speech of others.

This means taking a big-picture approach to communication, with a focus on fluent, confident speech that is accurate enough to succeed (Levis & Grant, 2003). As in sports, where the goal is to play and enjoy the game in a way that fits your skills, not to practice only in isolation, communication cannot solely rely on controlled practice. Teaching communicatively means building classroom practices that parallel real-life communication (Widdowson, 1972). This also means we need a wide variety of techniques, because being understood during communication, rather than simply being accurate, is the end goal. For this reason, pronunciation teaching should always include practice in which pronunciation is essential to the communicative goal.

Celce-Murcia et al. (2010) recognize that the learning (and therefore the teaching) of pronunciation requires techniques across a spectrum of cognitive and physical abilities. Activities must build cognitive understanding, perception, muscle memory, and the ability to pronounce while attending to other elements of communication. Traditional approaches emphasize the first three of these, and each continues to have its place in an intelligibility approach, just in the same way that athletes repetitively practice desirable actions (drills) or watch videos of performances and discuss what happened (cognitive understanding, perception).

It is the last item, however, that is most often neglected in pronunciation teaching. Celce-Murcia et al. divide this type of practice into guided and communicative practice, in contrast to the controlled practice of pronunciation features. The difference between the two is the amount of attention that learners pay to pronunciation form and meaning. In guided practice, attention to pronunciation form is possible, but this attention competes with attention to other aspects of language or modest communicative effort. This means that learners, especially in early stages of learning a new feature, will show more variable pronunciation accuracy because of the competition between form and meaning. In communicative practice, the focus is on communication of meaning, and attention to pronunciation form is difficult. It is in this type of practice that learners who show success in pronouncing new features are most likely to backslide into incorrect pronunciations, simply because the meaning is more important during communication. (In contrast, in controlled practice, learners can pay maximal attention to pronunciation and minimal attention to meaning, leading to greater accuracy in production.)

A corollary to this emphasis on meaningful production is the importance of perception, or listening comprehension. All speakers become listeners, and all listeners become speakers, trading roles in most normal types of communication. It is therefore essential that learners receive training in being able to hear normal, natural speech of varied voices, accents, and in varied contexts (Cauldwell, 2013; Field, 2014). Some of this listening may be one-way – that is, listening to lectures, videos, or conversations that are pre-recorded. But listening must also take place in interactive speaking and listening tasks that require pronunciation to be successful (Goodwin, 2005). In other words, pronunciation must have a purpose, including success in listening (Levis & Muller Levis, n.d.). As a bonus, there are close connections between improved perception and improved production (Bradlow, Pisoni, Akahane-Yamada, & Tohkura, 1997; Isbell, 2016)

Correct Rather than Incorrect

An intelligibility-based approach must be correct rather than incorrect. This may seem like an obvious criterion, and one that is not very different from the traditional approach with its emphasis on phonological and phonetic accuracy. However, correctness goes beyond phonological accuracy. For example, voicing is a critical phonological distinction in English that occurs in all environments, e.g., the /p/–/b/ distinction seen in *pat/bat, rapid/rabid, lap/lab*. While [+/– voice] is phonologically important, the phonetic distinction that allows speakers to distinguish voiced and voiceless sounds may be found not in voicing but in other areas. It is well-known that initial voiceless stops in English have a long-lag voice onset time (VOT) (Nagle, 2017). In other words, they are aspirated. In contrast, initial voiced stops typically have a short-lag VOT (that is, they are unaspirated but also voiceless). A small minority of native English speakers have negative VOT (that is, they are phonetically voiced), but most do not actually voice voiced stops. In medial and final positions, distinctions between voiceless and voiced obstruents are signaled primarily by the length of the preceding vowel rather than the voicing of the obstruent. This means that phonological distinctions in final stops can be heard and signaled by paying attention to vowel length rather than/in addition to consonant voicing. Thus, understanding phonetic detail can be important in correctly signaling phonological accuracy.

The second way in which correctness is important is the need to know what actually impacts intelligibility. Research suggests many features that are important, including high functional load segmental features, prosodic prominence, and certain issues with lexical stress. But most lists of features, even those with wide acceptance (e.g., Jenkins, 2000) are based on modest evidence applied to a particular group of listeners and speakers. Second, even though pronunciation is the major feature influencing judgments of intelligibility, there are other causes of unintelligibility that are barely discussed. Jenkins (2000), for instance, found loss of intelligibility due to non-pronunciation factors in 33 percent of her examples, including grammatical difficulties and word identification. Third, as I have argued before (e.g., Levis, 1999a), all pronunciation features in general are likely to include elements that are important for intelligibility and those that are not. It is not enough to proclaim that word stress should (or should not) be taught because of its effect on intelligibility (e.g., Dauer, 2005; Jenkins, 2000). Instead, treating all word-stress errors as equal is a fallacy (Richards, 2016). Some word-stress errors seem unimportant, while others are highly likely to cause loss of intelligibility. I would argue that this is true for all pronunciation features, and future research will help us specify the parts of an intelligibility syllabus more precisely.

In moving beyond intelligibility to judgments of comprehensibility, improvement is associated with features of L2 phonology, fluency, vocabulary and grammar use, and construction of discourse (Isaacs & Trofimovich, 2012; Trofimovich & Isaacs, 2012). It perhaps comes as no surprise that the amount of work listeners do in understanding a speaker is connected to many aspects of speech, some in the traditional linguistic features of vocabulary, grammar, and pronunciation, and some in how speech is produced and ideas are expressed.

Correctness is also important in saying no to particular features. Almost every pronunciation feature has its advocates, especially those sounds and features that are easiest to teach and notice, and evidence or reasons can be cherry-picked to justify inclusion of a sound or prosodic feature, especially when approaching pronunciation from the Nativeness Principle. But in an intelligibility-based approach there has to be a relative level of importance and a level below which teaching that feature is not a priority. Features are important not because they are teachable or learnable, but because of their likely effect on intelligibility for particular learners. Making such choices for pronunciation is not very different from what is done in any area of language teaching. All teachers have to make choices, whether it is in topics or exercises or according to what they believe a group of learners can do. An intelligibility-based approach simply asks that we make our reasons for including and excluding particular features explicit, and justify our reasons with evidence.

Finally, an appeal to correctness means that we need reliable information about best practices in teaching pronunciation, especially in teaching particular features. This is an issue of learnability rather than teachability. As discussed earlier, these two terms are often confounded, but there are many reasons for distinguishing them. Learnability refers to the ability of learners of a particular level to make a feature part of their speaking, first in controlled, then in form-focused contexts, and later in meaning-focused contexts. Learnability also refers to the ability of learners to achieve these ends within a relatively limited amount of time. Teachability, on the other hand, is largely a non-issue. Teachers with even a modest degree of skill can teach almost anything in an interesting way that has a significant effect in the short run. This fact may be behind the large numbers of studies that demonstrate improvement for pronunciation instruction (e.g., Lee et al., 2015). The more important question is whether such improvement lasts, and whether it becomes part of a learner's unmonitored speech.

Socially Significant Rather than Insignificant

An intelligibility-based approach to teaching pronunciation involves socially significant rather than insignificant features. This may mean particular social interactions with critical pronunciation features, such as self-introductions and the pronunciation of personal names or prominence patterns in repeated questions (Muller Levis & Levis, 2016). It may mean careful attention to taboo words as needed, such as *beach → bitch, piece → piss, sheet → shit, focus → fuck us*. These potential mispronunciations may or may not include important pronunciation features, but they can create social difficulties. Similarly, the pronunciation of key vocabulary is perhaps more important in "English for specific purposes" contexts, such as professional vocabulary for teaching assistants, faculty, or for medical professionals. In such cases, the way key vocabulary is pronounced may be the difference between comprehension and lack of comprehension in high-stakes communicative contexts. Socially significant features may also mean that learners' attitudes toward accent should be explicitly discussed individually or in the classroom, given learners' willingness to believe that their accents may be the cause of social stigma (Gluszek & Dovidio, 2010).

LeVelle and Levis (2014), playing off the LFC's image of centrality (Jenkins, 2000), call for a sociolinguistic core for pronunciation teaching and learning. As a first proposal, this sociolinguistic core calls for five elements for pronunciation instruction: interacting outside of one's comfort zone; using interactional strategies that match a desired social group; judicious use of sociolinguistic markers; looking like a speaker of the language (especially in regard to pronunciation-timed gestures); and taking a realistic view of accent and stigma. Several of these are not what would traditionally be included in pronunciation, but instead reflect the importance of situating pronunciation instruction and improvement within a context of spoken interaction. This social mindset is one of the central characteristics of exceptional pronunciation learners (Moyer, 2014). In one example of this kind of social grounding of pronunciation, Cutler (2014) discusses how immigrant youth in New York City take on pronunciation features of hip-hop culture even without knowing actual speakers of that variety. These youth immigrant learners decided that this was their intended model, and so chose its phonological markers over more standard accent features. Miller (2003) reports on immigrant youth in Australian high schools becoming audible to Australian peers when they take on markers of in-group identity (e.g., the use of quotative *like* in speech). Another part of the sociolinguistic core calls for looking like a speaker of the language. Based on Marx (2002), this may mean something as simple as dressing like target speakers, or it may mean incorporating body language that goes with communication in the target language (e.g., head shakes when using negation). Finally, the sociolinguistic core advocates honest discussion of the role of accent in social judgments made both by NSs and by NNSs. A realistic view of what can be achieved and what others may think when they hear an accent may not make a speaker more intelligible, but it will provide them with the ability to understand why listeners react as they do. This kind of knowledge can be empowering, especially for teachers (Golombek & Jordan, 2005).

Conclusions

Emphasizing intelligibility is the only practical approach to teaching pronunciation in most contexts. We teach pronunciation to make a difference in our students' ability to communicate, not to fill a certain number of minutes in the classroom. And teaching pronunciation, like teaching any other language skill, will have better results if teachers and learners pay attention to those things that make a difference while ignoring those that do not. This means that certain well-known, features (e.g., the vowel contrast in *Luke–look*) should be ignored while other little-known features (e.g., the use of prominence on the last content word of a phrase) should be taught and practiced repeatedly.

An intelligibility-based approach goes beyond unquestioning adherence to a reference accent and encourages learners to pronounce for successful communication. While there may be good reasons to adhere to a native accent in certain contexts (e.g., Bird, 2016; Cerreta &

Trofimovich, 2018), languages like English should celebrate diverse accents, especially since speaking with a particular accent does not make one more or less intelligible. Teaching for intelligibility is also refreshingly utilitarian. It is an approach that is interested in what works, not in adhering to traditional notions of social and linguistic privilege. For teachers, this means that an intelligibility-based approach is the only sensible path for the vast majority of speakers, both native and nonnative, who do not speak with a reference accent.

Although attempts to specify what should be included and what should be excluded in teaching pronunciation are central to teaching for intelligibility, such an approach must go beyond individual pronunciation features to also address the needs of learners and the effectiveness of how we teach. An intelligibility-based approach cannot be "one size fits all" since two learners rarely are the same size – that is, they will not have the same needs or same trajectory in learning to pronounce. Finally, it is especially important to question the ways that we teach and the techniques that we employ. For example, minimal-pair exercises may be abundantly available, but we have very little information about their relative effectiveness for promoting production (Field, 2014; Levis, 2016). The same could be said for most other common techniques for teaching pronunciation. Knowing what works is a new frontier in pedagogically based pronunciation research, and it is important not only to know what works in classroom or in technologically enhanced instruction, but also in how teachers use the materials they have available (Burri, Baker, & Chen, 2017; Sonsaat, 2017). Only by improving the effectiveness of teaching and learning opportunities, and by discovering what works for varied types of learners in varied contexts, can we improve the success of pronunciation learning.

10 *What Should and Should Not Be Taught*

An Intelligibility-Based Approach

Introduction

The previous two chapters present general principles for an intelligibility-based approach, but do not say what to teach and what to deemphasize in planning pronunciation teaching. That is the goal of this chapter. One of the most attractive and powerful aspects of the Lingua Franca Core (LFC) (Jenkins, 2000) is the certainty with which the core is presented. Certain features are put forth as essential for international intelligibility, and others are excluded from the core, with few gray areas (besides word stress). In this, Jenkins has set a standard which others should meet. However, intelligibility is context-sensitive, and a set of learners in one context will need certain features that learners in another context do not. Because of this context-dependence, principles are important in making decisions about what and how to teach pronunciation. But ultimately, it is important to take a stand on the importance of different features. In this chapter, I assume, as I have throughout the book, that all areas of pronunciation include more and less important elements. This means that no feature is, in general, always important, or never important. Word stress is sometimes important, and sometimes not important, always depending on what kinds of word-stress errors are present. Teachers need to be selective about what is taught and how it is taught. This should not be surprising, since teachers are always selective in what they present and emphasize. Pronunciation is no different in this way than other skill areas. Teachers may be implicitly selective by not teaching pronunciation at all, or by using some exercises but not others, or choosing one feature to teach while ignoring another. It is a challenge for pronunciation teachers and theorists to be clear about how to be selective. An intelligibility-based approach requires such knowledge.

I have argued elsewhere that what we need are evidence-based practices in L2 pronunciation teaching (Levis, 2017), including evidence from researchers, from teachers, and from L2 learners. Having such evidence will provide a strong basis for decisions about what and how to teach pronunciation. We actually have substantial evidence available from research, much from the wisdom of teachers, and much less from the successes of learners (such as Moyer, 2014). Indeed, we have enough evidence to make initial guesses about what is important for most English pronunciation features.

Selectivity, one of the principles from Chapter 9, means making choices from all the features that could possibly be taught. The Nativeness Principle (Levis, 2005a) makes no claim to selectivity. Everything is important, even though everything may not be important for learners from a particular L1. (Books like Swan and Smith [2001] and Avery and Ehrlich [1992] include features that are particularly likely to be important for speakers from different first languages, although the predictions are often mistaken in serious ways, e.g., Munro [2018].) Those who promote ideas and practices more in line with the Intelligibility Principle (Levis, 2005a), on the other hand, are explicitly selective in promoting an approach to learning and teaching that is limited yet leads to communicative results that are as good or better than the Nativeness Principle. Focus on these features, the Intelligibility Principle says, and leave the others untaught, and the result will be increased intelligibility. Of course, the nativeness and intelligibility approaches co-exist and overlap, and teachers and learners may follow a selective approach but still emphasize elements of pronunciation that they think will make them sound better, even if improvement on such elements has minor value for intelligibility. Rather than being inherently contradictory, as I have suggested (Levis, 2005a), these two principles often overlap in the features they teach and the practices they employ. The specifics of an intelligibility-based approach vary even among those who advocate it, because what we teach always depends on our teaching context, our learners, who we are as teachers, and the approaches we use to teach and learn.

Proposals for an intelligibility-based approach often argue for very different ideas of what should be taught. Jenner (1989), in one of the earliest attempts to specify important pronunciation targets, argued that features shared by all native speaker (NS) varieties of English were important, including both segmental contrasts and suprasegmental features. Those that were idiosyncratic to one or several varieties, in contrast, would be less important. Jenkins (2000) takes a different approach to intelligibility because she specifies a particular type of interaction (NNS–NNS communication) and rules out another type (NNS–NS). This second type is common, of course, especially in contexts in which English is the dominant language, but a great many interactions in English throughout the world take place between and among nonnative speakers (NNSs), and it is this context that Jenkins speaks to. As a result, many features that have been considered important in NNS–NS interactions are not addressed in Jenkins' LFC.

The research that Jenkins based the LFC on led to an argument against prevailing wisdom by focusing on the importance of segmentals and making suprasegmentals peripheral, at a time when most pronunciation teachers championed suprasegmentals and downplayed segmentals. The specificity of the LFC is one of its most appealing aspects, and it is one that I will attempt to imitate.

The Importance of Perception

Most of the following sections focus on what is important for production, since production is what teachers usually mean when talking about pronunciation. But perception is at least equally important to production. If an L2 speaker struggles with production, it is likely that their difficulties have roots in perception. Some difficulties in production (e.g., the production of <th> sounds in English) may not always be accompanied by difficulties in perception, but many consistent production problems, whether segmental or suprasegmental, are likely to be connected to an inability to hear the features or connect what is heard to its functions or meanings. This indicates that perception should be a priority in any language classroom. There are at least three reasons that perception should be a priority.

First, perception is critical for the neglected side of an intelligibility-based approach – that is, the ability of L2 speakers to understand those they are listening to. L2 speakers, like L1 speakers, need to be able to listen to speakers of different proficiency levels and from different L1s, not to mention being able to listen to L1 speakers with different accents. As L2 speakers increase in spoken proficiency, it is critical that they have the opportunity to listen to different speakers speaking in different ways. This may mean that learners need well-designed high-variability phonetic training to create new categories for L2 sounds (Qian, Chukharev-Hudilainen, & Levis, 2018; Thomson, 2018), but at the very least they need to listen to different speakers, especially from groups they are likely to interact with, to create flexibility in listening.

Second, perception improvement often leads to production improvement, even when there is no focus on production. Flege (1999), reviewing a variety of studies on the interface of perception and production, argues that errors in production often result from problems with segmental perception, but that not all production errors have a basis in perception. Flege's Speech Learning Model hypothesizes that perception accuracy limits production accuracy – that is, a sound contrast that is inadequately perceived is likely to be wrongly produced, especially when the L2 and L1 sounds are different yet highly similar. In another study, Bradlow, Pisoni, Akahane-Yamada, and Tohkura (1997) trained Japanese learners to better perceive the English /l/–/ɹ/ contrast. Improvements in perception resulted in improvements in producing the contrast, even though production was never trained. Sakai and Moorman (2017), in a meta-analysis of the perception–production connection, found that perception training led to small improvements in production, but that some types of sounds improved more than others.

The third reason to include perception is connected to perceiving sounds in context. Challenging sounds or features pronounced in isolation are often quite different than they are in sentences, in connected speech in larger discourse contexts, and in speech produced in different registers. This suggests that perception practice be carried out not only at the word level but also in environments that include varied speech rates and registers if possible, above the level of the sound or word. Hirata (2004), in a study of L2 perception of Japanese pitch and length contrasts, found that L2 learners of Japanese who were trained on sentence-level practice improved on the same contrasts at the word level. However, those trained at the word level did not transfer their improvement to perception of the same features at the sentence level.

What Else Is Important in an Intelligibility-Based Approach?

Any pronunciation difficulty, if frequent or unexpected enough, can be a potential target for instruction. For this reason, the following pronunciation topics have items listed as "more important" and "less important" rather than essential and peripheral. An underlying assumption of my lists is that all general phonological categories (e.g., consonants, word stress, intonation) include elements that are more and less important. Many of the recommendations are based on research discussed in earlier chapters, while others are based on my experience and the experience of others whom I have learned from. Each section is about a particular pronunciation or pronunciation-related topic, including tables followed by explanations about why items are evaluated as more or less important. I offer these recommendations to help specify what an intelligibility-based approach looks like and what that means for pronunciation teaching and learning. It should also be clear that some learners have idiosyncratic errors that may defy explanation, but that nevertheless are extremely damaging to intelligibility. For example, I had a student who produced all words with /ɛ/ as [aɪ], so *said* became *side, bed, bide, let, light*, etc. I could never get used to it. Similarly, another student used [j] for [ð], a completely unexpected deviation that required the teaching of a better option for an otherwise less important error (Tracey Derwing, personal communication).

Indirect Pronunciation Issues: What to Teach

This section includes language issues that are indirectly related to pronunciation, but which are nonetheless important for an intelligibility-based approach. Included are vocabulary, fluency, and orthography. Each of these is related to intelligibility, but may often be addressed separately apart from systematic attention to pronunciation.

Table 10.1 recognizes that pronunciation does not always mean teaching phonetics, but that individual words may be the organizing principle for pronunciation teaching. L2 learners often need to be able to pronounce specific words because they carry a high communicative value. One example of this could be called "The usually problem." One of the most common mistakes for Chinese learners is to say the word "usually" [juːʒuəli] as [jɜˑli]. A logical (but wrongheaded) way to approach this is to teach [ʒ], a relatively rare sound in English. It is my contention that it is more effective to teach them to say the word without consideration of other places the [ʒ] is used in English. There are a number of phonologically useful tricks to achieve this, none of which require extensive work on [ʒ]. One trick is to use knowledge of vowel lengthening before voiced consonants to help students use a "wrong" pronunciation that sounds right. It is well known that English listeners judge the voicing of consonants by the length of the preceding vowel. This means that Chinese learners can substitute [ʃ] if they say a lengthened initial vowel in the word. This work-around is

Table 10.1 Word-based pronunciation: the problem of difficult words

More important	Less important
Useful words ("the usually problem")	Words you are unlikely to use, learning vocabulary pronunciations just because you want to improve your vocabulary
Potential taboo words	
Professional vocabulary	
Personal names	Nonsense words

quite effective. Deterding (2009) suggested another trick that was also effective. He taught learners to use the phrase "You Shirley" with emphasis on the word "you" and the r-less pronunciation of British English. This is a case of re-spelling the problematic word to get an acceptable result, in the spirit of Hill and Beebe (1980) and Weinstein (1982). The principle represented by "usually" can be applied to many important words that do not require systematic phonetics training. Troublesome words may simply be troublesome words, and they should be treated as a pronunciation problem tied to the word. In another example of this kind of problem, I listened to (and was endlessly confused by) the pronunciation of the word "thrust" in a presentation on satellite power. The speaker pronounced the word as [zurist], with at least four errors in pronunciation, resulting in constant unintelligibility. Rather than being a reason to teach [θ], this calls instead for an intelligible pronunciation of what was a key word for the speaker, even if intelligible does not mean perfectly accurate. Another example for the importance of [θ] in words (when I would not teach the sound in general) might be in clusters, where simplifications are common, such as in ordinal numbers (e.g., *sixth, three-fifths*) or in the plural forms *months* and *clothes*. In these words, the interdental fricatives are typically not said, but L2 speakers often try to pronounce them, and paradoxically become less intelligible in their desire to be correct.

A second area of importance is the pronunciation of words that can sound like taboo words (e.g., *beach/bitch, sheet/shit, piece/piss, focus/fuck us, fork/fuck, peanuts/penis*). Because of their social impact, L2 learners need ways to either say these taboo sound-alike words clearly, or avoid them successfully, which is not always possible. For example, in English paper is counted in *pieces* and *sheets*, making such words often unavoidable in university contexts.

Professional vocabulary is also a central part of instruction for international teaching assistants (ITAs) in North America. ITAs often teach introductory classes, laboratory classes, or recitation sessions in a variety of disciplines at larger North American universities. Many ITAs have difficulty with the spoken forms of key vocabulary, and rather than systematic pronunciation instruction, are taught to pronounce the key disciplinary and academic vocabulary needed to communicate in academic contexts. Books designed for this population, such as that of Smith, Myers, and Burkhalter (1992), include extensive lists of discipline-specific words and general academic terms that are relevant to many fields. Similar sets with sound files can be found at https://grad.msu.edu/tap/team/resources. It is also possible to search for words and phrases using www.youglish.com, a site that provides lectures and other types of video examples from www.youtube.com. This approach to vocabulary learning, which is inspired by the English for Specific Purposes movement, may be quite important in an intelligibility-based approach. The pronunciation of important words and phrases, and perhaps the modification of those words/phrases so that the message is intelligible, is a way to approach pronunciation teaching in classrooms that have little extra time.

Finally, the pronunciation of names is important – both the L2 speakers' personal names and the names of others. Introducing oneself to others is an important gateway to further interaction, and thus to further opportunities for social interaction in the L2. I have known many L2 speakers who find it frustrating that people don't understand their names. They know how to say their names, obviously, but NS listeners don't always know how to hear their names. There are a variety of ways to address the issue of names, and learners and teachers have used different strategies for this. However, personal names are the place that L2 speakers have the greatest control. Names in English are prosodically patterned, with the last spoken part of the name being prominent. If an L2 speaker is communicating with NSs, their name will be heard more effectively if they produce it with a prosody that the NS expects. This may mean adjusting how their name sounds, which is not always easy (Muller Levis & Levis, 2014). This may sound like a somewhat radical recommendation, given the connections of names to identity, and other options may work as well or better, but it is important to be understood in these kinds of gatekeeping interactions.

Fluency and related issues (Table 10.2) are important in their own right, and the ability to produce speech comfortably while focusing on meaning is essential for intelligible and comprehensible speech. Although fluency is not by itself pronunciation, it may be less worthwhile working on some aspects of pronunciation if an L2 speaker struggles to produce speech. Lack of fluency may also be connected to excessive numbers of filled pauses, poor phrasing (this can seriously

Table 10.2 Fluency features for an intelligibility-based approach

More important	Less important
Working on general speaking skills so that production is comfortable. Thought groups (phrases) in reading aloud and in spontaneous speech	Attention to linking and connected speech in order to build more fluent speech

affect other suprasegmental features), and speech that is excessively slow. It is also possible that an L2 speaker may be excessively fluent, speaking at a rate that is faster than a listener can process, but this is less likely than speaking too slowly (Munro & Derwing, 1998). Fluency can be improved by allowing L2 speakers to plan what they are going to say (Ellis, 2009), to repeatedly present the same spoken text (the fluency circle technique; see Celce-Murcia, Brinton, & Goodwin, 1996, p. 291). For other fluency activities, see the work of Klippel (1984). The importance of fluency in an intelligibility-based approach is in line with Firth (1992), who suggested that teachers use a "Zoom Principle," starting from general speech production, then paying attention to pronunciation features that affect phrases, then words, then individual segments. Improved pronunciation has to fit within a communicative context, and it is essential that L2 speakers be able to speak comfortably as they work on many critical pronunciation issues. Jenkins (2000) argues that connected speech and linking instruction is sometimes put forth as a way to achieve fluency, but that such an approach is backward. This critique makes sense, and indicates that teaching students to pronounce connected speech features to increase fluency is unlikely to be successful. The pronunciation of connected speech features such as linking seems to be the result of greater fluency, rather than the cause of it.

A topic related to fluency, and foundational to an effective use of suprasegmentals, is the ability to speak in logical thought groups. Thought groups are the structure of spoken language and include syntactically connected groups of words. Thought groups refer to spoken phrases, and have been called by many names, such as tone units, breath groups, and sense groups. They are foundational to suprasegmentals because prominence is defined by its role in the thought group, tunes (final intonation) are at the end of each thought group, and rhythm is described by its alternations of stressed and unstressed syllables in the thought group. Murphy (2017) suggests that all speakers, native and nonnative, will benefit from understanding the ways that thought groups are used in speech, how they affect other aspects of speech (such as assimilation of one sound to be like another), and how they can be manipulated for greater intelligibility. Unfortunately, despite being the foundation for effective suprasegmentals, thought groups are rarely taught. They can be incorporated into speaking, however, through planned oral presentations, through copying other speakers in their presentations (such as TED Talks), and through use of dramatic scenes and subsequent role plays (Goodwin, 2005). An ultimate goal in these kinds of controlled activities is spontaneous thought groups that are logical and communicatively

Table 10.3 Orthography

More important	Less important
Basic skills in decoding written English into spoken, especially for vowels (Gilbert, 2012); changeable consonant letter/sound correspondences, and final grammatical endings such as –s/'s and –ed (Dickerson, 1989)	Complex spelling rules that have minor payoff, e.g., <th> spelling–sound correspondences

successful. This kind of performance is unlikely without speech that is sufficiently automatic (Gatbonton & Segalowitz, 1988).

Table 10.3 is about another non-pronunciation language feature that may be essential for pronunciation teaching. Many errors in pronunciation can be attributed to the ways in which L2 speakers negotiate the orthography/phonology connections of English. The most common view of spelling among English teachers is that spelling has no clear connection to how words are pronounced. This is unfair to L2 speakers, and it deprives them of the kinds of rules and regularities that can help them to pronounce new words. L2 speakers will continually encounter new words in reading, and it is essential that they be able to make intelligent guesses about what the words sound like.

Unlike Spanish or Turkish, English has a relatively opaque orthography. This means that the way words are pronounced is often not directly connected to the way they are spelled. It means that the same spelling can have multiple realizations (e.g., the <ch> in *character*, *chicken*, *machine*, and *choir* all sound different). It also means that the same phonetic realization may have multiple spellings (e.g., [ʃ] can be found in *sugar*, *social*, *shoes*, *nation*, *mission*, and *machine*). This does not mean that English is unsystematic in its spelling–sound connections. Chomsky and Halle (1968) argue that English spelling is close to ideal for English. By this, they mean that modern-day English is conservative in regards to spelling, and that morphemes with the same basic meanings are largely unchanging in different words (e.g., the *cav-* in *cave*, *cavity*, and *excavate* all have the same meaning, having to do with "a hole"). The pronunciation of vowels in related words is then dependent on whether the vowel is stressed and where the vowel occurs in the word. So cav– in *cave* is the only syllable, and is stressed, giving it a sound of [e] in English. The cav– in *cavity* is also stressed, but is the first syllable followed by two other syllables, giving a pronunciation of [æ]. Another pair of words like *cave/cavity* is *sane/sanity*. Finally, the –cav– in *excavate* is not stressed, giving it a pronunciation of [ə], the default unstressed vowel sound for English. This indirect connection of spelling and pronunciation makes it difficult to teach English pronunciation from spelling alone. But it also means that written English is nearly an ideal spelling system to allow written communication to be mutually intelligible across varieties and across space and time. For example, Australian, Nigerian, Scottish, Indian, South African, and North American writers can be understood anywhere in the world, despite vast differences in pronunciation. The nearly invariant English spelling system also means that modern readers can read texts from other centuries, even though the English of hundreds of years ago was pronounced very differently from today.

While pronunciation is often indirectly related to spelling, the relationships are regular enough that teachers should be confident in telling L2 learners that spelling is reliable. L2 learners from various languages are largely literate, and they will make use of spelling in learning to pronounce words; it is unfair to them to say that there is no system that they can understand (Kreidler, 1972). Instead, there are plenty of reasons to tell them about spelling regularities for consonants (Dickerson, 2013), vowels (Dickerson & Finney, 1978; Gilbert, 2012), and word stress (Dickerson, 1989; Hahn & Dickerson, 1999), among other features.

Segments, Syllables and Word Stress: What to Teach

Segments, syllables, and word stress are all features that are likely to impact intelligibility at the word level. Segments (consonants and vowels) are one of the features we know most about for intelligibility decisions. Segments also interact with each other. Lengthened vowels are an important cue to consonant voicing. For example, the vowel in *lose* is longer than the vowel in *loose*, helping listeners to interpret the final consonant as [z] and the second as [s]. The importance of syllables for intelligibility is closely tied to how consonant clusters are pronounced. Because not all languages allow the same range of consonant clusters that English does, L2 speakers may simplify clusters in English by inserting vowels to separate consonants (e.g., *shop* pronounced as *shopu*, making a CVC syllable into two CV syllables), or by deleting consonants (e.g., *clasp* pronounced as *class*, turning a CVCC syllable into a CVC syllable). Syllables are also affected by the addition of the grammatical endings –ed and –s (*walked*, *walks*), which can create clusters from single consonants in the root word. Finally, word stress affects word intelligibility. A wrongly stressed word can lead to an unintelligible pronunciation, especially if it changes the ways that consonants and vowels in the word are pronounced (*sentences* pronounced as [sənˈtʰɛnsəz] rather than the expected [ˈsɛnʔənsəz].

Tables 10.4 and 10.5 list principles related to segmentals. Consonants and vowels are especially important in determining word intelligibility. One of the more important measures is functional load (FL) – that is, a measure of how much work two sounds do in distinguishing different words in a language. Although FL means more than the number of minimal pairs two sounds participate in (see Sewell, 2017), the number of minimal pairs in different environments

Table 10.4 Consonants

More important	Less important
High functional load (e.g., /l/–/n/, /p/–/f/)	Low functional load (e.g., /d/–/ð/)
Lengthened vowels before voiced consonants or in open syllables (see Table 10.5 as well)	Allophonic variants that mark varieties, such as the flap/tap for intervocalic /t–d/ in American English, the labiodental approximant for /ɹ/ for some British English speakers.
Initial consonants	Medial consonants between vowels

Table 10.5 Vowels

More important	Less important
High functional load contrasts (e.g., /ɛ–æ/, /i–ɪ/, /ɑ–ʌ/)	Low functional load contrasts (e.g., /u–ʊ/)
Vowel quality distinctions rather than length as a phonemic distinguisher (see Table 10.4, however, for the importance of vowel length as a cue to voicing in consonants)	Vowel distinctions in syllables ending in <r> and those not before <r> (e.g., *paid/pair, feel/fear*)
Vowels in stressed syllables	Distinctions in which vowels have merged in certain varieties (e.g., distinguishing the vowels in *cot–caught*)
	Vowel distinctions in neutralizing contexts, especially before [g], [ŋ], and [ɫ] (e.g., *beg/bag, sing, pool/pull*)

can be used as a quick proxy for FL. Brown (1988) describes FL on a scale of one to ten, with ten being the highest FL measure and one the lowest. Qian et al. (2018) use five as the cut-off point for high FL contrasts (1–4 are considered low), but an appropriate cut-off score between high and low FL contrasts is not clear from the research on FL.

Not all high FL contrasts are likely to be important, especially if the two sounds are unlikely to be confused in perception. For example, /f–h/ has an FL of nine (Brown, 1988), meaning it has many minimal pairs, but the contrast is not very likely to be confused by many L2 learners besides Japanese learners of English because of the wide difference in place of articulation for the two fricatives. For a more complete list of FL contrasts, see Brown (1988) or Derwing and Munro (2014).

Vowel quality and length distinctions are complicated in their importance for intelligibility, though I argue that both are important. The tense vowels in pairs like /i–ɪ/ and /u–ʊ/ (the first vowel in each pair) are longer than the lax vowels (the second in each pair), but only if they are in the same linguistic environment. Thus the vowel in *beat* is longer than the vowel in *bit*, but not than the vowel in *bid* (which occurs before a voiced consonant, causing a lengthened vowel). Length is not phonemic in English, but it does serve an important function in helping listeners distinguish between following voiced and voiceless consonants. Hearing a longer vowel indicates that the following consonant is voiced rather than voiceless. Vowel length, however, does not reliably distinguish between tense and lax vowels across linguistic environments. For this reason, vowel length is included as important for consonants, while vowel quality distinctions in high FL contrasts are included as important for vowels. Some of these quality distinctions are high FL (e.g., /i–ɪ/), while others are low FL (e.g., /u–ʊ/). In general, however, English does not make distinctions between vowel phonemes on the basis of the length of the vowel. So-called long and short vowels are different in their quality, not in their length.

Initial consonants are especially important for intelligibility (Cutler, 2012), especially if they begin a stressed syllable, since they are especially influential in helping listeners decide among various words that are in competition for recognition. Medial consonants are less important, but final consonants are also important, partly because they are the placement of inflectional endings in English (Zielinski, 2008). Finally, stressed vowels are also critical for intelligibility (Bent, Bradlow, & Smith, 2007; Zielinski, 2008).

Certain types of consonant and vowel features are less important. First, vowels in neutralizing contexts (such as before voiced velar

Table 10.6 Consonant clusters and syllable structure

More important	Less important
Initial consonant clusters	Medial consonant clusters
Final consonant clusters, including those created with –ed and –s/'s endings	Complex consonant clusters when NSs simplify (e.g., *months* pronounced as [mʌnθs] rather than [mʌns], or *clothes* pronounced as [kloθz] rather than [kloz])
Vowels pronounced when no vowel is expected (e.g., *evening, temperature, chocolate* with all written vowels pronounced), unexpected vowels (e.g., *gift → gifuto*), or the insertion of unexpected vowels with grammatical endings (e.g., *walked → walk it*)	Well-attested epenthesis examples in NS speech (e.g., *ath(e)lete, real(a)tor*)
Unexpected sound or syllable deletions	Well-attested syllable deletions (e.g., *sent some, cost more*)

consonants) or which are not consistent across varieties of English (the merged low back vowel distinction which is lost in some major varieties, as suggested by Jenner [1989]), as well as the diphthongized vowel distinctions in r-less dialects (British English *fear, care, pure, four*) would all be part of the less important category.

In Table 10.6, consonant clusters and syllable structure are presented together because of the ways they interact in the speech of L2 speakers. Consonant clusters are among the most pedagogically neglected areas in pronunciation (Cardoso, 2017). They appear to be subject to many of the same principles that single consonants are. Clusters with high FL sounds such as /l/–/ɹ/ (e.g., *pray–play, grow–glow*) will be important like singles (e.g., *ray–lay, row–low*), although they are less likely to distinguish as many pairs of words (see Cutler, 2012, ch. 9). Clusters are especially important when they are initial (as are initial singletons) or final, but less so when they are found medially, since in medial position clusters can more easily re-syllabify into different syllables (e.g., the [nt] in *paint* can be pronounced in two syllables in *pain.ting*, effectively simplifying the cluster to single initial and final consonants).

The biggest difference between singletons and clusters is related to syllable structure. Clusters are more subject to changes that affect the syllable structure of words, specifically in deletions of one or more consonants (e.g., *sprain → spain*) or the insertion of vowels to break up clusters, thus changing the number of syllables in a word (e.g., *plastic* → *bilastik*). Any change in syllable structure has the potential to affect intelligibility, and should be a target of instruction.

It may also be the case that L2 speakers create difficulties with syllable structure by trying to say sounds that L1 speakers do not. This will lead to unexpected pronunciations that can be unintelligible. For example, the word *month* requires two consonants at the end, but when the word is plural, the <th> is either deleted or changed to [t] ([mʌnθs] → [mʌns/mʌnts]). Attempts to say the [θ] are not only unnecessary, they may make the word less intelligible because of changes to the expected syllable structure of the word, such as [mʌnθəs].

Finally, consonant clusters at the ends of words are often created because of –s/'s and –ed endings. For example, *laughs* [fs], *loved* [vd], *mourned* [ɹnd], *lapsed* [pst], and others create consonant clusters that carry grammatical meaning at the ends, and the grammatical endings of the clusters cannot be simplified. Because the morphemes are often spelled with <e>, sometimes in the case of <es> and always in the case of <ed>, this may lead learners to create a logical pronunciation that includes an extra syllable (e.g., *walked* → [wɒkəd], sounding similar to "*walk it*"). Such insertions can lead to loss of intelligibility.

The –ed and –s endings are a mainstay in pronunciation teaching materials, where they are taught from a rule-based approach that tells learners the three-way pronunciation patterns for –ed and –s/'s and assumes this will be sufficient to create accurate pronunciation. This does not seem to be true (Hawkins & Liszka, 2003). Only rarely are students told why it is important to say them in particular ways or what effects spoken errors for these forms may have (Dale and Poms [1994] is an unusual exception). Celce-Murcia, Brinton, Goodwin, and Griner (2010) include "description and analysis" as one of the critical elements in communicative teaching of pronunciation. Description and analysis needs to be extended beyond telling learners how to make sounds to telling learners why it is important, and letting them know that what is being taught is based upon research on intelligibility. This is a neglected part of pronunciation teaching, yet it is essential for an intelligibility-based approach. It is also something that those adhering to a nativeness approach cannot match.

Different grammatical functions are typically presented together because their phonological and written forms are the same, even though the same written forms serve multiple grammatical functions and have different acquisition trajectories (Luk & Shirai, 2009). This problem is especially flagrant with –s/'s suffixes, where three very different functions are presented together, as though their pronunciations were the only thing that were important. Although this is a special problem with the presentation of –s/'s, differential performance has also been documented with –ed endings. Bayley (1994) found, for example, that Chinese students produced –ed twice as successfully in perfective (i.e., past tense) compared to imperfective contexts (i.e., past participle), suggesting again that teaching the pronunciation of grammatical morphemes without attending to their role in the grammar is unlikely to target the actual reasons that learners mispronounce in spontaneous speech.

The morphophonological rules, although elegant in their simplicity, are not cognitively simple. Language learners need to know a number of things before they can apply the rules to their speech, and need additional practice for automaticity. For example, the extras syllable for –s/'s endings requires that learners be able to identify sibilant sounds ([s, z, ʃ, ʒ, t͡ʃ, d͡ʒ] at the end of the base word, either from pronunciation or from spelling patterns (Dickerson, 1989). If the final sound is not a sibilant, learners are told to identify whether the final sound of the base is voiced or voiceless, a difficult task that requires both linguistic sophistication and the ability to accurately hear and immediately analyze the phonetic detail in one's own private speech or the speech of interlocutors. Given the less than direct connection between sound and spelling in English, the task that learners have is quite complex and difficult, and is unlikely to show immediate success in the stream of speech without well-designed feedback (Yang & Lyster, 2010). In addition, there is a tendency for voiced sounds to devoice at word ends, and many English speakers do not fully voice stops in any environment. Nonetheless, almost every book presents the voicing distinction as essential for final grammatical morphemes as it is for final phonemes, but it actually appears to be rather unimportant for the pronunciation of morphemes (Dickerson, 1990).

Brutten, Mouw, and Perkins (1986) tested Dickerson's assertion with ESL (English as a second language) learners of varying proficiencies and L1s, and found that presenting the pronunciation of morphemes as a two-way choice helped improve the pronunciation of the morphemes. Their research, however, did not examine the comparative effectiveness of the three-way linguistic analysis. The two-way analysis, however, was promising for learning. It reduces the complexity of the system L2 learners have to use by creating a binary decision and assuming that normal voicing assimilation processes will result in adequate pronunciation for non-syllabic endings. Even where this does not happen, the meaning of the endings will still be apparent because an expected morphophonological variant is available. In some

Table 10.7 Word stress

More important	Less important
Rightward mis-stressings (e.g., *COMfort* said as *comFORT*; *FOLLow* as *folLOW*)	Leftward mis-stressings (e.g., *inSURE* said as *INsure*; *comPLETE* said as *COMplete*)
Minimal straightforward rules that do not require extensive morphological knowledge (e.g., stress the vowel before the i+Vowel ending as in *'nation, anti'social, 'radius* – see Dickerson, 1989)	Teaching stress patterns for large numbers of suffixes, especially those that don't affect stress (e.g., Dauer, 1993; see Chapter 5 for more)
Unpredictable minimal pairs (e.g., *innocence/in essence* – see Dauer, 1993)	Noun–verb stress pairs (e.g., *an INsult/to inSULT*) or numbers (e.g., *thirteen/thirty*)
Mis-stressings with changed vowel quality (e.g., *senTENces*)	Mis-stressings without changed vowel quality (e.g., *concenTRATE*)
Embodied practice for stress differences (Gilbert, 2001; Murphy, 2004) using tricks like stretching rubberbands	

varieties of English, the expected voicing assimilation does not occur in all cases, such as the past tense after some sonorants, e.g., *learnt, spelt.*

Word stress is a pervasive feature of English speech and its production and perception are critical for intelligibility (Table 10.7). Instruction on word stress should therefore play a central role in pronunciation teaching in all contexts. Jenkins (2000) argues that word stress is a gray area for intelligibility, but the research instead indicates that the importance of word stress ranges from absolutely critical (Isaacs & Trofimovich, 2012) to merely important (Field, 2005). It is important for L2 speakers who communicate with L1 speakers, as well as in ELF (English as lingua franca) contexts (Lewis & Deterding, 2018).

The pronunciation of words (including those with more than one syllable) is the middle ground between production at the segmental and syllable level, and rhythmic structure, prominence, and tune (the last two being aspects of intonation) at the suprasegmental level of speech. Stressed syllables often determine the placement of other important features for intelligibility. They are the location for aspirated stops, they have clear vowels, their orthographic connections to sounds are easier to identify, and they are islands of reliability (Dechert, 1980; Field, 2005) for listeners to identify words in discourse. Unstressed syllables and words are, in contrast, the background against which stressed syllables are more prominent. They are harder to hear, are orthographically less explicit, and are the places where connected speech modifications such as deletions, additions, and sound modifications are more likely to occur. In regard to suprasegmentals, the stressed syllables of words are most likely to be marked with pitch accents and prominence, where they are the beginning of intonational movement, and they help configure the rhythmic structure of the spoken phrase. In other words, many intelligibility-related pronunciation features are dependent on word stress in English, and pronunciation teachers can profitably use stress to teach these features. At the very least, these other important features cannot be taught without making clear how stress impacts them.

Because word stress has been heavily studied, it is both clear that certain things make it essential for intelligibility, and also clear that other elements of word stress are quite unimportant for intelligibility. Specifically, most awareness-building exercises currently found in teaching materials are unlikely to be helpful, both because they are overabundant and because they focus on things that are unlikely to impact intelligibility. The main topics connected to awareness raising are the stress of noun–verb pairs, adjective–noun/compound noun distinctions, *–teen/ty* numbers, phrasal verbs, and minimal pairs.

Research by Cutler (1986) and Small, Simon, and Goldberg (1988) show that modeling one word from noun–verb pairs that differ only in stress promotes lexical access of both noun and verb forms. These types of minimal pairs are rare in free-stress languages (Cutler, 1986, 2015), and because of their rarity, are likely not worth emphasizing. Even for those pairs that include vowel quality changes (e.g., *REcord/ reCORD*), most pairs include a rare word that is unlikely to compete for access (e.g., the noun in the *COMbine/comBINE* pair). Finally, given the importance of vowel quality changes in stress recognition, it may be unnecessary to emphasize the prosodic differences in these pairs.

The use of adjective–noun/compound noun distinctions (e.g., *the white HOUSE* versus *the WHITE House*), *–teen/ty* numbers, and phrasal verbs to raise awareness of stress importance suffers from the same kinds of issues as noun–verb pairs. In each case, stress differences are at best a distinction between primary and non-primary stress. They may indicate that the speaker has an accent, but accentedness does not necessarily affect intelligibility. Slowiaczek (1990) showed that these kinds of mis-stresses led to slightly slower processing under several noise conditions, but there was no difference in intelligibility, that is, listeners were equally successful in decoding mis-stressed as stressed words.

The use of *–teen/ty* words is a particularly problematic example for raising awareness of word-stress issues. Only in the most isolated examples can we propose that these numbers differ in stress, e.g., *thirTEEN/THIRty*. We know that –teen numbers regularly shift stress, as in the well-known *thirTEEN/THIRteen MEN* example. We also know that native listeners regularly have difficulty hearing these differences – neither stress nor segmental features (e.g., the /n/) are consistently reliable indicators of the intended word. Native listeners rely instead on communication strategies when there are questions about the number being used. For example, they may say "Did you say 'three-oh' or 'one-three'?"

Despite its importance as a general category, there is much that we do not know about word stress and its role in intelligibility. For example, we do not know exactly what word-stress problems are common for learners of various proficiency levels, which word-stress problems affect understanding for NS and/or NNS listeners, whether learners can perceive stress but not produce it, or vice versa. We do not know how many word-stress errors are too many, or how word-stress importance varies for different L1 backgrounds. For example, Peperkamp, Dupoux, and Sebastien-Galles (1999) proposed a Stress-Deafness model in which they argued that French learners are persistently "deaf" to stress distinctions in Spanish, a language that, like English, has variable stress on multi-syllabic words. This French L1 difficulty with word stress in L2 acquisition has also been documented for English (Isaacs & Trofimovich, 2012; Tremblay, 2008), suggesting that simply providing rules is unlikely to be successful when learners cannot hear word-stress. While French listeners may be extreme in terms of perception, Altmann's (2006) Stress Typology model argues that stress perception is strongly influenced by the learner's first language.

Suprasegmentals and Intelligibility: Why They Remain Important

A radical departure of Jenkins (2000) from commonly accepted views of pronunciation teaching was the contention that most suprasegmentals (apart from prominence) are unimportant for intelligibility. Although Jenkins argued that she only spoke for NNS–NNS intelligibility, her view of intelligibility was narrow, limited primarily to intelligibility at the word level. Despite the importance of this type of intelligibility, there are other ways that intelligibility can be compromised, especially at the level of the message and its interpretation (Smith & Nelson, 1985). It is at these levels that suprasegmentals are most important, and it is at these levels that the methodology employed by Jenkins was unlikely to demonstrate loss of intelligibility. Suprasegmentals are discourse-based features, and as such they are unlikely to affect the intelligibility of words. In the following sections, the importance of rhythm, prominence (nuclear stress in Jenkins, 2000), and intonation are presented as including both more and less important elements. A major argument is made that if we have a limited view of intelligibility, we are unlikely to recognize unintelligibility when it actually exists.

In Tables 10.8 and 10.9, rhythm and connected speech are treated together because of significant overlap in their recommendations, and because many connected speech phenomena are closely connected to

Table 10.8 Rhythm

More important	Less important
Perception training to identify key words in the stream of speech	Production of schwa in unstressed syllables
Lengthening of stressed syllables, and shortening of unstressed syllables	Distinctions in unstressed syllable quality, e.g., between [ə] and [ɪ]
Being able to guess unstressed function words from inadequate acoustic signals	
Connections of stress and word classes	
Weak forms of frequent function words	

Table 10.9 Connected speech

More important	Less important
Perception of connected speech features that result in unexpected segments, both in controlled contexts and in "jungle listening" (Cauldwell, 2013)	Producing most types of connected speech
Perceiving differences between full and reduced vowels (especially schwa) in normal speech, and being able to interpret speech based on full vowels	Producing reduced vowels, apart from durational differences between stressed and unstressed syllables
Perception of linking that does not change segments	
Contractions versus full forms (e.g., *I'm* versus *I am*)	

rhythm. Rhythm refers to relative length, clarity, and distinctiveness of syllables, at least for a stress-based language like English. Connected speech phenomena include a wide variety of features that are dependent both on the linguistic environment and the stress patterns of words and phrases. These features may reflect pronunciation variations that are the result of the linguistic environment, speech register, or dialect. For example, the <t> in *native, natural, nation,* and *nativity* will be pronounced (in American English) as [ɾ], [tʃ], [ʃ], and [tʰ], pronunciations that are dependent both on stress and the following sounds. Connected speech is often well-described when it is relatively controlled – that is, the connections are seen in short phrases or in relatively formal normal speech. However, research has also shown that modifications to connected speech often become quite unexpected when speech becomes more casual or quicker, and that speakers take unexpected shortcuts while preserving the stressed syllables (Johnson, 2004; Shockey, 2003). Cauldwell (2013) calls this "jungle listening," using the image of how plants grow differently within a single planter, a greenhouse, and a jungle. By the jungle (or natural) stage, plants grow over each other to the extent that it is often difficult to know where one ends and the other begins. In the same way, the shape of words may change unexpectedly from their citation forms when speech is least monitored. This provides a great challenge for listening comprehension, but it is a challenge that pronunciation instruction can help with.

Rhythm is central to a listener's ability to segment speech – that is, to identify words in the speech stream. Likewise, connected speech phenomena may change the shapes of words in ways that L2 speakers may find to be unintelligible. As a result, both of these pronunciation categories are critical for intelligibility for L2 listeners. It is in production that the primary difference is found in these two categories. Rhythm in English includes longer and shorter syllables, corresponding roughly to stressed and unstressed syllables. The length differences of vowels are critical in how listeners hear the speech of others, and anyone who will interact with NSs (that is, most learners at some point) will be more successful if they can produce alternations of longer and shorter syllables.

The rhythm of English also has a consequence for vowel quality distinctions. Unstressed syllables in NS varieties tend strongly toward schwa, and from a listening viewpoint, L2 learners must learn to recognize the presence of schwa as a marker of unstressed syllables, and therefore less likely to be the beginning of a word. It is unlikely, however, that L2 speakers need to produce schwa in all the places that L1 English speakers do. The one exception to this is the production of frequent weak forms (e.g., *a, an, on, in, and, of, from*). These weak forms are extremely frequent in speech (they are over-represented in the top 100 most frequent words) and their weak form pronunciation is the *normal* pronunciation. The full form, in contrast, is likely to be heard as carrying some kind of special meaning. Thus, L2 speakers should learn the normal pronunciation of these weak forms. In this recommendation, I disagree with Jenkins (2000) and Walker (2010), who say that weak forms are unimportant for intelligibility. If they mean that weak forms are unimportant for word intelligibility alone, I would have no problem. But intelligibility is not just the ability to identify words but also messages and intentions, and it is here that using full vowels instead of reduced vowels, or being heard to emphasize unexpected words, can lead to loss of intelligibility (Low, 2006).

Likewise, English has a regular connection between word classes and stress, and L2 speakers need to be made aware of this connection for both perception and production. Finally, some types of connected speech features are important because of the differences in meaning they can signify. In this, I include the difference between contracted and uncontracted forms. In speech, the contracted form (e.g., *I'm, you're*) is normal, and the uncontracted form (e.g., *I am, you are*) is marked, and may sound like some special meaning is being communicated.

Tables 10.10 and 10.11 include more and less important features for intonation, which includes prominence, tune, and pitch range in English (see Chapter 7). Intonation has many aspects that are critical for intelligibility and for comprehensibility, and even though it is often considered by teachers as hard to teach (Sonsaat, 2017), there is no

Table 10.10 Prominence

More important	Less important
Default prominence (i.e., the last content word of the thought group)	Exceptional patterns (e.g., when the final content word is an adverbial, e.g., *I'd like to LEAVE soon*)
Contrastive prominence (e.g., *I'd like the RED roses*)	Low-frequency patterns (e.g., event sentences such as *The KETTle's boiling*)
New information (e.g., *The singer is GOOD, but not THAT good*)	
De-accented given information (e.g., *The singer is GOOD, but not THAT good*)	

Table 10.11 Intonation

More important	Less important
Rising/falling distinctions on declaratives or incomplete sentences	Rising/falling on yes/no questions
Intonation across multiple phrases, with rising intonation early in extended speech and falling intonation at a pause break (Pickering, 2001)	Intonation on structures that are rarely used by L2 learners, e.g., tag questions
Perception of meaning on falling–rising contours and other nonfinal contours (e.g., level contours)	Intonation rules tied to grammatical structures
Liveliness of intonation and rhythmic variation for monologic speech (Hincks, 2003)	Intonation as determinative of emotional or attitudinal meaning
Topic-changing pitches (paratones) in speech. (e.g., *The **NEXT** topic we'll discuss in intonation*). These paratones signal changes in what is being talked about and are critical for intelligibility in both perception and for production	

lack of accessible ideas available for how to describe and approach the teaching of intonation (e.g., Allen, 1971; Bradford, 1988; Kenworthy, 1987; Wells, 2006). Prominence is widely agreed to be important for all types of English speech, but it is important for teachers and learners to be able to employ and understand certain widely used functions rather than infrequent patterns, no matter how linguistically interesting they may be for testing theories (e.g., Allerton & Cruttenden, 1979). Tune and range also have features that are more and less important, especially the contrasts between rising and falling tunes, signaling of topic changes through paratones, and perception of the meaning associated with particular tunes. Prominence and tune should be kept separate for teaching, since both contribute independently to the meaning of utterances.

More generally, intonation must be taught in context, preferably in genuine communicative contexts with actual language. In Levis (1999b), I argued that the teaching of intonation to L2 learners suffered from treating it as just another pronunciation feature, and advocated four changes to pedagogical materials. Unfortunately, the critiques offered then remain relevant. The first recommendation for teaching intonation was to teach intonation in explicit linguistic contexts. Intonational meaning makes sense only when it is used in appropriate contexts, and whenever it is presented as a phonological form only, learners are asked to understand exactly what they cannot understand. One of the most common types of exercises violating this principle is shifting-stress sentences, in which learners are led to believe that they can place prominence on any of the numbered words depending on the meaning they want to convey, as in (10.1). What this type of exercise does not typically do is provide contexts that sanction the prominence placements that allow meanings to make sense. They also do not point out that the contexts that license earlier prominence placements (e.g., Jane) are unlikely to license de-accenting the rest of the sentence, including all content words. Most important, this type of exercise pretends that L2 learners have access to the same kinds of contextual and pragmatic information that NSs do. But they don't, and telling learners that they can place prominence anywhere is educational malpractice.

(10.1)

Jane just bought a new red car.
  1 2   3   4   5   6

Second, I urged that teaching materials represent intonational meaning in generalizable ways. For L2 teaching, the meanings contributed by intonation may need to be limited to what is most likely to make sense. This means that only those features that are likely to promote better intelligibility should be included, and that many items interesting for linguistic analysis may need to be left out of L2 teaching. For example, L2 materials often represent intonation as being particularly influential in communicating emotions or attitudes. This seems attractive on the surface, but a dominant finding of research on intonation and emotion is that the connections between the two areas are indirect at best. NSs are not consistent in identifying the emotions that are communicated by speech, and intonation itself is multifaceted, making it difficult to identify clear connections between the two areas. Other ways of teaching intonation may present connections of pitch movement to grammatical structures, but these kinds of connections are unreliable (Levis, 1997). If features like prominence are used to package normal speech, or are rearranged to represent new and given information, or are used to call attention to contrasts, then those are the types of meanings that should be taught. And each should be taught separately and explicitly, and should not rely on the intuitions of NSs for their explanations. This may mean that L2 learners will not get the full explanation, but they can get enough to improve comprehensibility. Even linguists don't yet have the full explanations, and much that linguists do know is likely irrelevant for L2 teaching.

Third, I argued that teaching intonation must be done with communicative purposes in mind. The meaning of intonation is communicatively determined, and it must be taught in relation to communicative routines and goals if it is to make sense. As mentioned already, there is no right or wrong to intonation in the way that there is to segmentals or word stress. Statements can be spoken with rising or falling intonation, as can tag questions, WH questions, etc. Even yes–no questions, widely advocated in L2 teaching materials as being spoken with rising intonation, have long been shown to be spoken as often with falling as with rising intonation (Lee, 1980). This is why a strict connection between grammatical form and intonation is misguided. Instead, intonation variants can be either appropriate or inappropriate, given a particular context. A speaker may use rising intonation to reflect uncertainty or to sound more polite with yes–no questions (Thompson, 1995), while rising pitch and prominence on the WH word in WH questions may ask for repetition of what was said. These are only hints about the kind of upside-down approach to intonation that is needed. What I said in 1999 still holds true.

Explicitly joining intonation and communicative uses of language would greatly change the way intonation is taught. For pronunciation textbooks, it would result in a connection between intonation and specific communicative uses to which the intonation clearly contributes. For oral communication textbooks, intonation would have an explicit role in the syllabus, as it contributes to an overall ability to communicate (Levis, 1999b, p. 58).

Finally, I argued that we should teach intonation using realistic language. The final recommendation asks for something that has become far more possible than it was 20 years ago, which is to use realistic language (including incomplete utterances) to teach the communicative uses of intonation and the structures in which it occurs. With the increasing availability of spoken corpora, and a better understanding of how intonation, and other prosodic features, function within discourse (e.g., Szczepek Reed, 2012), it is now possible to connect prosody to language use in a way that even the best armchair-linguist-turned-language-teacher cannot. An example of this could be the case of tag questions, which are typically taught as polar opposites (rising stem, falling tag, and vice versa), but with no regard for who uses tag questions, when they use them, why, etc. (Asher & Reese, 2007), much less their functions (Holmes, 1982) and the variant forms that tags may take (e.g., *eh?, right?*). Ultimately, the use of more realistic language requires that teaching materials be created that indirectly reflect how speakers actually use language, rather than how materials developers think they should use language.

Conclusions

An intelligibility-based approach to improving spoken language production and perception primarily includes pronunciation, but it must also include other things that are addressed in this chapter. Jenkins (2000), for example, demonstrated that pronunciation was the cause of many examples of unintelligibility, but almost one-third of her examples were due to vocabulary and grammar. There is much more to be learned about how these other areas of language impact intelligibility. Pronunciation may affect intelligibility in a basic sense (e.g., saying /l/ when /n/ was intended can lead to misunderstanding that affects the identification of words), but the overall message or the interpretation of a message may also be impacted by mispronunciations. These are also losses of intelligibility, but may not be immediately identified as such. Pronunciation errors in suprasegmentals are likely to contribute to these other types of intelligibility problems, but they may not be heard as pronunciation errors but rather social ones (Gumperz, 1982).

Pronunciation, as important as it is, does not exist in a vacuum, but serves communicative abilities. When a word is unintelligible, it causes an impairment in communication. The quality of the spoken message is impacted, and the listener is left to interpret a message that is noisy, in that it is not delivered in a way that the listener expects. The quality of a spoken message is also impacted by other things besides pronunciation, including grammatical accuracy and appropriateness, pragmatic choices, the speech environment, familiarity with the accents of the speakers, the ways in which the perceptual systems of those talking influence what they hear, and a host of other issues. Even when intelligibility is not impacted, it may be difficult for listeners to understand each other because of the amount of work they have to do. Even if there is nothing in the speech that is unintelligible, an interaction may fail nonetheless if those talking are not willing to do the work needed to understand. This book has done far too little with comprehensibility, a concept that is ultimately as important to successful interaction as intelligibility.

Although I have written about how the listener's perspective is critical in judgments of intelligibility, this book does not do justice to the L2 listening side of the intelligibility equation. In L2 interactions, being able to understand the speech of others is just as important as being understood by others. This part of communicative interaction is closely tied to the pronunciation of connected speech and register variation, yet it is barely treated in the teaching of L2 listening comprehension.

Finally, an intelligibility-based approach must include a far better discussion of pronunciation teaching methodology than I have provided. It is encouraging that there is increasingly varied research addressing the importance of methodological choices such as focus-on-form (Saito & Lyster, 2012), shadowing (Foote & McDonough, 2017), drama (Galante & Thomson, 2017), high-variability phonetic training (Qian et al., 2018; Thomson, 2011, 2012), sensory-based training (Cerreta & Trofimovich, 2018), the use of cognitively oriented rules (M. Hahn, 2002; Sadat-Tehrani, 2017), gestures (Smotrova, 2017), visual feedback (Chun, Jiang, Myer, & Yang, 2015), and many other methodological choices. It makes sense that how we teach has at least as much importance as what we teach. However, many methodological choices remain unexamined, and this remains an important area of future development in the study of intelligibility.

References

Abercombie, D. (1967). *Elements of General Phonetics*. New York: Aldine Publishing Company.

Acton, W. (1984). Changing fossilized pronunciation. *TESOL Quarterly*, 18(1), 71–85.

Acton, W., Baker, A., Burri, M., & Teaman, B. (2013). Preliminaries to haptic-integrated pronunciation instruction. In J. Levis & K. LeVelle (eds.), *Proceedings of the 4th Pronunciation in Second Language Learning and Teaching Conference* (pp. 234–44). Ames, IA: Iowa State University.

Alameen, G. (2014). *The Effectiveness of Linking Instruction on NNS Speech Perception and Production*. Doctoral dissertation, Iowa State University.

Alameen, G., & Levis, J. (2015). Connected speech. In M. Reed & J. Levis (eds.), *The Handbook of English Pronunciation* (pp. 159–74). Boston, MA: Wiley-Blackwell.

Algeo, J. (1978). What consonant clusters are possible? *Word*, 29(3), 206–24.

Allen, V. F. (1971). Teaching intonation, from theory to practice. *TESOL Quarterly*, 5(1), 73–81.

Allerton, D. J., & Cruttenden, A. (1979). Three reasons for accenting a definite subject. *Journal of Linguistics*, 15(1), 49–53.

Al-Saidat, E. M. (2010). Phonological analysis of English phonotactics: A case study of Arab learners of English. *The Buckingham Journal of Language and Linguistics*, 3, 121–34.

Altmann, H. (2006). *The Perception and Production of Second Language Stress: A Cross-Linguistic Experimental Study*. Newark, DE: University of Delaware.

Anderson, J. I. (1983). Syllable simplification in the speech of second language learners. *Interlanguage Studies Bulletin*, 7(1), 4–36.

Anderson-Hsieh, J., & Koehler, K. (1988). The effect of foreign accent and speaking rate on native speaker comprehension. *Language Learning*, 38(4), 561–613.

Anderson-Hsieh, J., Riney, T., & Koehler, K. (1994). Connected speech modifications in the English of Japanese ESL learners. *Issues and Developments in English and Applied Linguistics (IDEAL)*, 7, 31–52.

Archibald, J. (1992). Adult abilities in L2 speech: Evidence from stress. In *New Sounds 92: Proceedings of the 1992 Amsterdam Symposium on the Acquisition of Second Language Speech* (pp. 1–16). Cambridge: Cambridge University Press.

Archibald, J. (1993a). Metrical phonology and the acquisition of L2 stress. In: W. Rutherford, H. Clahsen, & F. Eckman (eds.), *Confluence: Linguistics, L2 Acquisition, and Speech Pathology* (pp. 37–48). Amsterdam: John Benjamins.

Archibald, J. (1993b). The learnability of English metrical parameters by adult Spanish speakers. *International Review of Applied Linguistics*, 31(2), 129–41.

Archibald, J. (1997a). The acquisition of English stress by speakers of non-accentual languages: Lexical storage versus computation of stress. *Linguistics*, 35(1), 167–81.

Archibald, J. (1997b). The acquisition of L2 phrasal stress. In M. Young-Scholten & S. J. Hannah (eds.), *Focus on Phonological Acquisition* (pp. 263–90). Amsterdam: John Benjamins.

Archibald, J. (1998). Second language phonology, phonetics, and typology. *Studies in Second Language Acquisition*, 20(2), 189–211.

Arvaniti, A. (2009). Rhythm, timing and the timing of rhythm. *Phonetica*, 66(1–2), 46–63.

Arvaniti, A. (2012). The usefulness of metrics in the quantification of speech rhythm. *Journal of Phonetics*, 40(3), 351–73.

Asher, J. J. (1969). The total physical response approach to second language learning. *The Modern Language Journal*, 53(1), 3–17.

Asher, N., & Reese, B. (2007). Intonation and discourse: Biased questions. In S. Ishihara, S. Jannedy, & A. Schwarz (eds.). *Interdisciplinary Studies on Information Structure* (pp. 1–38). Potsdam: Universitätsverlag

Avery, P., & Ehrlich, S. (1992). *Teaching American English pronunciation*. Oxford: Oxford University Press.

Baker, R. E., & Bradlow, A. R. (2009). Variability in word duration as a function of probability, speech style, and prosody. *Language and Speech*, 52(4), 391–413.

Baker, W., & Trofimovich, P. (2006). Perceptual paths to accurate production of L2 vowels: The role of individual differences. *International Review of Applied Linguistics in Language Teaching*, 44(3), 231–50.

Baker, W., Trofimovich, P., Flege, J. E., Mack, M., & Halter, R. (2008). Child–adult differences in second-language phonological learning: The role of cross-language similarity. *Language and Speech*, 51(4), 317–42.

Bancroft, W. J. (1976). Suggestology and Suggestopedia: The theory of the Lozanov method. Retrieved from https://eric.ed.gov/?id=ED132857.

Bansal, R. K. (1969). The intelligibility of Indian English: Measurements of the intelligibility of connected speech, and sentence and word material, presented to listeners of different nationalities. Central Institute of English [available from Orient Longmans, Chennai].

Barrera-Pardo, D. (2008). The reality of stress-timing. *ELT Journal*, 62(1), 11–17.

Baumann, S., & Grice, M. (2006). The intonation of accessibility. *Journal of Pragmatics*, 38(10), 1636–57.

Bayley, R. (1994). Interlanguage variation and the quantitative paradigm: Past tense marking in Chinese-English. In E. Tarone, S. Gass, & A. Cohen (eds.), *Research Methodology in Second Language Acquisition* (pp. 157–81). New York, NY: Psychology Press.

Bell, P., Trofimovich, P., & Collins, L. (2015). Kick the ball or kicked the ball? Perception of the past morpheme –ed by second language learners. *Canadian Modern Language Review*, 71(1), 26–51.

Benrabah, M. (1997). Word-stress: A source of unintelligibility in English. *International Review of Applied Linguistics in Language Teaching*, 35(3), 157–66.

Bent, T., Bradlow, A. R., & Smith, B. L. (2007). Segmental errors in different word positions and their effects on intelligibility of non-native speech. In *Language Experience in Second Language Speech Learning: In Honor of James Emil Flege* (pp. 331–47). Amsterdam: John Benjamins.

Berg, T. (1999). Stress variation in British and American English. *World Englishes*, 18(2), 123–43.

Bing, J. M. (1985). *Aspects of English Prosody*. New York, NY: Garland Press.

Birch, S., & Clifton, C. (1995). Focus, accent, and argument structure: Effects on language comprehension. *Language and Speech*, 38(4), 365–91.

Bird, S. (2016). Pronunciation change in SENĆOTEN: An acoustic study of /k, kw, kw', q, q', qw qw'/ across generations of speakers. *Journal of the Acoustical Society of America*, 139(4), DOI: 10.1121/1.4950621.

Bishop, J. (2012). Information structural expectations in the perception of prosodic prominence. In G. Elordieta & P. Prieto (eds.), *Prosody and Meaning* (pp. 239–69). Berlin: Mouton de Gruyter.

Bock, J. K., & Mazzella, J. R. (1983). Intonational marking of given and new information: Some consequences for comprehension. *Memory & Cognition*, 11(1), 64–76.

Boersma, P., & Weeink, D. (2009). Praat: doing phonetics by computer [Computer program]. Retrieved May 1, 2017, from www.fon.hum.uva.nl/praat.

Bolinger, D. L. (1961). Contrastive accent and contrastive stress. *Language*, 37(1), 83–96.

Bolinger, D. (1972). Accent is predictable (if you're a mind-reader). *Language*, 48(3), 633–44.

Bolinger, D. (1986). *Intonation and Its Parts: Melody in Spoken English*. Stanford, CA: Stanford University Press.

Bongaerts, T., Planken, B., & Schils, E. (1995). Can late starters attain a native accent in a foreign language? A test of the critical period hypothesis. In D. Singleton & Z. Lengyel (eds.), *The Age Factor in Second Language Acquisition* (pp. 30–50). Clevedon: Multilingual Matters.

Bongaerts, T., Van Summeren, C., Planken, B., & Schils, E. (1997). Age and ultimate attainment in the pronunciation of a foreign language. *Studies in Second Language Acquisition*, 19(4), 447–65.

Bradford, B. (1988). *Intonation in Context*. Cambridge: Cambridge University Press.

Bradlow, A. R. (2008). Training non-native language sound patterns: lessons from training Japanese adults on the English /r/-/l/ contrast. In J. Hansen-Edwards & M. Zampini (eds.), *Phonology and Second Language Acquisition* (pp. 287–308). Amsterdam: John Benjamins.

Bradlow, A. R., & Bent, T. (2002). The clear speech effect for non-native listeners. *Journal of the Acoustical Society of America*, 112(1), 272–84.

Bradlow, A. R., Akahane-Yamada, R., Pisoni, D., & Tohkura, Y. (1999). Training Japanese listeners to identify English /r/ and /l/: Long-term retention of learning in perception and production. *Perception & Psychophysics*, 61, 977–85.

Bradlow, A. R., Pisoni, D., Akahane-Yamada, R., & Tohkura, Y. (1997). Training Japanese listeners to identify English /r/ and /l/: Some effects of perceptual learning on speech production. *Journal of the Acoustical Society of America*, 101, 2299–310.

Brazil, D. (1997). *The Communicative Value of Intonation in English*. Cambridge: Cambridge University Press.

Brazil, D., Coulthard, M., & Johns, C. (1980). *Discourse, Intonation, and Language Teaching*. Harlow: Longman.

Brinton, D. (2014). Epilogue to the myths: Best practices for teachers. In L. Grant (ed.), *Pronunciation Myths* (pp. 225–42). Ann Arbor, MI: University of Michigan Press.

Broersma, M., & Cutler, A. (2008). Phantom word activation in L2. *System*, 36(1), 22–34.

Broersma, M., & Cutler, A. (2011). Competition dynamics of second-language listening. *The Quarterly Journal of Experimental Psychology*, 64, 74–95.

Bronkhorst, A. W. (2000). The cocktail party phenomenon: A review of research on speech intelligibility in multiple-talker conditions. *Acta Acustica United with Acustica*, 86(1), 117–28.

Broselow, E., & Finer, D. (1991). Parameter setting in second language phonology and syntax. *Interlanguage Studies Bulletin (Utrecht)*, 7(1), 35–59.

Brown, A. (1988). Functional load and the teaching of pronunciation. *TESOL Quarterly*, 22(4), 593–606.

Brown, A. (1991). *Teaching English Pronunciation: A Book of Readings*: London: Routledge.

Brown, A. (2014). *Pronunciation and Phonetics: A Practical Guide for English Language Teachers*. London: Routledge.

Brown, G. (1977). *Listening to Spoken English*. London: Routledge.

Brown, G., Currie, K. L., & Kenworthy, J. (1980). *Questions of Intonation*. London: Croom Helm.

Brown, H. P. (1950). *American Speech Sounds and Rhythm: Intermediate*. New York: Audio-Forum.

Brown, R. (1973). *A First Language: The Early Stages*. Cambridge, MA: Harvard University Press.

Brown, J. D., & Kondo-Brown, K. (eds.) (2006). *Perspectives on Teaching Connected Speech to Second Language Speakers*. Mānoa: National Foreign Language Resource Center, University of Hawai'i at Mānoa.

Brutten, S. R., Mouw, J. T., & Perkins, K. (1986). The effects of language group, proficiency level, and instruction on ESL subjects' control of the {D} and {Z} morphemes. *TESOL Quarterly*, 20(3), 553–9.

Burns, T. C., Yoshida, K. A., Hill, K., & Werker, J. F. (2007). The development of phonetic representation in bilingual and monolingual infants. *Applied Psycholinguistics*, 28(3), 455–74.

Burri, M., Baker, A., & Chen, H. (2017). I feel like having a nervous breakdown. *Journal of Second Language Pronunciation*, 3(1), 109–35.

Campbell-Kibler, K. (2007). Accent, (ING), and the social logic of listener perceptions. *American Speech*, 82(1), 32–64.

Cardoso, W. (2017). English syllable structure. In O. Kang, R. Thomson, & J. Murphy (eds.), *The Routledge Handbook of Contemporary English Pronunciation* (pp. 122–36). New York: Routledge.

Cardoso, W., John, P., & French, L. (2009). The variable perception of /s/+ coronal onset clusters in Brazilian Portuguese English. In M. Watkins, S. Rauber, & B. Baptista (eds.), *Recent Research in Second Language Phonetics/Phonology: Perception and Production* (pp. 203–31). *Newcastle upon Tyne: Cambridge Scholars.*

Cardoso, W., & Liakin, D. (2009). When input frequency patterns fail to drive learning: The acquisition of sC onset clusters. In M. Watkins, A. Rauber, & B. Baptista (eds.), *Recent Research in Second Language Phonetics/Phonology: Perception and Production* (pp. 174–202). Newcastle upon Tyne: Cambridge Scholars.

Caspers, J., & Horłoza, K. (2012). Intelligibility of non-natively produced Dutch words: Interaction between segmental and suprasegmental errors. *Phonetica*, 69(1–2), 94–107.

Catford, J. C. (1987). Phonetics and the teaching of pronunciation: A systemic description of English phonology. In J. Morley (ed.), *Current Perspectives on Pronunciation: Practices Anchored in Theory* (pp. 87–100). Alexandria, VA: TESOL.

Catford, J. C., & Pisoni, D. B. (1970). Auditory vs. articulatory training in exotic sounds. *The Modern Language Journal*, 54(7), 477–81.

Cauldwell, R. (2002). The functional irrhytmicality of spontaneous speech: A discourse view of speech rhythms. *Apples: Journal of Applied Language Studies*, 2, (1), 1–24. Retrieved from https://jyx.jyu.fi/dspace/bitstream/handle/123456789/22698/Apples_2_1_2002_Cauldwell.pdf?sequence=1.

Cauldwell, R. (2013). *Phonology for Listening.* Birmingham: Speech in Action.

Celce-Murcia, M. (1987). Teaching pronunciation as communication. In J. Morley (ed.), *Current Perspectives on Pronunciation* (pp. 1–12). Alexandria, VA: TESOL.

Celce-Murcia, M., Brinton, D., & Goodwin, J. (1996). *Teaching Pronunciation: A Course Book and Reference Guide.* New York: Cambridge University Press.

Celce-Murcia, M., Brinton, D., Goodwin, J., & Griner, B. (2010). *Teaching Pronunciation: A Course Book and Reference Guide* (2nd ed.). New York: Cambridge University Press.

Cenoz, J., & Lecumberri, L. G. (1999). The effect of training on the discrimination of English vowels. *International Review of Applied Linguistics in Language Teaching*, 37(4), 261–76.

Cerreta, S. (2016). *Engaging the Senses: A Sensory-Based Approach to l2 Pronunciation.* Doctoral dissertation, Concordia University.

Cerreta, S. & Trofimovich, P. (2018). Engaging the senses: A sensory-based approach to L2 pronunciation instruction for actors. *Journal of Second Language Pronunciation*, 4(1), 46–71.

Chafe, W. L., & Li, C. N. (1976). Givenness, contrastiveness, definiteness, subjects, topics, and point of view. In C. Li (ed.), *Subject and Topic* (pp. 25–56). New York: Academic Press.

Chan, A. Y. (2007). The acquisition of English word-final consonants by Cantonese ESL learners in Hong Kong. *Canadian Journal of Linguistics/Revue canadienne de linguistique*, 52(3), 231–53.

Chan, M. (1987). *Phrase by Phrase.* Englewood Cliffs, NJ: Prentice Hall Regents.

Chela-Flores, B. (1998). *Teaching English Rhythm: From Theory to Practice.* Caracas: Fondos Editorial Tropykos.

Chen, A., Gussenhoven, C., & Rietveld, T. (2004). Language-specificity in the perception of paralinguistic intonational meaning. *Language and Speech,* 47(4), 311–49.

Chen, H. C. (2013). Chinese learners' acquisition of English word stress and factors affecting stress assignment. *Linguistics and Education,* 24(4), 545–55.

Chomsky, N. (1959). A review of BF Skinner's Verbal Behavior. *Language,* 35(1), 26–58.

Chomsky, N. (1965). *Aspects of the Theory of Syntax.* Cambridge, MA: MIT Press.

Chomsky, N., & Halle, M. (1968). *The Sound Pattern of English.* New York: Harper & Row

Chun, D. M. (1988). The neglected role of intonation in communicative competence and proficiency. *The Modern Language Journal,* 72(3), 295–303.

Chun, D. M., Jiang, Y., Meyr, J., & Yang, R. (2015). Acquisition of L2 Mandarin Chinese tones with learner-created tone visualizations. *Journal of Second Language Pronunciation,* 1(1), 86–114.

Clarey, E., & Dixson, R. J. (1947) *Pronunciation Exercises in English.* New York: Regents.

Clopper, C. G., & Bradlow, A. R. (2009). Free classification of American English dialects by native and non-native listeners. *Journal of Phonetics,* 37(4), 436–51.

Cole, J., Mo, Y., & Hasegawa-Johnson, M. (2010). Signal-based and expectation-based factors in the perception of prosodic prominence. *Laboratory Phonology,* 1(2), 425–52.

Coniam, D. (2002). Technology as an awareness-raising tool for sensitising teachers to features of stress and rhythm in English. *Language Awareness,* 11(1), 30–42.

Content, A., Dumay, N., & Frauenfelder, U. H. (2000). The role of syllable structure in lexical segmentation: Helping listeners avoid mondegreens. In *ISCA Tutorial and Research Workshop on Spoken Word Access Processes* (pp. 39–42). Retrieved from https://archive-ouverte.unige.ch/unige:82811

Cooper, N., Cutler, A., & Wales, R. (2002). Constraints of lexical stress on lexical access in English: Evidence from native and non-native listeners. *Language and Speech,* 45(3), 207–28.

Coppieters, R. (1987). Competence differences between native and near-native speakers. *Language,* 63, 544–73.

Couper-Kuhlen, E. (1996). Intonation and clause combining in discourse. *Pragmatics Quarterly,* 6(3), 389–426.

Couper-Kuhlen, E. (2001). Intonation and discourse: Current views from within. In D. Schiffrin, D. Tannen, & H. Hamilton (eds.), *The Handbook of Discourse Analysis* (pp. 13–34). Chichester: John Wiley & Sons.

Coxhead, A. (2000). A new academic word list. *TESOL Quarterly,* 34(2), 213–38.

Crowther, D., Trofimovich, P., Saito, K., & Isaacs, T. (2015). Second language comprehensibility revisited: Investigating the effects of learner background. *TESOL Quarterly,* 49(4), 814–37.

Cruttenden, A. (1990). Nucleus placement and three classes of exceptions. In S. Ramsaran (ed.), *Studies in the Pronunciation of English: A Commemorative Volume in Honour of AC Gimson* (pp. 9–18). London: Routledge.

Cruttenden, A. (2014). *Gimson's Pronunciation of English*. London: Routledge.

Crystal, D. (1969). *Prosodic Systems and Intonation in English*. Cambridge: Cambridge University Press.

Crystal, D. (2008). Two thousand million? *English Today*, 24(1), 3–6.

Cucchiarini, C., Strik, H., & Boves, L. (2000). Quantitative assessment of second language learners' fluency by means of automatic speech recognition technology. *Journal of the Acoustical Society of America*, 107(2), 989–99.

Cummins, C., & Rohde, H. (2015). Evoking context with contrastive stress: Effects on pragmatic enrichment. *Frontiers in Psychology*, 6, 1–11.

Cummins, F., & Port, R. (1998). Rhythmic constraints on stress timing in English. *Journal of Phonetics*, 26(2), 145–71.

Curran, C. A. (1961). Counseling skills adapted to the learning of foreign languages. *Bulletin of the Menninger Clinic*, 25(2), 78.

Curran, C. A. (1976). *Counseling-Learning in Second Languages*. Apple River, IL: Apple River Press.

Cutler, A. (1976). Phoneme-monitoring reaction time as a function of preceding intonation contour. *Attention, Perception, & Psychophysics*, 20(1), 55–60.

Cutler, A. (1983). Lexical complexity and sentence processing. In G. B. Flores d'Arcais & R. J. Jarvella (eds.), *The Process of Language Understanding* (pp. 43–79). Chichester: John Wiley & Sons.

Cutler, A. (1984). Stress and accent in language production and understanding. In D. Gybbon & H. Richter (eds.), *Intonation, Accent, and Rhythm: Studies in Discourse Phonology* (pp. 77–90). Berlin: Walter de Gruyter.

Cutler, A. (1986). Forbear is a homophone: Lexical prosody does not constrain lexical access. *Language and Speech*, 29(3), 201–20.

Cutler, A. (2009). Greater sensitivity to prosodic goodness in non-native than in native listeners. *Journal of the Acoustical Society of America*, 125(6), 3522–5.

Cutler, A. (2012). *Native Listening*. Cambridge, MA: MIT Press.

Cutler, A. (2015). Lexical stress in English pronunciation. In M. Reed & J. Levis (eds.), *The Handbook of English Pronunciation* (pp. 106–24). Boston, MA: Wiley-Blackwell.

Cutler, A., & Carter, D. M. (1987). The predominance of strong initial syllables in the English vocabulary. *Computer Speech & Language*, 2(3), 133–42.

Cutler, A., & Clifton, C. (1984). The use of prosodic information in word recognition. In H. Bouma & D. G. Bouwhuis (eds.), *Attention and Performance X: Control of Language Processes* (pp. 183–96). Hillsdale, NJ: Erlbaum.

Cutler, A., Dahan, D., & van Donselaar, W. (1997). Prosody in the comprehension of spoken language: A literature review. *Language and Speech*, 40(2), 141–201.

Cutler, A., & Darwin, C. J. (1981). Phoneme-monitoring reaction time and preceding prosody: Effects of stop closure duration and of fundamental frequency. *Attention, Perception, & Psychophysics*, 29(3), 217–24.

Cutler, A., & Fodor, J. A. (1979). Semantic focus and sentence comprehension. *Cognition*, 7(1), 49–59.

Cutler, A., & Foss, D. J. (1977). On the role of sentence stress in sentence processing. *Language and Speech*, 20(1), 1–10.

Cutler, A., Hawkins, J. A., & Gilligan, G. (1985). The suffixing preference: A processing explanation. *Linguistics*, 23, 723–58.

Cutler, A., & Norris, D. (1988). The role of strong syllables in segmentation for lexical access. *Journal of Experimental Psychology: Human Perception and Performance*, 14(1), 113–21.

Cutler, A., Smits, R., & Cooper, N. (2005). Vowel perception: Effects of non-native language vs. non-native dialect. *Speech Communication*, 47(1), 32–42.

Cutler, A., Weber, A., & Otake, T. (2006). Asymmetric mapping from phonetic to lexical representations in second-language listening. *Journal of Phonetics*, 34(2), 269–84.

Cutler, C. (2014). Accentedness, "passing" and crossing. In J. Levis & A. Moyer (eds.), *Social Dynamics in Second Language Accent* (pp. 145–67). Boston, MA: Degruyter.

Dale, P., & Poms, L. (1994). *English Pronunciation for International Students*. Englewood Cliffs, NJ: Regents/Prentice Hall.

Dalton, C., & Seidlhofer, B. (1994). *Pronunciation*. Oxford: Oxford University Press.

Dauer, R. M. (1983). Stress-timing and syllable-timing reanalyzed. *Journal of Phonetics*, 11, 51–62.

Dauer, R. M. (1993). *Accurate English*. Englewood Cliffs, NJ: Regents/Prentice Hall.

Dauer, R. M. (2005). The Lingua Franca Core: A new model for pronunciation instruction? *TESOL Quarterly*, 39(3), 543–50.

Davidson, L., & Shaw, J. A. (2012). Sources of illusion in consonant cluster perception. *Journal of Phonetics*, 40(2), 234–48.

Davis, S. M., & Kelly, M. H. (1997). Knowledge of the English noun–verb stress difference by native and nonnative speakers. *Journal of Memory and Language*, 36(3), 445–60.

de Bot, K. (1996). The psycholinguistics of the output hypothesis. *Language Learning*, 46(3), 529–55.

Dechert, H. W. (1980). Pauses and intonation as indicators of verbal planning in second-language speech productions: Two examples from a case study. In H. W. Dechert & M. Raupach (eds.), *Temporal Variables in Speech* (pp. 271–85). The Hague: Mouton.

Dellwo, V. (2008). The role of speech rate in perceiving speech rhythm. In *Speech Prosody*, 4(8), 375–8. Retrieved from https://pdfs.semanticscholar.org/34a9/91053d0c915d43327380ce02d10f671478ab.pdf

Derwing, T. M. (2010). Utopian goals for pronunciation teaching. In J. Levis & K. LeVelle (eds.), *Proceedings of the 1st Pronunciation in Second Language Learning and Teaching Conference*, Fall 2009 (pp. 24–37), Ames, IA: Iowa State University.

Derwing, T. M., Moulton, E., & Campbell, M. (2005). *Accent Doesn't Have to be an Obstacle: Final Report to University Teaching Services*. Edmonton, Alberta.

Derwing, T. M. & Munro, M. (1997). Accent, intelligibility, and comprehensibility: Evidence from four L1s. *Studies in Second Language Acquisition*, 19, 1–16.

Derwing, T., & Munro, M. J. (2001). What speaking rates do non-native listeners prefer? *Applied Linguistics*, 22(3), 324–37.

Derwing, T. M., & Munro, M. J. (2005). Second language accent and pronunciation teaching: A research-based approach. *TESOL Quarterly*, 39(3), 379–98.

Derwing, T. M., & Munro, M. (2009). Putting accent in its place: Rethinking obstacles to communication. *Language Teaching*, 42(4), 476–90.

Derwing, T., & Munro, M. (2014). Once you have been speaking a second language for years, it's too late to change your pronunciation. In L. Grant (ed.), *Pronunciation Myths: Applying Second Language Research to Classroom Teaching* (pp. 34–55). Ann Arbor, MI: University of Michigan Press.

Derwing, T. M., & Munro, M. J. (2015). *Pronunciation Fundamentals: Evidence-Based Perspectives for L2 Teaching and Research*. Philadelphia, PA: John Benjamins Publishing Company.

Derwing, T. M., Munro, M. J., Foote, J. A., Waugh, E., & Fleming, J. (2014). Opening the window on comprehensible pronunciation after 19 years: A workplace training study. *Language Learning*, 64(3), 526–48.

Derwing, T. M., Munro, M. J., & Thomson, R. I. (2007). A longitudinal study of ESL learners' fluency and comprehensibility development. *Applied Linguistics*, 29(3), 359–80.

Derwing, T. M., Munro, M. J., & Wiebe, G. (1997). Pronunciation instruction for fossilized learners: Can it help? *Applied Language Learning*, 8(2), 217–35.

Derwing, T. M., Munro, M. J., & Wiebe, G. (1998). Evidence in favor of a broad framework for pronunciation instruction. *Language Learning*, 48(3), 393–410.

Derwing, T. M. & Rossiter, M. J. (2002). ESL learners' perceptions of their pronunciation needs and strategies. *System*, 30, 155–66.

Derwing, T. M., & Rossiter, M. J. (2003). The effects of pronunciation instruction on the accuracy, fluency, and complexity of L2 accented speech. *Applied Language Learning*, 13(1), 1–17.

Derwing, T. M., Rossiter, M. J., & Ehrensberger-Dow, M. (2002). 'They speaked and wrote real good': Judgements of non-native and native grammar. *Language Awareness*, 11(2), 84–99.

Derwing, T. M., Rossiter, M. J., & Hannis, D. E. (2000). Enhancing social work students' willingness to listen to a foreign accent. *Canadian Social Work*, 2, 22–9.

Derwing, T. M., Rossiter, M. J., & Munro, M. J. (2002). Teaching native speakers to listen to foreign-accented speech. *Journal of Multilingual and Multicultural Development*, 23(4), 245–59.

Derwing, T. M., Thomson, R. I., & Munro, M. J. (2006). English pronunciation and fluency development in Mandarin and Slavic speakers. *System*, 34(2), 183–93.

Deterding, D. (2005). Listening to Estuary English in Singapore. *TESOL Quarterly*, 39(3), 425–40.

Deterding, D. (2009). The effects of intensive pronunciation teaching for students from China. Paper presented at Teachers of English to Speakers of Other Languages, Denver, CO.

Deterding, D. (2010). ELF-based pronunciation teaching in China. *Chinese Journal of Applied Linguistics*, 33(6), 3–15.

Deterding, D., & Kirkpatrick, A. (2006). Emerging South-East Asian Englishes and intelligibility. *World Englishes*, 25(3–4), 391–409.

Dickerson, W. B. (1989). *Stress in the Speech Stream: The Rhythm of Spoken English*. Urbana, IL: University of Illinois Press.

Dickerson, W. B. (1990). Morphology via orthography: A visual approach to oral decisions. *Applied Linguistics*, 11(3), 238–52.

Dickerson, W. B. (2013). Prediction in teaching pronunciation. In C. Chapelle (ed.), *The Encyclopedia of Applied Linguistics*. Boston, MA: Wiley Blackwell.

Dickerson, W. B. (2015). Using orthography to teach pronunciation. In M. Reed & J. Levis (eds.), *The Handbook of English Pronunciation* (pp. 488–504). Boston, MA: Wiley Blackwell.

Dickerson, W. B., & Finney, R. H. (1978). Spelling in TESL: Stress cues to vowel quality. *TESOL Quarterly*, 12, 163–75.

Dupoux, E., Sebastián-Gallés, N., Navarrete, E., & Peperkamp, S. (2008). Persistent stress 'deafness': The case of French learners of Spanish. *Cognition*, 106(2), 682–706.

Eckman, F. R. (1977). Markedness and the contrastive analysis hypothesis. *Language Learning*, 27(2), 315–30.

Ellis, N. C. (2002). Frequency effects in language processing. *Studies in Second Language Acquisition*, 24(2), 143–88.

Ellis, R. (2009). The differential effects of three types of task planning on the fluency, complexity, and accuracy in L2 oral production. *Applied Linguistics*, 30(4), 474–509.

English Language Services. (1961). *Drills and Exercises in English Pronunciation: Stress and Intonation*. New York, NY: Collier Macmillan International.

Esling, J. H., & Wong, R. F. (1983). Voice quality settings and the teaching of pronunciation. *TESOL Quarterly*, 17(1), 89–95.

Fayer, J. M., & Krasinski, E. (1987). Native and nonnative judgments of intelligibility and irritation. *Language Learning*, 37(3), 313–26.

Fear, B. D., Cutler, A., & Butterfield, S. (1995). The strong/weak syllable distinction in English. *Journal of the Acoustical Society of America*, 97(3), 1893–904.

Ferguson, S. H., & Kewley-Port, D. (2007). Talker differences in clear and conversational speech: Acoustic characteristics of vowels. *Journal of Speech, Language, and Hearing Research*, 50(5), 1241–55.

Field, J. (2003). Promoting perception: Lexical segmentation in L2 listening. *ELT Journal*, 57(4), 325–34.

Field, J. (2005). Intelligibility and the listener: The role of lexical stress. *TESOL Quarterly*, 39(3), 399–423.

Field, J. (2008). Bricks or mortar: Which parts of the input does a second language listener rely on? *TESOL Quarterly*, 42(3), 411–32.

Field, J. (2014). Myth 3: Pronunciation teaching has to establish in the minds of the learners a set of distinct consonant and vowel sounds. In L. Grant (ed.), *Pronunciation Myths* (pp. 80–106). Ann Arbor, MI: University of Michigan Press.

Fillmore, C. J. (1979). On fluency. In C. Fillmore, D. Kempler, & W. Wang (eds.), *Individual Differences in Language Ability and Language Behavior* (pp. 85–101). New York, NY: Academic Press.

Firth, S. (1992). Pronunciation syllabus design: A question of focus. In P. Avery & S. Ehrlich (eds.), *Teaching American English Pronunciation* (pp. 173–83). Oxford: Oxford University Press.

Fischer, J. L. (1958). Social influences on the choice of a linguistic variant. *Word*, 14(1), 47–56.

Flege, J. E. (1995). Second language speech learning theory, findings, and problems. In W. Strange (ed.), *Speech Perception and Linguistic Experience: Issues in Cross-Language Research* (pp. 233–77). Timonium, MD: York Press.

Flege, J. E. (1999). Age of learning and second language speech. In D. Birdsong (ed.), *Second Language Acquisition and the Critical Period Hypothesis* (pp. 101–31). Mahwah, NJ: Lawrence Erlbaum.

Flege, J. E., & Bohn, O.-S. (1989). An instrumental study of vowel reduction and stress placement in Spanish-accented English. *Studies in Second Language Acquisition*, 11(1), 35–62.

Flege, J. E., Bohn, O. S., & Jang, S. (1997). Effects of experience on non-native speakers' production and perception of English vowels. *Journal of Phonetics*, 25(4), 437–70.

Flege, J. E., Frieda, E. M., & Nozawa, T. (1997). Amount of native-language (L1) use affects the pronunciation of an L2. *Journal of Phonetics*, 25(2), 169–86.

Flege, J. E., MacKay, I. R., & Meador, D. (1999). Native Italian speakers' perception and production of English vowels. *Journal of the Acoustical Society of America*, 106(5), 2973–87.

Flege, J. E., Munro, M. J., & MacKay, I. R. (1995). Factors affecting strength of perceived foreign accent in a second language. *Journal of the Acoustical Society of America*, 97(5), 3125–34.

Flege, J. E., Takagi, N., & Mann, V. (1995). Japanese adults can learn to produce English /l/ and /l/ accurately. *Language and Speech*, 38(1), 25–55.

Flege, J. E., Yeni-Komshian, G. H., & Liu, S. (1999). Age constraints on second language acquisition. *Journal of Memory and Language*, 41(1), 78–104.

Fogerty, D., & Humes, L. E. (2012). The role of vowel and consonant fundamental frequency, envelope, and temporal fine structure cues to the intelligibility of words and sentences. *Journal of the Acoustical Society of America*, 131(2), 1490–501.

Fogerty, D., & Kewley-Port, D. (2009). Perceptual contributions of the consonant–vowel boundary to sentence intelligibility. *Journal of the Acoustical Society of America*, 126(2), 847–57.

Foote, J. A., & McDonough, K. (2017). Using shadowing with mobile technology to improve L2 pronunciation. *Journal of Second Language Pronunciation*, 3(1), 34–56.

Fromkin, V. A. (1971). The non-anomalous nature of anomalous utterances. *Language*, 47(1), 27–52.

Fuchs, R., & Wunder, E. M. (2015). A sonority-based account of speech rhythm in Chinese learners of English. In U. Gut, R. Fuchs, & E-M Wunder (eds.),

Universal or Diverse Paths to English Phonology (pp. 165–83). Berlin: Mouton de Gruyter.

Gabriel, C., Stahnke, J., & Thulke, J. (2015). Acquiring English and French speech rhythm in a multilingual classroom: A comparison with Asian Englishes. In U. Gut, R. Fuchs, & E-M Wunder (eds.), *Universal or Diverse Paths to English Phonology* (pp. 135–63). Berlin: Mouton de Gruyter.

Galante, A., & Thomson, R. I. (2017). The effectiveness of drama as an instructional approach for the development of second language oral fluency, comprehensibility, and accentedness. *TESOL Quarterly*, 51(1), 115–42.

Gallego, J. C. (1990). The intelligibility of three nonnative English-speaking teaching assistants: An analysis of student-reported communication breakdowns. *Issues in Applied Linguistics*, 1(2). 219–37.

Gatbonton, E., & Segalowitz, N. (1988). Creative automatization: Principles for promoting fluency within a communicative framework. *TESOL Quarterly*, 22(3), 473–92.

Gatbonton, E., & Segalowitz, N. (2005). Rethinking communicative language teaching: A focus on access to fluency. *Canadian Modern Language Review*, 61(3), 325–53.

Gilbert, J. B. (1991). Gadgets: Non-verbal tools for teaching pronunciation. In A. Brown (ed.), *Teaching English Pronunciation: A Book of Readings* (pp. 308–22). London: Routledge.

Gilbert, J. B. (1995). Pronunciation practice as an aid to listening comprehension. In D. Mendelsohn & J. Rubin (eds.), *A Guide for the Teaching of Second Language Listening* (pp. 97–112). San Diego, CA: Dominie Press.

Gilbert, J. B. (2001). Six pronunciation priorities for the beginning student. *The CATESOL Journal*, 13(1), 173–82.

Gilbert, J. B. (2012). *Clear Speech: Pronunciation and Listening Comprehension in North American English*, 4th edition, New York, NY: Cambridge University Press.

Gluhareva, D., & Prieto, P. (2017). Training with rhythmic beat gestures benefits L2 pronunciation in discourse-demanding situations. *Language Teaching Research*, 21(5), 609–31.

Gluszek, A., & Dovidio, J. F. (2010). Speaking with a nonnative accent: Perceptions of bias, communication difficulties, and belonging in the United States. *Journal of Language and Social Psychology*, 29(2), 224–34.

Golombek, P., & Jordan, S. R. (2005). Becoming "black lambs" not "parrots": A poststructuralist orientation to intelligibility and identity. *TESOL Quarterly*, 39(3), 513–33.

Goodwin, J. (2005). The power of context in teaching pronunciation. In J. Frodesen & C. Holten (eds.), *The Power of Context in Language Teaching and Learning* (pp. 225–36). Boston, MA: Thomson Heinle.

Gordon, J., & Darcy, I. (2016). The development of comprehensible speech in L2 learners. *Journal of Second Language Pronunciation*, 2(1), 56–92.

Goto, H. (1971). Auditory perception by normal Japanese adults of the sounds "L" and "R". *Neuropsychologia*, 9(3), 317–23.

Grant, L. (1993). *Well Said: Advanced English Pronunciation*, 2nd edition. Boston, MA: Heinle & Heinle.

Grant, L. (2007). *Well Said: Advanced English Pronunciation*, 3rd edition. Boston, MA: Heinle & Heinle.

Grant, L. (2012). *Well Said: Pronunciation for Clear Communication*, 3rd edition. Boston, MA: Thomson Heinle.

Grant, L. (2014). Prologue to the myths: What teachers need to know. In L. Grant (ed.), *Pronunciation Myths* (pp. 1–33). Ann Arbor, MI: University of Michigan Press.

Guion, S. G. (2005). Knowledge of English word stress patterns in early and late Korean-English bilinguals. *Studies in Second Language Acquisition*, 27(4), 503–33.

Guion, S. G., Clark, J., Harada, T., & Wayland, R. P. (2003). Factors affecting stress placement for English nonsense words include syllabic structure, lexical class, and stress patterns of phonologically similar words. *Language and Speech*, 46(4), 403–26.

Guion, S. G., Harada, T., & Clark, J. (2004). Early and late Spanish–English bilinguals' acquisition of English word stress patterns. *Bilingualism: Language and Cognition*, 7(3), 207–26.

Gumperz, J. J. (1982). *Language and Social Identity*. Cambridge: Cambridge University Press.

Gut, U. (2003). Non-native speech rhythm in German. In *15th Proceedings of the ICPhS Conference* (pp. 2437–40). Retrieved from https://pdfs.semanticscholar .org/4d21/5f8a298b180768341acea3c01296ebbb4847.pdf

Hahn, L. D. (2004). Primary stress and intelligibility: Research to motivate the teaching of suprasegmentals. *TESOL Quarterly*, 38(2), 201–23.

Hahn, L. D., & Dickerson, W. B. (1999). *Speechcraft: Discourse Pronunciation for Advanced Learners*. Ann Arbor, MI: University of Michigan Press.

Hahn, M. (2002). The persistence of learned primary phrase stress patterns among learners of English. Unpublished doctoral dissertation, University of Illinois at Urbana-Champaign.

Hairston, M. (1981). Not all errors are created equal: Nonacademic readers in the professions respond to lapses in usage. *College English*, 43(8), 794–806.

Halliday, M. A. K. (1967). *Intonation and Grammar in British English*. Berlin: Walter de Gruyter.

Halliday, M. A. K. & Hasan, R. (1976). *Cohesion in English*. New York: Longman.

Hansen, J. G. (2001). Linguistic constraints on the acquisition of English syllable codas by native speakers of Mandarin Chinese. *Applied Linguistics*, 22(3), 338–65.

Hardison, D. M. (2004). Generalization of computer-assisted prosody training: quantitative and qualitative findings. *Language Learning & Technology*, 8(1), 34–52.

Hardison, D. M. (2005). Contextualized computer-based L2 prosody training: Evaluating the effects of discourse context and video input. *Calico Journal*, 22(2), 175–90.

Hawkins, R. & Liszka, S. (2003). Locating the source of defective past tense marking in advanced L2 English speakers. In R. van Hout, A. Hulk, F. Kuiken, & R. Towell (eds.), *The Lexicon–Syntax Interface in Second Language Acquisition* (pp. 21–44). Amsterdam: John Benjamins.

Hayden, R. E. (1950). The relative frequency of phonemes in general-American English. *Word*, 6(3), 217–23.

Henderson, A. (2008). Towards intelligibility: Designing short pronunciation courses for advanced field experts. *ASp. la revue du GERAS*, 53–54, 89–110.

Hill, C., & Beebe, L. M. (1980). Contraction and blending: The use of orthographic clues in teaching pronunciation. *TESOL Quarterly*, 14(3), 299–323.

Hillenbrand, J. M., Clark, M. J., & Houde, R. A. (2000). Some effects of duration on vowel recognition. *Journal of the Acoustical Society of America*, 108(6), 3013–22.

Hincks, R. (2003). Speech technologies for pronunciation feedback and evaluation. *ReCALL*, 15(1), 3–20.

Hincks, R., & Edlund, J. (2009). Promoting increased pitch variation in oral presentations with transient visual feedback. *Language Learning and Technology*, 13(3), 32–50.

Hinofotis, F. B., & Bailey, K. M. (1981). American undergraduates' reactions to the communication skills of foreign teaching assistants. In J. Cameron Fisher, M. Clarke, & J. Schachter (eds.). *On TESOL '80: Building Bridges: Research and Practice in Teaching English as a Second Language*, (pp. 120–133). Washington, DC: TESOL.

Hirata, Y. (2004). Effects of speaking rate on the vowel length distinction in Japanese. *Journal of Phonetics*, 32(4), 565–89.

Hirschberg, J., & Litman, D. (1987). Now let's talk about now: Identifying cue phrases intonationally. In *Proceedings of the 25th Annual Meeting on Association for Computational Linguistics* (pp. 163–71). Morristown, NJ: Association for Computational Linguistics.

Hirst, D., & Di Cristo, A. (eds.) (1998). *Intonation Systems: A Survey of Twenty Languages*. Cambridge: Cambridge University Press.

Hockett, C. F. (1947). Problems of morphemic analysis. *Language*, 23(4), 321–43.

Holmes, J. (1982) Functions of tag questions. *English Language Research Journal*, 3, 40–65.

Hong, H., Kim, S., & Chung, M. (2014). A corpus-based analysis of English segments produced by Korean learners. *Journal of Phonetics*, 46, 52–67.

Hopp, H. (2010). Ultimate attainment in L2 inflection: Performance similarities between non-native and native speakers. *Lingua*, 120(4), 901–31.

Hu, X., Ackermann, H., Martin, J. A., Erb, M., Winkler, S., & Reiterer, S. M. (2013). Language aptitude for pronunciation in advanced second language (L2) learners: Behavioural predictors and neural substrates. *Brain and Language*, 127(3), 366–76.

Im, J., & Levis, J. (2015). Judgments of non-standard segmental sounds and international teaching assistants' spoken proficiency levels. In G. Gorsuch (ed.), *Talking Matters: Research on Talk and Communication of International Teaching Assistants* (pp. 113–42). Stillwater, OK: New Forums Press.

Ingels, S. A. (2011). The effects of self-monitoring strategy use on the pronunciation of learners of English. Doctoral dissertation, University of Illinois at Urbana-Champaign.

Ioup, G. (1984). Is there a structural foreign accent? *Language Learning*, 34(2), 1–17.

Isaacs, T., & Trofimovich, P. (2012). "Deconstructing" comprehensibility: Identifying the linguistic influences on listeners' L2 comprehensibility ratings. *Studies in Second Language Acquisition*, 34(4), 475–505.

Isaacs, T., & Trofimovich, P. (2017). *Second Language Pronunciation Assessment: Interdisciplinary Perspectives*. Clevedon, OH: Multilingual Matters.

Isbell, D. R. (2016). The perception–production link in L2 phonology. *MSU Working Papers in Second Language Studies*, 7(1), 57–68.

Iverson, P., & Evans, B. G. (2007). Learning English vowels with different first-language vowel systems: Perception of formant targets, formant movement, and duration. *Journal of the Acoustical Society of America*, 122, 2842–54. DOI: 10.1121/1.2783198

Iverson, P., & Evans, B. G. (2009). Learning English vowels with different first-language vowel systems II: Auditory training for native Spanish and German speakers. *Journal of the Acoustical Society of America*, 126(2), 866–77.

Jenkins, J. (2000). *The Phonology of English as an International Language*. Oxford: Oxford University Press.

Jenkins, J. (2002). A sociolinguistically based, empirically researched pronunciation syllabus for English as an international language. *Applied Linguistics*, 23(1), 83–103.

Jenner, B. (1989). Teaching pronunciation: The common core. *Speak Out*, 4, 2–4.

Johnson, K. (2004). Massive reduction in conversational American English. In *Spontaneous Speech: Data and Analysis – Proceedings of the 1st Session of the 10th International Symposium* (pp. 29–54). Tokyo: The National International Institute for Japanese Language.

Jones, R. H., & Evans, S. (1995). Teaching pronunciation through voice quality. *ELT Journal*, 49(3), 244–51.

Jones, T. (ed.) (2016). *Pronunciation in the Classroom: The Overlooked Essential*. Alexandria, VA: TESOL.

Jun, S. A. (ed.). (2006). *Prosodic Typology: The Phonology of Intonation and Phrasing*. Oxford: Oxford University Press.

Kachru, B. B. (ed.) (1992). *The Other Tongue: English Across Cultures*. Urbana, IL: University of Illinois Press.

Kaneko, E., Heo, Y., Iverson, G. K., & Wilson, I. (2015). Quasi-neutralization in the acquisition of English coronal fricatives by native speakers of Japanese. *Journal of Second Language Pronunciation*, 1(1), 65–85.

Kang, O. (2010). Relative salience of suprasegmental features on judgments of L2 comprehensibility and accentedness. *System*, 38(2), 301–15.

Kang, O., & Moran, M. (2014). Functional loads of pronunciation features in nonnative speakers' oral assessment. *TESOL Quarterly*, 48(1), 176–87.

Kashiwagi, A., & Snyder, M. (2010). Speech characteristics of Japanese speakers affecting American and Japanese listener evaluations. *Teachers College, Columbia University Working Papers in TESOL & Applied Linguistics*, 10(1), 1–14.

Katz, J., & Selkirk, E. (2011). Contrastive focus vs. discourse-new: Evidence from phonetic prominence in English. *Language*, 87(4), 771–816.

Katz, W. F., Beach, C. M., Jenouri, K., & Verma, S. (1996). Duration and fundamental frequency correlates of phrase boundaries in productions by children and adults. *Journal of the Acoustical Society of America*, 99(5), 3179–91.

Kelly, L. G. (1969). *25 Centuries of Language Teaching*. Rowley, MA: Newbury House.

Kennedy, S. (2012). When non-native speakers misunderstand each other: Identifying important aspects of pronunciation. *Contact Magazine*, 38(2), 49–62. Retrieved from www.teslontario.org/uploads/publications/researchsymposium/ ResearchSymposium2012.pdf

Kenworthy, J. (1987). *Teaching English Pronunciation*. Harlow: Longman.

King, R. D. (1967). Functional load and sound change. *Language*, 43(4), 831–52.

Kingdon, R. (1958). *The Groundwork of English Intonation*. London: Longman.

Kirk, C. (2008). Substitution errors in the production of word-initial and word-final consonant clusters. *Journal of Speech, Language, and Hearing Research*, 51(1), 35–48.

Kirkpatrick, A., Deterding, D., & Wong, J. (2008). The pronunciation of Hong Kong English. *English World-Wide*, 29(2), 148–75.

Klippel, F. (1984). *Keep Talking: Communicative Fluency Activities for Language Teaching*. Cambridge: Cambridge University Press.

Kochanski, G., Grabe, E., Coleman, J., & Rosner, B. (2005). Loudness predicts prominence: Fundamental frequency lends little. *Journal of the Acoustical Society of America*, 118(2), 1038–54.

Koffi, E. (2010). The pronunciation of <-ED> in coda clusters in Somali-accented English. In J. Levis & K. LeVelle (eds.), *Proceedings of the 1st Pronunciation in Second Language Learning and Teaching Conference* (pp. 119–34). Ames, IA: Iowa State University.

Kolly, M. J., & Dellwo, V. (2014). Cues to linguistic origin: The contribution of speech temporal information to foreign accent recognition. *Journal of Phonetics*, 42, 12–23.

Kormos, J., & Dénes, M. (2004). Exploring measures and perceptions of fluency in the speech of second language learners. *System*, 32(2), 145–64.

Krashen, S. D. (1981). *Second Language Acquisition and Second Language Learning*. Oxford: Oxford University Press.

Krashen, S. D. (1985). *The Input Hypothesis: Issues and Implications*. London: Longman

Krashen, S., Houck, N., Giunchi, P., Bode, S., Birnbaum, R., & Strei, G. (1977). Difficulty order for grammatical morphemes for adult 2nd language performers using free speech. *TESOL Quarterly*, 11(3), 338–41.

Krashen, S. D., & Terrell, T. D. (1983). The natural approach: Language acquisition in the classroom. Retrieved from https://eric.ed.gov/?id=ED230069 (June 16, 2017).

Krasner, L. (1978). The future and the past in the behaviorism–humanism dialogue. *American Psychologist*, 33(9), 799–804.

Kreidler, C. W. (1972). Teaching English spelling and pronunciation. *TESOL Quarterly*, 6, 3–12.

Kreidler, C. W. (2004). *The Pronunciation of English: A Coursebook*. Malden, MA: Blackwell.

Labov, W. (2001). Applying our knowledge of African American English to the problem of raising reading levels in inner city schools. In S. Lanehart (ed.), *Sociocultural and Historical Contexts of African American English* (pp. 299–317). Philadelphia, PA: John Benjamins Publishing Company.

Ladd, D. R. (1980). *The Structure of Intonational Meaning: Evidence from English*. Bloomington, IN: Indiana University Press.

Ladd, D. R. (1996). *Intonational Phonology*. Cambridge: Cambridge University Press.

Ladd, D. R., & Cutler, A. (1983). Introduction: Models and measurements in the study of prosody. In A. Cutler & D. R. Ladd (eds.), *Prosody: Models and Measurements* (pp. 1–10). Berlin: Springer.

Ladd, D. R., Silverman, K. E., Tolkmitt, F., Bergmann, G., & Scherer, K. R. (1985). Evidence for the independent function of intonation contour type, voice quality, and F 0 range in signaling speaker affect. *Journal of the Acoustical Society of America*, 78(2), 435–44.

Ladefoged, P. (1980). What are linguistic sounds made of? *Language*, 56(3), 485–502. DOI: 10.2307/414446

Lecumberri, M. L. G., Cooke, M., & Cutler, A. (2010). Non-native speech perception in adverse conditions: A review. *Speech Communication*, 52(11), 864–86.

Lee, J., Jang, J., & Plonsky, L. (2015). The effectiveness of second language pronunciation instruction: A meta-analysis. *Applied Linguistics*, 36(3), 345–66.

Lee, W. R. (1980). A point about the rise-endings and fall-endings of yes–no questions. In L. R. Waugh & D. L. Bolinger (eds.), *The Melody of Language: Intonation and Prosody* (pp. 165–8). Baltimore, MD: University Park Press.

Lenneberg, E. H. (1967). *Biological Foundations of Language*. Oxford: Wiley.

Lennon, P. (1990). Investigating fluency in EFL: A quantitative approach. *Language Learning*, 40(3), 387–417.

Lev-Ari, S., & Keysar, B. (2010). Why don't we believe non-native speakers? The influence of accent on credibility. *Journal of Experimental Social Psychology*, 46(6), 1093–6.

LeVelle, K., & Levis, J. (2014). Understanding the impact of social factors on L2 pronunciation: Insights from learners. In J. Levis & A. Moyer (eds.), *Social Dynamics in Second Language Accent* (pp. 97–118). Boston, MA: Degruyter.

Levis, J. M. (1994). Attitude as a description of intonational meaning. *Issues and Developments in Applied Linguistics (IDEAL)*, 7, 91–106.

Levis, J.M. (1997). Grammar and intonation: An alternative approach. *Speak Out!*, 21, 26–9.

Levis, J. M. (1999a). The intonation and meaning of normal yes/no questions. *World Englishes*, 18(3), 373–80.

Levis, J. M. (1999b). Intonation in theory and practice, revisited. *TESOL Quarterly*, 33(1), 37–63.

Levis, J. (2000). Bridging the gap between controlled and spontaneous speech. Paper presented as part of the Speech/Pronunciation Interest Section Academic Session, International TESOL, Vancouver, British Columbia, Canada.

Levis, J. M. (2001). Teaching focus for conventional use. *ELT Journal*, 55(1), 47–54.

Levis, J. M. (2005a). Changing contexts and shifting paradigms in pronunciation teaching. *TESOL Quarterly*, 39(3), 369–77.

Levis, J. M. (2005b). Comparing apples and oranges: Pedagogical approaches to intonation in British and American English. In K. Dziubalska-Kotaczyk & J. Przedlacka (eds.), *English Pronunciation Models: A Changing Scene* (pp. 339–66). Bern: Peter Lang.

Levis, J. M. (2006). Pronunciation and the assessment of spoken language. In R. Hughes (ed.), *Spoken English, TESOL and Applied Linguistics* (pp. 245–70). Basingstoke: Palgrave Macmillan.

Levis, J. M. (2013). *Intonation*. In C. Chapelle (ed.), *Encyclopedia of Applied Linguistics* (pp. 5443–49). Boston, MA: Wiley-Blackwell.

Levis, J. M. (2015). Learners' views of social issues in pronunciation learning. *Journal of Academic Language & Learning*, 9(1), A42–55.

Levis, J. M. (2016). Research into practice: How research appears in pronunciation teaching materials. *Language Teaching*, 49(3), 423–37.

Levis, J. M. (2017). Evidence-based pronunciation teaching. *Journal of Second Language Pronunciation*, 3(1), 1–8.

Levis, J., & Cortes, V. (2008). Minimal pairs in spoken corpora: Implications for pronunciation assessment and teaching. In J. Levis (ed.), *Towards Adaptive CALL: Natural Language Processing for Diagnostic Language Assessment* (pp. 197–208). Ames, IA: Iowa State University.

Levis, J. M., & Grant, L. (2003). Integrating pronunciation into ESL/EFL classrooms. *TESOL Journal*, 12(2), 13–19.

Levis, J. M., & Moyer, A. (eds.) (2014). *Social Dynamics in Second Language Accent*. Boston, MA: DeGruyter Mouton.

Levis, J. & Muller Levis, G. (n.d.). Pronunciation for a purpose. Unpublished materials.

Levis, J. & Muller Levis, G. (2018). Teaching high-value pronunciation features: Contrastive stress for intermediate learners. *CATESOL Journal*, 30(1), 139–60.

Levis, J., & Pickering, L. (2004). Teaching intonation in discourse using speech visualization technology. *System*, 32(4), 505–24.

Levis, J., & Sonsaat, S. (2016). Pronunciation materials. In M. Azarnoosh, M. Zeraatpishe, A. Favani, & H. R. Kargozari, *Issues in Materials Development* (pp. 109–19). Rotterdam: Sense Publishers.

Levis, J., & Sonsaat, S. (2017). Pronunciation in the CLT era. In J. Murphy, O. Kang, & R. Thomson (eds.), *The Routledge Handbook of Contemporary English Pronunciation* (pp. 267–83). London: Routledge.

Levis, J. M., Sonsaat, S., Link, S., & Barriuso, T. A. (2016). Native and nonnative teachers of L2 pronunciation: Effects on learner performance. *TESOL Quarterly*, 50(4), 894–931.

Lewis, C. & Deterding, D. (2018). How pronunciation learning and teaching functions in ELF contexts. *CATESOL Journal*.

Liao, S. (2009). Variation in the use of discourse markers by Chinese teaching assistants in the US. *Journal of Pragmatics*, 41(7), 1313–28.

Liberman, M. Y. (1975). The intonational system of English. Doctoral dissertation, Massachusetts Institute of Technology.

Lima, E. D. (2015). Development and evaluation of online pronunciation instruction for international teaching assistants' comprehensibility. Dissertation, Iowa State University.

Lin, Y. H. (2003). Interphonology variability: Sociolinguistic factors affecting L2 simplification strategies. *Applied Linguistics*, 24(4), 439–64.

Lindemann, S., Campbell, M. A., Litzenberg, J., & Subtirelu, N. C. (2016). Explicit and implicit training methods for improving native English speakers' comprehension of nonnative speech. *Journal of Second Language Pronunciation*, 2(1), 93–108.

Lippi-Green, R. (1997). *English with an Accent: Language, Ideology, and Discrimination in the United States*. New York, NY: Routledge.

Long, M. H. (1983). Linguistic and conversational adjustments to non-native speakers. *Studies in Second Language Acquisition*, 5(2), 177–93.

Long, M. H., & Porter, P. A. (1985). Group work, interlanguage talk, and second language acquisition. *TESOL Quarterly*, 19(2), 207–28.

Low, E. L. (2006). A cross-varietal comparison of deaccenting and given information: Implications for international intelligibility and pronunciation teaching. *TESOL Quarterly*, 40(4), 739–61.

Low, E. L. (2014). *Pronunciation for English as an International Language: From Research to Practice*. London: Routledge.

Low, E. L., Grabe, E., & Nolan, F. (2000). Quantitative characterizations of speech rhythm: Syllable-timing in Singapore English. *Language and Speech*, 43(4), 377–401.

Luk, Z. P. S., & Shirai, Y. (2009). Is the acquisition order of grammatical morphemes impervious to L1 knowledge? Evidence from the acquisition of plural -s, articles, and possessive 's. *Language Learning*, 59(4), 721–54.

Lybeck, K. (2002). Cultural identification and second language pronunciation of Americans in Norway. *The Modern Language Journal*, 86(2), 174–91.

Major, R. C. (1994). Chronological and stylistic aspects of second language acquisition of consonant clusters. *Language Learning*, 44(4), 655–80.

Major, R. C., Fitzmaurice, S. F., Bunta, F., & Balasubramanian, C. (2002). The effects of nonnative accents on listening comprehension: Implications for ESL assessment. *TESOL Quarterly*, 36(2), 173–90.

Marcus, G. F., Pinker, S., Ullman, M., Hollander, M., Rosen, T. J., Xu, F., & Clahsen, H. (1992). *Overregularization in Language Acquisition*. Malden, MA: Blackwell.

Marslen-Wilson, W. D. (1987). Functional parallelism in spoken word-recognition. *Cognition*, 25(1), 71–102.

Marslen-Wilson, W. D., & Welsh, A. (1978). Processing interactions and lexical access during word recognition in continuous speech. *Cognitive Psychology*, 10(1), 29–63.

Marx, N. (2002). Never quite a "native speaker": Accent and identity in the L2- and the L1. *Canadian Modern Language Review*, 59(2), 264–81.

McClelland, J. L., Fiez, J. A., & McCandliss, B. D. (2002). Teaching the /r/–/l/ discrimination to Japanese adults: Behavioral and neural aspects. *Physiology & Behavior*, 77(4), 657–62.

McCrocklin, S. (2012). The role of word stress in English as a lingua franca. In J. Levis & K. LeVelle (eds.), *Proceedings of the 3rd Annual Pronunciation in Second Language Learning and Teaching* (pp. 249–54). Ames, IA: Iowa State University.

McDonald, J. L., & Roussel, C. C. (2010). Past tense grammaticality judgment and production in non-native and stressed native English speakers. *Bilingualism: Language and Cognition*, 13(4), 429–48.

McGowan, K. B. (2015). Social expectation improves speech perception in noise. *Language and Speech*, 58(4), 502–21.

McNerney, M., & Mendelsohn, D. (1992). Suprasegmentals in the pronunciation class: Setting priorities. In P. Avery & S. Ehrlich, (eds.), *Teaching American English Pronunciation*, (pp. 185–96). Oxford: Oxford University Press.

Mehl, M. R., Vazire, S., Ramírez-Esparza, N., Slatcher, R. B., & Pennebaker, J. W. (2007). Are women really more talkative than men? *Science*, 317(5834), 82–3.

Melenca, M. A. (2001). Teaching connected speech rules to Japanese speakers of English so as to avoid a staccato speech rhythm. Doctoral dissertation, Concordia University.

Miller, J. (2003). *Audible Difference: ESL and Social Identity in Schools*. Clevedon, OH: Multilingual Matters.

Miller, J., Watson, C. S., Kewley-Port, D., Sillings, R., Mills, W. B., & Burleson, D. F. (2007). SPATS: Speech perception assessment and training system. *Proceedings of Meetings on Acoustics 154ASA*, 2(1), 050005.

Miller, S. F. (2000). *Targeting Pronunciation: The Intonation, Sounds, and Rhythm of American English*. Boston, MA: Houghton Mifflin.

Mines, M. A., Hanson, B. F., & Shoup, J. E. (1978). Frequency of occurrence of phonemes in conversational English. *Language and Speech*, 21(3), 221–41.

Morley, J. (1991). The pronunciation component in teaching English to speakers of other languages. *TESOL Quarterly*, 25(3), 481–520.

Moyer, A. (2004). *Age, Accent, and Experience in Second Language Acquisition: An Integrated Approach to Critical Period Inquiry*. Clevedon, OH: Multilingual Matters.

Moyer, A. (2014). Exceptional outcomes in L2 phonology: The critical factors of learner engagement and self-regulation. *Applied Linguistics*, 35(4), 418–40.

Mugglestone, L. (1996). *Talking Proper: The Rise of Accent as Social Symbol*. Oxford: Oxford University Press.

Muller Levis, G., & Levis, J. (2012). Learning to produce contrastive focus: A study of advanced learners of English. In J. Levis & K. LeVelle (eds.), *Proceedings of the 3rd Pronunciation in Second Language Learning and Teaching Conference* (pp. 124–33). Ames, IA: Iowa State University.

Muller Levis, G. & Levis, J. (2014). Using introductions to improve initial intelligibility. In J. Levis & S. McCrocklin (eds.), *Proceedings of the 5th Pronunciation in Second Language Learning and Teaching Conference* (pp. 145–50). Ames, IA: Iowa State University.

Muller Levis, G., & Levis, J. (2016). Integrating pronunciation into listening/ speaking classes. In T. Jones (ed.), *Integrating Pronunciation with Other Language Skills* (pp. 27–42). Alexandria, VA: TESOL.

Muller Levis, G., Levis, J., & Benner, S. (2014). Contrastive stress can be learned – but can it be taught at lower levels? Presentation at Pronunciation in Second Language Learning and Teaching, Santa Barbara, CA, September.

Munro, M. J. (1998). The effects of noise on the intelligibility of foreign-accented speech. *Studies in Second Language Acquisition*, 20(2), 139–54.

Munro, M. J. (2003). A primer on accent discrimination in the Canadian context. *TESL Canada Journal*, 20(2), 38–51.

Munro, M. J. (2018). How well can we predict L2 learners' pronunciation difficulties? *CATESOL Journal*, 30(1), 267–281.

Munro, M. J., & Derwing, T. M. (1995). Foreign accent, comprehensibility, and intelligibility in the speech of second language learners. *Language Learning*, 45(1), 73–97.

Munro, M. J., & Derwing, T. M. (1998). The effects of speaking rate on listener evaluations of native and foreign-accented speech. *Language Learning*, 48(2), 159–82.

Munro, M., & Derwing, T. (1999). Foreign accent, comprehensibility, and intelligibility in the speech of second language learners. *Language Learning*, 49(s1), 285–310.

Munro, M. J., & Derwing, T. M. (2001). Modeling perceptions of the accentedness and comprehensibility of L2 speech: The role of speaking rate. *Studies in Second Language Acquisition*, 23(4), 451–68.

Munro, M. J. & Derwing, T. M. (2006). The functional load principle in ESL pronunciation instruction: An exploratory study. *System*, 34, 520–31.

Munro, M. J., & Derwing, T. M. (2008). Segmental acquisition in adult ESL learners: A longitudinal study of vowel production. *Language Learning*, 58(3), 479–502.

Munro, M. J., Derwing, T. M., & Burgess, C. S. (2010). Detection of nonnative speaker status from content-masked speech. *Speech Communication*, 52(7), 626–37.

Munro, M. J., Derwing, T. M., & Saito, K. (2013). English L2 vowel acquisition over seven years. In. J. Levis & K. LeVelle (eds.), *Proceedings of the 4th Pronunciation in Second Language Learning and Teaching Conference* (pp. 112–19). Ames, IA: Iowa State University.

Munro, M. J., Derwing, T. M., & Thomson, R. I. (2015). Setting segmental priorities for English learners: Evidence from a longitudinal study. *International Review of Applied Linguistics*, 53(1), 39–60.

Munro, M. J., Flege, J. E., & MacKay, I. R. (1996). The effects of age of second language learning on the production of English vowels. *Applied Psycholinguistics*, 17(3), 313–34.

Murphy, J. M. (1991). Oral communication in TESOL: Integrating speaking, listening, and pronunciation. *TESOL Quarterly*, 25(1), 51–75.

Murphy, J. M. (2004). Attending to word-stress while learning new vocabulary. *English for Specific Purposes*, 23(1), 67–83.

Murphy, J. (2014). Myth 7: Teacher training programs provide adequate preparation in how to teach pronunciation. In L. Grant (ed.), *Pronunciation Myths* (pp. 188–224). Ann Arbor, MI: University of Michigan Press.

Murphy, J. (2017). Suprasegmentals. In J. Murphy (ed.), *Teaching the Pronunciation of English: Focus on Whole Courses* (pp. 31–69). Ann Arbor, MI: University of Michigan Press.

Murphy, J., & Kandil, M. (2004). Word-level stress patterns in the academic word list. *System*, 32(1), 61–74.

Nagle, C. L. (2017). A longitudinal study of voice onset time development in L2 Spanish stops. *Applied Linguistics*. DOI: https://doi.org/10.1093/applin/amx011

Naiman, N. (ed.). (1978). *The Good Language Learner.* Clevedon, OH: Multilingual Matters.

Nakatani, C. H., & Hirschberg, J. (1994). A corpus-based study of repair cues in spontaneous speech. *Journal of the Acoustical Society of America*, 95(3), 1603–16.

Nation, I. S. P. (2002). *Learning Vocabulary in Another Language.* Cambridge: Cambridge University Press.

Neri, A., Cucchiarini, C., & Strik, H. (2006). Selecting segmental errors in non-native Dutch for optimal pronunciation training. *International Review of Applied Linguistics*, 44(4), 357–404.

Neri, A., Cucchiarini, C., & Strik, H. (2008). The effectiveness of computer-based speech corrective feedback for improving segmental quality in L2 Dutch. *ReCALL*, 20(2), 225–43.

Niebuhr, O., Alm, M., Schümchen, N., & Fiscer, K. (2017). Comparing visualization techniques for learning second language prosody: First results. *International Journal of Learner Corpus Research*, 3(2), 252–79.

Nolan, F. (2002). Intonation in speaker identification: An experiment on pitch alignment features. *Forensic Linguistics*, 9(1), 1–21.

O'Brien, I., Segalowitz, N., Freed, B., & Collentine, J. (2007). Phonological memory predicts second language oral fluency gains in adults. *Studies in Second Language Acquisition*, 29(4), 557–81.

O'Connor, J. D., & Arnold, G. F. (1961). *The Intonation of Colloquial English.* London: Longman.

Ockey, G. J., Papageorgiou, S., & French, R. (2016). Effects of strength of accent on an L2 interactive lecture listening comprehension test. *International Journal of Listening*, 30(1–2), 84–98.

Ordin, M., & Polyanskaya, L. (2015a). Perception of speech rhythm in second language: The case of rhythmically similar L1 and L2. *Frontiers in Psychology*, 6, 1–15.

Ordin, M., & Polyanskaya, L. (2015b). Acquisition of speech rhythm in a second language by learners with rhythmically different native languages. *Journal of the Acoustical Society of America*, 138(2), 533–44.

Orion, G. F. (2002). *Pronouncing American English: Sounds, Stress, and Intonation*, 2nd edition. New York, NY: Newbury House.

Osberger, M. J., & Levitt, H. (1979). The effect of timing errors on the intelligibility of deaf children's speech. *Journal of the Acoustical Society of America*, 66(5), 1316–24.

Osburne, A. G. (1996). Final cluster reduction in English L2 speech: A case study of a Vietnamese speaker. *Applied Linguistics*, 17(2), 164–81.

Parish, C. (1977). A practical philosophy of pronunciation. *TESOL Quarterly*, 11, 311–17.

Pennington, M. C. (1989). Teaching pronunciation from the top down. *RELC Journal*, 20(1), 20–38.

Pennington, M. C., & Ellis, N. C. (2000). Cantonese speakers' memory for English sentences with prosodic cues. *The Modern Language Journal*, 84(3), 372–89.

Peperkamp, S., & Dupoux, E. (2002). A typological study of stress "deafness". *Laboratory Phonology*, 7, 203–40.

Peperkamp, S., Dupoux, E., & Sebastián-Gallés, N. (1999). Perception of stress by French, Spanish, and bilingual subjects. *Proceedings of EuroSpeech '99* (vol. 6, pp. 2683–2686). Budapest: Department of Telecommunications and Telematics.

Pickering, L. (2001). The role of tone choice in improving ITA communication in the classroom. *TESOL Quarterly*, 35(2), 233–55.

Pickering, L. (2002). Patterns of intonation in cross-cultural communication exchange structure in NS TA & ITA classroom discourse. In *The Seventh Annual Conference on Language, Interaction & Culture* (pp. 1–7). Santa Barbara, CA: University of California.

Pickering, L. (2004). The structure and function of intonational paragraphs in native and nonnative speaker instructional discourse. *English for Specific Purposes*, 23(1), 19–43.

Pickering, L. (2009). Intonation as a pragmatic resource in ELF interaction. *Intercultural Pragmatics*, 6(2), 235–55.

Pickering, L. (2018) *Discourse Intonation: A Discourse-Pragmatic to English for ESL/EFL Teachers*. Ann Arbor, MI: University of Michigan Press.

Pierrehumbert, J. B. (1980). The phonology and phonetics of English intonation. Doctoral dissertation, Massachusetts Institute of Technology.

Pierrehumbert, J. (2006). Syllable structure and word structure: a study of triconsonantal clusters in English. In P. Keating (ed.), *Phonological Structure and Phonetic Form: Papers in Laboratory Phonology* (pp. 168–86). New York: Cambridge University Press.

Pierrehumbert, J., & Hirschberg, J. (1990). The meaning of intonational contours in the interpretation of discourse. In P. Cohen, J. Morgan, & J. Pollack (eds.), *Intentions in Communication* (pp. 271–311). Cambridge, MA: MIT Press.

Pike, K. L. (1945). *The Intonation of American English*. Ann Arbor, MI: University of Michigan Press.

Piller, I. (2002). Passing for a native speaker: Identity and success in second language learning. *Journal of Sociolinguistics*, 6(2), 179–208.

Pincus, N. A. (2016). L2 perception and production of three English prosodic patterns. Dissertation, University of Delaware.

Pinker, S., & Ullman, M. T. (2002). The past and future of the past tense. *Trends in Cognitive Sciences*, 6(11), 456–63.

Piske, T., MacKay, I. R., & Flege, J. E. (2001). Factors affecting degree of foreign accent in an L2: A review. *Journal of Phonetics*, 29(2), 191–215.

Pisoni, D. B., Manous, L. M., & Dedina, M. J. (1987). Comprehension of natural and synthetic speech: Effects of predictability on the verification of sentences controlled for intelligibility. *Computer Speech & Language*, 2(3–4), 303–20.

Poldauf, I. (1984). *English Word Stress*. Oxford: Pergamon.

Port, R. F., Dalby, J., & O'Dell, M. (1987). Evidence for mora timing in Japanese. *Journal of the Acoustical Society of America*, 81(5), 1574–85.

Prator, C. H., & Robinett, B. W. (1985). *Manual of American English Pronunciation*, 4th edition. New York, NY: Holt, Rinehart, and Winston.

Preston, D. R. (1996). Whaddayaknow? The modes of folk linguistic awareness. *Language Awareness*, 5(1), 40–74.

Prevost, S. (1996). An information structural approach to spoken language generation. In *Proceedings of the 34th Annual Meeting on Association for Computational Linguistics* (pp. 294–301). Morristown, NJ: Association for Computational Linguistics.

Qian, M., Chukharev-Hudilainen, E., & Levis, J. (2018). A system for adaptive high-variability segmental perceptual training: Implementation, effectiveness, transfer. *Language Learning and Technology*, 22(1), 69–96.

Quené, H., & van Delft, L. E. (2010). Non-native durational patterns decrease speech intelligibility. *Speech Communication*, 52(11), 911–18.

Ramus, F., Nespor, M., & Mehler, J. (1999). Correlates of linguistic rhythm in the speech signal. *Cognition*, 73(3), 265–92.

Reed, M., & Michaud, C. (2005). *Sound Concepts: An Integrated Pronunciation Course*. New York, NY: McGraw-Hill.

Reed, M., & Michaud, C. (2015). Intonation in research and practice: The importance of metacognition. In M. Reed & J. Levis (eds.), *The Handbook of English Pronunciation* (pp. 454–70). Boston, MA: Wiley Blackwell.

Richards, M. G. (2016). Not all word stress errors are created equal: Validating an English word stress error gravity hierarchy. Doctoral dissertation, Iowa State University.

Riggenbach, H. (ed.). (2000). *Perspectives on Fluency*. Ann Arbor, MI: University of Michigan Press.

Riney, T. J., Takada, M., & Ota, M. (2000). Segmentals and global foreign accent: The Japanese flap in EFL. *TESOL Quarterly*, 34(4), 711–37.

Riney, T. J., Takagi, N., & Inutsuka, K. (2005). Phonetic parameters and perceptual judgments of accent in English by American and Japanese listeners. *TESOL Quarterly*, 39(3), 441–66.

Rivers, W. M. (1981). *Teaching Foreign-Language Skills*. Chicago, IL: University of Chicago Press.

Roach, P. (1982). On the distinction between "stress-timed" and "syllable-timed" languages. *Linguistic Controversies*, 73, 79–84.

Rossiter, M. J., Derwing, T. M., Manimtim, L. G., & Thomson, R. I. (2010). Oral fluency: The neglected component in the communicative language classroom. *Canadian Modern Language Review*, 66(4), 583–606.

Rubin, D. L. (1992). Nonlanguage factors affecting undergraduates' judgments of nonnative English-speaking teaching assistants. *Research in Higher Education*, 33(4), 511–31.

Sadat-Tehrani, N. (2017). Teaching English stress: A case study. *TESOL Journal.* DOI: 10.1002/tesj.332.

Saito, K. (2012). Effects of instruction on L2 pronunciation development: A synthesis of 15 quasi-experimental intervention studies. *TESOL Quarterly*, 46(4), 842–54.

Saito, K., & Lyster, R. (2012). Effects of form-focused instruction and corrective feedback on L2 pronunciation development of /ɹ/ by Japanese learners of English. *Language Learning*, 62(2), 595–633.

Saito, K., Trofimovich, P., & Isaacs, T. (2016). Second language speech production: Investigating linguistic correlates of comprehensibility and accentedness for learners at different ability levels. *Applied Psycholinguistics*, 37(2), 217–40.

Sakai, M., & Moorman, C. (2017). Can perception training improve the production of second language phonemes? A meta-analytic review of 25 years of perception training research. *Applied Psycholinguistics*, 39, 187–224.

Sardegna, V. G. (2009). Improving English stress through pronunciation learning strategies. Doctoral dissertation, University of Illinois at Urbana-Champaign.

Scovel, T. (1969). Foreign accents, language acquisition, and cerebral dominance. *Language Learning*, 19(3–4), 245–53.

Scovel, T. (2000). A critical review of the critical period research. *Annual Review of Applied Linguistics*, 20(1), 213–23.

Scharenborg, O. (2007). Reaching over the gap: A review of efforts to link human and automatic speech recognition research. *Speech Communication*, 49(5), 336–47.

Schmerling, S. F. (1976). *Aspects of English Sentence Stress*. Austin, TX: University of Texas Press.

Segalowitz, N. (2000). Automaticity and attentional skill in fluent performance. In H. Riggenbach (ed.), *Perspectives on Fluency* (pp. 200–19). Ann Arbor, MI: University of Michigan Press.

Segalowitz, N. (2007). Access fluidity, attention control, and the acquisition of fluency in a second language. *TESOL Quarterly*, 41(1), 181–6.

Selinker, L. (1972). Interlanguage. *International Review of Applied Linguistics in Language Teaching*, 10(1–4), 209–32.

Setter, J. (2008). Consonant clusters in Hong Kong English. *World Englishes*, 27 (3–4), 502–15.

Setter, J., & Jenkins, J. (2005). Pronunciation. *Language Teaching*, 38(1), 1–17.

Sewell, A. (2017). Functional load revisited: Reinterpreting the findings of "lingua franca" intelligibility studies. *Journal of Second Language Pronunciation*, 3(1), 57–79.

Shockey, L. (2003). *Sound patterns of spoken English*. Malden, MA: Blackwell.

Shuy, R. W., Wolfram, W., & Riley, W. K. (1968). *Field Techniques in an Urban Language Study*. Washington , DC: Center for Applied Linguistics.

Slater, T., Levis, J., & Levis Muller, G. (2015). Spoken parentheticals in instructional discourse in STEM and non-STEM disciplines: The interaction of the prosodic, ideational, and interpersonal resources in signaling information structure. In *Talking Matters: Research on Talk and Communication of International Teaching Assistants* (pp. 3–31). Stillwater, OK: New Forums Press.

Slowiaczek, L. M. (1990). Effects of lexical stress in auditory word recognition. *Language and Speech*, 33(1), 47–68.

Small, L. H., Simon, S. D., & Goldberg, J. S. (1988). Lexical stress and lexical access: Homographs versus nonhomographs. *Perception & Psychophysics*, 44(3), 272–80.

Smit, U. (2002). The interaction of motivation and achievement in advanced EFL pronunciation learners. *International Review of Applied Linguistics in Language Teaching*, 40(2), 89–116.

Smith, J., Meyers, C. M., & Burkhalter, A. J. (1992). *Communicate: Strategies for International Teaching Assistants*: Englewood Cliffs, NJ: Prentice Hall.

Smith, L. E., & Nelson, C. L. (1985). International intelligibility of English: Directions and resources. *World Englishes*, 4(3), 333–42.

Smotrova, T. (2017). Making pronunciation visible: Gesture in teaching pronunciation. *TESOL Quarterly*, 51(1), 59–89.

Sonsaat, S. (2017). The influence of an online pronunciation teacher's manual on teachers' cognitions. Unpublished dissertation, Iowa State University.

Stevick, E. W. (1976). *Memory, Meaning and Method: Some Psychological Perspectives on Language Learning*. Rowley, MA: Newbury House Publishers.

Stevick, E. W. (1978). Toward a practical philosophy of pronunciation: Another view. *TESOL Quarterly*, 12, 145–50.

Stevick, E., Morley, J., & Robinett, B. W. (1975). Round robin on the teaching of pronunciation. *TESOL Quarterly*, 9(1), 81–8.

Strevens, P. (1974). A rationale for teaching pronunciation: The rival virtues of innocence and sophistication. *ELT Journal*, 28(3), 182–9.

Sung, C. C. M. (2016). Exposure to multiple accents of English in the English language teaching classroom: from second language learners' perspectives. *Innovation in Language Learning and Teaching*, 10(3), 190–205.

Swain, M. (1993). The output hypothesis: Just speaking and writing aren't enough. *Canadian Modern Language Review*, 50(1), 158–64.

Swan, M., & Smith, B. (2001). *Learner English: A Teacher's Guide to Interference and Other Problems*, 2nd edition. Cambridge: Cambridge University Press.

Szczepek Reed, B. (2012). A conversation analytic perspective on teaching English pronunciation: The case of speech rhythm. *International Journal of Applied Linguistics*, 22(1), 67–87.

Szpyra-Kozłowska, J. (2015). *Pronunciation in EFL Instruction*. Clevedon, OH: Multilingual Matters.

Tajima, K., Port, R., & Dalby, J. (1994). Influence of timing on intelligibility of foreign-accented English. *Journal of the Acoustical Society of America*, 95(5), 3009.

Tajima, K., Port, R., & Dalby, J. (1997). Effects of temporal correction on intelligibility of foreign-accented English. *Journal of Phonetics*, 25(1), 1–24.

Tannen, D. (2005). Interactional sociolinguistics as a resource for intercultural pragmatics. *Intercultural Pragmatics*, 2(2), 205–8.

Taylor, D. S. (1981). Non-native speakers and the rhythm of English. *International Review of Applied Linguistics in Language Teaching*, 19(1–4), 219–26.

Terrell, T. D. (1977). A natural approach to second language acquisition and learning. *The Modern Language Journal*, 61(7), 325–37.

Terrell, T. D. (1989). Teaching Spanish pronunciation in a communicative approach. In P. Bjarkman & R. Hammond (eds.), *American Spanish Pronunciation: Theoretical and Applied Perspectives* (pp. 196–214). Washington, DC: Georgetown University Press.

Thomson, R. (2018). High Variability [Pronunciation] Training (HVPT): A proven technique that every language teacher and learner should know about. *Journal of Second Language Pronunciation*, 4(2). Publication due Fall 2018.

Thompson, S. (1995). Teaching intonation on questions. *ELT Journal*, 49(3), 235–43.

Thompson, S. (2003). Text-structuring metadiscourse, intonation and the signalling of organisation in academic lectures. *Journal of English for Academic Purposes*, 2(1), 5–20.

Thomson, R. I. (2011). Computer assisted pronunciation training: Targeting second language vowel perception improves pronunciation. *Calico Journal*, 28(3), 744–65.

Thomson, R. I. (2012). Improving L2 listeners' perception of English vowels: A computer-mediated approach. *Language Learning*, 62(4), 1231–58.

Thomson, R. I., & Derwing, T. M. (2015). The effectiveness of L2 pronunciation instruction: A narrative review. *Applied Linguistics*, 36(3), 326–44.

Thomson, R. I., & Isaacs, T. (2009). Within-category variation in L2 English vowel learning. *Canadian Acoustics*, 37(3), 138–9.

Tortel, A., & Hirst, D. (2010). Rhythm metrics and the production of English L1/L2. In *Proceedings of Speech Prosody*, May 10–14 2010, Chicago, IL.

Tremblay, A. (2008). Is second language lexical access prosodically constrained? Processing of word stress by French Canadian second language learners of English. *Applied Psycholinguistics*, 29(4), 553–84.

Tremblay, A., & Owens, N. (2010). The role of acoustic cues in the development of (non-) target-like second-language prosodic representations. *The Canadian Journal of Linguistics/La revue canadienne de linguistique*, 55(1), 85–114.

Trofimovich, P., & Isaacs, T. (2012). Disentangling accent from comprehensibility. *Bilingualism: Language and Cognition*, 15(4), 905–16.

Tseng, C., & Su, C. (2014). Prosodic differences between Taiwanese L2 and North American L1 speakers: Under-differentiation of lexical stress. Paper presented at Speech Prosody. Retrieved from www.ling.sinica.edu.tw/eip/FILES/publish/2013.09.16.023072.499933.pdf

Tseng, C.-y., Su, C., & Visceglia, T. (2013). Underdifferentiation of English lexical stress contrasts by L2 Taiwan Speakers. In *Proceedings of Speech and Language Technology in Education* (pp. 164–167). Retrieved from www.ling.sinica.edu.tw/eip/FILES/publish/2013.09.16.023072.499933.pdf

Turnbull, R., Royer, A. J., Ito, K., & Speer, S. R. (2017). Prominence perception is dependent on phonology, semantics, and awareness of discourse. *Language, Cognition and Neuroscience*, 32, 1017–33.

Tyler, A. (1992). Discourse structure and the perception of incoherence in international teaching assistants' spoken discourse. *TESOL Quarterly*, 26(4), 713–29.

Tyler, A., & Bro, J. (1992). Discourse structure in nonnative English discourse. *Studies in Second Language Acquisition*, 14(1), 71–86.

Tyler, A., Jefferies, A. A., & Davies, C. E. (1988). The effect of discourse structuring devices on listener perceptions of coherence in non-native university teacher's spoken discourse. *World Englishes*, 7(2), 101–10.

van Donselaar, W., Köster, M., & Cutler, A. (2005). Exploring the role of lexical stress in lexical recognition. *Quarterly Journal of Experimental Psychology Section A*, 58(2), 251–73.

Varonis, E. M., & Gass, S. (1982). The comprehensibility of non-native speech. *Studies in Second Language Acquisition*, 4(2), 114–36.

Venkatagiri, H. S., & Levis, J. M. (2007). Phonological awareness and speech comprehensibility: An exploratory study. *Language Awareness*, 16(4), 263–77.

Verdugo, D. R. (2005). The nature and patterning of native and non-native intonation in the expression of certainty and uncertainty: Pragmatic effects. *Journal of Pragmatics*, 37(12), 2086–115.

Vihman, M. M. (2015). Acquisition of the English sound system. In M. Reed & J. Levis (eds.), *The Handbook of English Pronunciation* (pp. 333–52). Malden, MA: Wiley Blackwell.

Visceglia, T., Tseng, C.-y., Su, Z.-y., & Huang, C.-F. (2010). Interaction of lexical and sentence prosody in Taiwan L2 English. Paper presented at the SLaTE Workshop, Interspeech. Retrieved from www.gavo.t.u-tokyo.ac.jp/L2WS2010/papers/L2WS2010_O3-01.pdf

Walker, R. (2010). *Teaching the Pronunciation of English as a Lingua Franca*. Oxford: Oxford University Press.

Walter, C. (2008). Phonology in second language reading: Not an optional extra. *TESOL Quarterly*, 42(3), 455–74.

Wang, X., & Munro, M. J. (2004). Computer-based training for learning English vowel contrasts. *System*, 32(4), 539–52.

Ward, G., & Hirschberg, J. (1985). Implicating uncertainty: The pragmatics of fall–rise intonation. *Language*, 61(4), 747–76.

Watson, P. J., & Schlauch, R. S. (2008). The effect of fundamental frequency on the intelligibility of speech with flattened intonation contours. *American Journal of Speech-Language Pathology*, 17(4), 348–55.

Wayland, R., Landfair, D., Li, B., & Guion, S. G. (2006). Native Thai speakers' acquisition of English word stress patterns. *Journal of Psycholinguistic Research*, 35(3), 285–304.

Weber, A., & Cutler, A. (2004). Lexical competition in non-native spoken-word recognition. *Journal of Memory and Language*, 50(1), 1–25.

Weinstein, N. J. (1982). *Whaddaya Say? Guided Practice in Relaxed Speech*. Boston, MA: Allyn & Bacon.

Wells, J. C. (2006). *English Intonation: An Introduction*. Cambridge: Cambridge University Press.

Wennerstrom, A. (1994). Intonational meaning in English discourse: A study of non-native speakers. *Applied Linguistics*, 15(4), 399–420.

Wennerstrom, A. (1998). Intonation as cohesion in academic discourse. *Studies in Second Language Acquisition*, 20(1), 1–25.

Wennerstrom, A. (2001). *The Music of Everyday Speech: Prosody and Discourse Analysis*. Oxford: Oxford University Press.

Werker, J. F., & Tees, R. C. (1984). Cross-language speech perception: Evidence for perceptual reorganization during the first year of life. *Infant Behavior and Development*, 7(1), 49–63.

White, L., & Mattys, S. L. (2007). Calibrating rhythm: First language and second language studies. *Journal of Phonetics*, 35(4), 501–22.

White, L., Wiget, L., Rauch, O., & Mattys, S. L. (2010). Segmentation cues in spontaneous and read speech. In *Speech Prosody 2010: Fifth International Conference*. Retrieved from http://speechprosody2010.illinois.edu/papers/100218.pdf (accessed September 15, 2017).

Wichmann, A. (2000). *Intonation in Text and Discourse: Beginnings, Middles and Ends*. London: Routledge.

Wichmann, A. (2004). The intonation of please-requests: A corpus-based study. *Journal of Pragmatics*, 36(9), 1521–49.

Widdowson, H. G. (1972). The teaching of English as communication. *ELT Journal*, 27(1), 15–19.

Wiget, L., White, L., Schuppler, B., Grenon, I., Rauch, O., & Mattys, S. L. (2010). How stable are acoustic metrics of contrastive speech rhythm? *Journal of the Acoustical Society of America*, 127(3), 1559–69.

Wilkins, D. (1976). Notional syllabuses. *Bulletin CILA (Commission interuniversitaire suisse de linguistique appliquée). Bulletin VALS-ASLA depuis 1994*, 24, 5–17.

Williams, J. (1992). Planning, discourse marking, and the comprehensibility of international teaching assistants. *TESOL Quarterly*, 26(4), 693–711.

Wilson, M. (2003). Discovery listening: Improving perceptual processing. *ELT Journal*, 57(4), 335–43.

Wolfram, W. (1974). The relationship of white southern speech to vernacular black English. *Language*, 50(3), 498–527.

Wong, J. W. S. (2013). The effects of perceptual and/or productive training on the perception and production of English vowels /ɪ/ and /iː/ by Cantonese ESL learners. In the *14th Annual Conference of the International Speech Communication Association* (pp. 2113–17). Red Hook, NY: Curran Associates, Inc.

Wong, R. (1987). *Teaching Pronunciation: Focus on English Rhythm and Intonation*. Englewood Cliffs, NJ: Regents Prentice Hall.

Woods, H. B. (2005). *Rhythm & Unstress*. Hull, Quebec: Canada School of Public Service.

Yang, C., & Chu, J. (2016). Testing rhythm metrics in L2 Mandarin Chinese. *Journal of Second Language Pronunciation*, 2(2), 208–24.

Yang, Y., & Lyster, R. (2010). Effects of form-focused practice and feedback on Chinese EFL learners' acquisition of regular and irregular past tense forms. *Studies in Second Language Acquisition*, 32(2), 235–63.

Yule, G. (1980). Speakers' topics and major paratones. *Lingua*, 52(1–2), 33–47.

Zahn, C. J., & Hopper, R. (1985). Measuring language attitudes: The speech evaluation instrument. *Journal of Language and Social Psychology*, 4(2), 113–23.

Zhang, Y., & Francis, A. (2010). The weighting of vowel quality in native and non-native listeners' perception of English lexical stress. *Journal of Phonetics*, 38(2), 260–71.

Zhao, Y. (1997). The effects of listeners' control of speech rate on second language comprehension. *Applied Linguistics*, 18(1), 49–68.

Zielinski, B. W. (2006). Reduced intelligibility in L2 speakers of English. Unpublished dissertation, Macquarie University.

Zielinski, B. W. (2008). The listener: No longer the silent partner in reduced intelligibility. *System*, 36(1), 69–84.

Zielinski, B., & Yates, L. (2014). Myth 2: Pronunciation instruction is not appropriate for beginning-level learners. In L. Grant (ed.), *Pronunciation Myths* (pp. 56–79). Ann Arbor, MI: University of Michigan Press.

Index

Printed in Great Britain
by Amazon